John Waters FAQ

John Waters
FAQ

All That's Left to Know About the Provocateur of Bad Taste

Dale Sherman

APPLAUSE
THEATRE & CINEMA BOOKS
Guilford, Connecticut

Published by Applause Theatre & Cinema Books
An imprint of The Rowman & Littlefield Publishing Group, Inc.
4501 Forbes Blvd., Ste. 200, Lanham, MD 20706
www.rowman.com

Distributed by NATIONAL BOOK NETWORK

The FAQ series was conceived by Robert Rodriguez and developed with Stuart Shea.

All images are from the author's collection unless otherwise noted.

Book design and composition by Snow Creative

Library of Congress Cataloging-in-Publication Data available

ISBN 978-1-4950-7665-7

♾™ The paper used in this publication meets the minimum requirements of American National Standard for Information Sciences—Permanence of Paper for Printed Library Materials, ANSI/NISO Z39.48-1992

Printed in the United States of America

Dedicated to all outsiders who have found a place for their dreams
and to those still searching.

Contents

Acknowledgments   ix

Introduction   xi

1 The Filthiest Man Alive: The Evolution to Smut Peddler   1

2 Dreamlanders: The Recurring Cast and Crew of John Waters   28

3 Teach Me to Be Divine: The Short, Sweet History of Divine   59

4 If I Had to Pick One Place to Live: The Various Hometowns   78
   of John Waters

5 Extreme Behavior: Ten Filmmakers and Ten Movies   92
   That Influenced John Waters

6 *Eat Your Makeup*: The Short Films of John Waters   117

7 A Gutter Film: The Making of *Mondo Trasho*   129

8 And George Figgs as Jesus Christ: The Making of *Multiple*   139
   Maniacs

9 Like a Septic Tank Explosion: The Making of *Pink Flamingos*   151

10 Cha-Cha Heels: The Making of *Female Trouble*   171

11 Backwards Day: The Making of *Desperate Living*   185

12 The Wonders of Odorama: The Making of *Polyester*   201

13 Killing People or Eating: Working at the Patuxent Institution 217

14 How to Tease: The Making of *Hairspray*   220

15 Take the Kids: The Making of *Cry-Baby*   245

16 Fashion Has Changed: The Making of *Serial Mom*   263

17 Full of Grace: The Making of *Pecker*   275

18 DeMented Forever: The Making of *Cecil B. DeMented*   286

19 Let's Go Sexing: The Making of *A Dirty Shame*   298

20 Nobody Would Give Me the Money: The Lost Projects   312

21 If They Don't Have Books: Books Written by John Waters   319

22 Hardy Har: John Waters and His Artwork   328

23 Hawaiian Shirts: Actor in Films and Television   332

24 Santa Claus Is a Black Man: The Musical Collections of John Waters 341

25 A Lifetime of Penning Trashy Screenplays: The Awards   346
    of John Waters

26 Not the Sleaze King: Nicknames That John Waters Does Not   350
    Want on His Tombstone, and One He Does

Bibliography   351
Index   361

Acknowledgments

Thanks to Jill, Maddie, Mike, Brian, Marybeth, and everyone at Applause for their patience.

Special thanks to Josh McCullough of Trashytravels.com and Kyle Lords for their expertise and help in the making of this book.

Extra special thanks to Mr. Waters and all the members of his various casts and crews who made these memorable movies.

A hello to Josh McCullough, James C. Falcon, and all the fellow fans at All Things Dreamland—hope you enjoy the journey here.

Introduction

They like to see an outsider win, no matter who that outsider is. And they don't have to be a member of that outsider group as long as that outsider group makes fun of the people that harass outsiders.

—John Waters describing the universal theme
of his films (*Cups Magazine*, Winter 1998)

W hat can be said about John Waters?
Seriously, that's what many of you are thinking at this point while looking at this book. Moreover, not necessarily in delirious mockery. Of course, there are and always will be a number of people who—if they know him from his movies at all—think of Waters as a deranged pornographer who probably has done unspeakable horrors over the years that even he would not venture to put on the screen. It isn't even necessary for these people to have seen any of his films or heard him talk; it is simply clear that the man is a danger to society. To them, what can be said at all about such a madman or, better yet, said in a way that wouldn't produce a queasy feeling for the next few hundred pages?

Then there are the devout: the fans who already know everything that Waters has done. They know he's written and directed multiple movies, created artwork that has been shown in galleries throughout the world, and narrated and acted in a number of films. Plus, there are the numerous books he has written over the years as well as various appearances he's made on television talk shows and in documentaries. Those fans know all that, but they have all those guest appearances and interviews in their collections to review any time they wish.

And speaking of those interviews—boy, does he love to talk. At one time early in his career, Waters may have been a stringy- and long-haired loner in shades, mumbling his way through interviews, but he happily and quickly changed in the 1970s when he began pursuing the press in order to promote his later films. With aggressiveness came the persona of John Waters we have come to know and love over the years: the man with a twinkle in his eyes and a story on his lips—a man determined to amuse us while talking about the trashiest things. It is what we've come to expect of Waters, and it is evident in his written work as well as in his interviews, his live talks, and his lectures, which are more like one-man comedy shows (there's a reason many of his early shows were done in comedy clubs) than the typical, dry film studies that many filmmakers would give to audiences.

With this vast volume of documented material—the books and inter-views—we're back to the original question: What can be said about John Waters? Here is a man who has given us in-depth, behind-the-scenes details of the making of his early films in his book *Shock Value* (discussed in greater detail in chapter 21), in documentaries such as *Divine Trash*, in his DVD audio-commentaries, and in his one-man shows. He is a man who has dis-cussed his obsessions and his public life in a number of documentaries as well as in his books *Crackpot* and *Role Models*.

Yet, even with all that material already available, there are still aspects of Waters's career that need closer examination. After all, *Shock Value* only covers his career up to 1980 and focuses on just three of his films—*Pink Flamingos*, *Female Trouble*, and *Desperate Living*—along with a brief mention of what would have been, at the time, his latest film, *Polyester*. We can readily see his interest in the work of such filmmakers as William Castle—a man Waters would portray in the television miniseries *Feud* in 2017—as well as H. Gordon Lewis, but one could easily miss the remarkable debt Waters owes to the Kuchar Brothers and their underground films from over the years. Much has been written about popular Waters film star Divine, but rarely does the discussion turn to the work Divine did outside of Waters's films, nor has there been much written about the work of other members of the Dreamland actors and crew outside of their involvement in Waters's filmography.

We hear stories of Waters's influence in movies and television, but not much discussion of where one can see examples of such. Censorship affected his work over the years, but there is evidence that it was more than just a simple love-hate relationship with the censor board of Maryland that cropped up in Waters's career. Furthermore, there are other controversies and achievements that are ignored due to flashier—and sometimes grosser—elements of his career.

There certainly has been plenty said about a career that is nearly fifty years on, but there is much more to say. Throughout *John Waters FAQ*, buried treasures will be uncovered and newfound connections will be made in the close inspection of a career that demonstrates how the outsiders are typically the ones that make the rules for those that follow. John Waters came into the film industry from a direction that should only have been found in the movies themselves, and an examination of his career may help enable others to step outside of the norm and toward success as well.

John Waters FAQ

The Filthiest Man Alive

The Evolution to Smut Peddler

At the premiere of *Hairspray* on Broadway, Harvey Fierstein's mom said to my mom, 'Didn't we raise great sons?' and my mother just started sobbing, because I'm sure they'd both been through other nights when people didn't say that.

—John Waters to Terri White

What we know of John Waters, we know through John Waters. Not that Waters isn't a wallflower when discussing his past, but what he does discuss is obviously in very controlled allotments. A comparison of his anecdotes in his books to those told in interviews clearly shows that he has a set number of stories about his background that he wants to tell. These are the ones that he has perfected and feels worthy of sharing. John Engstrom of *The Advocate* once stated, "Waters is an engaging but elusive fellow . . . (he) presents himself primarily as a storyteller and entertainer," and we as his audience buy into that—or, rather, perhaps we settle for that—because the stories are so funny and vivid. What we get is enough to satisfy our curiosity.

Sometimes, however, Waters will slip in a story that may seem out of the norm of his standard stories about growing up, but such moments are rare gems. As noted throughout much of this book, for someone who has ballyhooed his life for decades, Waters is, in many ways, a very private man. He is also like most other storytellers in that if a story needs a slight tweak in order to make it funnier or connect with another story more effectively, so be it. It is tempting at times to even wonder if certain stories are merely that—stories—rather than the truth.

Yet over the years, there have been enough facts that have leaked through about John Waters's life, and these facts can help give us a somewhat better understanding of the man, or, better yet, an understanding of how a man who came from a wholesome, pedestrian background could end up becoming the man who would create films that would shock us so much as well as make us laugh. Thus, to really understand a journey through Waters's films, it's best to take a look at certain elements of his life before and even a little into his career.

Of course, in that regard, family should always come first.

Family

John Samuel Waters Jr. was born on April 22, 1946, in Baltimore, Maryland, the first of four children for John Samuel Waters (1917–2008) and Patricia Ann Whitaker Waters (1924–2014), and a troublemaker from day one. "I was even born six weeks too early, premature," Waters mentioned in an interview with James Egan in 2010. "The first child. They were scared of me, basically, because I weighed a pound or something. So I caused trouble from the very beginning."

Waters's father grew up in Baltimore and earned a degree in economics from Johns Hopkins University—a college that would later be the location of one of his son's biggest mishaps while filming. After military service during World War II, where John Sr. obtained the rank of corporal as an Army finance officer, he worked for a short time as a stockbroker until 1947, when he started the Fireline Corporation, a company that sells and services fire extinguishers and fire-prevention equipment. "We would deliver the fire extinguishers on the way to school in the morning," John Jr. told the *Guardian* in 2015. Although Waters would reflect in some interviews that his father had eyes on Waters taking over the company someday, his parents told the *New York Times* in 1991 that Waters only lasted three hours before he was asked to leave. "I worked there for one day," Waters told the *Guardian*, "but I had bleached hair and I was listening to rhythm and blues music with the workers."

Born in 1924, Waters's mother, Patricia, lived in Victoria, British Columbia, until the mid-1930s, when her family moved to Guilford in northern Baltimore. In early February 1944, the *Baltimore Sun* announced Waters Sr.'s engagement to Patricia Ann Whitaker, and they married in June of that same year, just days after she graduated from Sweet Briar College with a degree in French. In 1947, a year after the birth of John Jr., the family moved to a home in what is now part of the Lutherville Historic District, located north of Baltimore.

John Jr. summarized the family in various interviews as "upper-middle-class at best," although they lived in a large home with an acre of land surrounding it, so they were doing quite well for themselves. As such, it was not completely illogical for the family to have their own maid; Waters has discussed how he, as a child, once scared their maid while dressed as Captain Hook from *Peter Pan*. In later years, after the children were out of the house, Waters's parents were well off enough to vacation for a month each year in rural England—clearly a sign that the pair had little difficulty with finances. It is also evident from Waters's book *Shock Value* that his mother's side of the family came from money and influence, with Patricia's brother, John C. Whitaker, eventually working as an aide to President Richard M. Nixon while he was in office as well as helping to form the Environmental Protection Agency. Such juxtaposition of the careers of John C. Whitaker and his nephew John Waters appeared to cause little strain on the family, however. "We called him Uncle Buddy," Waters recalled to the *Baltimore Sun* in 2016, "and he always gave me incredible support in my career. He was hilarious. I loved to hear his inside stories about the Nixon reunions, and he loved to hear mine."

Further evidence of a higher level of upbringing comes from both John Sr. and Patricia regularly receiving notices in the society pages of the *Baltimore Sun*, including their engagement notice in 1944, the announcement of their move to Lutherville in 1947, and the notice of each of their children being born over the years. John Jr. was the first in 1946, with their first daughter, Kathleen Neville Waters, born in 1951. After Kathleen came the birth of Stephen Bosley Waters in 1952 and then finally Patricia Whitaker Waters Jr. in 1955.

Of his siblings, Stephen would have the most involvement in John Jr.'s films, appearing in three: *Multiple Maniacs*, *Pink Flamingos*, and *Polyester*. He was also involved behind the scenes in Waters's early film ventures, taking charge of ticket sales when the movies ran in the University of Baltimore auditorium. "Steve was the only person I would trust to run the box office for my early films," Waters recalled to the *Baltimore Sun* in 2009. Once it was clear that John Jr. had no interest in succeeding his father, Stephen took over Fireline Corp. in 1982 and continued to run the company until his death due to a brain tumor in 2009. (Stephen's daughter, Anna Waters Gavin, replaced him and thus kept the company within the family.) Kathleen (commonly referred to as Kathy) appeared briefly in Waters's short film *Roman Candles* as one of the models. Patricia Jr. (typically listed as Trish) also popped up in *Roman Candles* as well as in Waters's first short film, *Hag in a Black Leather Jacket* (as a flower girl in the wedding scene), and *Mondo Trasho* (as the schoolgirl that David Lochary's character tries to grab near the end of the film). Trish eventually moved on to work in the art world, both at the Baltimore Museum of Art and the Phillips Collection in Washington, D.C.; she also at one time was dating Vito Zagarrio, who directed the 1985 documentary about Divine and John Waters, *Divine Waters*.

Perhaps surprisingly for some readers, the Waters could not have been a more traditional portrait of a nuclear family, with John Sr. working and being home by six o'clock each night for a home-cooked meal prepared by Patricia. Both parents were involved with various clubs and activities, making them popular people in the area, which sometimes caused annoyances for them once their son became popular due to his films. In his book *Shock Value*, Waters noted that once, when his mother was showcasing her home to a reporter for a story, she exhaustedly admitted that the man who did *Pink Flamingos* was her son, and that John Sr.—because they shared the same name—had to field television calls from several of John Jr.'s more crazed admirers. Neither parent was quite sure what to make of their first-born, admitting to others that he was an "odd duck" even as a youngster. An example of such that Waters has mentioned: after first going to kindergarten, Waters would arrive home and tell his mother about "this weird kid" who drew only in black crayons and didn't speak to the other kids, only for his mother to find out from his teacher that the boy was Waters himself.

Waters also showed an early interest in what some would consider a rather macabre subject: car crashes. This interest started innocently enough as playtime with toy cars but then escalated. "I . . . used to be obsessed by car accidents. I used to make my parents take me to junkyards and look at wrecked cars. I think that was the first time my mother called the child psychologist," Waters recalled to the *Soho Weekly News*. Even though his parents were concerned, however, Waters's mother would drive to such scrap yards and nervously ask the bemused owners if her son could play among the wrecks. (Waters would later outrageously exaggerate this interest in a scene in *Female Trouble*, where even Dawn Davenport thinks a child acting that interested in automobile accidents is extreme.) Other times, he and his father would chase after fire trucks to see the fires they would have to put out, which Waters sensed his father enjoyed as much as he did, although his father never admitted to it. "I always felt closest to my father when we stood together and watched a neighbor's house burn to the ground," Waters reflected in his book *Shock Value*.

Waters's father tried to steer his firstborn toward more "normal" activities, including sports, but his son took little interest. Once, when his parents reviewed old home movies with a writer from the *New York Times* and saw footage showing a young John ignoring a football while playing with his father, Patricia scolded her husband, saying, "I don't know why you felt you had to play football with the child all the time." Participation in school sports only led to Waters usually being picked last and placed in positions that afforded the team little damage from his neglect, of which he had plenty to give. "Right field was perfect because no balls came there," Waters recalled to Gerald L'Ecuyer in 1990. "I could just stand and daydream." Attempts to get their son interested in watching sports led nowhere as well, with Waters being bored and contemplating disasters, such as baseballs slamming into the heads of spectators at baseball games. As for football games, he told the *New York Post*: "I remember sitting there the whole time trying to imagine what would happen if the stands collapsed and every person would die. And I pictured thousands of ambulances coming in. That's how I'd sit there, imagining destruction and death, with my father."

"Our other kids are normal," Waters's father jokingly put it to the *Baltimore Sun* in 1998, but parents typically clash with their children even in the best of times, and it certainly was not different with Waters and his parents. As Waters became a teenager and, naturally, wished to rebel, he found his upright parents as easy targets to pick on. Waters would later joke about baiting his father at the dinner table with comments about joining a Black Panther rally and rioting just to see him verbally explode. Yet, at the same time, it is easy to see that Waters's father somewhat enjoyed the back-and-forth tirades as well. Waters Jr. also would be truthful in saying if he were on drugs if asked, even though he knew his parents didn't really want the answers. Nevertheless, through multiple articles, interviews, and his own books, Waters made clear that his father and mother were always there for him, despite his shenanigans. In *Shock Value*, he wrote: "No matter how much trouble I got into, they never threw me out of the house. Despite all the hassles, I knew I could count on them if real traumas arose and I think this kept me from taking the final plunge to the deep end."

Waters later recalled his mother driving him to Martick's, a bar in Baltimore, when he was underage so he could hang out, which may seem strange on the surface. "She knew I couldn't get in the bar," Waters told Steve Birmingham in 2010. "She knew I wasn't twenty-one and that the owner knew that and she also knew my friend Pat Moran worked there. But it is amazing when I look back on it. She said, 'Maybe you'll find people here that you can get along with,' and I did and they ended up in my movies. It was an incredibly loving and risky thing to do."

Waters expanded on this to *Time Out*: "It takes a long time to realize that they made me feel safe when I lived a life which was very not safe. You know, I don't know how I made those movies. I went out every single night; I smoked pot every single day. I drank. We did everything, but I never became a drug addict or an alcoholic. Other friends are dead, many of them."

"It was a magical childhood," Trish Waters said after the passing of Patricia Waters in 2014. In the same *Baltimore Sun* article, John Waters reflected on his mother: "She taught us to have a good work ethic and a sense of humor. We were a very close family and she always made us feel safe, which really is the only job a parent has to do, and she did it so well." Waters realized that his father had imprinted upon him as well. "I'm a weird gay version of my father," Waters told the *Guardian* in 2015, "and I got my work ethic from him . . . By the time they died, we had worked out everything and the things that we didn't, I turned into a career." As to work ethics, Waters has described his own work schedule as regulatory and precise, just like his father's regiment of normal working hours through the week. His schedule involves getting up at six o'clock in the morning, with reading and writing in strict time allotments until midday, and having his evenings and weekends free, although he's usually in bed by ten o'clock. "I'm a Swiss person trapped in an American's body. I like a very orderly life," Waters told *Vanity Fair* in 2010.

Even so, a need to rebel stemming from his upbringing would become the catalyst to his later creative career. "Once I had a shrink who said, 'Your parents are the fuel you run on,' because I was raised on the tyranny of good taste," Waters told *Time Out* in 2014. "If my parents hadn't taught me all that, I couldn't have made fun of it." Further, his father helped support Waters's dreams of making movies by helping to finance his films up through *Pink Flamingos*, a debt that Waters always paid back and would, in retrospect, find surprisingly supportive. Waters later reflected that his parents probably hoped he wouldn't have been able to pay them, however. "I think I'm probably the only person that, when the parents lent me money to make the movie, they wished I had not paid them back. They could have said, 'No,' and it would have ended and I would have gotten a real job," Waters told the *Baltimore Sun* in 2017. After his father's death, Waters would discover that his father kept all the repayment notes Waters had written in a safety deposit box, which he found touching. Even so, they rarely saw his films, which suited Waters fine. "Why force my parents to [sit] through *Pink Flamingos*? That's parental abuse," Waters told *The Australian* in 2014. In 2015, he expanded on this: "What parent would be happy—like Divine's mother—what mother would be happy that their son is in drag eating dog shit? Really, no parent's that liberal."

His parents did relent on a few occasions, with his mother seeing some of his earlier films first. As Waters recounted in *The Talks*, upon seeing *Mondo Trasho*, Patricia went in tears to her son, saying, "You're going to die, end up in a mental institution, commit suicide, or OD." Waters responded, "Oh, you liked it?" His father once told him, as Waters remembered in *Shock Value*, "You're going to be shot one day, boy. I don't mean assassinated—you're not that famous—just shot." However, as the films became more mainstream, starting with *Polyester* (as will be discussed in a subsequent chapter) and especially with the success of the PG-rated *Hairspray*, Waters's parents would attend the premieres in Baltimore. Later, at a retrospective of Waters's films at the Baltimore Museum, the pair attended a showing of *Female Trouble* (Water's 1974 film), which proved somewhat embarrassing. "We had to stand up, remember?" Patricia asked John Sr. in an interview with the *New York Times*. "And then they showed a movie. And every time there was anything questionable, all these young people would turn around and look at us to see how we were reacting."

Overall, Waters's family took it with good grace and humor, especially upon seeing Waters achieving success. Waters recounted to the *Guardian* that when he told his parents that the subject matter of his 2004 film *A Dirty Shame* would be about sex addiction, his mother replied, "Maybe we'll die before that one comes out." His father's response upon seeing it was, "It's funny, but I hope I never see it again."

Ultimately, no matter what Waters did on the screen, no matter if it was disturbing or disgusting, the family was always there for him—even if his father would joke, "When you do interviews, tell them that you're an orphan."

Schooling

With the Waters family doing financially well, it is not surprising to discover that John Jr. went to a private school, Calvert School in Roland Parks, located ten miles south of Lutherville. "There were only 27 kids, and you went to school with them every year for six years. In the morning, when you walked in, you had to shake hands with the principal. Girls had to curtsy," Waters explained to Gerald L'Ecuyer in 1990. "It's the only place where I ever learned anything. I wish I could have quit school after sixth grade—I'd know as much as I do today."

A move up to the seventh and eighth grade saw Waters entering Towsontown Junior High School (usually referred to in biographical material as Towson Junior High School). It was in this public school setting that Waters met up with kids from the other side of the tracks—specifically delinquent girls who, according to Waters in his book *Shock Value*, "were wasting time until they could legally quit school, run away, and become full-time skags." Skags being a term that would best describe angry, jobless women who end up drinking beers and smoking cheap cigarettes in front of their trailer homes early in the morning. Dawn Davenport and her school friends in *Female Trouble*, which Waters made years later, are good examples of such characters, and Waters was irresistibly attracted to their sense of danger— besides being "so tired of being good."

It was this taste of another world, among other aspects, that would convince Waters he needed to rebel by the time he entered Calvert Hall College High School as a freshman. "I decided I was a beatnik and began wearing jeans with elaborate bleach stains and sandals that wrapped up to my knees," Waters stated in *Shock Value*. "I never washed my hair and bleached the front of it a sickly orange." This type of behavior would have caused problems in the early 1960s even at the more liberal schools he had previously attended. Now he was entering a boys-only Catholic school that was strict about preparing the boys for college and certainly did not need Baltimore's own Maynard G. Krebs (a beatnik character from the comedy series *The Many Loves of Dobie Gillis* portrayed by Bob Denver) in the school. Forced to "clean up" and dye his hair back to normal, Waters soon tired of the school's strictness.

He also had little patience for the school's emphasis on Catholicism in its teachings, which antagonized him. Although both of Waters's parents believed in a Christian God, they were of different religions, with his mother being Roman Catholic and his father not, and that separation of faith led to conflict early in Waters's life. "When I was at Calvert [School], I had to go to Catholic Sunday school where they had the nuns, and they were evil," Waters said to James Egan. "These women should be locked up. They knew my parents weren't sending me to Catholic school and would say, 'They're going to Hell.' I mean, tell a seven-year-old that?" Waters began to vocally question the religion even if he liked some of its other elements. "Don't get me wrong," Waters told the *Miami News* in 1988, "I'm not at all sorry I was brought up Catholic because it gave me that warped view of things that all Catholics have. And a sense of theatricality. But the thing that I like best about Catholicism, the most ludicrous aspect, is that whenever some awful senseless thing happens that can't be logically explained, what do they invoke? Original Sin." Even so, as he told James Egan, "Once a Catholic, always you remember it. I don't believe in what the Catholic Church believes in. I believe they are my enemy."

The move to a strict Catholic high school ("It wasn't even a good Catholic high school," Waters reported in the same interview) only helped to firmly establish his love–hate relationship (with an emphasis on the hate part) in with the religion. Such sentiment would later flare up in his films: from the delinquent nun in his early short *Roman Candles* to the Virgin Mary ventriloquist doll in *Pecker* and especially to the notorious "rosary job" in *Multiple Maniacs*. "I'm proud to be a Catholic-basher," Waters told the *Santa Fe Reporter* in 2013, "because they are against women and gay people; they're against gay marriage, abortion, they are against everything that I am for and they are quite militant in trying to stop everyone else." The Catholic Church was also instrumental in the direction Waters took with the movies he saw, but more about that in Chapter 5.

As to other students, Waters found little trouble from them in high school. "Having people think you were nuts was part of it," Waters determined years later to the *New York Times*. It was namely with the Brothers who taught the classes that he came in conflict—typically by mouthing off about some religious aspect being ham-fisted into the school day. Always on his own, and tired of the draconian attitude in the classroom, Waters began playing hooky to find things to do. "My father would drop me off in the morning and I'd watch him drive away and then hitchhike downtown, approach any woman in her early twenties (I soon learned that hairdressers were the best), and ask her to call the school and impersonate my mother," Waters reported in *Shock Value*. He spent such days going to various theaters and watching "trashy films" until it was time for school to let out, and he would then return home so no one would find out that he skipped school.

Waters reported in *Shock Value* that the Brothers finally gave up on teaching him anything when he did make it to school and instead would give him "the lowest possible passing grade" if he just kept to himself and did not disrupt the class with antics or jokes. For a time this worked, as Waters would sit in the back of the class and read various books, but at some point it appeared that the jig was up, and his parents moved him from Calvert Hall College High School to Boys' Latin School of Maryland to obtain some semblance of a standard education. Although Waters's writing in *Shock Value* would suggest he graduated from Calvert Hall ("The Christian Brothers refused to let me graduate on the stage."), most sources list Boys' Latin as the high school from which Waters graduated in 1964.

Waters went on to take classes for a year at the University of Baltimore, and his grades had improved enough that he was accepted into the film school at New York University (NYU) in the fall of 1965. "I got into NYU because, I remember, in the interview, I talked about Edward Albee [author of *Who's Afraid of Virginia Woolf?*] the whole time, and I guess that worked," Waters told the *Baltimore Sun*. He had hoped that the school would help him in his career as a filmmaker, but classes were disappointingly "academic," with students not even allowed to offer up their own films for review until they had been there for over a year. "It was film school, but all we had to do was watch the Odessa steps sequence [the famous scene from Sergei Eisenstein's 1925 film *Battleship Potemkin*] over and over," Waters told Michael Musto in 1977. "I'd already seen that, so I just went to 42nd street every day and saw all the exploitation films. I think I got a better education on 42nd Street."

Depending on the source, Waters lasted anywhere from three weeks to three months before NYU asked him to leave in January 1966. At the time, rumors flew that Waters and a few other students had been smoking marijuana in the dorm rooms on the Washington Square campus. Although never discovered in the act of doing so, a number of students (Waters stated in *Shock Value* it was seven students) were summoned to the dean's office and were then expelled from the school. "We were told to never tell anyone what had happened, and guards were placed outside our dorm rooms so we couldn't flee [before the arrival of parents]," Waters recounted in his book. Instead, Waters called the *New York Daily News*, and reporters arrived before the parents could, leading to parents fleeing with their children and hiding their faces from the cameras as well as leading to the university having a scandal on its hands, with students who felt the dean's office had conducted "an inquisition." The event would be written about in an article by Richard Goldstein for the *Saturday Evening Post* ("Drugs on Campus: Why Marijuana Use Surged in the 1960s," from the June 4, 1966, issue) and in his 1966 book *1 in 7: Drugs on Campus*. Even with the moment of triumph, however, Waters claimed to the *Baltimore Sun* in 1998 that the trip back from NYU after being expelled was the roughest moment between him and his parents. Waters attempted to keep a positive spin on the event, telling the press in March 1966 that he planned to return to NYU at some point in the future, but he gave no hint that his expulsion was the reason he left in the first place (and the reason he could probably never return). NYU would be his last attempt at a proper education, and not long after his expulsion Waters had already found himself a new path that was evolving from his trips to 42nd Street.

Books Come to the Rescue

Inspiration came from other sources, such as books, with his first love being *Slovenly Peter* by Heinrich Hoffman, as he told Shelf-awareness.com in 2017: "[The] illustrated German children's classic that taught valuable lessons: suck your thumb and a scary man will charge into your house and cut it off with a giant pair of scissors. Play with matches? You'll catch on fire just like the little girl did in the drawing. See the flames? See her screaming in pain?" It seems a natural fit for the child that would grow up to be the John Waters we know.

However, school sabotaged his interest in books for a time. "Grade school ruined reading for me," Waters told the *New York Times* in 2017, "by demanding book reports for such snore-a-thons as Benjamin Franklin's biography written for children." When he found himself with free time in class as a teenager, however, things changed. "It wasn't until I was a teenager and Grove Press came along and introduced me to [William S.] Burroughs, Marguerite Duras, and Marquis de Sade that I became a real bookworm." With these and other authors, it is clear that Waters fixates on subjects that are out of the ordinary, albeit not necessarily in a light and/or fantastic manner. "I don't want to 'escape' when I read a book," Waters told the *New York Times*. "I want to enter a new world that disturbs me."

Other authors who have disturbed Waters over the years have been Jean Rhys (*Good Morning, Midnight*), Denton Welch (whose *In Youth Is Pleasure* is covered extensively in Waters's book *Role Models*), and Patrick White (Waters has cited White's novel *Voss* as an influence and even stole a line of White's dialogue to use in *Serial Mom*). He also has a special place in his heart for Grace Metalious, the author of *Peyton Place*, a book he first read when he was ten and which he has called "the first dirty book I ever read."

An author that Waters has commonly mentioned near the top of his list—and one he discovered in his youth—is the playwright and novelist Tennessee Williams. Waters was first attracted to Williams's material due to the writer's unusual name and the unique titles of his work, such as *A Streetcar Named Desire* and *Cat on a Hot Tin Roof,* and Waters felt that Williams's writing enabled him to accept himself as a teenager. "When I was about fourteen, Tennessee Williams saved my life," Waters told *Out* magazine in 1997. "I read him in the library and thought, 'Oh, thank God there are other people like me and I don't have to care what other people think.' He made me feel fine about myself, just by his very subject matter." Waters also has listed the 1968 film *Boom!*—scripted by Williams and based on his play *The Milktrain Doesn't Stop Here Anymore*—as "the best film ever made," although he admitted to *Vice* that this was namely because "it's so awful it's perfect."

Waters's taste in literature has obviously played into his career as a filmmaker, with influences seeping into his work to the point of parody. The hyperbole of dialogue in both Williams's and Metalious's work can easily be spotted in Waters's films, especially in Waters's ability to throw in occasional five-dollar-words within sentences full of cacophony. More evident is how Waters's taste in "disturbing" books featuring leading characters that are murderers, hustlers, and thieves play into many of Waters's film plots. One such influence came from Jean Genet's novel *Our Lady of the Flowers*—a book that Waters later realized he may have subconsciously borrowed from when he named Glenn Milstead "Divine." (He would later deny this possibility, however, stating that his character's name came to him from his Catholic background and not from the book). One major element of the book—detailing the virtues of crime—no doubt influenced Waters's film *Female Trouble*.

Waters mentioned in his book *Role Models* that as of 2010 he had "8,425 books, all catalogued but no longer in complete order on my shelves." His interest ranges from the most serious of biographical studies and fiction to the obscure and even jokey. "I collect weird sex pulp paperbacks, especially with the outdated slang word 'chicken' [young gay man] in the title. I have fifty-two of them," Waters told the *New York Times* in 2017. His interest in true-crime books has fallen off in recent years. "Lately there's been nothing published in that field that sends me over the moon," Waters told the *New York Times*. Yet other than that, and science fiction—a genre he is quoted as saying he "never understood"—Waters obviously loves the written word and has adorned his films with people reading books in various scenes. It has also led to one of the most famous recent quotes about reading, which Waters has used in his one-man show: "We need to make books cool again. If you go home with somebody and they don't have books, don't fuck them."

Bohemian Hooky

By the age of sixteen, Waters was frequenting areas of downtown Baltimore as often as possible, usually to see movies—up to four a day—and check out various places such as Martick's, a popular bar on W. Mulberry Street, where both Pat Moran and Maelcum Soul worked at one time or another. Although Waters was not old enough to drink, he hung around in the alley behind the bar to talk to the artists, writers, and beatniks that often came to the bar. He also began hitchhiking to New York—although in 2013 he admitted to the *Guardian* that he essentially gave up the practice when he was sixteen. Either by hitchhiking or by taking a Greyhound bus, Waters would go with friends to see underground films from artists like Kenneth Anger and Andy Warhol, check out "happenings on the Lower East Side" (as Waters referred to them in *Shock Value*), and pester people to crash in their homes in Greenwich Village.

Along with underage drinking also came drugs, and Waters has never shied away from either topic when discussing his glorious, misspent youth. His one big arrest as a teenager was due to underage drinking at Carlin's Drive-In. "I got arrested in Carlin's Drive-In for underage drinking with a mixed group of black and white teens, and the cop said in court that the girls were urinating outside the car," Waters said to James Egan. "I'll never forget my father's expression when he heard that. 'Well, it's a long walk to that concession stand.'" After that arrest came a number of drug experimentation, which he placed in chronological order in his book *Carsick*: "Hash, pot, LSD, amphetamine, morning-glory seeds, glue, heroin, MDA, opium, mushrooms, and cocaine." Yet most were disappointing once he experienced them. "I tried heroin," Waters told *Time Out* in 2014. "I shot up in high school,

Movie poster for Tennessee Williams's *A Streetcar Named Desire*. Williams's writing would be a lifesaver for Waters as he entered his teens.

but I just thought it was so dreary: puking and nodding . . . Coke didn't last long enough; it gave me a hangover for two weeks for being high for ten minutes." Instead, Waters's drug preferences centered on pot, LSD, and speed. "I was on black beauties all the time," Waters admitted to *Time Out*, and he would admit in various interviews that he even sold amphetamines to make money back in the late 1960s. "On a bicycle I sold diet pills that I'd gotten from [a doctor in Provincetown]. I sold them to friends," Waters told Gerald Peary in 1997. "It wasn't that I was a major dealer, but it was once the only way to raise money for underground movies." Waters also has stated that he smoked marijuana every day until the middle of the 1970s, when he gave it up for the most part. "I'll have pot in my home for guests—I'm polite!" Waters joked to *Time Out*. "But I don't sit around and smoke by myself, ever. Not like I did when I was young."

He has also discussed poppers in his one-man shows. Poppers are small bottles of alkyl nitrites—typically amyl nitrite and sometimes amyl nitrate (leading to a memorable line in *Multiple Maniacs*: "This is even better than amyl nitrate!")—which writers often describe as creating "a feeling of excitement and a quick high." For a writer/director who has visualized people huffing glue and cleaning supplies in his films, poppers certainly were not anything out of left field, and Waters has even gone so far as to mention having "popper parties" at the annual Provincetown Film Festival, which did give him some concern. "The *Boston Globe* somehow found out and asked me about it this year right before I had it," Waters told the *Santa Fe Reporter* in 2013, "and I thought, 'Maybe I'll get busted'—because poppers are illegal in Massachusetts. Now wouldn't that be a good photo-op? Us being chained; taken away to the Provincetown Police Station for a popper bust?"

LSD has always had Waters's strongest support from his own personal history. "I never had a bad LSD trip," Waters told James Egan, "and it was a wonderful bonding experience for me and my friends." As Waters emphasized in this interview with Egan and in other interviews as well, LSD created a moment of clarity for him when it came to his film career. "LSD made me think, 'I can do what I want to do.' . . . It came to me that 'I could do this. Be a filmmaker. This is gonna happen.' I'm not saying every kid should take LSD and you're gonna have your career bubble come through."

Even with his matter-of-fact attitude about his own drug use and the benefits he saw from it, Waters has always been quick to point out that there was a downside as well. "I can't do anti-drug ads. I can't be that much of a hypocrite," Waters told Gerald Peary in 1997. "But I'm not pro-drugs because many of the people who took them with me, including David Lochary, are dead because of drugs. Cookie [Mueller] and I were estranged for a while because of her use of drugs, but we made up later in life." Waters was also quick to point out in interviews that he had no problems with drugs while writing a script, but once filming started, he had no time for it, nor was he happy to see others using on his sets. Drugs meant attention diverted from the film—a loss of control for Waters, who admitted he could be like a dictator when filming. There was no tolerance for diversions on the set, either in the early years when money was scarce or later when studio financing was tight. Waters also found that his interest in drugs became more limited as the films became more successful. Life was fulfilling, thanks to the films, and thus the need to escape beyond that to relax with friends on occasions became more infrequent, and drug-addiction escaped him due to his more intense habit to create.

As mentioned above, drug use appears in many of his films. That's not too far-fetched for underground films of the late 1960s and into the "hip" comedies of the 1970s. What is different, however, is how Waters portrays such drug use in his films. Many films—even studio films—glamorized the use of drugs by the early 1970s; pot and cocaine were standard punch lines in comedies of the later 1970s (an old lady snorting a line, a cop looking for a roach to smoke, etc.). Waters, on the other hand, rarely showed people going with the drugs thought by Hollywood to be harmless. (Admittedly, people thought cocaine was "fun" at the time.) Pot occasionally turned up, but fleetingly; cocaine was even rarer. The drugs of choice in Waters's films were nastier and dirtier—people shooting up on-camera or huffing from bags and rags for cheap highs. These were lower-level highs that fit into the filthy world of his characters and were done by people who no one ever wanted to be like. People may have gotten a thrill in seeing Al Pacino in *Scarface* with a mountain of cocaine in front of him, but no one wanted to associate themselves with the rag-sniffing, foot-fetishizing Dexter from *Polyester*. And the man shooting up by the church alter in *Multiple Maniacs* now seems more depressingly transgressive than even the "rosary job" seen just before it. If anything, it could be said that Waters's depictions of drug use possibly deterred more people from drugs than some of the films Hollywood made over the years that showed drug usage.

The Draft

Waters, like many young people in the mid- to late 1960s, was against the Vietnam War that was raging at the time. He even received coverage in the *Baltimore Evening Sun* in October 1965 by having marched in a protest in New York, although he would confess later that attending protests and riots came more from having something exciting happening than wanting social justice. At least, that is how he would present his actions later on in life. "All the cute boys were at the riots," he would joke when discussing such days. Further, one could say even the article in the 1965 paper was more to advertise his film work than his righteous indignation about the war.

Nor did Waters hesitate when it came time to go to the draft board. After he checked everything on the form handed to him that would suggest he was unfit—including bed-wetter, drug-user, and homosexual—"they didn't even make me take a physical," Waters told John Ives. Ironically, after Waters tried his best to get out for mental reasons, the board determined there was a physical reason to not take him. "I was one pound too thin. You had to be a hundred and thirty and I weighed a hundred and twenty-nine." Classified as 1Y—"basically it means after hairdressers they'll take us," Waters once joked—Waters later discovered, when filming *Cry-Baby*, that singer/actor Iggy Pop had been classified the same. The Gulf War was just starting at the time and Waters joked with Pop, saying: "God, we're 1Y, do you think they'll call us?"

His Mustache

Waters first began working on his legendary pencil-thin mustache back when he was sixteen, having been influenced by the mustache worn by one of his idols, a rock and roll superstar and a man who might as well put a saloon door on his closet: Little Richard. "I wanted to be Little Richard as a child. I wanted to be the only white man to have one," Waters told *Cups Magazine*. Of course, the style—in minor variations—had been around for years before that, as it was common among movie stars and other famous figures, and it seemed to be a fixture of many villains in the crime movies of the 1930s up through the bad exploitation films of the 1950s and 1960s.

This cut-rate "bad guy" image was a primary reason Waters continued working on the look off and on until he made it part of his look permanently in 1970 while promoting *Multiple Maniacs* in California. "I dressed like a hippie pimp," Waters told the *New York Times* in 2016. "I had long hair and wore ridiculous thrift-shop shirts. The mustache just went along with my sleazy look."

The look, however, took some time to get right. "It's tough for a white man who isn't that hairy to grow one," Waters joked in his book *Role Models*. The shaving wasn't an issue—"every day, shave down; twice a week, scissors on the bottom"—it was simply a lack of hair to make it look full, and a possible nick could make it look botched and uneven. It was at that time in 1970 that Mink Stole's sister told him, "Just put a little pencil on it." What this meant was to get an eyeliner pencil (Waters strongly recommends Maybelline Expert Eyes in Velvet Black in *Role Models*) and pencil in the areas that were not full. In other words, the mustache is real, just with some additional effects to help.

The pencil works wonders, but the downside is that it comes off easily, and the pencil has to be sharp, which is hard to do if one is missing a pencil sharpener. Plus, as Waters told *Cups*, "As I get older, I might have to use more pencil because it is getting gray." Yet even with the minor annoyances the mustache brings with it, he can't see ever getting rid of it after close to fifty years, especially as he recognizes that the mustache has worked in his favor. Talking to Steve Appleford in 2007 about being approached for acting jobs, he said: "I don't go to auditions. It's not like I have a headshot that I sent out. My mustache gets every part I've ever had."

He's gotten used to people trying to wear such a mustache in tribute when meeting him, although he prefers not to make mention of it, just to see their reactions. "I've had little kids come up to me; I've seen people dressed

Waters in a promotional still to promote the twenty-fifth anniversary of *Pink Flamingos*. Styles may come and go, but a pencil-thin mustache is a joy forever and a signature look for Waters as the 1970s began.

like me on Halloween. In a look-alike contest, usually lesbians wear it. It's easy to be me," Waters told the *New York Times*.

"The only time I would shave it off," Waters replied when asked by the *New York Times*, "is if I was going to prison, because I wouldn't have the proper tools." Besides, he concluded, "I bet if I shaved it off now there would be a mark there, or a scar, because I've had it for so long. Why would I get rid of it now?"

Death of the Peanut Man

Leslie Van Houten was a follower of Charles Manson and directly involved in the murder of Rosemary LaBianca on August 9, 1969. Waters would later become friends with her while she was in prison and writes about her in his 2010 book, *Role Models*, which deals with people who have made a connection or an impression on Waters over the years. In his book, and elsewhere, Waters sees Houten as someone who could have easily been part of his circle of friends making movies in the late 1960s and into the 1970s. Only instead of falling in with a group of crazy moviemakers, she fell in with Manson and ended up involved in a crime for which she has since felt remorse.

In reflecting on being the perpetrator of a death, Waters describes in *Role Models* about an incident in 1970, when he accidentally killed a man while driving his car. "It's something I never told anybody," Waters told *Word Magazine* in 2011, "but it seemed like the proper time to reveal it because it was the only thing I could think of to try and imagine how terrible Leslie felt for what she had done—even though it was not my fault."

It was a Sunday afternoon in 1970, and Waters was driving with Mink Stole up Broadway, near the Broadway Market—a marketplace full of food vendors in the Fells Point area of Baltimore. As they were driving, an older man stepped off the curb, right in front of Waters's car. Waters was unable to avoid hitting the man, who "flipped up and landed on the hood with his face pressed toward mine through the driver-side windshield," as Waters described it in *Role Models*. It was unavoidable, and fortunately for Waters, a police officer had witnessed the entire incident, as he knew it could have easily looked otherwise. "Thank God the cop saw it—my God, it was like a guardian angel, it really was, an angel in a police uniform who could stand as my witness at court, because I really did look incredibly disreputable at the time," Waters told *Word Magazine*, referring to the greasy hair and "trashy pimp" clothes he wore, not to mention the reputation he had already earned with his early films by 1970.

Waters would end up having to go to court for manslaughter, which he did with his parents by his side, but the hearing quickly ended after testimony from the police officer cleared Waters. Although obviously innocent of any wrongdoing, Waters was naturally bothered by the incident even though it was, according to everyone who had witnessed it, clearly an accident. "It was a horrible experience causing someone's death, even if it was a complete accident," Waters told *Word Magazine*. "It was even worse when I found out it was the old man who sold peanuts at the Broadway Market. The Peanut Man."

Deadly automotive incidents appeared in Waters's films before the real-life accident occurred—the plot of *Mondo Trasho* (1969) hinges on Divine's character accidentally hitting Mary Vivian Pearce's character while driving, for example—but he has acknowledged they became an established moment in most of his films afterward. "It's there in every movie," Waters told *Word Magazine*. "In *Polyester* when they run over Tab Hunter at the end and he lands on the windshield. In *Cry Baby* with the lollipop lady, in *Serial Mom* when she runs over the teacher, in *Cecil B. DeMented* when Fidget falls off the marquee and lands on his parent's windshield. I hate the phrase 'creative process' and it's a term I'd never utter out loud, but anything that happens to you, if you're a creative person, ends up in your work in some way."

Trial Groupie

Speaking of trials, Waters readily called himself a trial groupie when discussing an article he was writing about such people to *Provincetown Magazine* in 1977: "I go to all these trials all the time. I went to Patty Hearst's trial, the Manson trial, and the Watergate trial. It's a humorous article on the people who go to trials all over the country. They say, 'Oh, hi, I saw you at the Angela Davis trial.'" As Waters gained the freedom of money and travel, he turned to his interest in crime—namely spectacular, newspaper-headlining, and national-interest crimes. A fascination with these trials, as well as famous crime scenes and even a handful of mementos of famous criminals, comes from trying to understand how people crossed the line from the imaginative—as in his films, which he has called "his crimes" when discussing them with a group of prisoners in the 1970s—to the real. "Trials are the only theater I like," Waters told the *New York Times* in 1988. "When I go on like this about, say, the Manson family," Waters told David Shute in 1981, "I certainly mean no approval of what they did. But I also think that what they did to themselves was a tragedy to allow that to happen. I'm interested in people who lost control, who did act out those fantasies, because I wonder why . . . I think these criminals, the really lunatic ones, have very little choice in what happens to them."

That attitude, and his inclination to treat it all as a big joke in his films and interviews, changed as time went on and as he became friends with people like Leslie Van Houten and later Patricia Hearst. Suddenly the jokes in *Multiple Maniacs* about killing Sharon Tate, or those in his chapter about going to trials in his book *Shock Value*, took on a personal tint that made them not as funny now that he had come face-to-face with the people involved. He also had to stop going "because they recognize me," as he stated in his one-man show *This Filthy World*. He became too famous to sit among the crowd and study the people involved, as he found himself too often the study of others. Even so, that interest in criminals and how others are attracted to the most notorious of them would become the basis of his film *Female Trouble* and certainly an element in *Pink Flamingos* as well.

Jobs

As a young teenager, shoplifting was a source of easy income for Waters, although it seems that many times he did it more for the kicks of doing it than for the money. "For some reason, Hutzler's (a department store in Baltimore) used to get one copy of *Variety* and I used to shoplift it," Waters said to the *Baltimore Sun*. "I don't know why, it wasn't that expensive, but I shoplifted it every week. They must have known—they only got the one copy." He also reflected on earning money while at NYU by stealing textbooks from the university bookstore and selling them back to the store for quick cash. One adventure in shoplifting paid off even greater—Waters was in the process of shoplifting a record at a Korvettes department store when he noticed that the store detective had spotted him. Managing to put the record back without the detective seeing him, the detective apprehended Waters when he left the store. With no stolen merchandise on him, Waters sued the store and received a quick settlement—money he used to help pay for trips to New York and more trips to the theaters.

As mentioned previously, Waters's simple requests for money or favors worked for a time, and he benefitted as well from having a girlfriend who could get cash for various trips and activities. While briefly living in New York, Waters also used what he called "the tennis shoe rip-off" to earn extra cash. It involved wearing pre-ripped tennis shoes and then walking into various department stores, claiming that the escalator in the store had ripped his shoe, and demanding ten to fifteen dollars compensation for the damage. "They knew you were lying," Waters said in 1997 to the *New York Times*, "and you had to complain for twenty minutes before they finally gave you the money. Worse, sometimes they just gave you a new pair of tennis shoes."

Waters and his friends in the 1960s and into the 1970s shoplifted food and clothes for money and thrills, and became more daring as time went on. In *Shock Value*, Divine mentions in an interview of once walking out of a hardware store with a chainsaw and an electric drill for no other reason than just to do it; Waters, meanwhile, became so friendly with the staff at a store he was stealing clothes from that they came close to offering him a job. There were also small cons to make money, such as Mary Vivian Pearce getting an official UNICEF kit to "collect money, and we'd buy LSD with it," as Waters said to John Ives in 1992. Waters even admitted in the same interview that he used fake credit cards (not stolen, but fake) in order to help pay for phone calls to his distributor in the early 1970s. Yet these were seen as small, harmless crimes against companies with money, driven somewhat in protest against "the man," perhaps ("All that kind of rip-off shit was considered politically correct then," Waters told Ives), but mostly because it was more fun than having to work.

Over time, however, Waters knew that he had to find a real job. There was only so long you could pull the tennis shoe rip-off or shoplift clothes before every store knew you, and bumming for money had diminishing returns. The group of friends he ran around with during the summer of 1966 in Provincetown became so notorious for their shoplifting that they were known as "the Hillbilly Rip-offs." He also needed to look for financing for his films, as he couldn't—and didn't want to—continue turning to his father for money to make them.

Discussed earlier was Waters's few hours of working for his father at the family business before he was asked to leave. He then briefly worked for a survey company, where he would go door to door with magazines with fake ads and then ask people a series of questions about the advertising for a Gallup poll. The job itself was fine, but Waters ran into problems with cooperation of the participants. "No housewives ever let me in . . . because I had real long hair and looked weird," Waters told Ives in the same interview. "So I made up every one of the answers. I had to be so many different people; it was really a good way to develop characters. I never got caught, so I think they believed them."

Summer excursions to Provincetown, Massachusetts, from 1965 into the 1980s saw Waters looking for work to cover expenses. An attempt to work at a clothing store called No Fish Today in 1966 only lasted a week due to Waters being uncooperative with the patrons. "I was fired after a week," he told Gerald Peary, "because [the owner] would come in and I'd be sitting there reading. I think she expected me to say to the customer how great they looked in our Levi's. I wasn't very good at the job." That same year, he moved on to the East End Bookshop, where he only worked when it rained because that was when the store would become busy. He loved the owner, Molly Malone, due to her attitude about customers and books. "I saw Molly snatch a book out of someone's hand and say, 'Get out!' I was very impressed. I thought, 'This is my kind of job.'"

Waters must have made an impression, for when he came back to Provincetown in the summer of 1967, he was offered a full-time job working for a competing bookstore, Provincetown Bookshop. "They sought me out, I don't know why, but probably because I was passionate about books," Waters told Gerald Peary. The pay was good—one hundred dollars a week, the equivalent of over five hundred dollars in 2017. In addition, because the bookstore closed each winter, unemployment was available to Waters while he crisscrossed the country in order to promote his early films. The owners also allowed Waters to use the storefront window to promote his films and have his friends in the store without running them off for loitering. It was a dream job for Waters, and he would remain with the bookstore for years, even past the time of starting to receive national attention with *Pink Flamingos*. The bookstore job would also be the last "nine to five" job he would have before devoting his full-time attention to his movies, writing, and other personal projects.

There was one other job Waters would have while growing up.

Puppetry

As a youngster, Waters was engrossed with playacting, saying in *Lapham's Quarterly*, "[My parents] built me a stage at the top of the second-floor steps on a landing outside my bedroom so I could act out whatever show-business fantasies I was entertaining." Later, to Todd Solondz in 2004, Waters would admit that the little stage built by the Dashers for Dawn in *Female Trouble* was based on his own stage as a child. After tormenting neighborhood kids and "Aunt Rachel" with his antics on the stage, Waters then decided to expand his work to something bigger as he got older: a haunted house.

"I printed up handbills advertising 'John Waters's Horror House' and taped them to telephone poles along our street." The "horror house" itself was actually the garage of his parent's house, which he had decorated with traditional Halloween gimmicks. "But I knew that wasn't enough to really scare anybody," he went on. "I needed to make it dangerous. At the last minute, when the customers were lining up outside, I turned off all the flashlights and installed little trip wires that would be invisible in the dark." For twenty-five cents, kids could go in and get a blast of chemical powder from a fire-extinguisher in the face and a kick in the shins, and then proceed to stumble through the dark garage, falling over trip-wires. "But you know what? They loved it! They'd laugh, get right back up, grope their way through the rest, fall several more times, and then race back outside and get in line all over again to give me their money." It was as if "being weird" was already providing Waters with an audience. Then there came the puppets.

The musical film *Lili* came out in 1953 and starred Leslie Caron as a young woman who becomes the hostess in a carnival puppet act, which is performed by a man who hides his affections for her behind the puppets she loves. The movie, probably best remembered today for the clip of Caron signing "Hi Lili, Hi Lo" with the puppets, made an impression on John Waters, who already was a fan of *The Howdy Doody Show* on the NBC network. Waters's parents recognized his interest and, thrilled to find it one so wholesome and not lethally oriented, got then nine-year-old Waters into the Peanut Gallery on the *Howdy Doody* program. Considering he knew from *Lili* that the puppets were being manipulated by people behind the scenes and that the story was always about the ones pulling the strings rather than the dolls themselves, the visit was everything he could have wanted it to be. "I remember going in," Waters told the *Lincoln Journal Star*, "and seeing it was all a lie. I was the opposite of disillusioned. I knew this was what I was going to do. Other kids were disillusioned. They wanted to go to Doodyville. I was at NBC Studios, and that's where I wanted to be. I was really excited to be in on the magic."

Soon enough, Waters began creating his own puppets shows and hiring himself out to perform at parties for other kids. By the age of twelve, he was popular enough that he was making up to twenty dollars a show and performing sometimes up to four times a week. Essentially variations on *Cinderella* and *Punch & Judy*, Waters's productions were good, but as he got older, he became less enthused. "It was too mortifying to be a puppeteer," Waters told John Ives. "It was so uncool, I would never tell anybody. I was too embarrassed. When I was a kid it was great; when I was a teenager, it was really embarrassing."

He soon began improvising in his show, ending them with his characters eaten by his "favorite dragon character." He would then come from behind

Lili (1953), a musical from MGM, featured Leslie Caron and a plot dealing with puppets, which would lead to young John Waters's interest in puppetry.

A DVD collection of later *Howdy Doody Show* episodes. The series fascinated Waters when he was a child in the 1950s, and when he found out how
the show was done, he became interested in hearing more about television
and films.

the stage and offer each child a bite from the dragon for "good luck"—sometimes chasing uncooperative, crying kids around the room until they finally
gave up and let the dragon bite them. The parents and children saw it as a bit
odd. "I would try out things," Waters told Ives, "and the children would just
look at me confused. You know, it wasn't like they were upset. It was just
'Huh?' Then I realized I'd better get another job."

With performance in his blood by this point, he became interested in
using a movie camera, including one that belonged to his father. It was

enough to convince his grandmother to give him an 8 mm Brownie movie camera of his own on his seventeenth birthday. "I guess she figured it would keep me out of trouble," Waters stated in his book *Shock Value*, "and since I was such a show-off, she might as well encourage my career in show business."

The pieces were starting to fall into place for Waters's eventual career. Yet to make films, one needs people to help behind and to perform in front of the camera. That would mean convincing friends to help out—friends that would help with his films for years to come and would be commonly referred to by everyone, even by those friends themselves, as the Dreamlanders.

2

Dreamlanders

The Recurring Cast and Crew of John Waters

There's a lot of ghosts in those early films.

—John Waters to the *Baltimore Sun*, discussing the various
actors who appeared in his films and have died.

Every kid who picks up a camera needs to put something in front of the lens if they want to get anything done, and unless you really want to do it alone as an animator, your main option is to convince friends, relatives, and anyone else hanging around to perform for you.

Waters was fortunate enough to have friends who enjoyed performing in public in order to freak out innocent bystanders, and thus they had little qualms in doing so in front of the camera. Some only stayed on as long as the early 8 mm films, some just into the 1970s, while a few have managed to stay part of Waters's team up through his last film, *A Dirty Shame*, in 2004.

As to being called a Dreamlander? It's a name that the fans and a certain segment of the press has used for the continuing band of friends that Waters has featured in his films over the years—obviously based on the name of Waters's production company, Dreamland. It was not, however, a name that the people involved ever used for themselves at the time, but one which they have fallen back on in the years since, and certainly in light of so many other people calling them such.

Over the course of sixteen films directed by Waters, there have been more than 300 people who have worked on at least two of his films, which goes to show how much loyalty existed between Waters and those individuals in working together so often. To name them all here would be a book in itself. Instead, listed here are the main members that left their mark, both big and small, on the films of John Waters:

The cast from *Pink Flamingos* (1972) and most of the core members of the Dreamlanders. *From left to right*: Divine, Mary Vivian Pearce, Mink Stole, Danny Mills, John Waters, Edith Massey, and David Lochary.

Mary (Bonnie) Vivian Pearce (Born 1947)

Films with Waters: *Hag in a Black Leather Jacket* (1964); *Roman Candles* (1966); *Eat Your Makeup* (1968); *Mondo Trasho* (1969); *The Diane Linkletter Story* (1970); *Multiple Maniacs* (1970); *Pink Flamingos* (1972); *Female Trouble* (1974); *Desperate Living* (1977); *Polyester* (1981); *Hairspray* (1988); *Cry-Baby* (1990); *Serial Mom* (1994); *Pecker* (1998); *Cecil B. DeMented* (2000); *A Dirty Shame* (2004)

Always known as Bonnie to friends, Mary Vivian Pearce first met Waters when they were nine years old. They eventually became such good friends that they were bad influences on each other—from shoplifting together to

Waters trying to bleach Pearce's hair with Clorox—leading to the parents of each trying to stop them from seeing each other. That didn't stop them, and it was common in their later teens for Bonnie to solicit dates with boys in order to be allowed out of the house by her parents and then ditch the boys down the road where Waters would be waiting in his car. Waters would revisit this concept in his film *Polyester*, where the daughter character, Lu-Lu, uses the same method in order to meet up with her real boyfriend. (In fact, in the film Mary Garlington looks as if she could pass for the younger sister to Pearce.)

Waters and Pearce seemed inseparable for a time, becoming notorious at teenage parties for causing such havoc—stealing items and drinking until they got sick—and becoming personae non gratae to some of their school friends. Losing friends was fine by them, as they would make their own fun by going to underground films and plays and even twice dancing together on *The Buddy Deane Show* and getting in trouble for dancing the "Bodie Green" (the "Dirty Boogie" seen in *Hairspray*).

Pearce went through a period where she tried to make herself look as much like Jean Harlow as possible, making her a lightning rod for attention in the late 1960s. (Waters more than once said that she would always cause a riot when walking through stores with the way she looked.) "I cut it short, began wearing red lipstick and looking like Jean Harlow," Pearce told Gerald Peary. "It was kind of harsh, not as pretty as Marilyn Monroe, who I really wanted to look like." It is this look that she is best remembered for in Waters's films, although she would dispense with it after *Pink Flamingos*.

With a family background in horses and the racetrack, she understandably met and married a "jockey at Saratoga" at the age of eighteen, although she would later state: "[It was a] fake marriage to get me out of the house. I'd taken all our wedding presents back and bought books and records." The marriage would last three months before Pearce was gone, with Waters picking her up in his father's station wagon. Her husband told her family that she had run off with beatniks. "I was so pissed at him for telling," she told Gerald Peary years later.

Pearce would film roles for every single film that Waters has done over the years, although her role went from being the costar in *Mondo Trasho* to one of the players in *Multiple Maniacs* and *Pink Flamingos* and finally to cameos in every film since *Polyester*. "I started at the top," Pearce joked to the *Baltimore Sun* in 1994, "and I'm clawing my way to the bottom." This was not to distance her from Waters; rather, it was a mutual agreement between the two. According to Waters, speaking to Scott MacDonald in 1982, Pearce "had absolutely no desire to be an actress. She sort of dreaded doing the films." She went on to multiple careers, including working for a time in the 1990s as a bicycle courier; she also worked as a clocker for the *Daily Racing Form*, where she would time racehorses. In 1999, she suffered a stroke while having brain surgery to remove a tumor, leaving the left side of her face paralyzed. Nevertheless, she filmed her cameo in *Cecil B. DeMented* just weeks afterward and was doing nude modeling for art classes within the year, writing about it for the *Baltimore Sun* in May 2000. Pearce earned a Masters of Fine Arts degree in Creative Writing in the late 1990s as well. Of the many so-called bohemians that Waters hung around with, Pearce has spent a lifetime coming the closest to being a true one.

Mona Montgomery (Date of Birth Unknown)

Films with Waters: *Hag in a Black Leather Jacket* (1964); *Roman Candles* (1966); *Eat Your Makeup* (1968)

There is little known about Waters's high school girlfriend, Mona; even her name is not her real one. Waters and other Dreamlanders have always referred to her as Mona, but Waters admitted in 1997 to Gerald Peary that this was not her real name, saying: "I changed her name to Mona Montgomery in my book, *Shock Value*, because I don't know where she is today. She's not in show business and she's not a public figure."

Waters met Mona in high school when she was fifteen. She would be his only serious girlfriend, and the pair was much like how Waters was with Pearce—in fact, it is common in some reviews of Waters's early films that feature Mona to get her and Pearce confused in descriptions of actors. Waters and Montgomery were known for their shoplifting escapades, including stealing signed art prints right off the walls of galleries, and the pair would travel together to New York and to Provincetown, MA—sometimes rooming with Pearce—in the mid- to late 1960s. The relationship finally went sour after a few years when Mona found Waters asleep in bed with another man and dumped a trashcan of garbage on the pair.

Mona would appear as the bride in *Hag in a Black Leather Jacket* and then in smaller roles in *Roman Candles* and *Eat Your Makeup*. She also supplied the 8 mm film for *Hag* by stealing it from the photo supply shop she worked for at the time. Beyond that, not much is known about Mona, although at least one book about Waters appears to hide her name in plain sight.

Bob Skidmore (Born 1947)

Films with Waters: *Hag in a Black Leather Jacket* (1964); *Roman Candles* (1966); *Eat Your Makeup* (1968); *Mondo Trasho* (1969); *Multiple Maniacs* (1970); *Pink Flamingos* (1972); *Pecker* (1998)

Skidmore met Waters in the eighth grade and became friends with him and Bonnie Pearce. Although typically not credited with *Hag in a Black Leather Jacket*, Waters had a number of school friends appear in the film, and it would not be surprising if Skidmore were one of them. Waters's book *Shock Value* mentions Skidmore early in the book as simply "Bob."

Skidmore would work as a production assistant on *Mondo Trasho* and *Multiple Maniacs*. He mostly appeared in incidental roles in Waters's films, taking a twenty-six-year break between films, going from playing a delivery boy in *Pink Flamingos* to a delivery man in *Pecker*. In an interview about *Multiple Maniacs* with the *Baltimore Sun*, Skidmore remembered filming a Waters movie, saying, "We would all pile into a station wagon and we would just go do something."

Margie Skidmore (Born 1949)

Films with Waters: *Eat Your Makeup* (1968); *Mondo Trasho* (1969); *Multiple Maniacs* (1970); *Pink Flamingos* (1972); *Female Trouble* (1974)

People may remember Margie Skidmore best as the school snitch in *Female Trouble*, who tells the teacher about Dawn sneaking a meatball sub into class. Probably filmic karma for having gotten shot by Divine's character in the Cavalcade of Perversion from *Multiple Maniacs*. She also played the Virgin Mary in *Mondo Trasho*. In the DVD commentary for *Female Trouble*, Waters mentions that he stayed with (then-husband and wife) Bob and Margie Skidmore at various times, and also mentioned that Margie was nothing like the character she played in *Female Trouble*. At the time of the commentary's recording, Waters stated that Margie had moved on to become a talented tattoo artist.

Pat Moran (Born 1942)

Films with Waters: *Roman Candles* (1966); *Eat Your Makeup* (1968); *Mondo Trasho* (1969); *The Diane Linkletter Story* (1970); *Multiple Maniacs* (1970); *Pink Flamingos* (1972); *Female Trouble* (1974); *Desperate Living* (1977); *Polyester* (1981); *Hairspray* (1988); *Cry-Baby* (1990); *Serial Mom* (1994); *Pecker* (1998); *Cecil B. DeMented* (2000); *A Dirty Shame* (2004)

Moran met Waters back in 1964 at the Mount Vernon Flower Mart, and she didn't think much of him. "I remember he was awfully skinny and had an awfully long neck," she told *Baltimore Magazine* in 2013. Interestingly enough, Moran also met future early Waters star Maelcum Soul at the Mount Vernon Flower Mart around the same time, and it was Moran who introduced Soul to Waters. Older by a handful of years, Moran had experienced things a bit more than many of the other Dreamlanders and had already been married and divorced twice—and with a son—by the time Waters met her in 1964.

Her father, Johnny Moran, was a popular big band leader and owned a grocery store with Pat's mother in Catonsville. (The store was used for the setting in *Pink Flamingos* where Divine shoplifts the steak.) Pat was raised to be a "proper" domestic housewife, but she broke out of such a mold in the early 1960s through friendship with a group of gay men at a bar called Leon's. "They introduced me to a whole new world of style and taste," Moran told *Baltimore Magazine* in 2013. "Gay men liberated me from Middle America." She began working nights at Martick's, where she ran into Waters again. They soon found that they had been following the same journey in life. "We had both ventured downtown and found the world we were looking for," Waters told *Baltimore Magazine*. "Pat may have worked at Social Security by day, but she was a beatnik goddess at night."

Although Waters would have many close female friends over the years, he and Moran would become almost inseparable—at least when it came to Waters's films—and Moran was certainly the most dedicated of the Dreamlanders. "Pat did whatever was needed," Waters told John Lewis in 2013 when discussing what Moran did on his films. Although cast as Dorothy in the aborted *Dorothy, the Kansas City Pot Head*, Moran mostly played small supporting parts in Waters's films from *Roman Candles* through *Desperate Living*. Her contribution became greater behind the scenes, however; her assistance during the filming of *Pink Flamingos* led to her being the production manager or production associate of many of

Waters's films after that point. She would also be an associate producer on every film since *Hairspray*. Most importantly, she would help cast many of Waters's movies, placing casting ads in the *Baltimore Sun* in the early 1970s when Waters was about to film and officially taking on the title starting with *Polyester*. She also ran the Charles Theater—one of Waters's favorite movie theaters—for a time in the 1970s.

Among the Dreamlanders, Moran has had the most successful career in films, thanks to working with director and Baltimore native Barry Levinson in some casting for his 1990 film *Avalon*. Levinson brought Moran back to help cast the series *Homicide: Life in the Street* between 1993 and 2000. (Vince Peranio, another Dreamlander, also worked on the series, while several other people connected to Waters—and Waters himself—appeared on the Baltimore-based program over the years.) She has continued to work as a casting director in a number of television series and films, including *Red Dragon* (2002), *Wedding Crashers* (2005), *State of Play* (2009), and the comedy series *Veep* (2012–2015).

Her husband, Chuck Yeaton, who works as a home contractor, typically steered clear of involvement in the Waters films, but he did appear briefly in *Pink Flamingos*, *Desperate Living*, *Polyester*, and *Hairspray*. Her daughter, Greer Yeaton, has also worked in production, starting with *Homicide: Life in the Street* and working on such programs as *Oz* and *Damages* (2007–2011). Her son, Brook Yeaton—who appeared briefly in *Desperate Living* as Peggy's son at the beginning of the film—has worked as a property master for such shows as *NCIS: New Orleans* (2014–2017) and *The Wire* (2002–2006).

David Lochary (1944–1977)

Films with Waters: *Roman Candles* (1966); *Eat Your Makeup* (1968); *Mondo Trasho* (1969); *The Diane Linkletter Story* (1970); *Multiple Maniacs* (1970); *Pink Flamingos* (1972); *Female Trouble* (1974)

While Pat Moran found success in the movies outside of Waters, David Lochary was a case of a very talented performer who never found his niche outside of the films he made with Waters. Born in 1944, Lochary became friends with Harris Glenn Milstead, who would eventually become Divine, either when they met while attending the Marinella Beauty School in 1963 or—according to Divine in *Shock Value*—when they were over at the house of a mutual friend, Carol Wernig. Lochary had wild ideas about fashion and hair and introduced Milstead to the idea of drag, leading to the creation of Divine (but more about the man behind the character in the next chapter). Already with a receding hairline in his mid-twenties, Lochary would go against form and instead of hiding it, drew attention to it with multi-color dye jobs and a clipped mustache that became more outrageous as the years went on. Lochary's passion went beyond hair and makeup, which he did for Divine and sometimes for others in the early Waters films, to clothing and set design as well. It was through Divine that Waters would meet Lochary.

According to Waters in his book *Shock Value*, Lochary was liked by many of the parents of the Dreamlanders "because he was polite and knew how to turn on the charm," although he confused them at the same time by somehow obtaining a British accent from "living in suburban Baltimore." Nevertheless, Waters's mother in particular loved Lochary, once telling her son, "I like David. He's the only lady you've ever brought home." Lochary was a high-school drop-out and willing to pull scams like the rest of the Dreamlanders to make easy money in the 1960s. "His favorite thing to do in the ripoff years was to get a job in a Provincetown restaurant," Waters told Gerald Peary in 1997, "and then the second day throw himself on the floor and say he hurt his shoulder. He'd

David Lochary and Mink Stole as the Marbles in *Pink Flamingos*. Both were official Dreamlanders, although Waters would know Lochary for some time before being introduced to Stole.

get workmen's compensation. I saw him spend a whole summer in a fake neck brace, but he couldn't go down to the beach because of insurance agents, who thought there was nothing wrong with him."

Beyond such tomfoolery, however, Lochary was also serious about proving himself. In 1968, Lochary was featured in a two-page article in the *Baltimore Sun Magazine*, where he discussed trying to put together a "state-wide arts festival" as well as marketing designer clothes based on the comic book superheroine Wonder Woman. (The article featured photos of Judy Boutin, who appears in Waters's first three films, wearing two of the outfits Lochary designed.) Naturally enough for Lochary, the article featured his demands that the wearer of his designer dresses should think of it "as a total look, complete with curly short hair dyed blue-black." He also admitted that he had at that point sold the dress to only two women. "One's twenty-two, and one is thirty-one," he proclaimed in the article.

Lochary was also set to be the creator and director of the first Baltimore Theater Festival in early 1970, which was a "means whereby some local groups other than the established theaters could find a large audience," as he told the *Baltimore Sun*. The concept was that theatrical groups would be given a hall for their use—"the old Poly auditorium in what is now the Calvert Education Center"—and the committee running the festival would promote the shows, while the theatrical groups would cover all other costs (costumes, sets, etc.). Out of twenty offers, five groups submitted proposals—including Mink Stole appearing as Jean Harlow in a production of Michael McClure's controversial play *The Beard*—and work was going ahead. However, financial and personal issues soon saw Lochary on the outs. The production of *The Beard* was rejected, and then the festival closed with little fanfare in early April 1970.

Lochary began to focus more time on his acting and eventually would move to New York City to pursue work on the stage there. This made sense when the films he made with Waters in the 1970s began appearing around the country, giving some recognition to his name. He also clearly had ability: onscreen, Lochary drew the audience's attention, much like Divine, and this magnetism was not just based on looks or how large their roles were. Rather, it was because they were clearly serious about acting their roles, even in the early 8 mm films of Waters. However, it was also evident that Lochary could be difficult to work with at times. In the documentary *I Am Divine*, Pat Moran stated, "He probably had a fight with every single person in Dreamland except for me," and Lochary's growing drug addiction was affecting his output as well. By 1977, he was "smoking a lot of Angel Dust" (PCP). While his death, on July 29, 1977, is commonly described as a drug overdose, several sources state that Lochary fell onto either some furniture or a mirror and cut himself deeply while high on PCP and bled to death. A sad ending for an actor that would have found work as a character actor before or after his brief time on the national screens.

Nancy (Mink) Stole (Born 1947)

Films with Waters: *Roman Candles* (1966); *Eat Your Makeup* (1968); *Mondo Trasho* (1969); *Multiple Maniacs* (1970); *Pink Flamingos* (1972); *Female Trouble* (1974); *Desperate Living* (1977); *Polyester* (1981); *Hairspray* (1988); *Cry-Baby* (1990); *Serial Mom* (1994); *Pecker* (1998); *Cecil B. DeMented* (2000); *A Dirty Shame* (2004)

Her name is Nancy Stoll, but she is known by many today from the name Waters gave her while filming *Roman Candles*—Mink Stole. Mink may not have had quite the continuous career of Pat Moran, or the bohemian experiences of Mary Vivian Pearce, but she has appeared in every Waters film after *Hag in a Black Leather Jacket*. She has gone on to appear in many other films and television over the years, making her one of the most successful of the Dreamlanders that appeared in front of the camera.

While most of the first Dreamlanders were friends by around 1964–65, Mink did not meet Waters until 1966. By that time, Waters was in Provincetown for the summer and staying with Mink's sister, Sique, when Mink arrived. "I was at loose ends, and I was looking for adventure," Stole told *Slant Magazine*. "And along came John Waters." The two roomed with others for the summer and then went back to Baltimore in the fall of 1966. "Then he calls me up one day and says, 'Do you want to be in this movie I'm making?' And I said yes, and that was it."

The film was *Roman Candles*, and from that point onward, she would appear in every one of Waters's films—many times in large supporting roles, such as in *Hairspray* and *Polyester*, and once even starring (*Desperate Living*). Admittedly, at one point she did feel that working for Waters had been a "mixed bag," as she told the *Baltimore Sun* in 1994: "It's given me access to some things and denied me access to others. I've scared a lot of casting directors because of the over-the-top characters I've played." However, that opinion shifted by 2013, as she mentioned to *Slant*, "I'm proud of the work, especially in recent years, because I've been told by so many people what an impact this work has had on their lives."

In the late 1970s and into the 1980s, Stole worked in the New York theater scene with Charles Ludlum and John Vaccaro. In 1990, she began branching out by performing in television and in other films not related to Waters, such as a fondly remembered episode of Chris Elliott's comedy series *Get a Life* (1990), the comedy *But I'm a Cheerleader* (1999), and even a drag-remake of *Hush, Hush, Sweet Charlotte* called *Hush Up Sweet Charlotte* (2015). She has continued to work in theater, and in 2001 she began performing as a singer, fronting a band called Her Wonderful Band and releasing a CD of music in 2013 called *Do Re Mink*.

Patricia Ann (Maelcum) Soul (1940–1968)

Films with Waters: *Roman Candles* (1966); *Eat Your Makeup* (1968)

Although Mary Vivian Pearce came before and after there, Waters called Maelcum his "first real star" in his book *Shock Value*. She is featured prominently in two of his early films; first as a heavily made-up nun who makes out with her boyfriend in *Roman Candles* (the photo of Soul in the nun habit seen in Waters's *Shock Value* is one of the most famous stills from his early films), and then as an evil nanny/governess who kidnaps models to pose to death in *Eat Your Makeup*.

Pat Moran introduced Soul to Waters at Martick's, the bar both Waters and Moran frequented in the 1960s. According to Moran, both she and Waters were underage at the time, but Moran was able to enter with her fake I.D., while Waters would have to wait in the alley behind the business until the owner had left before Moran and Soul would then sneak Waters into the place. Soul was older and intimidating in her own way that would resonate in the later Dreamland era by all who knew her ("Even Divine was in awe of Maelcum Soul," Waters said in the short video documentary *The Maelcum Soul Story*). She wore vintage clothes, many layers of makeup, heavy eye shadow, bright red hair, an eight-point star drawn on one cheek, and—most importantly—she didn't care if anyone was shocked by it, even if she went out wearing a blue mask of makeup on her face. "Maelcum was the most astonishing bohemian I've ever known, and she influenced my twisted vision of how women should look more than any film, book, or painting," Waters stated in *Shock Value*.

In 1965, Soul made national news by posing for twenty-six portraits shown at Matrick's in November of that year. Twenty-five of the twenty-six drawings and paintings were nudes, and the display was called "The Maelcum Show." In early 1966, Waters convinced Soul to help out with his movies and even posed for some publicity photos as the Wicked Witch for Waters's intended film *Dorothy, the Kansas City Pot Head*. That film was never completed. Instead, she appeared in Waters's next two films. Soul (who went by the family nickname of Maelcum) would die of kidney failure in 1968 at the age of twenty-seven.

Mark Isherwood (1948–2013)

Films with Waters: *Roman Candles* (1966); *Mondo Trasho* (1969); *Multiple Maniacs* (1970); *Pink Flamingos* (1972)

Isherwood was a high school friend of Waters and appeared in miscellaneous roles in four of Waters's films. He's probably remembered best for his role as the nude hitchhiker in *Mondo Trasho*. Isherwood would move on after appearing in *Pink Flamingos* in 1972, eventually residing in Bristol, Massachusetts, where he worked as an independent painting contractor.

In 2014, Waters mentioned in an interview with Johns Hopkins University that he had only recently, in 2013, heard about Isherwood's death from natural causes and that they had not talked in twenty-five years. The obituary for Isherwood would mention that, "while in Baltimore he appeared in a John Waters movie," but there was no mention of Isherwood's notoriety from his most famous role.

Paul Swift (1934–1994)

Films with Waters: *Multiple Maniacs* (1970); *Pink Flamingos* (1972); *Female Trouble* (1974); *Desperate Living* (1977)

Swift first turned up in *Multiple Maniacs* as Cookie's militant boyfriend but probably will be forever known as the "Eggman" in *Pink Flamingos*. A former roommate to Susan Lowe, Swift was known in Fells Points for spending many evenings getting drunk at Ledbetter's and dancing naked on top of the bar. He stopped appearing in Waters's films after *Desperate Living* in

1977 and worked in retail in Baltimore, most notably at a store called Oh Susannah's on South Broadway. He died from AIDS in 1994.

Marina Melin (Born 1940)

Films with Waters: *Eat Your Makeup* (1968); *Mondo Trasho* (1969); *Multiple Maniacs* (1970); *Pink Flamingos* (1972); *Female Trouble* (1974); *Desperate Living* (1977); *Polyester* (1981)

Waters met Melin in Provincetown through Mona Montgomery, who was working in the same dress shop with Melin. According to Waters in his book *Shock Value*, Melin was an ex-painter from Sweden whom Waters persuaded to come back with him to Baltimore in the fall of 1967 to be in his next movie, *Eat Your Makeup*. Marina played the main model that is chained up and later forced to model herself to death. Waters goes on to say in his book that, due to a breakdown, Melin ended up in the hospital soon after making the film, but she would be back to perform in five of his next six films. Her last appearance was as the last victim of Dexter at the supermarket before being apprehended in *Polyester*.

George Figgs (Born 1947)

Films with Waters: *Eat Your Makeup* (1968); *Mondo Trasho* (1969); *Multiple Maniacs* (1970); *Pink Flamingos* (1972); *Female Trouble* (1974); *Desperate Living* (1977); *Polyester* (1981); *Serial Mom* (1994); *Pecker* (1998); *Cecil B. DeMented* (2000); *A Dirty Shame* (2004)

One can't be a fan of Waters's films without knowing that Figgs was once Jesus Christ.

Figgs met Waters when he was seventeen, outside of Matrick's, "looking for beatniks" and hoping someone would buy them drinks. While Figgs was involved with Waters as early as the ill-fated *Dorothy, the Kansas City Pot Head*, where he was to play the Grassman, his proper introduction into Waters's movies came with *Eat Your Makeup*, as Prince Charming. He would appear in every Waters film between *Mondo Trasho* and *Polyester* in small roles, with his biggest being that of Jesus in the blasphemous Passion play seen in *Multiple Maniacs*. As Figgs joked to the *Baltimore Sun* in 2016: "Back in those days, I actually thought I was Jesus Christ. I was taking a lot of acid and everything ... I just said, 'Yes, of course I'll play Jesus. I am Jesus." Although he would stop appearing onscreen for Waters after *Polyester*, Figgs would work as a projectionist for the dailies done on the last four films Waters directed. He continues to do interviews about his work with Waters and in particular about his role as Jesus Christ in *Multiple Maniacs*.

For a time, Figgs worked as an assistant manager and projectionist at the Charles Theater. Then, in 1990, he originated and ran the Orpheum Cinema, an eighty-seat theater on the second floor of a row house in Fell's Point. It was one of the first theaters to adopt a rear-projection system for the showings (something much more common nearly thirty years on). The theater eventually closed in 1999, but during those years and beyond, Figgs gained a reputation as a film historian, a commentator on Fell's Point, and a conspiracy theorist on the death of Edgar Allan Poe.

Laura (Susan) Lowe (Born 1948)

Films with Waters: *Mondo Trasho* (1969); *Multiple Maniacs* (1970); *Female Trouble* (1974); *Desperate Living* (1977); *Polyester* (1981); *Hairspray* (1988); *Cry-Baby* (1990); *Serial Mom* (1994); *Pecker* (1998); *Cecil B. DeMented* (2000); *A Dirty Shame* (2004)

Lowe was attending the Maryland Institute College of Art (MICA) as a painter in 1967 when she began dating George Figgs, who introduced her to Waters. Subsequently, Lowe would later introduce Waters to Edith Massey, Vincent Peranio, and Van Smith, whom she knew from the college (leading to Waters once referring to her as his "first talent scout"). She had already worked as an actor in plays at the college, so it was only natural for her to join in on the antics in Waters's films, usually in small role. Her best remembered role was also her biggest—that of Mole in *Desperate Living*, wearing Van Smith makeup that disturbed her husband and kids at the time. Her then-newborn son, Ramsey, appears as newborn Taffy in *Female Trouble*.

Lowe has appeared in ten of Waters films, while also painting and working with ceramic sculptures. Her artistic work has appeared many times over the years in the Baltimore area, and she has also taught art history at MICA, the University of Maryland, and Catonsville Community College.

Van Smith (1945–2006)

Films with Waters: *Pink Flamingos* (1972); *Female Trouble* (1974); *Desperate Living* (1977); *Polyester* (1981); *Hairspray* (1988); *Cry-Baby* (1990); *Serial Mom* (1994); *Pecker* (1998); *Cecil B. DeMented* (2000); *A Dirty Shame* (2004)

Under John Waters's guidance, both Vincent Peranio and Van Smith defined the look of his films over the year—Peranio with set and art design, and Van Smith with the costumes and makeup of the characters in the movies. While David Lochary was the first to give Divine a look in makeup and hair, it was really once Van Smith came along and created a makeup style Waters has referred to often as "a combination of Jayne Mansfield and Clarabelle the Clown" that Divine's image became an icon.

Smith graduated from the Maryland Institute College of Art with a degree in fashion arts. (One of his illustrations for a dress design appeared in an April 1967 issue of the *Baltimore Sun* while he was still a student at the college.) Moving into production design and fashion in the fast-paced fashion world of New York, Smith very quickly grew tired of the competition and returned to Baltimore. Around 1970, Smith and Waters met at the Marlboro Apartments, close to the Maryland Institute College of Art. Both he and Peranio soon became part of the "Hillbilly Rip-offs" entourage that went to Provincetown every summer.

In 1970, *Multiple Maniacs* became a sensation at the Palace Theater in San Francisco, leading to Divine being invited to appear live onstage. Smith went with Divine, with the suggestion that he do "something outrageous" with Divine's makeup, while Waters told Smith to "do something weird with his hairline." Smith would shave off the eyebrows and shaved Divine's head halfway back in order to exaggerate the eye makeup on Divine's face. Really exaggerate. "There wasn't enough room on the human face for the amount of eye makeup that Van wanted [Divine] to wear," Waters joked in the documentary *I Am Divine*.

With that success came Waters working on the production that would become *Pink Flamingos*. Smith was working for *Women's Wear Daily* as a fashion illustrator at the time, but he hated the commute. That was when Waters told him, "Look, I can give you a couple of dollars, do you want to do the movie?" Smith agreed and it would be a partnership lasting through the rest of Waters's movies. "Van Smith is the only costume designer with whom I've ever worked," Waters told Mary Vivian Pearce for *Paper Magazine*. "He's hard-core Dreamland royalty, a fashion terrorist who understands what my characters would wear before and after I write them. His costumes have been a huge part of any success my films have had."

Smith's style was the antithesis of what would have been the norm for most artists. Where many would try to find the beauty, Smith would look for the deformities—the outrageous clothes, the emphasis on pockmarks, and scars on the characters' faces. Smith's work, along with Peranio's, created an otherworldly look in Waters's films that made them seem consistently nightmarish even in the bright sunshine of *Pink Flamingos*. Many have pointed out how Smith's work would forecast the punk look of the later 1970s. As Richard Cardone, who was the national artistic director for Clairol in 1994, stated in an article about Smith for the *Baltimore Sun*, "Who would have thought shaved heads, torn clothes, and hooker makeup would be seen on the runaways of the top designers?"

In later days, Smith would wistfully recall the earlier days of the Dreamland productions. "I really enjoyed the early movies," Smith told Vida Roberts, while working on *Serial Mom*. "It was a great creative outlet, creating a character, a totally different venue. I got work as a result of the early Waters notoriety from people who wanted that crazy look." Smith continued to do illustrations and at one time had a twentieth-century antiques shop, and he did some work for *Homicide: Life in the Streets* as well. He only appeared once on-camera in a Waters film, as a party guest in drag in *Pink Flamingos*. He passed away in 2006 from a heart attack.

Vincent Peranio (Born 1945)

Films with Waters: *Multiple Maniacs* (1970); *Pink Flamingos* (1972); *Female Trouble* (1974); *Desperate Living* (1977); *Polyester* (1981); *Hairspray* (1988); *Cry-Baby* (1990); *Serial Mom* (1994); *Pecker* (1998); *Cecil B. DeMented* (2000); *A Dirty Shame* (2004)

Peranio came a little later than most of the first generation of Dreamlanders, arriving in time to help design Lobstora so that it could rape Divine near the end of *Multiple Maniacs*. An establish painter in the Baltimore area by 1969, Peranio graduated from the Maryland Institute with a Fine Arts degree in 1968. He and several other artists moved in together at a place called the Hollywood Bakery, which was right next door to Pete's Hotel, a bar where Edith Massey worked. Young and artistic, the group would have frequent parties, which led to Peranio meeting Waters for the first time. "During one of the parties, John Waters, Mink, Divine, Bonnie Pearce, David Lochary, Van Smith, and Pat Moran showed up. A friend of ours, Susan [Lowe], brought them. They had just finished doing a movie called *Mondo Trasho*," Peranio said to Bruce Goldfarb.

Later in the year, Waters began working on *Multiple Maniacs*. Calling up Peranio (in a 2016 interview with the *Baltimore Sun*, Peranio said Waters actually sent him a card instead of calling him), Waters asked Peranio if, since he was an artist, he could create a fifteen-foot lobster. "My whole thing is that I never say no," Peranio told Bruce Goldfarb. "That's why I got in this business. You never say no in this business." Peranio worked on the lobster with his brother Ed and operated it in the film while also appearing as one of the freaks early on in *Multiple Maniacs*. He then went back to doing art.

Then Waters contacted him to work on *Pink Flamingos*, for which he designed the sets and other aspects of the production. "I thought, well, *Pink Flamingos* is a fun little thing and might play at some colleges, something like that." Soon, Peranio got used to alternating between spending half a year painting and the other half of the year making films with Waters "until eventually the film career took over."

Besides appearing briefly on-camera in *Pink Flamingos* and *Female Trouble* (he dies for Dawn's art near the end of the film), Peranio has worked as a designer on every one of Waters's films since *Multiple Maniacs*. His wife, Delores Deluxe, has contributed to Waters's films as an assistant art

Lobstora attacks Divine in *Multiple Maniacs* (1980). The giant lobster was the creation of Vincent Peranio and his brother, Ed. Vincent Peranio would work behind the scenes on every Waters film thereafter.

director on *Desperate Living* and *Polyester*, an art director on *Cry-Baby*, and an assistant title designer on *Female Trouble*.

Peranio began working on films not connected to Waters in 1979, working on two Tim Conway–Don Knotts films in a row: *The Prize Fighter* (1979) and *The Private Eyes* (1980). He continued to work on films centered in Baltimore, such as *Homicide: Life on the Street* and *The Wire*.

Delores also appeared in *Desperate Living* as the nurse at Johns Hopkins. Ed Peranio also appeared on film a few times for Waters: as a party guest in *Pink Flamingos*; as Wink, a hairdresser at the Lipstick Beauty Salon in *Female Trouble*; and as one of Queen Carlotta's goons in *Desperate Living*.

Edith (Edie) Massey (1918–1984)

Films with Waters: *Multiple Maniacs* (1970); *Pink Flamingos* (1972); *Female Trouble* (1974); *Desperate Living* (1977); *Polyester* (1981)

Massey made only five movies with Waters, and her first appearance (in *Multiple Maniacs*) was more of a cameo than a role. She was overweight, had bad teeth, seemed to be in her own little world, and had an obvious issue with reading her lines, but she projected such an air of sweetness even in her most evil appearances (like her role in *Female Trouble*) that it was impossible to not love her.

Massey was born in New York City, but when her father and then her mother died, she and her five siblings—four brothers and a sister—moved to an orphanage. At sixteen, she ran away from a foster home—"I was going to be one of the family. It turned out I was the maid," Massey noted in an article for the *Baltimore Sun*—and ended up in Los Angeles. She had learned tap-dancing while in the orphanage and used it to land a job working in a nightclub in LA and eventually in San Francisco.

After work descended into being a B-girl and then a madam as the 1950s wore on, and after a failed marriage, Massey moved to Baltimore. It was there that she worked for a time in "The Block," an area full of sex shops and strip clubs, and then eventually as a bartender at Pete's Hotel. It was at Pete's Hotel where Vincent Peranio introduced her to Waters, according to a *Baltimore Sun* article in 1973. (Waters, in a 1978 interview with *Evening Magazine*, stated it was Susan Lowe who did the introduction.) "She worked in a wino bar that we used to hang out in because drinks were ten cents," Waters told Scott MacDonald. "I thought, 'God, she looks so good!'"

After *Multiple Maniacs*, where she played a version of herself along with the Virgin Mary in the Passion Play segment of the film, Massey opened her own secondhand clothing store called Edith's Shopping Bag in lower Broadway, using money she had gotten from her sister. She continued operating the store for years until her move to LA in the early 1980s.

In the late 1970s, Waters assisted Massey in creating her own "punk" band, which featured Ann Collier—of the popular Baltimore band Rhumboogie—and future Go-Go's drummer Gina Schock. Massey sang lead for the band, which was called Edie and the Eggs (referencing her role as the Egg Lady in *Pink Flamingos*). The band would perform in various places in Baltimore, Philadelphia, San Francisco, and Los Angeles, obtaining gigs based on Massey's popularity in the Waters films. The touring would convince Schock to relocate from Baltimore to LA, which led to her joining the Go-Go's. Massey would record two songs in 1982 that were released as

Edith Massey as the Virgin Mary in *Multiple Maniacs* (1970). It was her first film with Waters, and although she was a struggle to work with when it came to remembering her lines, she was so endearing that everyone who filmed with her loved her.

a single: "Big Girls Don't Cry" (originally done by the Four Seasons) and "Punks, Get Off the Grass." When performing in her band, Massey would sometimes wear an outfit similar to the black outfit she wore in *Female Trouble*, although she stated during the filming of the movie that she hated wearing the outfit. She also appeared as the "love interest" in John Cougar Mellencamp's 1980 music video for "This Time" and appeared on the cover of his 1980 album *Nothin' Matters and What If It Did*. "She was pretty funny," Mellancamp told Kurt Loder in 1980 about having Massey appear on the cover with him. "We'd get a call from her at ten in the morning and she'd say, 'I'm at the corner of Santa Monica and someplace, and I don't think I can walk back.'" In the late 1970s, she also appeared as a model in a series of racy greeting cards, which she sold in her shop.

In the early 1980s, after appearing in *Polyester*, Massey moved to Venice, California, and opened a new version of her secondhand store there. Massey never improved much as an actor in the films and was well known for having difficulty in learning her lines—she either read stage directions as if they were dialogue or simply forgot her lines. (In a *Baltimore Sun* interview from 1973, Massey recalled that, while she was freezing in the baby crib in *Pink Flamingos*, Waters once snapped at her in frustration, telling her, "We're going to stay here until we get it right.") She was also known to be in her own world at times when talking to others; sometimes she didn't even register what people were saying to her as she made conversation in her own way. Even so, it's clear that her sunny attitude is what brought people to visit her in her shop and love her on the set. "[She was] the eccentric grandmother everybody wished they had had," Waters told the *Baltimore Sun* in 1984. In a way, it's fitting that her final character in a Waters film turned out to be the fortunate and eternally happy Cuddles in *Polyester*. She deserved that kind of happiness in her life even if she seemed fine with whatever came her way. Best of all, in the end she achieved stardom through her fans and her friends. When she died in 1984 due to cancer of the lymph nodes, friends old and new surrounded her, and while some told of the news as if the "Egg Lady" had died, many, many more simply thought of losing their friend, Edie.

Howard Gruber (1942–1993)

Films with Waters: *Eat Your Makeup* (1968); *Multiple Maniacs* (1970); *Pink Flamingos* (1972)

Little seen in the Waters film, Howard Gruber was one of the original Dreamlanders, eventually residing in Provincetown, where he operated the Front Street Restaurant from 1974 through 1987. He would open Gruber's Bayside Restaurant in 1988.

He is best remembered for playing John F. Kennedy to Divine's Jackie Kennedy in *Eat Your Makeup* and for attacking Divine while wearing a dress and huffing glue with Susan Lowe in *Multiple Maniacs*. He also appears briefly in *Pink Flamingos*. He died in 1993 of complications from AIDS.

John Leisenring (1947–1989)

Leisenring appeared in only one of Waters's films, *Mondo Trasho*, where he played Prince Charming and—memorably—"The Shrimper" early in the film. Leisenring was Waters's boyfriend at the time and they lived together for a while in Provincetown in the summer of 1968. Waters told Gerald Peary, "People always ask me if I sleep with people in my movies. I think besides him there was only one other person in my movies I slept with. No, not Divine."

He later became a cook, working for years in San Francisco preparing Chesapeake Bay seafood dishes. He returned to Baltimore in 1987 and worked as a cook at the Belvedere Hotel before dying of liver disease in 1989.

Dorothy Karen (Cookie) Mueller (1949–1989)

Films with Waters: *Multiple Maniacs* (1970); *Pink Flamingos* (1972); *Female Trouble* (1974); *Desperate Living* (1977); *Polyester* (1981)

Mueller sometimes went by her middle name Karen, although mostly she used the nickname she was given "before [she] could walk," as she mentioned in her book *Walking Through Clear Water in a Pool Painted Black*. She never seemed to be sure how she got the name, but she said, "It didn't matter to me, they could call me whatever they wanted." Mueller was a traveler, moving from place to place and from experience to experience.

Mueller met John Waters in March 1969 when his film *Mondo Trasho* premiered at the Emmanuel Church in Baltimore. A contest occurred at the premiere, with the door prize of "dinner for two at one of the sleaziest hamburger shops in town," as Waters referred to the Little Tavern in his book

Shock Value. Mueller was the winner and drew in Waters immediately with her "hard-as-nails attitude" and her mention of being released from a mental hospital. She quickly became friends with Waters's friends and wound up playing the role of Cookie, Divine's daughter, in Waters's next film, *Multiple Maniacs*.

Mueller would continue to work in Waters's films up until *Polyester*, and her son Max appeared as the newborn in *Pink Flamingos*. She also gave Waters the name of one of his movies when she became ill and he went to visit her in the hospital. When asked what was wrong, Mueller told Waters, "Just a little female trouble, hon." Mueller was one of the few members of the original Dreamlander actors to work in films other than Waters's, albeit her parts were typically small: a barmaid in *Underground U.S.A.* (1980) and an actress in a horror film in Susan Seidelman's *Smithereens* (1982). Mueller had always been a writer: at the age of eleven she wrote a book about the Johnstown, Pennsylvania, flood, which was over 300 pages long and which

Cookie Mueller as one of Dawn's gang in *Female Trouble*.

she snuck into her local library and put on a shelf. Into the 1970s and onward, she wrote about a variety of topics—mostly nonfiction. She wrote a regular column called "Ask Dr. Mueller" for the magazine *East Village Eye* in the 1980s and briefly worked for *Details* magazine as an art editor. Much of her writing is collected in various books published before and after her death and all are well worth obtaining. Her short piece "Abduction and Rape— Highway 31, Elkton, MD—1969," about a hitchhiking trip to Provincetown with Mink Stole and Susan Lowe that went horribly wrong, has been reprinted numerous times over the years and appears in the volume *Ask Dr. Mueller* (1997).

Waters commented in his 1997 interview with Gerald Peary that he saw little of Cookie for a time in the 1980s due to her drug use, but they reconciled later in the 1980s. In 1986, Mueller married an Italian artist named Vittorio Scarpati, who would die less than seven weeks before Mueller did in 1989, both from complications related to AIDS. On the back of the posthumous collection of her writing, *Walking Through Clear Water in a Pool Painted Black*, Waters said of Mueller, "She was a writer, a mother, an outlaw, an actress, a fashion designer, a go-go dancer, a witch doctor, an art-hag, and above all, a goddess. Boy do I miss that girl."

Bob Adams (Born 1947)

Films with Waters: *Pink Flamingos* (1972); *Female Trouble* (1974); *Desperate Living* (1977); *Polyester* (1981); *Hairspray* (1988); *Cry-Baby* (1990); *Serial Mom* (1994); *Pecker* (1998); *Cecil B. DeMented* (2000); *A Dirty Shame* (2004)

Described by John Waters as being the "ultimate Dreamland archivist," Bob Adams has been friends with Waters since the late 1960s. His association with Waters on his films began in 1971 with the filming of *Pink Flamingos*, where he allowed Waters to set up Divine's trailer in the film on a 200-acre farm that he was housesitting. He also appeared in the film as a policeman who gets shot and worked as a soundman on the film. He returned in *Female Trouble* as Ernie, the gay man Massey's character uses in an attempt to entice her nephew. His main function for Waters is in an everyman role—appearing as an extra in films, taking photos on the sets, and even finding odd items to populate the sets.

At one time, Adams ran a secondhand store co-owned by Edith Massey called Flashback, which contained a certain amount of archival pieces from

Waters's films. The store closed many years ago, but Adams is still known as the man who has the largest stash of Dreamland material connected to the films.

Susan Walsh (1948–2009)

Films with Waters: *Mondo Trasho* (1969); *Multiple Maniacs* (1970); *Pink Flamingos* (1972); *Female Trouble* (1974)

Walsh appeared in four Waters films. Her best role came in *Female Trouble*, where she played Chicklette, one of Dawn Davenport's classmates and a criminal henchperson. She later married and had two daughters. She passed away in 2009 from natural causes.

Channing Wilroy (Born 1940)

Films with Waters: *Pink Flamingos* (1972); *Female Trouble* (1974); *Desperate Living* (1977); *Pecker* (1998); *Cecil B. DeMented* (2000); *A Dirty Shame* (2004)

An actual former dancer on *The Buddy Deane Show*, the dance program Waters used as the basis for the show in *Hairspray*, Wilroy met up with Waters in the mid-1960s. He eventually moved to Provincetown for good in 1969 and, when interviewed in 1997 by Gerald Peary, stated that he runs a "cottage colony" there. Wilroy's biggest role was as Channing the Butler in *Pink Flamingos*. He also worked as a musical consultant on *Cry-Baby*, with his collection of 1950s rhythm and blues records.

Jean Hill (1947–2013)

Films with Waters: *Desperate Living* (1977); *Polyester* (1981); *A Dirty Shame* (2004)

"Jean Hill was my only African-American star. She was a talented comedian, a brave actress, and a much valued member of the Dreamland acting gig I worked with in my movies," Waters told the *Baltimore Sun* in 2013. Hill was a latecomer to the films Waters made in the 1970s, appearing first as Grizelda Brown, the maid who murders the husband at the beginning of

Desperate Living. It would be her largest role in a Waters film, although she also has a memorable role in *Polyester* as the gospel singer who hijacks the bus. She last appeared in *A Dirty Shame* in a small role as a woman on a fire escape.

Hill was working as a teacher for special education students while also working as an actor around Baltimore—namely with the Arena Players—when Pat Moran placed a wanted ad in the Baltimore Sun looking for a "black actress over 200 lbs." (not "400 pounds," as listed by many sources). At the auditions, many of the actors quickly disappeared when Waters mentioned that there would be brief nudity and they would have to dye their hair blonde, but Hill was game. "I've got a lot to show, honey," Waters remembers her telling him at the time of the audition. Hill would also appear as a model on a number of "humorous" and raunchy greeting cards found at stores such as Spencer's Gifts. She died of renal failure at the age of sixty-seven.

Ricki Lake (Born 1968)

Films with Waters: *Hairspray* (1988); *Cry-Baby* (1990); *Serial Mom* (1994); *Cecil B. DeMented* (2000); *A Dirty Shame* (2004)

A true second generation of Dreamlanders started with the film *Hairspray* and the emergence of Ricki Lake in the role of Tracy Tumblad. Her role became secondary in subsequent Waters films, but she always returned when available. She was also supposed to appear in *Pecker* but had to bow out when she could not negotiate time away from the weekday talk show she did at the time. Her talk show, *Ricki Lake*, lasted eleven seasons and was followed by a different show, which lasted one season. She has appeared in a number of television series since *Hairspray* and even made an appearance in the live version of the *Hairspray* musical done for NBC. She is still looked upon as one of the many success stories of those who have participated in Waters's movies.

Patricia Hearst (Born 1954)

Films with Waters: *Hairspray* (1988); *Cry-Baby* (1990); *Serial Mom* (1994); *Cecil B. DeMented* (2000); *Pecker* (1998); *A Dirty Shame* (2004)

Ricki Lake from *Serial Mom* (1994). Although not an original Dreamlander, Lake has been in nearly all of Waters's films in some capacity ever since starring in *Hairspray* (1988), making her a second-generation Dreamlander, of which there are only a few.

Waters first saw Hearst in person at her trial in 1976 for her involvement in the infamous Hibernia Bank robbery. "That was the hardest trial to get into since the Lindbergh baby," Waters told James Grant in 1994, when discussing his fascination for being an eyewitness to various criminal trials. "People waited three days in sleeping bags and stuff. I waited twelve hours, easy."

Hearst is the granddaughter of the famous newspaper publisher William Randolph Hearst. In 1974, the Symbionese Liberation Army (SLA), a radical guerilla group that sustained itself through robberies and murder, kidnapped her. Two months after the kidnapping, an audiotape appeared of her saying she had joined the SLA, and a few days later she took part in the robbing of a bank, with surveillance video showing her participation. Arrested in September 1975 and put on trial, Hearst faced a heavy public assumption that she was a willing participant, although later evidence strongly suggested that she had been brainwashed for a time to become involved. After being convicted of the robbery, Hearst went to prison. She was released in

1979 but only pardoned in 2001. In 1981, she wrote a book about her past called *Every Secret Thing*.

In 1988, Paul Schrader directed the film *Patty Hearst*, which was based on Hearst's book. The film premiered at the 1988 Cannes Film Festival, where Waters saw it. Hearst was also there at Cannes to help promote the film and met Waters, who mentioned to her that he would love for her to be in his next movie. Hearst then received the script for *Cry-Baby*. "Oh, no, he was serious," Hearst said to the *Hartford Courant* in April 1990. Reading the script and thinking it may be fun to do, she agreed to come out and audition for the part. Although she thought she did a terrible job with the reading, Waters cast her for the role of the mother of Traci Lords's character in the film.

Hearst has appeared in every one of Waters's films after *Cry-Baby*, making her a Dreamlander, although not in the traditional sense of the original gang of low-level radicals and criminals of Waters's past—even if they wanted her to be like them in some ways at the time. "Patricia has said to me: 'It's because of people like you that I went to jail, because you wanted me to be something that I was not.' And she's right," Waters told James Grant. "We wanted her to be this bad-girl heiress when really she was brainwashed and a horrible thing happened to her."

Alan J. Wendl (Born 1933)

Films with Waters: *Hairspray* (1988); *Cry-Baby* (1990); *Serial Mom* (1994); *Cecil B. DeMented* (2000); *Pecker* (1998); *A Dirty Shame* (2004)

An actor, director, and producer of plays in Baltimore—mostly for the Oregon Ridge Dinner Theatre—Wendl also was a regular on the live comedy series *Crabs*, which ran for seven years on MPT (Maryland Public Television). Wendl appeared in Waters's last five films, making him pretty much a second-generation Dreamlander, and is best remembered as Mr. Pinky in *Hairspray*. Wendl also appeared in episodes of *Homicide: Life on the Street* and *The Wire* as well as the in the films *Men Don't Leave* (1990) and *He Said, She Said* (1991). He alternated between being listed as Alan Wendl and Alan J. Wendl on various projects over the years.

His wife, Joyce Flick Wendl, who also acted and directed for the Oregon Ridge Dinner Theatre, appears in Waters's last three films as well.

Traci Lords (1968)

Films with Waters: *Cry-Baby* (1990); *Serial Mom* (1994)

Born Nora Louise Kuzma, Traci Lords became national news in 1986 when it was discovered that she had been appearing in pornographic films in the mid-1980s while underage. In 1987, she transitioned to strictly non-pornographic roles in low budget films such as a remake of the science fiction film *Not of This Earth* (1988) and a Jim Varney comedy, *Fast Food* (1989). She was next cast through an audition for *Cry-Baby*, where she got to both get away from and parody her earlier history: "I get to make fun of my so-called image as a sex symbol and ex-porno-film queen," Lords told *Rolling Stone* magazine. Ironically, the one scene that truly showed her character as only acting the role of a "bad girl" and really being a "good girl" at heart was dropped from the film before its release. While working on the film Lords began dating Pat Moran's son, Brook Yeaton, who was working on the film as the property master. The two married and later divorced in 1995.

She appeared briefly in Waters's follow-up film, *Serial Mom*, and appeared in a number of films and television series, including the early Marvel Comics film *Blade* (1998), Kevin Smith's *Zack and Miri Make a Porno* (2008), and as a regular in the series *First Wave* (2001) and the comedy-crime series *Swedish Dicks* (2017). She also recorded an album, *1000 Fires* (1995), and wrote an autobiography, *Traci Lords: Underneath It All* (2003).

In the documentary on the *Cry-Baby* DVD, as well as discussed by Waters in print and in his one-man shows, that federal agents at one point arrived on the set of *Cry-Baby* to serve papers to Lords in order for her to appear in a trial. The cast and crew tried to hide Lords from what they saw as a humiliating exhibition by the agents to shame a woman trying to move past an event in her childhood. To cheer her up, it was mentioned that "everyone has gone to prison at one time or another" who was working on the film, with cast and crew discussing the times they had been arrested, including Polly Bergen (who was arrested for protesting in favor of gun control in the 1960s). "And, you know, they just started telling these stories," Lords said in the documentary *It Came From Baltimore*, "but it was beyond that. It was the fact that so many people rallied around me and were willing to just, kind of, stand up and say: 'You know what? It's not just you.'" "It was a bonding experience," Waters stated in the same documentary, and this experience makes Traci Lords one of the second-generation Dreamlanders.

Kim McGuire (1955–2016)

Films with Waters: *Cry-Baby* (1990); *Serial Mom* (1994)

McGuire only appeared in one film for Waters but was such a stand-out performer in the film, and was mentioned so often in Waters's subsequent one-man shows, that it seems appropriate to list her here with the other Dreamlanders. Her role as Hatchet-Face in *Cry-Baby*, with her makeup and actions making her look and sound like the demented love-child of Edith Massey and Divine. "I think she's one of Van's best creations," Waters told *SF Weekly* in 1990. "In real life Kim's like a blank: she's very pale and her hair's white. So it was like drawing on a face. And she understood the role perfectly. Van drew her face on crooked, and she moved her body crookedly."

McGuire subsequently made a cameo appearance in *Serial Mom*. However, beyond a regular role in the odd-but-quickly-cancelled comedy series by David Lynch, *On the Air*, her film and television roles were few. She subsequently became an attorney following the career path of her father. She and her partner, producer Gene Piotrowsky, also had the unfortunate luck of living in Los Angeles during the 1994 earthquake there, New York City at the time of the 9/11 attack, and New Orleans at the time of Hurricane Katrina.

She returned to be interviewed for the retrospective documentary on the 2005 "Director's Cut" DVD release of *Cry-Baby* and continued to work as an attorney. She and Piotrowsky eventually settled in Naples, Florida, and it was there in September 2016 that she was admitted into a hospital with pneumonia and died from cardiac arrest. Her acting career was brief, but due to just one role, McGuire was immortalized in film in a way that can never truly be duplicated.

Johnny Knoxville (Born 1971)

Films with Waters: *A Dirty Shame* (2004)

Knoxville appeared in only one film for Waters, playing the costarring role of Ray-Ray in *A Dirty Shame*, but Waters obviously saw a kindred spirit in Knoxville, noting the subversive nature of Knoxville's popular MTV stunt series *Jackass* (2000–2002) and subsequent film spin-offs. Knoxville has appeared in a number of films, including *Men in Black II* (2002), *The Dukes of Hazzard* (2005), *Elvis & Nixon* (2016), and, of course, the various *Jackass* films.

Waters would go on to appear in *Jackass Number Two* (2006) and had plans to star Knoxville in his follow-up to *A Dirty Shame*, to be called *Fruitcake*, but the film never got past the script stage. All the cards are there for Knoxville to be a second-generation Dreamlander, but they never were quite dealt out the way Waters planned.

And Some Other Memorable Players . . .

Lizzy Temple Black

In an attempt to parody the name that the famous child star Shirley Temple used as an adult—Shirley Temple Black—Waters named his own child star "Lizzy Temple Black." The ten-year-old girl appeared in *Eat Your Makeup* as a Girl Scout and later appeared as the Virgin Mary's assistant in *Mondo Trasho*. Maelcum Soul had been the girl's governess and so Waters asked the father of the girl if she would appear in his film, which he agreed to do. Lizzy appeared in only the two films and stopped after that. Waters, naturally enough, does not give her real name in interviews, although he does state in *Shock Value*, "I still see her on the street, grown into a seemingly very serious young lady, but she never says hello. I wonder if she has fond memories of that marvelous day in the pigpen?"

Berenica Cipcus

Cipcus appeared in *Eat Your Makeup, Mondo Trasho* (as Dr. Coathanger's nurse), *Multiple Maniacs, Pink Flamingos,* and *Female Trouble*. She is best remembered as one of the two women in the park—the other played by Margie Skidmore—who David Lochary exposes himself to in *Pink Flamingos*.

Alan Reese

Meeting Waters in the early Provincetown years, Reese appeared as an extra in six of Waters's movies: *Mondo Trasho, Multiple Maniacs, Pink Flamingos, Desperate Living, Pecker,* and *Cecil B. DeMented*. He later became a school teacher in Baltimore County.

Rick Morrow

Another early Provincetown recruit, Morrow appeared in only two movies for Waters: *Mondo Trasho*, as a reporter, and *Multiple Maniacs*, as Ricky, Divine's assistant who spends most of the movie bumming out on the couch. Waters—in his 2005 collection of scripts, *Hairspray, Female Trouble, and Multiple Maniacs*—states that Morrow later worked as a cab driver and a poet in Springfield, Oregon. He later moved back to the Baltimore area and passed away in December 2017 from lung cancer.

George Stover

Stover was another later member of the Dreamland group of actors, appearing first as the chaplain in *Female Trouble* and more prominently as the husband of Mink Stole's character in *Desperate Living*. He also made small appearances in *Polyester* and *Hairspray*. In an interview with Robert Long II, Stover noted that he knew Waters when they were kids, long before meeting again to appear in his films, saying: "I had lost touch with him and was never sure whether that guy from junior high school was the same person as the filmmaker I had been reading about in the Baltimore newspapers. On Monday morning back in eighth grade homeroom, John and I would often discuss the episode of *The Twilight Zone* that had been on TV the previous Friday evening." As a young man, Stover was also involved with early movie fanzines, working on self-published magazines called *Black Oracle* and later *Cinemacabre*.

An actuary for the state government when not working as an actor, Stover has made a career out of playing small- to medium-size roles for a number of other directors over the years. He is especially known for appearing in low-budget science fiction films for Don Dohler—*Galaxy Invader, Nightbeast, The Alien Factor*—and Fred Olen Ray (*Attack of the 60 Foot Centerfold*). In February 2012, he was shot through the neck by a robber in his home, but he survived with a flesh wound—the bullet managed to miss anything vital—and gave a description of the shooter to police, who captured the man. He still appears in low-budget movies today.

Of course, there are many other members of Waters's cast and crew who, over the years, have had a vital impact on his films. One in particular was so important that a whole chapter must be devoted to her work. And that is, of course, the work of the most beautiful woman in the world.

Almost.

3

Teach Me to Be Divine

The Short, Sweet History of Divine

I love making people laugh. I just happen to do it dressed as a woman.

—Divine, to the *Chicago Tribune*, 1985

In an age where we as a society try to show some enlightenment as to how to address people of different backgrounds, cultures, and sexual orientation, how is it best to define Divine? Was Divine a transgender person? Would it be best to refer to Divine as "they" instead of "he" or "she"?

The first step in arriving at such a definition is to remember that most interviews and articles discussing Divine while alive occurred at least thirty years ago—some even closer to fifty (and, yes, that does seem a bit hard to believe until you count the years). Closing in on a couple of generations ago, if you physically identified as a male but dressed as a female, it was acceptable to be called a transvestite, while today the term would be seen as insulting by many. Current GLAAD Media guidelines strongly suggest not even using the term unless the person being discussed uses the term themself. Divine in the 1970s would sometimes refer to being a transvestite but later would disavow being one. "I'm not just a fat transvestite. In fact, I'm not really a transvestite at all," Divine told *The Face* in 1984. "It's just a role I play."

The term more commonly used was "drag queen." This age-old term, and off-shoots such as "being in drag," are still common today but almost always used in the case of someone sex-assigned as male who dresses as female for a performmance. (The same is true for drag kings—women who dress as men to perform for audiences—a topic Waters himself has written about in various places.) Outside of that function, however, such a term could be offensive. After all, to dress as another sex because it makes one comfortable should not expose the person to suggesting that they are there strictly for our amusement.

Certainly in light that the term "drag queen" tends to evoke images of comic performances rather than serious ones.

Yet all this does help to identify Divine as a drag queen but not as a cross-dresser, as photos of Divine outside in everyday wear shows that women's clothing was not a norm in personal life (loose clothing that may be considered gender-neutral, perhaps, but oftentimes not definable one way or another). Divine only wore those outfits when working, sometimes even for interviews—which was still work time in a sense—but never outside of performance (and the interviews "in character" mostly stopped by the early 1970s). Even the early days, when David Lochary was helping with the wigs and costumes, were all about looking good for people at a party or event, never in private. And everyone who knew Divine well knew that it was only that—a costume. "When he wasn't on-camera," Waters stated in the documentary *I Am Divine*, "he would get that shit off. You know, it was uncomfortable. It was hot." In the same documentary, Pat Moran stated, "Did he want to be a woman? Never. He never, ever wanted a sex change. He never ever wanted to become a woman. It was a J-O-B." Even Holly Woodlawn (1946–2015), a transgender performer famed for working with Andy Warhol and immortalized in Lou Reed's song "Walk on the Wild Side," stated in the documentary, "He never wanted to be a woman, are you kidding? No, no, no. He just wanted to be a movie star. There's a difference."

Early on there were moments where Divine considered going further. Waters remembered Divine going

The movie poster for the 2013 documentary *I Am Divine*.

through a period of about a month where there was nothing but women's clothing in his life, including dresses for Christmas Mass one year. Actress Jean Hill, in an interview in Jack Sevenson's book *Desperate Visions 1: Camp America*, claimed that Divine regaled people in Pete's Hotel with stories of getting a sex-change operation, only for Hill to expose the lies. There is also an interview with Divine in Waters's *Shock Value*, where Divine admitted to considering augmentation while making *Pink Flamingos*, saying, "I thought about having hormone injections so I could have big breasts." There was no reconsideration after the time of filming *Pink Flamingos*, and Divine appeared happy with that decision. "When I wipe my make-up off, I wipe Divine off," Divine told *The Face* in 1984.

The above quote points out another element today as to what pronoun to use when discussing Divine. Although Waters once mentioned in an interview with *Interview* magazine that Divine preferred the term "shim," it appears to be a joke and not a serious reference. It is also interesting to note who calls Divine "she" and who uses the term "he": those who only worked with Divine onstage for a short time use the term "she"; those who grew up with him, worked with him for many years, and got to personally know him offstage always refer to Divine as "he" or "him." Admittedly, there are very early interviews with Waters where he sometimes referred to Divine as "she," but he tended to follow the lead on what pronoun the interviewers used first. After the early 1970s, it was always "he," "him," and "man." Divine was also quite happy to appear in male roles in Waters's films (such as in *Female Trouble* and *Hairspray*) as well as in other films and on television. As the 1980s progressed, he wanted recognition as a character actor who could play both male and female roles rather than simply as the "character" Divine, and he jumped at the chance to play male roles.

Thus, while it is possible that Divine today would use more up-to-date word choices, it is best to stick with what we know about the actor. Divine's friends felt comfortable in using male pronouns when referring to the man playing Divine. (In context of the scripts' character, it was always she, but in terms of making the films, he was always playing the role). Further, when appearing in interviews from the mid-1970s on, he always appeared as a man—eventually wearing dress clothes and suits to further that identity. For this reason, when discussing Divine in this book, it is best to go with what Divine himself preferred—that he was not transgender but strictly a male actor who cross-dressed in his role as a popular female character.

With that said, let's get back to who was there before Divine.

Born October 19, 1945, Harris Glenn Milstead was the only child for parents Harris Bernard and Diana Frances Milstead, who owned a children's day care service in Towson, Maryland, and then later in Lutherville after moving there when Glenn was twelve. The boy grew up using his middle name, Glenn, just as his mother went by her middle name, Frances. As pointed out in other sources, it is ironic that, for a family who catered to taking working parents' children into their nursery business, Glenn was commonly passed on to his grandmother to watch him during the day. Nevertheless, in Bernard Jay's book about Divine, *Not Simply Divine*, Frances spoke about how she spoiled Glenn as a child: "I had never had a toy in my lifetime and I loved him dearly. I was a possessive mother and I really wanted to do the best for him." Frances and even Glenn himself would later reflect on growing up spoiled, with his parents readily giving in, which would become a problem as he got older.

Divine looking his Elizabeth Taylor best in *Multiple Maniacs* (1970).

Out of concern for keeping Glenn safe, when a doctor told Frances that Glenn did not like exercise because he was afraid of getting hurt, physical activities simply became a thing of the past. Coupling the lack of exercise with his love of eating—his grandmother sometimes would prepare him a dinner before Glenn met up with his family for dinner some evenings— Glenn quickly obtained a weight problem. Frances also had other concerns: "When Glenn was ten years old," Frances stated in *I Am Divine*, "I took him to a pediatrician, and he told me that Glenny was more feminine than he was masculine. When

Dr. Anderson told me about Glenn, I cried. And Glenn, he would say, 'Mom, what did he tell you was so bad?' I said, 'Glenn, no matter what that doctor told me, you'll always be my baby and I'll always love you.'"

Glenn's father, who suffered from muscular dystrophy, was an officer in a local Baptist church, and, between that and the daycare center, Glenn's life revolved around the church and being helpful at home into his teen years. It was a happy childhood until he got into school, where his weight and tendency to act in a more feminine manner led to beatings after school. "Gangs of boys used to wait to beat me up after school because I wasn't one of them," he told the *Baltimore Sun* in 1981. "I certainly wasn't gay or anything. I didn't even know what that word meant." The situation escalated when his parents heard about the fights and complained to the school, leading to suspensions for several of the boys and Glenn having to be driven to and from school because of the threats that came after that.

His safety net was in the home, where being with his family meant no judgment and little concern about his eating or his actions. They were a tight, happy family, which was fine by Glenn for a time at least. "I never went out of the house," Divine told Waters in *Shock Value*. "I was with my parents always. Always. Until I was fifteen years old I was constantly with my mommy and daddy." Still, Glenn did attempt to fit in. He tried to look like others and even went on a diet in his final years of high school, dropping his weight from 180 pounds to 145 pounds. In some ways, it did work—there was a feeling of acceptance with his fellow students, and he began to be invited to participate. Yet the abuse he had suffered before that left him feeling cold about his change of luck with kids his own age. "People talked to me, but I didn't like them anyway. They were just talking to me because I lost eighty pounds or sixty pounds or whatever. But I did have more fun that year. I did go to the school dances and things like that, which I had never really done before."

Glenn also had girlfriends, such as Diana Evans, whom he steadily dated between 1959 and 1965. He also began working, first in a florist shop when he was fifteen—where he briefly considered studying horticulture before losing interest in the field—and then in cosmetology. "Glenn used to come in the [beauty] shop and wait with me," Frances explained in *I Am Divine*. "And while he was there he would fool around with the wigs. I said to Glenn, 'I'll tell you what—I'll make a deal with you. I'll let you go to the beauty school.'"

It was at the Marinella Beauty School that he became good friends with David Lochary, a fellow student who Glenn had met previously at the house of mutual friend, Carol Wernig. Lochary would mold Glenn—Glenn's girlfriend Diana felt Lochary "was a little possessive of Divine" and found him a bit suspect—introducing him to the concept of "drag," helping him find wigs and makeup, and borrowing dresses for him to use. From early photographs, it was clear that Glenn had a fixation on looking like a particular actress as much as possible. "He wanted to be Elizabeth Taylor," Waters stated in *I Am Divine*. "That's all he cared about. He smoked Salems because she did." A visit to a psychiatrist told him that he was attracted more to men than women, and Glenn soon decided to embrace the gay culture in Baltimore.

Homosexuality was still illegal at the time, but there was an active underground scene, with many male hairdressers being involved. With Glenn's involvement at the beauty school, it was only natural to find himself exposed to this new world and liking what he saw. Lochary also introduced Glenn to drag balls, which were held in Washington, D.C., and featured men crossdressing in competition. And, contrary to how some people outside of drag view it to be over-the-top, the competition was to be glamorous, striking, and perfect. Glenn was serious about the drag balls for a time, but his weight and earlier resistance of being part of the norm—even the norm created at a drag ball—left him wanting to rebel. "After a while," Divine told Waters in *Shock Value*, "I saw the others were ridiculous and I couldn't get into it, so I decided to have fun. That's when I got comic and they really hated it, 'cause they thought I was making fun of them." As Waters mentioned in the documentary *I Am Divine*, "He wore clothes that you would never wear when you're overweight, and that's when he realized the attention was so much more. Now I encourage this heavily because he was making fun of drag."

Soon school friends began to fade away, as Glenn developed into a new, more open person as he gained new friends, including John Waters, who lived six houses down from where the Milsteads had moved to in Lutherville. Waters famously tells about first seeing Glenn when he was seventeen, which he expounded on again in *I Am Divine*: "My father used to take us to school and I was angry and hating every moment in school, just defiant. And I would see Divine waiting for the bus and my father would shudder. And Divine was dressed in a little preppy outfit just waiting for the bus, but like with that look of nelly-ness." They eventually met through their mutual friend Carol Wernig and became friends, leading to Glenn meeting Mary Vivian Pearce, Bob Skidmore, and several of the others. That affiliation led to drinking beer with the others, shoplifting, and eventually doing drugs, although it was slow in coming. "I used to put it down at first," Divine told Waters in *Shock Value*. "I thought if you smoked grass you were a junkie. But then I tried it and it was a whole other ball game." He would become a lifetime marijuana smoker, which only increased his appetite. (According to friends he finally gave up the habit near the end of his life.)

Between the cross-dressing, the realization that he preferred men to women, the drugs, and his newfound friends, it was like a dam had burst open. While the others could pass for "normal" when needed, Glenn wanted nothing to do with being something that he had tried for so long to imitate and found he didn't like. Instead, he became even more uninhibited in his own ways than the others. By the fall of 1964, he had split from Diane Evans and focused his attention on hairstyling, his new friends, and the world of the drag balls.

On December 3, 1964, Glenn got together with Pat Moran and another friend by the name of Sally Patricia Crough. They were at Glenn's home for a time before going back to Crough's apartment in Catonsville to do some hairstyling and left her home about one o'clock in the morning on December 4. Sometime between then and the following afternoon, someone entered Crough's apartment and killed her. Early reports stated that she appeared to be strangled by a pair of scarves that were tied together around her neck, but otherwise there was no indication of a struggle. The next day saw reports that her hands were tied together at one point and that there was a struggle. Then it was suggested that she wasn't strangled but had been smothered to death. By early 1965, the police officially announced that Crough had been raped, which hardly matched initial reports claiming the victim had not been assaulted. By February 1965, the police believed that the victim may have asphyxiated when a girdle was pulled over her head during the assault, which was found over her face, or possibly with a pillow found nearby. Whatever changed about the case over time, one thing was sure: Glenn and Pat Moran had been two of the last people to see Crough alive.

The police picked up Glenn at the beauty parlor where he worked, putting him in handcuffs and demanding to know "Why did you kill Sally?" "I was with the cops for thirty-six hours without a break," Divine told Waters in *Shock Value*. Glenn, Moran, and three other people were interrogated by the police, given lie detector tests, and eventually released. However, an attempt to keep the possible suspects' names out of the paper failed, when, on December 7, the *Baltimore Sun* listed the names and addresses of three of the suspects, including Glenn and Moran. Worse, the paper listed Glenn's name as "Harris Milstead," which is what his father went by, causing many people to think, if only for a moment, that it was Glenn's father who may have murdered the woman. Glenn's mother faced harassment from neighbors who finally had a clear chance to tell her how they had always thought something was wrong with Glenn, while Glenn himself hid away at home for a long period afterward.

In February 1965, a thirty-five-year-old man was arrested. The police believed he had been involved with a series of burglaries—assaults that were similar to the Crough case—although there were no further details about the case in the *Baltimore Sun* after February 8, 1965. Waters, in *Shock Value*, states that the police never found the killer, but Bernard Jay's book, *Not Simply Divine*, states that the killer was caught. Either way, both Pat Moran and Glenn were cleared of the crime. This experience did allow Moran to mention being accused of murder as the reason she went to jail when discussing jail time during the making of *Cry-Baby*. (See Traci Lords's entry in Chapter 2 for more details.)

As mentioned, his mother readily admitted that they indulged Glenn more than they should have, loaning him money for cars and even paying to set him up with his own beauty salon, where he was "Mr. Glenn" to his customers. For a time, it worked in helping to ground Glenn, but it was clear he had no concept of money beyond spending it, and the pressure of running a business was leading him to a breakdown. "I was just going crazy," Divine told the *Baltimore Sun* in 1981. "I'd be doing hair and then I'd be in the bathroom for three hours crying because I didn't want to do anybody's hair. I didn't know what I wanted to do. I wanted to be a movie star, but I thought it was hopeless."

Waters by this point had done his first 8 mm short, *Hag in a Black Leather Jacket*, and was looking to try out his camera, taking it to Glenn's birthday party to film some footage that later turned up in his second film, *Roman Candles*. Waters, encouraged by how Glenn played to the camera—and after seeing Glenn dance the "Dirty Boogie" (a.k.a. the "Bodie Green") at a party—thought Glenn would be good in his films. When putting together *Roman Candles*, Waters suggested that Glenn use the name "Divine" as a stage name in the film. Waters had no particular reason behind the name, although Glenn suggested in interviews "he thought I was divine," (however, see Chapter 1 for further details as to why the name popped into Waters's head), and it was not a big deal. Waters mentioned the name, Glenn said yes, and that was it. "We didn't have a christening or anything," Waters joked in *I Am Divine*.

Waters quickly turned around and made his third film, *Eat Your Makeup*, the following year, with Glenn returning for a dream sequence that involved a reenactment of the Kennedy assassination. Glenn, as Divine, played Jackie Kennedy in the car; he wore a pink dress-suit and a pillbox hat and had to try to climb out of the back of the car before being driven away. The scene was shot on the street where they lived, and only two years after the assassination had occurred, horrifying neighbors who witnessed the event.

Yet Glenn managed to keep most of this second life hidden from his parents, even if it only furthered his stress. "I was leading a double life," Divine told the *Baltimore Sun*. "There I was on Sundays dressed up like Divine and during the week I was Mr. Glenn and I couldn't really talk to all those women about what I was doing." To compound things, Glenn had gotten into the habit of catering huge, glamorous parties for himself and his friends in fancy halls, restaurants, and hotels and charging them to his parents, only to get the mail and tear up the bills before his parents could see them. This naturally affected the very conservative Milsteads's credit and led to legal problems for them. Even then, however, his parents stood by him. When he would profess ignorance to the bills or shrug them off, they believed him.

At the age of twenty-three, Glenn abandoned the beauty salon—under a doctor's advice that the stress of the business was too much for him—and made his way to Provincetown for the first time to spend the summer with his friends who made an annual summer trek to the town. He worked at a gourmet kitchen shop, selling utensils, and, as Vincent Peranio said to Gerald Peary in 1997, Glenn "stole like crazy from these people, for his fiestas." In the same article, Waters went on to say: "He did not bother to cover it up. At the end of the summer, when they asked, 'Where are the books?' he said, 'I lost them.' His reputation was pretty strange."

The following summer, in Provincetown, Divine opened a secondhand store called Divine Trash, which was full of clothes and odd items that he had purchased from other stores or found in the local dump. The rent was paid for by Glenn's parents, who also gave him a new station wagon to use. When the shop closed due to Divine not having a permit, he was able to move it to another location and reopen thanks to public support pushed by Mink Stole, but it didn't last long. Christmas that year saw Divine and Cookie Mueller cutting down a tree that was already decorated on the front lawn of a house belonging to the sheriff. In one of his last moves before leaving Provincetown in early 1971, he auctioned off all the furniture in the furnished apartment he was renting, keeping the money. "His landlady was Carey Seamen," Channing Wilroy recalled in 1997, "a lawyer-real estate agent, quite old with lots of money and cheaper than shit. Divine was no longer there when the warrant was issued, but it lasted for seven years." It was time for Glenn to find a new home, as he was obviously making himself unwelcome in Provincetown.

Through all these shenanigans, Divine continued to trust in Waters and his films, becoming the star of his next project, *Mondo Trasho*, in 1969, and then *Multiple Maniacs* in 1970. Waters, who finally had two full-length 16 mm films completed, had begun traveling with his films across the country, locating theaters that would play his films like the exploitation film marketers of old that he read about in *Variety*. This led to Waters taking his films to San Francisco, where a theatrical group called the Cockettes—"a bearded transvestite theater group that believed the revolution was coming," as Waters described them—raved about Divine to their manager, Milton Miron, who was better known by the name of Sebastian. "A guy named Sebastian ran it, he was the booker. He had the Palace Theater, and later a place called the Secret Cinema, which was a movie theater in a loft—it was great," Waters told John Ives in 1992. "He showed *Multiple Maniacs* at both, and the audience went nuts for it. They all went nuts for Divine. So Sebastian said, 'Let's fly Divine here.'" Waters called Glenn about the news and, with Provincetown looking less than fun at the moment, a trip to San Francisco seemed promising.

It was then that Waters suggested a change to Divine's look. Up to that point, Divine's makeup had been somewhat traditional, even into *Multiple Maniacs*, where it may have been layered a bit think but was still within reason. She may have looked like a crazed version of Elizabeth Taylor gone to seed, but it was still a takeoff of the traditional drag scene. The Cockettes had moved beyond that type of drag makeup, becoming visions of people in makeup that went beyond a clash of color into some type of psychedelic *Twilight Zone*. Waters and Smith both believed that, with the outrageous look of the men and women in the Cockettes, if Divine showed up with makeup like he had in *Multiple Maniacs* and *Mondo Trasho*, then they would think he's "just another drag queen," according to Glenn in *Not Simply Divine*. Instead, he had to burst out of the plane looking as if he came from a planet even further out than the one containing the Cockettes. This meant shaving off Glenn's eyebrows and a good portion of his hair in order to create the Divine look—with the oversized eyebrows and the enormous forehead—that would remain for *Pink Flamingos* and *Female Trouble*. It would also be how

Divine in *Pink Flamingos* (1972), showcasing the outrageous makeup style created by Van Smith to push Divine's looks far past that of the standard "drag queen."

many remember Divine's makeup, even though it would fall back to a more common, pedestrian look by the time of the filming of *Polyester* in 1980.

Changing into his outfit and in makeup on the plane, Glenn took the flight to San Francisco without a penny in his pocket. "When we got off the plane in California," Divine told the *Baltimore Sun*, "there were several hundred people there. John screamed, 'There she is.' And I remember people saying 'Divine, Divine, Divine. We want Divine, Divine, Divine. I wish you were mine.' I'll never forget it. It was like stepping into another world." Surrounded by the Cockettes and whisked to a limousine, Glenn realized that he suddenly found his dream of movie stardom coming true. "He never really took it seriously until he came to California and he saw fans, and then in his mind he never, ever went back to being Glenn Milstead," Waters said in *I Am Divine*: "And he realized it could be true and he could have a career doing this, and he could live his life as Divine."

The show done for the crowd at the theater featured Waters dressed "like a hippie pimp" (hence, as mentioned in a previous chapter, the newly created pencil-thin mustache that he had recently grown and that would become Waters's trademark physical trait), introducing "the most beautiful woman in the world." The act was one Waters and Divine had performed at other colleges when promoting his films, and later only slightly rewritten for Dawn Davenport's monologue to the theater in *Female Trouble*. This included Divine pushing a shopping cart of dead fish to throw into the audience, while telling the audience of her offenses against the world: from killing Sharon Tate to eating white sugar. It went over amazingly well, but they soon returned to Baltimore for the next film.

And, yes, at this point, it was Divine that returned, not Glenn. When he arrived at his parents' home, they were in for a shock. "They saw me and I had no eyebrows and my hair shaved back," Divine states in *I Am Divine*: "That's the day I told them everything. I told them I was gay. I told them I smoked dope; that I had tripped. I just got it all off because I couldn't live two separate lives, and they just did not understand."

While his physical look may have been shocking, his announcement that he was gay probably was not that much of a jolt, as Frances knew that there was talk about Glenn, even from doctors she knew. What seemed more of an issue was that there was a feeling Glenn was avoiding responsibilities, with his new look and continuing blasé attitude about money being the conclusive proof of his disinterest in what they saw as reality. As mentioned earlier, he had traditionally passed off bills for his various escapades to his parents without concern, and rarely did his parents try to say no to him. Finally, according to Bernard Jay's book, there was an incident in May 1971 when Divine had charged expensive repairs to his station wagon while in Baltimore, but did not even visit them. It was the final break for his mother and father, who felt he viewed them strictly as a money source. They told Divine that they would no longer be taken advantage by him and were selling the car. "And I said," Frances related in *I Am Divine*, "so just keep on going and forget you have a mother and father. I remember saying that, and I felt so bad after I said it." Divine arrived at their home, packed his belongings, and left. It would be several years before Divine would see his parents again.

With a new image, Divine was in Baltimore in the fall of 1971 to film the movie that both set Divine up as a national icon and stymied him and Waters: *Pink Flamingos*. More details about the making of this film will appear in a subsequent chapter, but for Divine the main element discussed even before filming began was that the film would end with his character picking up a dog turd and eating it on-camera. Divine even mentioned the idea in interviews while out in San Francisco earlier in 1971. Of course, it is quite possible that he believed it was nothing more than a joke between the two of them, for when filming began and Waters reminded Divine of his promise to eat dog feces in the film, Divine was somewhat surprised he meant it. "I thought he was kidding," Divine stated in *I Am Divine*. "A year later he said, 'Okay, now tomorrow you have to eat the dog turd.' I thought, 'Oh, this is great, he wasn't kidding.' He said, 'Well, listen, do you want to be famous?'"

"It was done for anarchy and it worked for that," Waters replied in the Divine documentary. The point was to find something to do in the film that was transgressive—something that had never been done in a film but that wasn't illegal either. Oddly enough, for a film that involves such moments as people having sex with a chicken and a character (Divine again) giving oral sex to her own son, it was always the dog scene that people thought was going too far. It would be the thing that pushed the film into one people had to see to believe, and *Pink Flamingos* would start the rumblings for Waters and Divine to become bigger successes as the 1970s rolled on.

However, that was in the future in 1971 when filming wrapped and Waters went away to edit the film and try to find a distributor for the movie. Instead, needing work, Divine and Mink Stole went back to San Francisco, where they joined members of the Cockettes in a number of shows at the Nocturnal Dream Shows, together and on their own. (Stole appeared in a continuing show as Nancy Drew, in 1973, for example.) The Cockettes would perform musicals full of a mishmash of music, props, and people in odd outfits with all the enthusiasm of kids putting on a show in their barn—like the Little Rascals but as college kids on quaaludes. Divine fit right in, and his first appearance came in a show in February 1972, when he played a crab monster in *Journey to the Center of Uranus* who sings "A Crab on Uranus Means You're Loved." After this came Divine headlining in the show *Divine Saves the World* and then *Vice Palace* (a parody of *The Masque of the Red Death* with Divine playing "Divina" and costarring Mink Stole). "I did another play with him around the same time in San Francisco that we renamed *Ladies in Retirement*," Stole recalls in Jay's *Not Simply Divine*. "In that, we both played older women. It was a situation where he had to play a character. He couldn't be a larger-than-life brassy, big woman. And he was absolutely convincing."

Waters eventually landed distribution for *Pink Flamingos*, leading to the film slowly spreading across the country ("Like a cancer," as Waters's father described it). The growing interest in *Pink Flamingos* also demonstrated there was enough interest in Waters to help him land financing for his next movie, *Female Trouble*, which would begin casting in December 1973 and would start filming at the beginning of 1974. The film would be the best starring role for Divine—perhaps not his best acting role in a Waters film but certainly the biggest role he ever had. As traditional, all of the Dreamlanders who could appear came back to Baltimore for the filming. Divine then returned to San Francisco for a time to perform onstage, including starring in *The Hearbreak of Psoriasis* for Sebastian in 1975.

Early 1976 saw Divine joining the cast of the off-Broadway comedy *Women Behind Bars*, written by Tom Eyen (1940–1991), which had first been attempted in 1975 with Pat Ast, an Andy Warhol regular who eventually would play a similar matron in the 1986 film *Reform School Girls*. The play was a parody of earlier women-in-prison films that usually involved some innocent becoming a hardened criminal after rough treatment from other women—prisoners and guards alike. Divine was brought in to play the Matron, the evil head of the prison, when the play was revived in Washington, D.C., during February 1976 and then moved to the Truck and

Divine in a rare publicity photo of himself not in drag. While there was no denying that his drag character got him noticed, Divine never shied away from wanting to be known as a character actor that could play both male and female parts, which he often did in Waters's films.

Warehouse Theater in New York, where it played for most of the year. He then moved with the show to London, where it had a mostly different cast, in June 1977, and the show lasted until November of that year. This was followed by Divine starring in a new off-Broadway comedy written by Tom Eyen called *The Neon Woman*, which had Divine as a strip club owner in 1962. The play opened in 1978 and moved on to San Francisco in 1979 for a time.

In hopes of getting an album contract, Divine ended 1979 by recording two songs: an old Shirley Ellis song called "The Name Game" and one written by Tom Eyen and Henry Krieger that was originally called "Cheap" but was then changed to "Born to Be Cheap" and released by the Chicago label Wax Trax. Besides all this, Divine was working with his new manager, Bernard Jay, to start appearing at gay clubs around the U.S. and elsewhere with an act that mostly involved Divine insulting the audience between disco songs.

Divine found some success as a recording artist, producing several singles between 1980 and 1987, some of which reached the charts in other countries, although only two broke through the Top 40 in the US Dance charts: "Native Love (Step by Step)" at twenty-one and "Shoot Your Shot" at thirty-nine. His best-selling single was 1984's "You Think You're a Man," which reached the Top 10 in Australia and Sweden and No. 16 in the United Kingdom. The success in the United Kingdom led to a controversy with the British television series *Top of the Pops*, on which Divine appeared and sang "You Think You're a Man," leading to many phone complaints about having a man wearing women's clothing on the show. His performance is very sedate actually, but still there were some concerns, and the story goes that Divine was simply not asked back rather than being banned from the program.

All this work outside of Waters's films kept Divine from appearing in Waters's 1977 film, *Desperate Living*, in which, supposedly, Divine was to play the part of Mole (which went to Susan Lowe instead). Waters, however, harbored no ill feelings about the split from his memorable star. "I was always for it," Waters stated in *I Am Divine*, "because I couldn't make a movie every year. I couldn't get it together. I couldn't get the money to make it, so I hoped Divine found a way to get other work." This break also gave both him and Divine a chance to spread their wings and see how they would do without the participation of each other at a time when they seemed to be close to becoming a double-act and inseparable in the public eye.

Divine returned in 1980 to costar in Waters's next film, *Polyester*, along-side famous 1950s teen-heartthrob Tab Hunter. It was remarkable in a way, beyond that of having a star like Hunter working in a Waters film, as it set

Picture sleeve cover for Divine's musical single "You Think You're a Man."

Divine up to play a character, Francine Fishpaw, completely different from what fans had become used to when seeing Divine in . . . anything, really. Here was a woman on the edge of a nervous breakdown, struggling to be normal in a world gone mad around her, and some fans were less than happy to see their crazed leader playing a character so docile.

On the other hand, it was a smooth production for Waters, and Tab Hunter enjoyed working with Divine so much that when Hunter got the chance to make a western parody called *Lust in the Dust*, he asked for Divine to be cast in the film with him. Also asked to join the film was Waters as the director and Edith Massey in the part of "Big Ed," but Massey died before filming began and Waters passed, since it was not an original project for him. Instead, popular cult director Paul Bartel (*Eating Raoul, Death Race 2000*) directed, and what could have ended up looking like John Waters-lite became the first major film for Divine outside of Waters's influence. The movie did not do particularly well at the box office, but there were strong positive critical notices for Divine in the reviews.

Divine followed up the film with an appearance in the 1985 movie *Trouble in Mind*, directed by Alan Rudolph. By this point, Divine wanted to show Hollywood that he could play roles beyond that of women or, rather, characters other than the crazy dog-turd-eating Divine of *Pink Flamingos*. "I never set out in the beginning to play just female parts," Divine said in *I Am Divine*. "But they were the only parts that came my way. They were written especially for me, and they were the leads of films. As a young aspiring actor you don't turn down the lead in the movie. It made me a star of sorts with a cult status, but then a cult status isn't enough. You can't get by on that. You can't make any money." When given a chance to play a man in *Trouble in Mind*, Divine was happy to be able to show he could easily play such a part. He also played a male part in an episode of *Tales from the Darkside* ("Seymourlama") in 1987 and made a cameo appearance as a police detective in the film *Out of the Dark* (produced by Paul Bartel, who directed Divine in *Lust in the Dust*).

Divine continued to work, including playing clubs when possible, which was hard work for someone in excellent health and even more so for a large man like Divine. In late 1987, he returned to work on Waters's 1988 film *Hairspray*, with an eye on playing a double-role as both Tracy and her mother. Yet everyone was older now than when Divine played a teenage Dawn Davenport in *Female Trouble*, and the producers felt the film really had to feature a person of the proper age of the character, especially since the character of Tracy appears in romantic situations with a boy in the film. Naturally, Divine was disappointed to find that she was no longer to be the focus of a Waters movie but was excited to have two roles to play—that of Tracy's mother and then the racist television station owner, Arvin Hodgepile.

The film was a smash and many critical reviews pointed out how good Divine was in a role that showed him as a mother more worried about her work and daughter than her looks (a status that some of his friends cringed at, but that Divine took as a sign of his ability to play the role: "I did fit right in and I did look exactly the way I was supposed to."). Soon after came an opportunity to play a part on the Fox Television series *Married . . . with Children*, which excited him because it was another male role and one that could lead to more work on the series. There was even talk about trying to find a series for Divine over at NBC. Things were looking up for Divine, who now appeared to be catching a second wind in his career, with good reviews and more opportunities in front of him.

Yet that was not to be. On March 7, 1988, he was found dead in his hotel room—where he was preparing for his *Married . . . with Children* rehearsal the next day—due to an enlarged heart. He was forty-two. Although large, his friends were surprised to hear about his death. At the end of *I Am Divine*, Waters concluded his thoughts by saying: "We were stupefied that he died.

I've never gotten over the shock of it. I'm still shocked he's dead. I wake up sometimes and I'm amazed by that."

Ironically, for a man who grew up conflicted about his hometown and happy to be in cities like New York or San Francisco where life could be glamorous, Divine ended up back in Towson, Maryland, buried next to his grandmother in the Prospect Hill Park Cemetery. He won't be alone forever, however. "We're going to spend eternity with him," Waters told *Baltimore Magazine* in 2015, "because I bought a gravestone where Divine's buried. So did Pat, so did Mink Stole, so did Dennis Dermody. We call it 'Disgraceland.' So we'll all be together." Friends until the end and after.

Divine came into the world as a blessing for his parents and remarkably made a mark upon the entertainment business and society. There were drag queens in films and television before Divine, yet as mentioned early in this chapter, they were usually the butts of jokes. Milton Berle in drag, or Flip Wilson as Geraldine—a little racier, but still obviously a guy in a costume. Divine moved the goalpost—his characters was dangerous, threatening, and yet still funny; eventually they became lifelike and we believed him as a woman in *Polyester* and *Hairspray* because he was willing to play women who were not the "goddesses" too often attempted in drag. Further, he was simply a good actor—one of several friends of Waters who had natural acting ability and helped push his films beyond the norms of an underground film. When Divine loses his mind at the end of *Multiple Maniacs*, we laugh at first but then wonder how long he can keep it going (spoiler—until Divine gets killed by the soldiers is how long). When Dawn Davenport is being ratted out for eating a meatball sub, she is so credible a teenage girl giving the other girl the evil eye that we momentarily forget it's a nearly thirty-year-old man playing the role.

Divine has become part of our culture. He even became a Disney villain, as Ursula in *The Little Mermaid*, which was based on his appearance and acting; he was that easily identifiable. The downside is that he never got to experience that newfound layer of stardom that would have come his way thanks to the success of *Hairspray*, but he at least went out on top—which is how he would have liked it. He also mended a few bridges along the way.

As the 1970s went on, Divine had no contact with his family for several years. Things had calmed down a bit since Glenn walked out the door in 1971. Divine himself, in an interview in July 1981 with the *Baltimore Sun*, stated that he began hearing from them around 1976 when one Christmas Waters's mother told Divine that Frances had been asking about him. They began talking to each other on the phone and Divine began sending them postcards—some of which have been collected in a 2011 book called *Postcard from Divine*, which commences with cards from 1977 onward. Later in the 1970s his parents went to see *Female Trouble*, where some men in the lobby confronted them, suggesting they wouldn't want to see the movie. When Frances told them that she was Divine's mother, they asked for her autograph.

There were still issues, according to Divine in the 1981 interview. "They saw me on the Tom Snyder Show and they said, 'We'd love to see you. Would you come home? But could you wear a toupee and would you wear your eyebrows and sideburns?' And I said, 'No, I'm not willing at this age to change my looks completely with glue-on things just to make you two happy for a few hours.' They wanted me to drive the car into the garage to let me out."

The movie poster for *Lust in the Dust*, a 1985 comedy directed by Paul Bartel that reunited Tab Hunter with Divine after they appeared together in *Polyester* (1981). Hunter started the project in hopes of reuniting most of the team from *Polyester* but instead made a film that was a unique showcase for Divine outside of the scope of Waters's movies.

In the early 1980s, either Frances contacted Divine or vice-versa, and it was decided that Divine would come to his parents' home in Florida for a visit and to "be a family again." According to those interviewed in *I Am Divine*, a banner was hanging over the front door saying "Welcome Home Divine," which Divine found very moving. Glenn was home.

And it was Divine.

4

If I Had to Pick One Place to Live

The Various Hometowns of John Waters

I would never want to live anywhere but Baltimore. You can look far and wide, but you'll never discover a stranger city with such extreme style. It's as if every eccentric in the South decided to move north, ran out of gas in Baltimore, and decided to stay.

—John Waters, from his book *Shock Value*

There's no doubt about it—Baltimore is John Waters's city. If it wasn't, it certainly would not have been the location for every one of his films, with references to streets, businesses, and the general tone of the people included in every one. Waters may parody American culture in his movies, but at of the heart of his films is his hometown. Yet, like many great loves, sometimes you just need to get away in order to come back home.

While Waters has lived in Baltimore all of his life, he is most definitely a traveler. Starting with hitchhiking trips to New York City and later Provincetown, Massachusetts, Waters expanded to other areas of the country as he started shopping his early movies. The typical method—and one Waters himself has referred to several times over the years—was one called "four-walling." It refers to a classic method for low-budget studios to take their films city-by-city and locate theater owners who would agree to show the films for a day or more. The film owner gets all or most of the box-office receipts from ticket-buyers, while the theater owner gets cash from concession sales and perhaps a percentage of the box office as well. In other words, the studio, or in this case Waters himself, gets the four walls of the theater to show his films—hence "four-walling."

Waters had done this on a smaller scale with his first few 8 mm films, typically around either Baltimore or Provincetown, where Waters would spend nearly every summer starting in the mid-1960s. By the 1970s, Waters had two 16 mm full-length films done—*Mondo Trasho* and *Multiple Maniacs*—which allowed him the opportunity to throw the reels in the back of his car and drive across the country, searching out theaters to show them. "I use to travel with a car full [of stuff]," Waters told John Ives. "I traveled with furniture, like a gypsy, you know, I lived in that car. I drove back and forth across the country, all five major routes. I mean, I did *On the Road* to death." The driving was grueling, but there were fringe benefits from such diverse travels, such as being able to take in the Manson Trials that ran from mid-1970 through early 1971.

There were other stops along the way as well. Waters once spent part of a year in New Orleans while waiting for the release of *Pink Flamingos*, living with Mary Vivian Pearce and Danny Mills (who played Crackers in the film) in an apartment on Rampart Street across from an all-night supermarket and eating beans and rice every night. "It was the poorest I had ever been in my entire life," Waters told the *Huffington Post*, "and then I got the call from the distributor that the movie was going to open in New York, and I drove away from New Orleans. My life kind of changed, but I always have fond memories."

Four cities: Baltimore, Provincetown, Manhattan, and San Francisco have been cornerstone locations for Waters in his career and personal life and a reason why he continues to own houses, studios, and/or apartments in each. Having such choices also allows for a certain amount of freedom: "I can go wherever I want," Waters told *New York* magazine in 2008. "So much better if you go to their house and they can come to yours. If you have a fight, you can get away, there's no pouting room." Further, people who live there recognize Waters as one of their own, even if he will never depart from the idea that Baltimore is where he was born and raised, and where he will be buried one day.

Baltimore, Maryland (Est. 1729)

As mentioned in Chapter 1, Waters moved to Lutherville, Maryland, when he was a one-year-old. Lutherville is part of Baltimore County, directly north of downtown Baltimore, and was founded back in 1852 by two Lutheran

Waters's old home, which he used as the Marbles's home in *Pink Flamingos*.

ministers, Benjamin Kurtz and John Morris, who wanted to build a female seminary in the area. The first house Waters lived in was at 1401 Clark Avenue, where Waters took his first steps into exploring the side of life people tend to want to avoid. "They were building the beltway near my parents' house and we used to crawl down in the drain pipes really deep," Waters told the *Guardian* in 2014. "So dangerous, now that I think about it, but that was my first journey."

Waters's family lived at the Clark Avenue house for several years before the family moved in the late 1950s to 313 Morris Avenue, a street named after John Morris, one of the founders of the area. In fact, the cottage Morris built in Lutherville—Oak Grove—would be the house where Waters would spend his teenage years. Soon enough, Waters would meet Glenn Milstead, who had moved just a few houses down from Waters. Although Waters would eventually move out later in the 1960s, his parents continued to live at Oak Grove for the rest of their lives. The house on Morris Avenue appeared in several of Waters's early films:

- *Hag in a Black Leather Jacket*: Among the scenes shot there is that of the finale, the wedding scene, which was filmed on the rooftop of Oak Grove.
- *Roman Candles*: Certain segments of the film took place around the house and in Waters's bedroom, which he called Dreamland Studios.
- *Eat Your Makeup*: The Kennedy assassination reenactment occurred on Morris Avenue, and some filming was done at the house as well.
- *Multiple Maniacs*: Cavalcade of Perversion was filmed just outside the house.
- *Desperate Living*: The opening sequence showing Peggy losing it was filmed in Waters's parents' bedroom and around the house.

Waters would have a series of apartments and homes in both Provincetown and Baltimore between 1966 and the late 1980s. Many of these he shared with roommates—typically female friends like Mink Stole or Mary Vivian Pearce—until close to when filming began on *Female Trouble* and he came to a realization, which he recounted in *Shock Value*: "I could be a better fanatic if I lived alone." The residences of interest to readers, of course, would be those in Baltimore that made their way into his films. This practice occurred mostly because it was easier to film "on location" than anywhere else, and, for a time at least, every new place became the home of Dreamland Studios. "There were central heating, adequate electrical outlets, and real bathrooms, so the cast was always relieved to hear we'd be shooting a scene [there]," Waters remembered in *Shock Value*.

In late 1967, Waters moved to an apartment on 25th Street, between North Calvert Street and Guilford Avenue. It soon became an area affected by the Baltimore Riots that occurred after the assassination of Martin Luther King Jr. between April 6 and 11, 1968, with fires, several people dead, and Governor Spiro Agnew gaining favor with Richard Nixon for the upcoming election that year. "My first apartment in Baltimore was on 25th Street and Calvert, and there were tanks outside of my house. Everywhere was burning," Waters told the *Daily Beast* in 2015. This apartment served as the interior of Lady Divine's residence in *Multiple Maniacs*, with the room decorated exactly like Waters's apartment at the time. While the location allowed for convenience during filming for the actors, it did have one minor issue, which Waters discussed with the *Daily Beast*: "We lived in this place that had a plumbing school underneath it. To get to our apartment, you had to walk

The Senator, a movie theater in Baltimore that has hosted numerous premieres for Waters's films over the years and that even makes an appearance in *Cecil B. DeMented* (2000).

right through the plumbing place. Divine would walk through in full drag—a gold lamé toreador outfit—while these student plumbers would be working on their pipes."

In the early 1970s, Waters moved to another recognizable place from his films—this time to a dwelling fans refer to as "The Marbles's House." This home, at 3900 Greenmount, is a normal row house "on the outermost boundaries of the nicest neighborhood in Baltimore" that, at the time, "faced a semi-ghetto neighborhood," according to Waters in *Shock Value*. When filming *Pink Flamingos*, Waters shared the house with Mink Stole, and the house became the setting for the house of the villains, the Marbles, played by Mink Stole and David Lochary, with Connie Marbles's office being Mink Stole's room. What we see in the film is pretty much how Waters furnished the house, with movie posters on the walls and other oddball items around the house.

While Waters kept a low profile while living there, the neighbors were quick to note that something was different about the man. A friend of

Waters, Carol Alexander, recalled in 1973 to the Baltimore newspaper the *News-American* what a coworker had told her about her new neighbor: "She said she was always seeing people of indeterminate sex leaving and entering the house … and then there were the wild flashing lights. I didn't make the connection at first, but finally I realized she lived next door to John—so I could put her mind at rest about whatever she imagined was going on and explained they were making a movie." While filming *Pink Flamingos* in the home, Waters's landlady misheard dialogue being rehearsed in the house, which caused issues. "The landlady went around and told all the neighbors that Mink had a baby and sold it. And she was always so nice to me when I lived there," Waters told the *News-American*. "What if I had ever used her for a reference? Can you imagine?"

Even with the notorious history of the house—or maybe because of it—the house still is a private home today, although there's been no mention of if the banister has been changed over time. "It's exactly the same," Waters exclaimed to the *Guardian* in 2014. "The woman that owned it ran a fancy wine shop and had never seen *Pink Flamingos*. I said, 'Well, you should see it!' She freaked out afterwards. She said, 'Divine was licking my banister!' Then she moved."

By the time of working on *Female Trouble* in late 1973, Waters had moved on as well—this time to the Temple Gardens apartments on Madison Ave., very close to Druid Hill Park Lake. He remained at Temple Gardens for several years, up through the making of *Hairspray* and *Cry-Baby*. Then, with money that he earned from *Cry-Baby*, he decided to seek out the dream home of his youth.

In a 1991 article with the *New York Times*, Waters remembered traveling at the age of nine with his mother to where she used to live on Whitfield Road in the Tuscany-Canterbury neighborhood of Baltimore, close to Johns Hopkins University. On the trip, Waters noticed a creepy four-story home that "looked like Dracula's house" just a few blocks away and became fascinated with the place. "I knocked on the door and began nagging the owner to sell me the house," Waters told the *Wall Street Journal*. "Five years later she finally did. The house looks European, but the lawn is wooded and overgrown, like the small grounds of a private mental institution." Although Waters had never filmed any of his movies at the house, he has invited many writers to interview him there over time, showing off his extensive collection of oddball items, such as the electric chair from *Female Trouble*, fake food that litters tables and shelves, the sunglasses that Patty Hearst was arrested in, and even a baby doll that Waters refers to as his "son" and calls Bill. "I had his portrait done," Waters told *Vanity Fair*. "It's in my San Francisco apartment." That and over 8,000 books that are "carefully catalogued."

Waters also rents a studio in Hampden to use when working on artwork he exhibits at shows throughout the country. While it may seem odd to have a separate place just for his artwork, there is a reason behind doing so. "I work on the photo pieces in a separate studio," Waters told Todd Solondz in 2004, "because the photographic work is very separate in my mind. What I'm trying to do is not so different from one medium to the other, but it's a very, very different kind of theater."

Of course, these are just some of the places where Waters lived in Baltimore. All of his movies take place in areas within and surrounding the city. It's possible to spend days driving around Baltimore to see all the places that have turned up in Waters's movies, and there's even a website, Trashytravels.com, created by Josh McCullough, that shows off many of the places Waters filmed in the city through the years. Better yet, many of his films involve scenes either shot on the streets of Baltimore or include establishing shots of buildings that are still around. Of course, it would be virtually impossible to find the pit of pig manure that Divine crawls through in *Mondo Trasho*, although no doubt some fans have tried, but not everything has changed from the locations filmed decades before. As mentioned, the Marbles's House is still sitting there on Greenmount for gawkers, although it's covered by trees and bushes to some extent, and, with a vast history behind it, Oak Groves obviously remains. For every location that is gone, one is still standing. Pete's Hotel, seen in *Multiple Maniacs* and which was located at 721 S. Broadway, is long gone, having lost out to efforts to make the Fell's Point area more tourist-friendly in recent years. There is still the Drinkery at 205 W Read Street, where Divine turns the corner and spots the dog that changes the destiny of everyone involved with *Pink Flamingos*. The bridal shop in Highlandtown that was changed into Hefty Hideaway for *Hairspray*, at 3309 Eastern Ave, has been wiped out by renovations to the buildings on the street, but there's still Philly's Best, where Pecker worked, at 1101 West 36th Street in Hampden. And just a few blocks away from Philly's Best is the most recent location for Atomic Books, where John Waters has all his fan mail sent and where one can see a wall of Waters's infamous Christmas cards sent to friends every year. There's the Hippodrome at 12 N. Eutaw Street, where Cecil and the gang hung out; the Senator Theatre at 5904 York Road, where many of Waters's movies have premiered; and Holiday House from *A Dirty Shame*, at 6427 Harford Road (and just three miles straight down East Northern Parkway from The Senator). And if you want to visit the sights, it is worth checking out the American Visionary Art Museum at 800 Key Highway, where the ten-foot tall statue of Divine, created by Andrew Logan, is located (among other Waters-related pieces).

There's more as well, with many side streets and houses in outer parts of Baltimore that have been used in Waters's movies. There are even tours of the area based on where Waters has shot as well as the tours Waters has given to cast and crew members before filming the Baltimore he knows. On why he takes his cast on such tours before filming, Waters explained to the *Baltimore Sun*: "No matter what you tell them, after they come and see it, it makes everything better. It makes it realer." Reporters have constantly been after him over the years to show them the sights and where to go, to the point that he has mentioned in some

Atomic Books, where Waters has his fan mail sent and which includes a wall covered in the various Christmas cards that Waters sends out every year.

interviews that he dreads giving any more tours for interviewers, but nine times out of ten, he'll do it all over again when asked. The love for the city and its surrounding area is obvious in his films, and it is hard to resist showing it off when asked. "Baltimore to me is what I write about, what inspires me," he told the *New York Times* in 2002.

But every kid needs to spread their wings eventually.

Provincetown (Est. 1700)

Provincetown is a town up at the furthest tip of Cape Cod, in Massachusetts, about 500 miles northeast of Baltimore. The area was first discovered by Europeans in 1602, and the Pilgrims aboard the Mayflower landed there in 1620. The area would become a major port for ships as well as an excellent location for fishermen. (There's a reason it's called Cape Cod, after all.) Because of its scenic beauty and isolation in the winter months due to climate, it rapidly developed into an artist colony in the late nineteenth century and continued to build on that reputation in the twentieth century. This burst of creativity, along with cheap rent and citizens who were tolerant of those who stand outside of the norm, naturally attracted young people, including the beatniks and hippies of the 1960s. The gay community also found a home and tolerance in Provincetown, starting back in the 1920s, making it a prime summer vacation spot for people of other sexual preferences. In 1978 the town's business guild began promoting Provincetown as a summer spot for gay tourists, leading to a number of people from the gay community moving to the town over the past few decades.

Waters first heard of Provincetown in 1965. "I was in Baltimore in the summer of 1965, and that had been a bizarre year for me," Waters explained to Gerald Peary. "I'd been expelled from NYU for pot, and they told my parents I needed extensive psychiatry. I was very confused, and somebody said to me, 'Have you ever been to P-Town? It's a very weird place.'" Hearing about the beatniks in Provincetown, which Waters longed to be, he hitchhiked with his girlfriend, Mona Montgomery, in the summer of 1965, staying a total of two weeks. The first person he saw upon arriving was Victor "Moulty" Mouton, the drummer for the band the Barbarians, who had a song called "Are You a Boy or Are You a Girl?" in 1965 that peaked at No. 55. Regarding Moulty, Waters said to Gerald Peary: "[He] had hair to his waist, a two-year-growth, which meant that he'd starting growing long hair before anyone else in the world. Plus, he had a hook instead of a hand, which is something I always wanted. I was so impressed."

Waters almost immediately fell in love with the town but ran out of funds and had to return quickly that summer. He came back the next summer with Mona and Mary Vivian Pearce, and Waters got his first regular job at a local bookstore. From then on out, Waters made it a priority to return each summer to Provincetown, becoming a regular. Both *Mondo Trasho* and *Multiple Maniacs* premiered at the Arts Cinema there. "I would rent this 35 mm theatre and sit in the back with a 16 mm projector after flyering all week. [Provincetown] was the first place outside of Baltimore the films caught on," Waters wrote in 2014 for the *Civilian*. The bookstore where he worked would even allow him to use a storefront window in order to advertise the showing of his movies. Waters has continued to be actively involved with showing his films in the town over the years as well as participating in the yearly Provincetown Film Festival, which is held in June and features many popular writers, directors, and actors discussing films.

In 1967, Waters lived in one of the more notorious places in Provincetown, a "tree fort" that belong to gay rights activist Prescott Townsend. "Living in that tree fort was like Swiss Family Robinson," Waters said to Gerald Peary. "It was part an old abandoned submarine, a lunatic had built it, and there was no roof, so when it rained it poured in. But you could live there for free if Prescott liked you, and I can remember it as some of the happiest moments of my life; of complete freedom for the first time." While Waters and others had fun living there, many considered the tree fort an eyesore, and eventually it was torn down (with many regretting never taking a picture of the place).

With Waters coming to Provincetown, many of his friends joined him for the summer and became quite well known in the town for their various pranks and stunts to make money, as discussed in previous chapters, earning them the title of the "hillbilly rip-offs." Divine lived there for a time but eventually left after having conflicts with the law enough times, only to return in the mid-1970s with a production of *Women Behind Bars* performed onstage. Cookie Mueller, Susan Lowe, Mary Vivian Pearce, and others came to the town, and there was even one winter romance where Mink Stole and Vince Peranio shared a Christmas in Provincetown together. Some eventually moved there for years, but others only traveled there a few summers before leaving and never returning. Waters, however, would make it a yearly ritual, coming from Memorial Day through Labor Day each year.

Not that he sees it as a summer vacation spot as many tourists do these days. "People often ask me if I'm having a good vacation and I'm not really vacationing, I'm working here," he said to Peary. Waters follows a variation of his schedule that he has kept everywhere he goes: up at six o'clock in the morning to write until noon, then traveling around the town on a bicycle and going to the beach for strictly a half hour each day. "I go for half an hour a day with no sunblock on and my dermatologist says it's okay. Now of course I'll probably die of skin cancer and the irony will be immortalized in print." Waters spent many summers working on scripts for his next film projects in Provincetown while working at the bookstore there. He'd then return to Baltimore in the fall to make his next film based on said scripts, while collecting unemployment from the bookstore. (This also explains why so many of his early films seem to take place in the winter—because they did.) Waters even admitted that the town was the inspiration for one of his films. "I wrote *Desperate Living* here," Waters said to *Civilian Magazine*, "which is about an isolated town outside of the rest of the community—just like P-town." There is another odd connection with Provincetown in one of his early films: "Do you remember in *Multiple*

Maniacs where I had that giant lobster rape Divine?" Waters asked Gerald Peary in 1997. "That was from the postcard they sold in P-Town for twenty years of the big lobster over the sky at the beach."

Waters continued staying in various apartments during the 1970s and for the entire summer, then for shorter periods in the 1980s, usually staying at Howard Gruber's place or a bohemian hotel called the White Horse Inn. Finally, he returned to spending full summers in Provincetown, settling in an attic apartment belonging to artist Pat de Groot that he rents. He had offers over the years to go elsewhere for the summer but has declined. "I have friends in the Hamptons, but with P-town you don't give up a summer rental or someone else inherits it. And it's way too late for me to go to another summer resort," he told Peary.

While Baltimore continues to be where his heart is, Waters has conceded that he has fallen for Provincetown as well. "I'd like to have a house there; that's my fantasy! And I still haven't missed a summer since 1965, even if it's just being there a weekend. Something bad would happen to me if I missed."

Greenwich Village, New York (Est. 1696)

Typically, Waters's apartment in Manhattan is referred to as being in West Village, but Waters, in an interview with the *Villager* in 2015, corrected that assumption: "It's not the East Village, it's not the West Village—historic Greenwich Village!" As a seventeen-year-old, he would hitchhike to the neighborhood from Baltimore (admitting in one interview that he did it as a runaway), staying at a place called Hotel Earle, which would eventually be renovated and turned into the Washington Square Hotel. In 1990, he began renting an eighth-floor apartment that he uses when in the area, which is frequent enough due to various promotional work and art shows. While the area has memories for him, he is sorry to see how New York has cleaned itself up over the years. "I miss the lunch counter at Bigelow. I remember the Women's House of Detention. I remember the Eighth Street Bookshop. In a way, no kid today could come and hitchhike here and wander around the Village and find a place to crash. There isn't really a place to do that anymore."

Waters is quite set on routine, even down to how he arranges his New York apartment. "My New York apartment is exactly like my Baltimore house. I wake up sometimes and I don't know which place I'm in," Waters told *Index Magazine.* The *New York Times* mentioned in an article in 2002 that Waters hired decorator Henry Johnson to get his apartment in New York in order. "I told him, I just wanted a symphony in puke green, and I got it. When I was a child, I wanted my skin to be that color, like the Wicked Witch of the West. Now, as I get older, it's getting close. It'll match the apartment."

As with his Baltimore and Provincetown residences, Waters sticks to his regiment of writing Monday through Friday from six o'clock in the morning until noon. (The *New York Times* article has Waters admitting that he writes from eight to eleven-thirty in the morning in his New York apartment, however.) This is followed by drinking on Friday nights, hangovers on Saturdays, reading in bed on Sundays, and back to the routine each Monday. Waters once referred to the regiment as being "like a coal miner," but it works well for him and keeps him active, not to mention his afternoons free.

Waters had longed to live in the city ever since his days of hitchhiking there and going to the exploitation theaters that at one time populated Time Square. But before 1990 it was always as a guest rather than in his own place, even during a stretch where he lived there in 1973. "I always wanted to live in New York, but I didn't want to live badly in New York. I wanted to wait until I could get a nice place," Waters told the New York Times in 2002. The money made off of *Hairspray* and *Cry-Baby* helped him pay for the chance to live in New York and do what he considers the most fun things to do. "All I ever do in New York anymore is go to art galleries and bookshops, but that's plenty," Waters continued. "That's why I keep an apartment here."

Nob Hill, San Francisco (Est. 1855)

As mentioned when discussing his New York apartment, Waters now has a place in the Nob Hill neighborhood of San Francisco. It would be the last of the "permanent" residences for Waters in his favorite cities, although Waters spent plenty of time in San Francisco before that.

Waters first ventured into San Francisco in early 1970 when the Palace Theater at 1731 Powell Street in the North Beach neighborhood ran *Mondo Trasho*. That film went over so well that *Multiple Maniacs* came next, along with a return of *Mondo Trasho* and the appearance of Divine at the theater covered in Chapter 3. Waters remembered the reaction to *Multiple Maniacs* when it played at the Palace: "It was made as a movie to offend hippies, in the greatest way," Waters told *SFGATE* in 2016. "But the hippies wanted to be offended. And the hippies turned into punks, and bikers came. It certainly caught on at the Palace Theater with the Cockettes and later at the Secret Cinema, which was a wonderful place that a promoter named Sebastian ran."

Waters came for the films, only to remain in San Francisco for a time, heading back to Baltimore in 1971 to film *Pink Flamingos* before returning to the city afterward. With the city and the people he became acquainted with in San Francisco at the time, it was easy to get enticed to stay. "Van Smith and I spent some of our most insane nights in San Francisco in the '70s," Waters told the *San Francisco Chronicle*. Waters found similarities to that of Provincetown, with not only the liberal and openly gay communities there but also the climate and view. "It's my favorite weather," Waters told *SFGATE*. "I hate hot weather. I love the views every second no matter where you are. I love how when you walk here, it's exercise. I can tell how many days I've been here by how winded I am on each hill walking home."

Living out of his car when he first came to San Francisco—his home away from home when "four-walling" his films around the country in the very early 1970s—he later moved to a commune, which came with its own unique problems. "There were people who led communes who sort of said, 'Okay, you can't eat meat.' And they'd go around and tell other communes they shouldn't eat meat. So we did a raid on one of them and threw white sugar all over the floor," Waters told John Ives. He secured his first apartment in the city near 18th and Church Street. Still, he never felt he had a permanent place in the area until 2008, when he bought a one-bedroom apartment in Nob Hill from a friend thanks to money he earned from the *Hairspray* musical—both the Broadway version and the 2007 film musical. In a 2010 interview with *SFGATE*, Waters admitted that he keeps the same hours in San Francisco as he does everywhere else. "I would probably be easy to kidnap, because I leave my apartment to get the newspapers within thirty seconds of the same time every day. I do have four different lives that I really like, and four different sets of underwear, in every city. But it doesn't matter where I am. I have to work every day."

Waters admits that he gets recognized no matter what city he is these days. It does make people-watching for his books and scripts difficult, but he ultimately doesn't mind. "I've never once complained about any kind of fame I've had. I have little patience for people who do," Waters told *SFGATE*. "I mean, so what? People take my picture without me knowing it on the cable car. I don't understand people who get into show business and pretend they don't want to be noticed. Why do you think it's called show business?"

It is clear that the cities he calls home have influenced Waters as much as his friends and his family upbringing. Yet, speaking of show business, there is still one area of Waters's past that has influenced his career and life in a very large way—the movies he saw growing up and, even more so, the creators of those films that drove Waters to become not only a filmmaker but a hustler for his films as well, as will be discussed in the next chapter.

5

Extreme Behavior

Ten Filmmakers and Ten Movies
That Influenced John Waters

> I was the only kid in the audience that didn't understand why Dorothy would ever want to go home. It was a mystery to me. To that awful black-and-white farm with that aunt who was dressed badly, with smelly farm animals around, when she could live with winged monkeys, and magic shoes, and gay lions. I didn't get it.
>
> —John Waters, from his one-man show *This Filthy World*

In Chapter 1, it is clear some aspects of television Waters saw as a child swayed his interest in entertainment. *Lili* and *The Howdy Doody Show*, for example, steered him toward puppetry and showed him the workings of creating a show for an audience, as he attended the shooting of an episode of the *Doody* program when he was a youngster. Cyril Ritchard's performance as Captain Hook in the various Mary Martin productions of *Peter Pan* that appeared on television in the 1950s and 1960s fascinated him in general, and the over-the-top villainous role in these films would lead to many similar types of roles in his own work. However, it was film—not television—that influenced his mind the most, and the movies that made their biggest impact on him were those that he wasn't supposed to ever even think about, let alone see.

In 1933, the American Catholic Church founded the National Legion of Decency. Its objective? To review films made by Hollywood (and elsewhere) and let Catholics know if the films were okay to see or if they were offensive, with "condemned films" deemed morally objectionable. In some ways, such a code was as an earlier version of the rating code used today, only with much more personal jeopardy involved. For example, an R rating by the Motion Pictures Association of America today means that no one under seventeen without a guardian can see a film, and if you were under seventeen and did so, well . . .

boy, you were in trouble and were probably asked to leave the theater. Be Catholic and see a condemned movie? "You will definitely go to hell if you see these movies," Waters remembers the nuns telling the kids in Sunday School. That seems a bit harsher than being chased out of a theater.

The National Legion of Decency would review films and give them a rating of A, B, or C. (An "A" rating could have extended designations, such as "A-II" and onward to note films acceptable for particular age groups.) Essentially, anything labeled with an A rating was okay, within reason. A "B" rating meant that there were portions of the film that were "morally objectionable" for everyone, but the entire film wasn't objectionable, so one only needed to nip out for popcorn during those select scenes. For example, *Abbot and Costello Go to Mars*—a film one commonly would not think of being objectionable except by those who hate Abbott and Costello—was given a "B" rating in 1952 because the female costumes were considered too "suggestive." A "C" rating meant "condemned," and there was no way you should be seeing such a film. In 1978, the NLD combined "B" and "C" ratings to become "O," which still meant "morally objectionable," but the point is still the same; it mostly just knocked two letters down to one ominous one. "If you saw one of those movies," Mink Stole told *Provincetown Magazine* in 2017, "and then left the theater and got hit by a bus and didn't confess it before you died, you went to hell. I think they've lightened up a bit these days, but back then a lot of stuff sent you straight to hell."

And every week the list to hell would be updated, with Catholic newspapers—as well as communications made within the church and in Catholic schools—announcing the films that would send you "straight to hell." To a kid who had increasingly rejected his Catholic upbringing, like Waters had in his teen years, a new list of condemned films was like Pandora's Box waiting to be opened every single week of the year. Waters craved finding out what he "shouldn't see," just as many other Catholics did. (There were arguments within the Church at the time that the list probably drove more people to see the films rather than scare them off.)

The first condemned film that came to Waters's attention was the 1956 film *Baby Doll*. (See later on in this chapter for more details about the film.) The Legion of Decency's review of the movie stated: "The subject matter of this film is morally repellent both in theme and treatment. It dwells almost without variation or relief upon carnal suggestiveness in action, dialogue, and costuming. Its unmitigated emphasis on lust and the various scenes of cruelty are degrading and corruptive. As such, it is grievously offensive to Christian and traditional standards of morality and decency." Now who could resist that type of review? Even more important was the film making headline news in the *Baltimore Sun* in 1956, with Cardinal Spellman appearing in St. Patrick's Cathedral in New York and personally condemning the film "under pain of sin." According to Waters in *Shock Value*, when the film turned up at the Stanley in Baltimore in December 1956—and then in 1957 at the Rex, an art theater that Waters would commonly go to in his teen years—he "immediately sneaked downtown to see *Baby Doll* and made a point, from then on, to see every condemned film [he] could."

Around this time, Waters also started getting the weekly version of *Variety*, which covered all types of films, including those condemned by the church. "It was a whole new world opening up, and I devoted all my time to the exploration of cinematic garbage," Waters went on to say in *Shock Value*. Waters also lived close to a huge drive-in, the Timonium, over on Greenspring Drive. The Timonium had a movie screen so large that cars parked a quarter of a mile away could easily see the action. That screen's size also gave a young Waters a chance to walk over to a construction site on a hill near his house and watch movies through binoculars. (Speaking of which, research shows that most of the films playing at the Timonium during these years were mainstream studio films and were rarely exploitation movies; certainly none were "X-rated," as has been claimed in some biographical studies about Waters. I suspect people have misinterpreted Waters's comments about what movies he did eventually see at other drive-ins, such as Carlin's. These were R-rated action and horror films that were sometimes promoted as "adults-only" films, but that did not mean they included pornography, which an X rating normally suggests.) Once he was able to drive, Waters spent many nights at the drive-ins (including the one time he was arrested, which is covered in Chapter 1), sometimes nightly, and in any season. "We went in the dead of winter too. I've been to the drive-in in the snow," Waters explained to John Ives. "Those drive-in years are where my film knowledge came from, in one direction—all the exploitation movies. I saw those movies many, many times; we'd go every night of the week."

Waters has talked at length in interviews about certain theaters and drive-ins of his early years. The Timonium (torn down for a Holiday Inn) and Carlin's (knocked down in 1978 for businesses) were popular drive-ins for Waters, while the Bengies Drive-In—admittedly a bit opposed to Waters's tastes at the time—was used in *Cecil B. DeMented*. As for rooftop theaters in the city, the Senator of course is one where he has held many premieres for his movies, while the Charles was a personal favorite and one that Pat Moran ran for a time. There was the Rex (later a porn theater before closing in the mid-1970s), the Stanley (torn down for a parking lot in April 1965), and the Playhouse (transformed into a church in 1989) for art and foreign films back in the 1950s and 1960s. And that was only the local scene. Toss in excursions to New York for films on 42nd Street and the various theaters and bars where underground films were proliferating at the time.

Also included in the list of condemned films, besides exploitation movies, were artistic endeavors that attempted to be adult in nature. This included many European films that were starting to become more prominent in the art theaters around the country in the 1950s and onward. Thus, by leading Waters to this list of films, the Catholic Church pointed him as well to the work of artists like Ingmar Bergman, Jean-Luc Godard, and Luis Buñuel. It is within this mixture of what many consider the bottom of the barrel when it comes to movies—sex and violence of exploitation films—along with these avant-garde filmmakers that would lead Waters to the underground film movement of the 1960s, with such individuals as Andy Warhol, Paul Morrissey, Kenneth Anger, and the Kuchar Brothers. Seeing movies like *Blood Feast* at the drive-ins was only a gateway drug to the underground film movement in New York, and . . . well, it just goes on from there. "I tried to make exploitation films for art theaters" is how Waters described his career to *Esquire* in 2016.

Waters enjoys movies and has always been ready to support other creators in print, in interviews, and at festivals. Obviously, not every artist or film that Waters has recommended over the years can be covered in one chapter. The list below highlights filmmakers and movies that had an early influence on Waters and perhaps gives us a brief understanding of some things he did in his own films when creating them.

Howard (Kroger) Babb (1906–1980)

A newspaper man out of Wilmington, Ohio, Kroger Babb got into the movie business in the 1940s, working to promote exploitation films that usually were amazingly dull dramas about a then-shocking topic, like illegal drugs or sex. Babb was one of several promoters who would buy up these films, cut out some of the boring stuff and throw in some additional titillating material, and then travel around the country, four-walling the films in small towns and playing them in halls, churches, and perhaps—if lucky—a theater or two. Promoters like Babb, typically referred to as "the forty thieves," were film hustlers, pandering to the basic emotions of everyone and looking for suckers to take a dollar or two off of in the process.

Babb's biggest success was a film called *Mom and Dad* (1945), which deals with a young woman who has sex and becomes pregnant (neither action mentioned by name) with a man who dies—conveniently off-camera—before they can marry. The film then cuts to a lecture about aspects of sex education, and there would be a live lecture in the theaters by "Elliot Forbes," who would have "nurses" sell pamphlets to the rubes in the audience. As mentioned in many other sources, Babb would sometimes have dozens of "Elliot Forbes" working around the country—young men who learned the routine and went on the road to work the picture for Babb.

The main attraction of Babb to Waters was his ability to make money through promotion on films that he could play for years around the country due to their lewd subject matter. Better yet, Babb could play them without being run out of town on a rail because the films always played to the side of proper civil actions and decency: the girl should have learned about sex in order to not get pregnant, the kids taking drugs in *She Shoulda Said No!* would learn in the film to avoid marijuana, and so forth.

There was another reason that Waters was attracted to *Mom and Dad*, and the reason it was condemned by the Legion of Decency—the main attraction that brought people in was that it showed a real birth. "The only way they could show frontal female nudity in the '40s was by showing the birth of a baby," Waters told the *Guardian*. "So dirty old men just looked at the vagina and ignored the baby," which Waters thought was a brilliant way to "square up" the film for those wanting to see something "dirty" while still appearing to make the film educational and therefore legit (and also to avoid being tarred and feathered before leaving town).

He also bought films from other markets and recut them for the exploitation market in America; the most notorious was that of Ingmar Bergman's 1949 film *Summer with Monika*. For this one, he had a good half hour cut, leaving the brief bits of nudity in it, sold it as *Monika, the Story of a Bad Girl* and promoted it with tidbits of the nudity therein. It would be the first Bergman film Waters would see, thanks of course to it being condemned. An associate of Babb, David Friedman (1923–2011)—who made nudie films in the 1950s and, later on, harder sex films (but never outright pornography)—also traveled around with *Monika* until he was sued to stop. When Friedman was mentioned in an interview, Waters replied: "I knew Friedman. He had hilarious stories. He was a carny! I was influenced by all those guys because of *Mom and Dad.*"

Besides briefly mentioning Babb in his book *Crackpot*, Waters also discussed Babb in his one-man show; he spoke mostly about *Mom and Dad* but also about Babb's jab at the Catholic Church for condemning his films by always threatening to make a film called *Father Bingo*. The movie, never made, was heavily advertised as about to go into production and was to be a comedy about a priest who runs a fixed bingo game. In 2017, Waters reflected in *Pasatiempo* on his career as a filmmaker and a man who does live one-man shows with *Pasatiempo*, saying: "I always said I wanted to make exploitation films for art theaters, and now I've turned into Kroger Babb. He was the one that toured the country with a nurse—and they would show sex education films, so they could show the birth of a baby—and he would come out and talk. Well, that's me. I am Kroger Babb. But I'm still doing what I always do, which is telling stories."

H. Gordon Lewis (1926–2016)

Speaking of David Friedman, Friedman had an early association with Herschel Gordon Lewis, who became known as the "King of Gore." Lewis was working in advertising when he began directing television commercials in the 1950s, which led to starting his own production company and making his first film, *The Prime Time*, in 1959. Working on that film with him was David Friedman, who would form a partnership with Lewis over several additional films. The movies stood out for their use of nudity and were some of the first in a genre—the nudie-cuties—that played in independent art theaters throughout the country. Such films had plots that were mostly built around getting people undressed to do little more than walk around or jump in the air. Many were set in nudist camps and purported to tell stories about the clean, fresh, innocent life of nudists, while cameras ogled the buttocks and breasts of people playing cards and badminton and taking long strolls.

Lewis directed most of the films he produced after *The Prime Time*. (Some say he directed that one as well.) Then, as Waters states in *Shock Value*, "Realizing the nudie film was a dead-end street, Mr. Lewis decided to appeal to the lowest common denominator in the least-discriminating audiences' taste—blood lust. Instead of nudity, his following paid to see tongues being ripped out, eyeballs being squashed, and various other forms of creative mutilation." As with his earlier films that actually showed nudity rather than implied it, Lewis went one step further than most filmmakers did by actually showing gore onscreen instead of insinuating it with cutaways and off-camera movements. His gore films, such as *Blood Feast* and *Two Thousand Maniacs*, were just as over-the-top as his earlier nudie films. For example, they included an infamous shot of a woman having her tongue cut out—a tongue that was obviously a sheep's tongue (which has to be sprayed with Pine-Sol due to the smell)—and the dismembering of a victim in *Two Thousand Maniacs*. In *Shock Value*, Waters would go on to say, "When I saw teenage couples hopping from their cars to vomit, I knew I had found a director after my own heart."

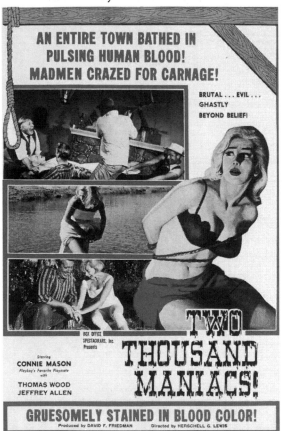

Two Thousand Maniacs! (1964), an early gory film written and directed by Herschell Gordon Lewis, whom Waters would eventually interview in his book *Shock Value* (1981).

Friedman split off from Lewis after the 1965 film *Color Me Blood Red* to go back to producing skin-flicks and a few roughies (a sub-genre mixing sex with violence). Meanwhile, Lewis continued to make his gore films until 1972, along with an occasional film of a different genre, including two movies made for children. Later in the 1970s came a revival of horror films with gory special effects, rekindling an interest in Lewis's earlier movies and a search for the man who seemed to vanish. Waters tracks him down for an interview that appears in *Shock Value*, which led to Waters appearing as "The Reverend" in Lewis's last full directorial job, *Blood Feast 2*, in 2002. Waters has also gone on record as saying that the title of *Multiple Maniacs* came from the title of Lewis's movie *Two*

Thousand Maniacs and that the "vomit bags" sometimes handed out to audiences for *Pink Flamingos* were based on the same idea used in a couple of Lewis's films as well.

Russ Meyer (1922–2004)

"Russ Meyer is the Eisenstein of sex films," Waters states in *Shock Value*. Yet, what made his films memorable—especially since none ever reached the point of being hardcore pornography—is his editing style, comedic sense, and unpredictable stories.

Meyers started taking photos and films while a combat cameraman in World War II. When he came back to the United States, he struggled to find work as a filmmaker while working on some early pictorials for *Playboy* in the 1950s. Caught up in the nudie-cuties market, Meyers made his first movie, *The Immoral Mr. Teas* (1959), and stuck with rather traditional storytelling in such films until he got to *Lorna* (1964), which showed the emerging style of Meyers, including his use of dramatic storylines along with rapid-fire editing techniques.

Waters saw *Faster, Pussycat! Kill! Kill!* (1965) in 1966, probably at Carlin's Drive-In, and fell in love with the film; typically listing it as one of his top ten favorite movies ever. Waters wrote extensively about the film in *Shock Value* and tracked down both Tura Satana and Russ Meyers for interviews in the book. Waters would also claim in 1980 that *Beyond the Valley of the Dolls* (1970, and written by film critic Roger Ebert) is "the funniest film ever made, and I think in 1999 this film will still be shown and enjoyed in much the same way as *Golddiggers of 1933* is today." (Considering that, at the time of his comment, 20th Century Fox seemed embarrassed by the film and rarely allowed it to be shown—only to now have it in various releases on DVD and Blu-ray, including Criterion—he wasn't far off.)

William Castle (1914–1977)

Unlike the previous filmmakers mentioned, William Castle was a director-producer who worked within, rather than outside of, the studio system. Not that Castle didn't crank them out over the years as well.

Castle, born William Schloss Jr. had a brilliant mind for promotion and often would use it in the films he produced. He also was known for being able to work well in the studio system, completing films under-budget and without any flare-ups of discord. He also had a love of horror and mystery films, and most of his films would either be one of those two, or a western, throughout his career.

Specifically, what drew Waters's interest to Castle were the publicity stunts connected to his films. As Waters points out in his book *Crackpot*, Castle's 1958 movie *Macabre* was simply "a rip off of *Diabolique*." Castle, however, got the idea to have ticket-buyers insured by Lloyd's of London for $1,000 in case of death by fright. Following the lineage of Kroger Babb before him, Castle arranged to have fake nurses standing by in theaters and even hearses outside the theaters. *Mr. Sardonicus* (1961) featured a "Punishment Poll," during which the audience was given a card that allowed them to decide the fate of the villain at the end of the film by either giving him a "thumbs up" or "thumbs down." Fans of Castle's work still argue if the director ever filmed a "thumbs up" version, as every audience wanted to see the villain get what was coming to him and always voted "thumbs down." *House on Haunted Hill* (1959) was sold on the gimmick called "Emergo," which was supposed to be greater than 3-D but was actually just a skeleton flown on a wire above the audience at a certain point in the film. "When I first saw *House on Haunted Hill* as a kid in Baltimore and the skeleton went out on the wire and the thousand kids in the audience went crazy . . . My whole life, I've tried to at least equal that cinema anarchy," Waters told Indiewire. com in 2017. Waters's attempts to duplicate Castle's outlandish promotional stunts go back as far as his puppetry days, which just confused the kids, and continued into stunts like the Odorama cards given to audience members for *Polyester*. "I came close with the end of *Pink Flamingos*, but I didn't tie with it. He still beat me." There was also, of course, *The Tingler* and its gimmick, described in more detail below.

Castle also produced and directed the Joan Crawford horror film *Strait-Jacket* (1964), which was recreated in 2017 in the miniseries *Feud*, about the Joan Crawford–Bette Davis feud. When *Strait-Jacket* was released, Castle took Joan Crawford with him on a publicity tour for the film, and to play the part of Castle in the miniseries, the producer remembered reading about how Waters had attended one of the showings that featured Crawford in attendance and about his love for all things Castle. Waters was then asked to play the part of Castle in the episode featuring a restaging of the tour.

"When they asked me to do it," Waters told Indiewire.com, "I was like, 'Well, I'm not fat, should I wear a fat suit?' and they were like, 'No, we just like the conceptual idea of you playing him.'"

In the pages of *Crackpot*, Waters stated, "I wish I were William Castle." Thanks to *Feud*, he fulfilled that wish.

Federico Fellini (1920–1993)

So far, the filmmakers listed have been those who have worked in exploitation films or variations of such. If people in the general public hear names like Castle, Lewis, or Babb, they probably will say, "Who is that?" If they had heard of them, the question would be, "Why would anyone look up to people like that?" But Fellini remains a giant in cinema and one that has influence many filmmakers over the years, including Waters, who typically mentioned Fellini as one of his favorite directors.

Oddly enough, while Waters has often mentioned Fellini as one of his influences, he rarely has spoken much about what exactly has influenced him, but it is somewhat easy to see when comparing the output of the two. Fellini appeared in the 1950s with films such as *La Strada* and *Nights of Cabiria*, which were lyrical dramas with occasional light touches. The two movies also both play with oddity and confusion, along with a common crowd made up of an assortment of people who look different or clownish. Fellini's *8½* was a big influence on Waters, and the film's odd assortment of people who band together inspired Waters's later work. It is easy to perceive the Cavalcade of Perversion in *Multiple Maniacs* fitting into a Fellini film, and some of the grotesque makeup of the people in Waters's films (although this was more likely an influence from the Kuchar Brothers) found its genesis in Fellini's work. There is also the back-and-forth pull of Catholicism and the acceptance and rejection of religion in Fellini's films, which quickly worked its way into Waters's movies.

Waters has talked more than once about going to see *8½* at the Charles in Baltimore in August 1963, where he and other members of the audience were given a promotional item of a ruler that was eight and a half inches long. Waters has also noted how his fascination with one character in *8½*—the large, insane-looking Saraghina, who dances with the protagonist as a youngster—obviously influenced his look and work with Divine in his early movies. Waters would later do an art piece called *8 1/2*, which was a giant ruler measuring eight and a half feet rather than inches. "I loved that movie. Fellini was a little lofty for a teenage boy, but certainly he was a huge influence," he told the *Guardian* in 2015. "He inspired me because he had a local cast in his movies, people who typically weren't movie stars. That's what I did too."

Ingmar Bergman (1918–2007)

As with Fellini, Ingmar Bergman is one of the most important filmmakers in motion picture history. Born in Sweden, Bergman began writing and directing films in the 1940s. He became best known for serious, dramatic films that sometimes took a magical bent, such as a soldier playing chess with Death in *The Seventh Seal* (1957), demons attacking the protagonist in *Hour of the Wolf* (1968), and the miraculous transportation of the children in *Fanny and Alexander* (1982). Over the years, his movies have been influential for many directors, including Waters, Woody Allen, and Robert Altman. Waters has often stated that *Brink of Life* is his favorite Bergman film.

Bergman's films also tended to deal with subjects that were darker in tone, although his films usually showed a search for beauty and happiness either within or as an outcome of subjects like death and insanity. "They released all the Ingmar Bergman movies in Baltimore when I was growing up," Waters told *Entertainment Weekly* in 2005. "And Ingmar Bergman, I know it might be hard to see, was a huge influence on me. He always had vomit and suicide and adult subject matter in his films."

One particular incident that Waters remembers was that of seeing *The Hour of the Wolf* in a theater with Divine. "I used to make Divine go see Ingmar Bergman movies with me when we were on LSD, and we were tripping during that scene where the woman rips her face off and it scared the shit out of us. I will always remember the wonderful moment on LSD when Ingmar Bergman really became an artist to me," Waters jokingly told Daniel Rothbart in 2000.

Luis Buñuel (1900–1983)

The films of Spanish-born writer–director Luis Buñuel used strong surrealism to tell stories that at first appeared to be almost normal before descending into dreamlike worlds where things make sense within the framework of the "dreams" themselves. Buñuel also was raised Catholic and later not only abandoned the faith but even parodied aspects of Catholicism in several of his films.

Buñuel's contribution to the art of surrealism, and even some aspects of what could be seen as the later underground movement, came as early as his first film, *An Andalusian Dog* (*Un Chien Andalou*), from 1929, which features the still-shocking image of a razor blade slicing through a woman's eye. (The effect was done through editing to make it appear to be the woman's eye.) His 1930 film *L'Age d'Or* caused a riot soon after its premiere due to its images.

Buñuel's international career really took off around 1962 with his film *The Exterminating Angel*, which features a story about rich socialites who seem unable to exit a dinner party and begin to turn against each other. Buñuel went on to make such films as *Belle de Jour* (1967), *The Discreet Charm of the Bourgeoisie* (1972), and *That Obscure Object of Desire* (1977).

Many have pointed out that Waters's surrealistic parodies of Catholicism (such as that of the rosary job in *Multiple Maniacs*) are similar to those of Buñuel—an observation that Waters himself agrees with. When *Pink Flamingos* was released, *New York* magazine referred to it as "the nearest American film to Buñuel's *Andalusian Dog*," a quote that was later used in advertising for the film.

Kenneth Anger (Born 1927)

After digging into foreign films and art films, it was only natural for Waters to venture into seeing "underground films." In *Sight & Sound*, Waters said: "Somehow I got my hand on the *Village Voice* and started reading Jonas Meka's column and that opened up the world of underground movies that I knew nothing about. I used to run away to New York all the time, on the greyhound bus, and make up lies that I was going to a fraternity weekend or something and then go see these movies. I wanted to be an underground filmmaker."

At the time Waters was discovering them in the 1960s, underground films were films created by artists who dealt with subjects and actions that would not be included in commercial films. Such films were shown in little theaters, clubs, and elsewhere but were typically not available in normal theaters. The films of Andy Warhol, Paul Morrissey, the Kuchar Brothers, and others were all part of the scene in the 1960s, with Kenneth Anger being one of the better-known names of the movement.

Anger was born Kenneth Wilbur Anglemyer, and he began making his own films when he was a youngster. His fascination with the occult along with his coming out in an era that still considered homosexuality to be an illegal act were to become themes in his films, starting with the short *Fireworks* in 1947. Anger's true rise in the underground movement came with the success of such titles as *Scorpio Rising, Inauguration of the Pleasure Dome, Lucifer Rising*, and *Invocation of My Demon Brother* over the years. His use of popular music as his soundtracks to his otherwise silent movies was perhaps most intriguing and led to much commentary on the music's juxtaposition to the actions onscreen. This would progress to the point where Anger convinced artists such as Mick Jagger and Jimmy Page to contribute soundtracks to his films.

It is easy to see how Anger's use of popular music influenced Waters. "I love Kenneth Anger. I saw him, certainly probably, in 1964. Kenneth Anger did pop music in films before anybody," Waters told *Crave* in 2016. Waters has used popular songs in all of his movies; in fact, the main reason *Mondo Trasho* has no official release on DVD or Blu-ray is due to copyright issues with the music used without permission in the film. Waters's early shorts also incorporate a number of images cut together in a mishmash fashion—a technique that appeared in Anger's early work as well. Finally, it is also intriguing to see the rather splashy opening credits to Anger's shorts and note how similar they are to those Waters would use in his films of the 1970s. Mary Vivian Pearce can also be seen reading the original French version of *Hollywood Babylon*, a book written by Anger, in *Mondo Trasho*.

Andy Warhol (1928–1987)

A world-famous artist who made a career out of taking the ordinary and reworking it into pieces of art with subtle twists, Andy Warhol helped popularize the silk-screening process in his work, which repeated images within the same piece but changed their looks through blotches of color not always "within the lines." As his popularity grew, Warhol began to work in other mediums, such as pushing the career of the musical group the Velvet

Underground, developing *Interview* magazine, and creating experimental movies that were part of the whole underground scene.

He also made films between 1963 and 1968, some in association with filmmaker Paul Morrissey, who would continue on with their association when making *Andy Warhol's Dracula* and *Andy Warhol's Frankenstein* in the 1970s. (Warhol's association on the films had more to do with hanging his name on the two features rather than doing anything connected with creating the films.) Warhol's early films were very experimental and—as typical—usually did nothing more than show everyday things and events in real time onscreen, such as his 1963 film *Sleep*, which showed a man sleeping for over five hours. The film *Eat* is forty-five minutes of a man eating a mushroom. *Blue Movie* (1969) was more than ninety minutes of two people having sex, and in some corners it is considered an early pornographic film in the "golden age of porn."

One of the male stars of his films, and later of several films by Morrisey for Warhol, was Joe Dallesandro, who appeared as one of the parents in *Cry-Baby*. Waters has also pointed out that his second film, *Roman Candles*, which was three films running at once on one screen, came about after seeing Warhol's *Chelsea Girls* (1966), which showed two films side by side for close to three and a half hours. Waters admired the way Warhol could promote and was even given an early Warhol print from his girlfriend back in the mid-1960s. There were limits to Warhol's influence, however, as Waters told John Ives: "Warhol's influence on me was giving me the confidence that I could [make films] with my friends, for no money. But I didn't want to do things like filming just one person doing something. Who influenced me most was the Kuchar Brothers, because their films were lurid melodramas."

George Kuchar (1942–2011) and Mike Kuchar (Born 1942)

Twin brothers born in New York City, George and Mike Kuchar became well-known underground filmmakers. Their work together and apart—especially George's solo work—was an obvious influence on Waters. "Both of them—they made me want to make films. They are the reason," Waters told Jack Stevenson. "Because they were like—and I hadn't even seen Douglas Sirk yet—they were the first people that ever idolized Douglas Sirk, they were so ahead of their time. And their films were that lurid color and they were the biggest influence on me, of the underground filmmakers."

Their films featured poor acting and were obviously put together more with imagination than with proper costumes and props. George also had a tendency to put his female characters into makeup that made them look more like they were in drag, with eyebrows that looked to have been drunkenly put on with magic maker in a dark room (and yet this obviously influenced Van Smith with the look he would later give Divine). The titles of their films were crazy, such as *Pussy on a Hot Tin Roof, Unstrap Me*, and *The Naked and the Nude*, and their films became memorable hits in the underground movement. George Kuchar's short film, *Hold Me While I'm Naked* (1966), was voted one of the 100 Best Films of the twentieth century by the *Village Voice*. He also wrote and costarred in (and obviously heavily influenced the look of) the epic comedy-horror-mystery-porno *Thundercrack!* (1975). Mike Kuchar did the well-remembered futuristic *Sins of the Fleshapoids* (1965).

What made them exciting and unique was not their obvious lack of funds but their imagination. As pointed out in the documentary *It Came from Kuchar*, many of the artists working in underground films in the 1960s were looking strictly for imagery without telling a story, or going so far as the things Warhol did, which was having nothing happen at all in his films. The Kuchars, on the other hand, were trying to make Hollywood-style films—much like the colorful melodramas of Douglas Sirk (*Written on the Wind; All That Heaven Allows*) on the cheap. The very, very cheap. Along the way, they managed to convey warmth and energy that involved the audience in their dreamlike worlds. Better yet, George worked for nearly forty years at the San Francisco Art Institute, transferring his passion of filmmaking—and doing it no matter what resources are available to you—onto students. When he died, the institute asked Mike to take his place, knowing what an asset the Kuchar touch was to the students. He continues to pass on that passion to the new filmmakers today, just as the brothers passed it on to Waters back in the early 1960s.

Yet, it was simply not any one person that motivated Waters with his work. In the John Ives interview, when asked if Warhol was a prime motivator, Waters reflected on how all of these creators came together to steer him toward his career. "[The Kuchars], along with Russ Meyer and trashy Herschell Gordon Lewis gore movies, were a stronger influence than Warhol. And Kenneth Anger was a huge influence. All put together, it was the New York underground school meets the drive-in movies, with Ingmar Bergman giving them some fervent angst." Yet, for any true artist, influence reflects in one's work, but only so far.Waters went his own direction, away from his movie mentors, to become a filmmaker that would influence others after him.

Beyond admiring the body of work and careers of others, Waters also reveres specific films he has seen over the years. Every year sees at least one new "best of" list from Waters for the year, and it makes for good fodder for writers and gives Waters a chance to promote movies he liked in the year. Some films like *Lili* have already been discussed, but below are ten films that Waters has referred to multiple times over the years as being some of his favorites:

Cinderella (1950)

This is the Disney animated version of the story of Cinderella, which was the first movie Waters remembers seeing as a child. It also features the first movie villains that Waters admired as well: "Every time the stepmother and stepsisters came on, I was happy, because Disney villains were always the best," Waters told Mikki Brammer. This can be plainly seen in *Desperate Living*, when one character transforms herself into the evil queen from *Snow White* by the end of the film.

The 78 rpm record released for the movie also has a special place in his heart. "I played the record over and over and over. Especially when the stepmother comes and says, 'Cinderella . . .' and the music goes Da-DADA-Da-DADA. I wanted that music to play whenever I stepped into a room for the rest of my life."

Cinderella, her stepsisters, and the glass slipper are all parodied in *Mondo Trasho* during the scene when Mary Vivian Pearce's character is being "shrimped" by her Prince Charming.

Wizard of Oz (1939)

Another classic children's film that Waters saw as a child. "I don't remember how old I was, and it wasn't the first movie I saw, but it was close to it," Waters told *The Today Show* in 2011. As the film did have a major rerelease in 1955, Waters probably saw it in August of that year at the Loew's Century in downtown Baltimore. "It was a complete, complete obsession from the very, very beginning."

Like he did with the evil stepmother in *Cinderella*, Waters sympathized with the villain as well as the look of the film. "*The Wizard of Oz* opened me up because it was one of the first movies I ever saw. It opened me up to villainy, to screenwriting, to costumes. And great dialogue. I think the witch has great, great dialogue." In the same interview, Waters would quote his favorite line, that which the Wicked Witch of the West said as she was slowly melting because Dorothy threw water on her: "'Who would have thought a good little girl like you could destroy my beautiful wickedness.' That line inspired my life. I sometimes say it to myself before I go to sleep, like a prayer."

His fascination with the witch led to Waters dressing up like the character for a birthday party as a kid. "The only time I've ever been in drag in my entire life," Waters chuckled in the interview. In 1965, Waters would begin work on a short film that parodied *The Wizard of Oz, Dorothy, the Kansas City Pothead*, of which a little of the footage can be found on the *John Waters DVD Scrapbook* that was available via mail order through New Line in 2001. Waters would use some of the music from the film in *Mondo Trasho* and would have Mary Vivian Pearce's character use her new bird feet to tap three times and be transported away. Also, Waters compared the final party scene in *Desperate Living* to the film when interviewer Scott MacDonald suggested it reminded him of scenes from Bergman's *The Seventh Seal*, saying: "I think it's more like *Oz*. The end is like, 'Ding, dong, the wicked witch is dead.'" Most importantly, Waters feels that in the movie it is easy to see characters that would be antagonists in one movie to be protagonists in another. "The fat girl gets the guy; the good killer is *Serial Mom*," Waters told Scott MacDonald. "It's always the reverse character in other people's movies that are heroes. I realized that I was never going to be like the other kids; that I wasn't going to fit in, but it didn't bother me. It was a secret society to know that the villains were just much more fun."

Trog (1970)

Trog is a science fiction movie that was Joan Crawford's last theatrical film. Some aspects of the filming were recreated in the 2017 miniseries *Feud*, which features an appearance from John Waters, but for those who have never heard of it, here's a quick synopsis: Crawford plays a scientist who finds that a troglodyte—in other words, a caveman—is alive in a nearby cave. She works to educate the caveman, but a big ol' mean businessman (played by Michael Gough) hates "Trog" and gets Trog killed, but not before Trog kills him and a few other people … kinda proving his point about how dangerous Trog is, actually.

In 2015, the British Film Institute had a retrospective of Waters's movies, and along with those, the BFI asked Waters to put together a program of British films that he would like others to see. Of the six movies picked, two are amazingly bad—but fun—films: *Trog* and the next movie on this list, *Boom!* Waters enjoys how serious Crawford is in a role where she has to talk to a guy wearing a variable of an ape mask and wooly suit for ninety minutes. "You kind of feel sorry for her, and then you don't because she was Joan Crawford," Waters told *Vice* at the time.

In the same interview, Waters said that the film taught him something for his own movies: "Get a star and build a vehicle around her. That's how to get your movie made." With *Desperate Living* onward, Waters has followed that advice and has made progressively bigger films each step of the way once he started doing it.

Boom! (1968)

It's Tennessee Williams, a favorite of Waters, with a screenplay based on Williams's play *The Milk Train Doesn't Stop Here Anymore.* The film features Elizabeth Taylor as a rich woman who is dying. A gigolo, played by Richard Burton, arrives at her island residence and they spend their time whispering, talking, and screaming at each other. Taylor's character soon realizes that the gigolo has been seen with various women before they died, making him a type of "angel of death." Noel Coward turns up as a gossipy friend of Taylor's character, nicknamed "the Witch of Capri." Taylor's character is supposed to be much older, Burton's much younger, and Coward's a woman. Not that any of it really matters, as it's Taylor, Burton, and Coward saying Williams's worst dialogue for 112 minutes.

Waters loves the movie, viewing it as a good example of a "bad movie." "I show it to every person I think I'm falling in love with—if they hate it, I don't talk to them anymore," Waters told the *Baltimore Sun* in 1998. Waters has shown the film at various festivals, pleased to have full audiences for

together
they devour
life

TAYLOR
AND
BURTON

in
TENNESSEE WILLIAMS'
most powerful
drama since
"Cat on a Hot
Tin Roof"!

BOOM!

ELIZABETH TAYLOR   RICHARD BURTON
NOEL COWARD

Boom! (1968), starring Elizabeth Taylor and Richard Burton, was adapted from a play by Tennessee Williams. Waters has repeatedly listed it as one of his favorites.

a movie that "bombed" at theaters when it was released in 1968. "It's so awful, it's perfect," Waters told *Vice*. "It's a staggering movie and it's worth seeing it with a live audience because you just don't know how to react at the beginning. You think, 'What is the tone of this?'"

Waters stated in the *Vice* interview that *Boom!* influenced *Pink Flamingos*: "I saw [*Boom!*] right before making that, and in the movie Goforth is writing her memoirs, and in *Pink Flamingos*, Divine is writing her memoirs in the trailer. [This footage was cut from the finished film but appears as an extra in the twenty-fifth anniversary edition of the movie.] No one would notice that, though. I'm such a big Liz Taylor fan and so was Divine. At the end of *Boom!*, Liz Taylor looked like Divine, and Divine always looked like Elizabeth Taylor at the beginning of her career."

Years after becoming a fan of the film, Waters met Elizabeth Taylor on Labor Day in 1997 and told her how much he loved the film. To *Vice*, Waters said: "She got real mad and shouted, 'That's a terrible movie!' And I said, 'It isn't! I love that movie! I tour with it at festivals!' Then she realized I was serious." Nevertheless, Waters noted in 1998 to the *Baltimore Sun*, "She didn't ask me back this Labor Day."

Baby Doll (1956)

Already discussed in earlier chapters, *Baby Doll* was the first condemned movie that Waters ever saw. Directed by Eliza Kazan (*On the Waterfront*; *A*

Streetcar Named Desire), the film's script came from Tennessee Williams and so impressed a young Waters that he began checking out Williams's work from the library (as described in Chapter 1) and became a ferocious reader.

The film's plot is rather mild by today's standards. Karl Malden plays a cotton gin owner, Archie, who is feuding with another cotton gin owner, Silva, played by Eli Wallach. Malden's character is in a marriage with a young woman, Baby Doll, played by Carroll Baker. Their marriage is unconsummated, as Archie must wait until Baby Doll is twenty, according to an agreement with her father. When Archie is desperate for work, he burns down Silva's cotton gin. Silva then seduces Baby Doll into signing an affidavit saying Archie did it. Archie is arrested, Silva abandons Baby Doll, and Baby Doll finally wises up a little.

The film is ripe with seduction scenes between Silva and Baby Doll, but nothing is seen, and what is suggested—such as Baby Doll asking Silva why he was doing what he was doing in a close-up shot, implying his hands are not where they should be—could be seen as meaning something else. Nevertheless, it caused a controversy due to its condemnation by the Catholic Church, which led to the banning of the movie in parts of the country and in areas around the world. As one of its stars, Eli Wallach once commented to *Entertainment Weekly*, "People see it today and say, 'What the hell was all the fuss about?'"

Waters has never outright said it, but it has been suggested that the seediness of *Pink Flamingos'* trailer digs and the feud set up by the Marbles against Divine is reflective of the movie. Further, both feature grown but dimwitted female characters in cribs—as if Baby Doll would eventually end up like Edith Massey's character in the later film.

The Bad Seed (1956)

Patty McCormack plays the title role, Rhonda Penmark, which she also played in a 1954 Broadway play that was based a novel by William March. Rhonda is an eight-year-old sociopath who torments others, kills a classmate for a penmanship award, and then murders the caretaker at her house when he discovers her secret. By the end of the film, even God is fed up with her and kills her with a bolt of lightning.

As can be expected, the film is one of Waters's favorites from his childhood years, and he has collected material about the film. He also spends a chunk of his book *Role Models* talking with Patty McCormack, with whom he later became friends, and discussing the film. Waters would use a photo of Patty McCormack as Rhonda for one of his Christmas cards, and a framed photo of Rhonda can be seen in documentary footage of his home. It also would be the influence for one of his casting choices in *Cry-Baby*: "Traci Lords looks like Patty McCormack. That's what Iggy Pop told me and I said, 'You're right! I never even thought of that. It's like Patty McCormack grown up.'"

"I wanted to be Rhonda Penmark," Waters joked in his book and in interviews. "I wanted to be feared like Rhonda. Other people maybe liked Robin Hood or Batman, but I liked little Rhonda Penmark."

Faster, Pussycat! Kill! Kill! (1965)

This Russ Meyer movie was covered a bit previously in this chapter, but for those who have never seen what is probably Meyer's second biggest movie (*Beyond the Valley of the Dolls* being just a tad more popular among fans), here's the plot: Three female criminals (we see them briefly as go-go dancers at the beginning of the film, but that seems to be more of a hobby for them) kill a guy and kidnap his young girlfriend in the desert. They arrive in a ghost town with their hostage and discover that the wheelchair-bound owner of a gas station has money hidden somewhere in the area. The three stick around and generally abuse everyone in sight until one by one they get knocked off. The leader, Varla (played by Tura Santana), is the last to die, being hit by a truck driven by the hostage.

"It's a great action movie," Waters told *New York* magazine, "with the kind of movie stars we're hard-pressed to find anymore." Reflecting on when he first saw it back in the 1960s at Carlin's Drive-In, he said: "I went back every night and took different people. Divine and I saw it many, many times. It was certainly an influence—and Russ would probably be surprised to hear this—on the Divine character." Waters is of course referring to Varla, the rough leader of the gang who takes no guff from anyone around her, although she respects a worthy opponent when found (like the one son of the old man who manages to stop her from killing him with a car, causing her to walk off rather than finish him when she could have). It may take a bit of an imagination, but one could see Divine playing the same character in a film without much of a change beyond costume fittings. The strong female villains obviously sat in Waters's mind when he was writing *Female Trouble*, as Dawn and her schoolmates, like Varla, also go on a crime spree.

The Girl Can't Help It (1956)

Another Waters favorite that he saw as a child. He went in mostly to see the rock and roll acts that were advertised as being in the movie—especially Little Richard, whom he idolized—but he came out converted and was now a fan of the film. "This wasn't a movie that my boy classmates wanted to see or cared about," Waters told Margy Rochlin in 2009. "They weren't interested in discussing Jayne Mansfield's complete lack of roots. I really had no one that I could be enthusiastic with about it. So it was a private secret of mine, this movie."

The film stars Tom Ewell as a press agent, Tom Miller, who is paid by a gangster named "Fats" Murdock (Edmond O'Brien) to make his girlfriend Jerri (Jayne Mansfield) a singing sensation. Intercut in the comedy of Miller trying to promote Jerri are several rock and roll acts performing for the camera, including Little Richard, Eddie Cochran, the Platters, and Gene Vincent. "This affected me more than anything ever," Waters said in an interview with the Directors Guild of America, referring to seeing Little Richard performing in the movie. "I still have the mustache today because of this scene."

The clever thing about the film is that, although Jerri supposedly is a bad singer, she turns out to be talented and smarter than most of the other characters in the film. It's also a very colorful film, with hues that are brighter than natural life, which works well for a movie that takes place nearly all on sets at the studio. Director and coscripter Frank Tashlin had worked as an animator at Warner Brothers years before making the film, and it is obvious that the look and several of the gags come from a person used to work in a medium one or several steps away from reality. "If only my bedroom looked like that," Waters said to the Directors Guild of America. "If only the world looked like that! I wanted to live my real life in that kind of over-the-top color. It's so ... it's so ... it's so ... fake!"

Waters has admitted taking many elements from *The Girl Can't Help It* and putting them into his films:

- Divine's first appearance in *Mondo Trasho* features the Little Richard theme song, "The Girl Can't Help It," as Divine drives down the road.

- Divine's walk down the street in *Pink Flamingos* also features the same song, and used in a similar manner as the scene in the Tashlin film when Jayne Mansfield walks down the street to the same song.
- A man who sees Divine in *Female Trouble* has his (fake) eye pop out, just as the men who ogle Mansfield all have comic physical reactions to Mansfield when they see her.
- Waters's promotion for his early films take a leaf from Miller's playbook. Waters told the DGA, "When Divine and I first started, I'd make him get all dressed up and we'd ride the subway or walk through cheesy restaurants just to get people talking and it worked!"
- Divine was always Waters's Jayne Mansfield in his films. "Well, Jayne Mansfield mixed with Godzilla," Waters joked to the DGA.
- The opening of the film where Tom Ewell talks directly to the audience and the screen widens to demonstrate CinemaScope was parodied in *Polyester* as the scientist finishes his speech and the screen opens up.

As with other films listed here, Waters has promoted the movie many times over the years and feels a connection to it. Pointing to how Frank Tashlin photographed Mansfield in the film, Waters said to the DGA: "He loved her—and you can feel that, you can feel how he shot her. So what this movie is about is the chemistry between a director and a glamour girl. That was always incredibly important to me. I'm not comparing myself, I'm saying we parodied this and I only parody the things I love."

The Tingler (1959)

Produced and directed by William Castle, who is covered earlier in this chapter, *The Tingler* was another childhood favorite that Waters has returned to many times in interviews. Waters refers to the film as Castle's masterpiece in his book *Crackpot*, mostly because of the gimmick Castle came up with for the film.

The film's plot is about a pathologist, Dr. Chapin (played by Vincent Price), who discovers that at the time of extreme fear a parasite—a "tingler"—grows on a person's spine and will kill them unless they scream. The movie also features Vincent Price's character taking LSD in order to induce the tingler on himself—an early introduction of the drug Waters and his friends would be using in just a few years.

The film leads up to a situation where a tingler has gotten loose and is about to attack someone in a darkened theater. At that point, the screen goes black, and Price can be heard telling the audience in the theater watching *The Tingler* that the creature is loose and they all need to scream in order to stop it. At that point, Castle used his gimmick, "Percepto." What this turned out to be was a little electronic buzzer that was placed on the bottom of random chairs in the theater. Just as Price finishes his speech to the audience in the film, the projectionist would turn on the buzzers, causing people in those seats to feel a tingling sensation and propel them to yell.

"I went to see it every day," Waters remembers in *Crackpot*. "Since, by the time it came to my neighborhood, only about ten random seats were wired, I would run through the theater searching for the magical buzzers. As I sat there experiencing the miracle of Percepto, I realized that there could be such a thing as Art in the cinema."

All That Heaven Allows (1955)

Waters once was asked by *Vanity Fair* what he would like to come back as after death. His reply was "a mirror in a Douglas Sirk film." Mirrors appear many times in Sirk's films, especially his later films that are in luscious color (Waters once compared the unreal color in *The Girl Can't Help It* to that of many of Sirk's films), and reference an image of oneself rather than the real person.

All That Heaven Allows deals with a suburban widow, played by Jane Wyman, who falls in love with a younger man, played by Rock Hudson, who loves only the natural life. Her children do not like the idea of their mother hanging out with the man and his friends and eventually force a breakup (leading to a scene where the children buy her a television set to keep her company, and the widow sees her reflection trapped inside the darkened mirror image of the television screen). The young man has an accident that the widow sees him through, and, with the children finally on her side, the widow and the man reconcile.

Sirk made big, colorful melodramas that had blatantly unsubtle symbolism everywhere one looked, such as the bride finding out that the husband has a very small pistol under his pillow on their wedding night in *Written on the Wind*. Waters stays away from parodying the symbolism, but he does play with the usage of overly complicated personal dramas that persist through

All That Heaven Allows (1955), a film by Douglas Sirk that influenced Waters in his films, especially *Polyester* (1981).

Sirk's films in his film *Polyester*, where everything that can go wrong for Francine does. This includes her children not understanding her, a town turning against her, and a young man rekindling romance in her life—just like in *All That Heaven Allows*. Sure, it all goes a bit haywire, with the man turning out to be a criminal trying to drive her insane—oh, if only we had gotten a scene where Francine sees a deer through the picture window of her house and smashed through the glass to frighten it off—but the references are there.

Such references in Sirk's films, as well as other films and filmmakers listed in this chapter, helped refine Waters's choices later in his movies, just as his life growing up and his friendships with the Dreamlanders led him to the direction he would follow in later years. With those elements in mind, it's time to go back to 1964, when Waters decided to make his first short film, *Hag in a Black Leather Jacket*, which would put Waters on the road to the memorable films that were to follow.

6

Eat Your Makeup

The Short Films of John Waters

People thought it was arty. I don't even know if you could do that today. When I saw the footage, I thought, 'What's this? They gave me somebody else's roll of film.

—John Waters, on the double-exposed footage
in his first film, *Hag in a Black Leather Jacket*

Seventeen years old and feeling embarrassed that he was still working as a puppeteer as a teenager, Waters was thrilled to get an 8 mm camera from his grandmother. By that point he had started reading Jonas Mekas's column in the *Village Voice*. Mekas was an early champion of the underground movie scene in the New York area, and, as mentioned in chapter 5, through reading and seeing those films, Waters realized that this was what he wanted to do. "I realized you didn't need any money. You could use your friends. I wanted to try that," Waters told Matt Patches in 2014. "I thought underground movies were controversial. They broke barriers. They caused trouble. They had beatniks and hippies—a world I wanted to be in."

He jumped into the world with both feet, putting his friends and family to work in his short films. Even more interesting is that, unlike other starting filmmakers who do a few little movies that only they see and then pack away, Waters took the route of William Castle and Kroger Babb before him, trying to get his films seen by an audience immediately—even when he really didn't know what he was doing yet when it came to filming. "I sent ads for [*Hag in a Black Leather Jacker*] to try to get the drive-in to book it," Waters told John Ives, "not knowing that a drive-in couldn't show an 8 mm movie."

His early films, his first two shot with 8 mm film and then progressing to 16 mm with his third and fourth film, are all essentially shorts. They range from fifteen to forty-five minutes in length and feature audio recorded on a reel-to-reel tape machine that is played somewhat in sync with the film. It was because of this audio setup that Waters had reason not to commercially release them (besides concerns of having used unlicensed music in the films). "I remember the torture of doing that, of thinking that I could synch a whole movie with a tape," Waters told John Ives. "You know, different projectors run at slightly different speeds—a tiny bit threw the whole thing off because it was closely synchronized."

The films appeared briefly when first finished and then only on special occasions ever since, in retrospectives and touring art exhibit. He explained his reasoning for allowing them to be seen in such context to Todd Solondz in 2004: "The reason I think they'll work in the show is that besides getting to see Divine when he's seventeen years old, people will be able to see the seeds of what interested me then, and still interests me now—Catholicism, my obsession with the press, assassins, race relations, shoplifting, obscure pop music, and taking scenes from other movies and using them." The first of these appearances came in his art exhibit *Change of Life*, which toured between 2004 and 2006. Three rooms in the exhibit are set up to play his first three short films: *Hag in a Black Leather Jacket*, *Roman Candles*, and *Eat Your Makeup*. These films also appeared in the 2014 retrospective at the Lincoln Center in New York, "Fifty Years of John Waters: How Much Can You Take?" and in the BFI program from 2015, "It Isn't Very Pretty ... The Complete Films of John Waters (Every Goddam One of Them)."

Because of the sparseness of their viewings, it is not easy to see these short films unless you happen to go to one of these special events. Only the fourth film, *The Diane Linkletter Story*, has crept into view on YouTube and other online video sites, and it is one that Waters tends to dismiss from his filmography due to its production; but more about that later on in this chapter.

Although there is little available for fans to see, it is possible to get a good idea of what occurs in each one thanks to information gathered by such sources as John G. Ives's book *American Originals: John Waters*, Michael Cohn's "John Waters: Change of Life" in the *NY Arts Magazine* from 2004, Joe Blevins's review of the "Change of Life" exhibit on his Dreamlandnews. com website (which includes research into what music appears with each film), as well as comments Waters and others have made about the films over the years.

Hag in a Black Leather Jacket (1964)

The very first John Waters movie was shot with 8 mm film stolen by his girl-friend, "Mona Montgomery," (although an article from the October 20, 1965 edition of the *Baltimore Evening Sun* about the film states that Waters got the film from his grandmother) who also stars in the film as a white woman who elopes with a black man. The man arrives at the woman's house in his car with a trash can in the front seat. The woman leaves with him and does a mild striptease in front of the man as she changes into a ballet outfit. The man then gets into the trash can and the woman has to place the trash can with the man inside into the car.

The pair arrive at a house and climb up to the roof to be married by a man sitting on the edge of the chimney and wearing a Ku Klux Klan robe. The woman wears a bridal gown, and the wedding guests are an odd assortment of people, including a woman in an American flag dress, a man in drag, and a girl with weird hair. The man throws pieces of wedding cake off the roof to those below, and the newlyweds leave in the car with the Klansman standing on the hood of the car as it takes off. With Waters's mother playing "God Bless America" on the piano, Mary Vivian Pearce steps forward and does the "Bodie Green" (a.k.a. the "Dirty Boogie") as the film ends.

Starring in the film was Bobby Chappel as the groom, "Mona Montgomery" as the bride, Bob Skidmore and Mary Vivian Pearce as wedding guests, and Trish Waters as the girl helping with the wedding dress. The *Baltimore Evening Sun*, on October 20, 1965, mentioned that someone named Judy Boutin played a "star role" in the film as well. Boutin would appear in Waters's first three films and would later model dress designs by David Lochary in an article from 1968 before disappearing from Dreamland.

Filmed in the fall of 1964, the location of the seventeen-minute short was the house belonging to Waters's parents. Over the years, the film's budget is stated to have been anywhere from five to eighty dollars, but as Waters said to James Grant in 1994: "[The film] really cost no money because the leading lady stole the film. And the developing." At one point, Waters didn't realize he had put a roll of film he had already used back into the camera, creating an unintentional double-exposure effect that people liked. Waters used the family reel-to-reel recorder to make the sound for the film, which did work as long as the film was played on the one 8 mm projector with the reel-to-reel player he had at the time, and with a tape that had not been stretched from overuse. In other words, after a handful of times playing it, the synch would be off no matter how hard one tried (although one would assume that some work was done to fix this problem for the videos made to be shown in the later retrospectives). The music in the film includes pop songs like "He's Sure the Boy I Love" by the Crystals and "The Leader of the Pack" by the Shangri-Las," along with "The Mickey Mouse March," "Supercalifragilisticexpialidocious," and, of course, Waters's mom playing "God Bless America." (Blevins)

"It's barely a real movie. That was very much influenced by Theater of the Absurd," Waters told Thedissolve.com in 2014. "I didn't even know there was editing! I guess I put a few cuts in it? I had no idea what I was doing. Absolutely none." The one moment from the film that Waters always discusses as being fun is that of watching Mary Vivian Pearce dancing the Bodie Green at the end of the film, saying, "For no reason. It has nothing to do with the plot."

The film was shown once in a coffee shop on Howard Street, where Waters "passed a hat" around for donations and made his first profit. (Waters stated to Scott MacDonald that the film "grossed a hundred dollars," but he also said that the film cost eighty to make, when he would later remember it costing nothing, so the profit amount should be taken with a grain of salt.) The coffee house went out of business soon afterwards, although it is safe to assume that it wasn't due to *Hag in a Black Leather Jacket*. Waters told The *Baltimore Evening Sun* in October 1965 that he planned to take the film to New York in an attempt to get it played in one of the underground movie houses there, but as Waters never mentions such a showcase happening in any interviews, it is safe to assume that he never got far with that venture. Certainly the drive-ins were not interested.

But there was the upside—he could make a film. He could get people into a room, get them to sit through the finished product, and get them to pay him something for it. Best yet—he could make a profit off his creative outlet. It may have been only thirty dollars or so, but it was a profit. The wheels were turning, and he was already thinking ahead to his next film when life got in the way for a bit.

Dorothy, the Kansas City Pothead (1966; Never Completed)

Then there was NYU, which found Waters in New York for a few weeks, battling against the Man and spending his days on 42nd Street seeing movies.

Before his departure to college, he told the *Baltimore Evening Sun* that his next movie would be a parody of *The Wizard of Oz*. By early 1966, he was back in Baltimore and looking to start up another movie while "planning to return to NYU in the fall" (though this may have just been hyperbole by Waters in an interview in March 1966 with the *Baltimore Sun* to show himself to be "mature" and dedicated to his education). Using an 8 mm camera with color film—an Associated Press article at the time stated that Waters borrowed his father's camera—Waters gathered together a handful of friends to begin filming *Dorothy, the Kansas City Pothead* in March 1966. "It's a comedy, not a message," Waters told Tom Briley of the Associated Press at the time. "You couldn't [convey a message] with such a film. It would just be laughed at. It would cost too much to try to say anything."

In the same interview with Briley, Waters explained the plot of the proposed forty-five-minute half-color/half-black-and-white movie as followed: Dorothy takes LSD, causing her to be transported to the land of Od, where "Munchins" perform a ballet "dressed in leotards and orthopedic oxfords." A narcotics agent is the evil "wicked witch" of Od, who uses "winged junkies" to try to capture Dorothy. The film was to end with Dorothy safe back home, only to be arrested along with Aunt Ann and Uncle Henry on "drug raps." It all seems a bit too ambitious and with a plot far too obvious, but readers should keep in mind that it came from the mind of a kid just out of his teens with dreams just a little too big for his experience and equipment.

No doubt, Waters quickly realized how overambitious he was once he began filming. Pat Moran was cast as Dorothy, Maelcum Soul as the Wicked Witch, George Figgs as "Grassman" (a drug parody of the scarecrow), and friend Gilbert McGill as the "Wizard of Od." Others were sure to join at some point, but Walters abandoned the project after a day of filming with Moran and Figgs (footage of which has since floated around on the Internet). "I didn't know what I was doing," Waters told the *Chicago Tribune* in 2011. "I thought I could lip-sync with a reel-to-reel tape recorder, which was completely impossible. So we only shot a day of it." That didn't stop him from meeting with the press about the proposed movie, however, and earning a write up with the Associated Press and photos in the *Baltimore Sun* about the project. Waters mentioned in *Shock Value* that the famous photo of him crouched down over an 8 mm camera in the middle of a street that has been seen in documentaries about his career was taken by the *Baltimore Sun* for their *Dorothy* article without the newspaper's writer and photographer knowing that there was no film in Waters's camera. Waters, Moran, McGill, and Soul posed for the photos, perhaps in hopes of restarting the project soon—Waters even said that he planned to finish the movie in April 1966 and "show it at a local espresso coffee house"—but it was not to be.

Still, Waters wasn't feeling defeat. He still had another project in mind that he had already started working on and would now concentrate on finishing—a film tentatively titled *Beat Me and Kick Me* that would emerge as *Roman Candles*.

Roman Candles (1966)

With *Dorothy, the Kansas City Pothead* no longer in the works, Waters turned his attention to a number of rolls of home movie footage he had taken of his friends, a practice he had started as a means to test out the new camera (as mentioned in the documentary *I Am Divine*). While in New York to see underground films, Waters had seen Andy Warhol's *Chelsea Girls*, a nearly three-and-a-half-hour long film made up of two films shown side by side, with many of the personalities from Warhol's Factory. Waters decided to do something similar, only with three films playing together to do Warhol one better. "It was copying *Chelsea Girls*," Waters told Thedissolve.com in 2014, "having random footage of people doing fucked-up things. I was in my parents' bedroom. It was hardly the Chelsea Hotel."

Waters did fulfill his promise to make a forty-minute film, however, with projectors set up to show the films in a square format and with three films playing in one of the four corners of the screen, although not always in the same corners. The material is random footage of Waters's friends doing a variety of ordinary and not so ordinary things. The film was the first to be called a Dreamland production, although Waters has since stated he does not know why he decided to use that as the name of his "studio" (which was his bedroom at the time). It is also the first to feature many Dreamlanders, including Divine, who plays hide-and-seek with Maelcum Soul near the end of the footage. Speaking of which, Divine and Mink Stole both get their new stage names with this movie as well. Appearing with them are David Lochary, Bob Skidmore, Pat Moran, Mark Isherwood, "Mona Montgomery," and Mary Vivian Pearce, as well as Waters's sisters, Trish and Kathy. As mentioned in Chapter 2, Waters saw Soul as his first "star," and she does appear several times in the footage.

The film really is composed of random images and situations, on three separate parts of the screen, making a complete synopsis of the film a tad difficult. Here are some highlights, however:

- Mary Vivian Pearce as a woman attacked by Bob Skidmore with an electric fan.
- Judy Boutin as a bride-whipping a man who models stolen clothes and appears in a simulated sex scene with Bob Skidmore and Mark Isherwood.
- Pat Moran playfully spanking Mink Stole and at one point dancing to "These Boots Are Made for Walking" with her boyfriend, who is tied up in the scene. This was the scene that led to the initial film title of *Beat Me and Kick Me.*
- Mink Stole praying at a grave and then breaking down in tears.
- Alexis, a large woman who was a Dreamlander friend, eating fruit.
- David Lochary reading *The Wizard of Oz* to Maelcum Soul. (It is easy to wonder if this may have been abandoned footage for the *Dorothy* project.)
- Maelcum Soul as a nun who makes out with a priest, played by her boyfriend at the time.
- A man takes off his belt and then shoots up on-camera.
- Random "found" footage from a Mighty Mouse cartoon, *The Creature Walks Among Us*, *The Undead*, and news footage of the Pope.
- Included in the reel-to-reel audio—which did not have to match up with any narratives on the screen, saving Waters the trouble of synching up to the film—was an excerpt of an interview with Lee Harvey Oswald's mother, several rock and roll songs, and an ad for Mr. Ray, a famous pitchman for his hair-weaving store whom Waters would later ask to narrate *Pink Flamingos*. When Mr. Ray turned him down, Waters did the narrative himself in a manner similar to Mr. Ray.

The film was completed in time to be shown during the annual Flower Mart in the neighborhood of Mt. Vernon in May 1966. The Flower Mart is where Waters met some of the other Dreamlanders for the first time (as described in Chapter 2) and is an annual event in Baltimore that is used to promote ways of beautifying the city. As one could suspect in the 1960s, this naturally would attract a certain number of beatniks and hippies, such as the Dreamlanders. One of Waters's friends knew the reverend of the Emmanuel Episcopal Church in Mt. Vernon, and Waters managed to get use of the church hall for a showing of *Roman Candles*. The cast then went to work at the Flower Mart, passing out flyers for the three showings of the film project. The showings were in the same "pass the hat" fashion as done for *Hag in a Black Leather Jacket*, leaving Waters once again with a small profit on a film that cost largely nothing due to film once again being stolen for his use. Waters would put together a trade advertisement for the film that featured quotes from those who reviewed the showing at the church. (Leo Cedrone of the *Baltimore Evening* Sun called it "Junk," which Waters proudly displayed in the ad.) The ad helped get the film shown in a couple of additional underground theaters in Baltimore. People were still interested in what he was doing, and there was no reason to back down now.

Eat Your Makeup (1968)

After two films that were more about images than a true storyline, Waters decided to do something more structured in his next film, the forty-five-minute long *Eat Your Makeup*. The film was made in the fall of 1967 using "a few hundred dollars, which today would be maybe $7,000" (*Time Out*). In the film, David Lochary and Maelcum Soul play a deranged couple in a similar vein to the Marbles in *Pink Flamingos* and the Dashers in *Female Trouble*. This sinister twosome kidnaps young women and chains them up in the woods, where the only nourishment for those kidnapped comes in the form of makeup. An audience of friends of the couple comes to watch the women model until they die from exhaustion. Marina Melin, wearing her "Story of O" dress (as Waters calls it in *Shock Value*), Mary Vivian Pearce, and Judy Boutin play the kidnapped women.

Also featured in the film is a long dream sequence in which Divine dreams of being Jackie Kennedy in a reenactment of the Kennedy assassination. There is also a carnival scene that involves a "cheapskate Spook House," as Joe Blevins calls it in his review. After the women die, Prince Charming (George Figgs) appears and kisses Marina Melin's character, bringing her back to life, and they live happily ever after.

Other cast members were Bob and Margie Skidmore, Otts Munderloh, Howard Gruber as President Kennedy, Lizzy Temple Black as the Girl Scout scaring people in the Spook House, and Berenica Cipcus (under the name of Extreme Unction) as the starving model crawling across the sands and pleading for makeup.

The film was done with a 16 mm camera, although the audio was still done afterward. Waters came up with the idea for the film while in Provincetown for the summer in 1967: "I got the idea from the candy store, the Penny Patch," Waters told Gerald Peary, "which I still go to in Provincetown. They sold candy lipstick with the little slogan, 'Eat Up Your Make Up.'" The film was made in the front yard of Waters's parents' house. It was also the first film Waters did where he borrowed money from his father to help pay for it. "He said, 'Don't ever tell anybody I lent it to you,'" Waters remembered to Steve MacDonald years later. In *Shock Value*, Waters talks of trying to synch up the starving model's voice screaming for makeup with the visual and driving everyone in his apartment building crazy with the noise. In fact, according to Waters, it was the noise that contributed to his room-mate at the time, Marina Melin, ending up in a hospital after she admitted that she actually ate her makeup.

Waters entered the completed film into a student film competition, which turned out to be a bit of a mistake. "In the middle [of the film] the judges started screaming, 'Get this shit off!' They didn't even watch it all the way through," Waters told Scott MacDonald. Waters had already set up a showing for February 23 and 24, 1968, at the same church where he had premiered *Roman Candles*, with two showings each night and featuring an animated film by "8-year-old David Wise" called *Short Circuit*. Wise would become a writer of animation, helping to launch *Teenage Mutant Ninja Turtles* for television and writing for *Transformers*, *Batman: The Animated Series*, and the 1970s live-action *Wonder Woman* series.

The judges of the film festival contacted the church in an attempt to stop the film and, when the church refused to do so, called in the IRS to make sure that no admission fees were charged, leading to Waters having to ask for donations. Waters would have better luck when it premiered in Provincetown that summer, with Mary Vivian Pearce and Waters going around with the candy and offering it to people as a way to promote the film: "I used to hand people a flyer; she'd hand them a candy lipstick and say, 'Eat it, read it, and come.' People thought we were giving them acid and would say, 'No, no, get away from us!' but it was good promotion, and we didn't have any money for advertising." It worked, as well, as the church in Provincetown where the movie played sold out for its performance. Waters tried to take it to take it to New York but only found interest from one theater—the Gate Theater—where it was ignored when screened by Elsa Tambellini. Waters was told, "We'll call you if we want it." He never heard from them.

It didn't really matter—Waters made the money back he had borrowed from his father and paid him back. The shorts were working, and Waters was feeling confident enough in his work to think he could make a full-length feature. But there was still one more stop along the way beforehand.

The Diane Linkletter Story (1970)

This is the shortest of Waters's films, running just a little under ten minutes in length, and is usually skipped over when Waters discusses his filmography. The film was an experiment in order to make sure the equipment was working properly, and it mushroomed into an added feature that played frequently alongside *Mondo Trasho* and *Multiple Maniacs* in theaters over several years.

Diane Linkletter was the daughter of famous actor and announcer Art Linkletter, who did a number of shows where he was the folksy emcee to a program where adults (on *People Are Funny*) and children (in a segment on a series called *House Party*) were made to do and say embarrassing things. On October 4, 1969, Diane Linkletter jumped from the window of her apartment building, dying less than two hours later from injuries sustained in the fall. Art Linkletter, who had recorded a duet called "We Love You, Call Collect" with Diane just a few months before that time, quickly announced to the press that his daughter had died due to being on LSD. He would then direct attention to Timothy Leary as being the cause of her death and put out a book about drugs, all of which left Waters feeling as if Linkletter was using his daughter's death to promote his own agenda. "[Linkletter] put out a book, *Drugs at My Doorstep*. So he didn't waste any time in turning her death by drugs into product, which I found more offensive than what we did. We felt like we were her, because all our parents said if you take LSD, you're going to go crazy. It wasn't until twenty-some years later that I found out that she wasn't even on LSD when she jumped."

Waters, angry over the news, decided to use it as a way for the Dreamlanders to test the 16 mm sound camera recently acquired for his next film, *Multiple Maniacs*, which he planned to start filming in the late fall of 1969. "It was the day that we got the equipment to test for *Multiple Maniacs*, the first time I had ever had lip-synched sound," Waters told Geraldine Visco in 2014. "And the day before or something, this had

John Waters setting up the passion play segment from *Multiple Maniacs* (1970), a part of the film that is in many ways reminiscent of Waters's earlier shorts, which he did between 1964 and 1970.

happened. So we said, 'Let's do it! Divine can play Diane Linkletter!" There was no script—a first and last for Waters—and everyone improvised their lines. "Divine doesn't even have makeup on," Waters went on to say in the interview. "She just has a day-old beard, my bathrobe and a two-dollar wig from a thrift shop. So it was not a movie that was written or planned. It was technically a camera test."

The film has Divine as Diane, David Lochary as Art Linkletter (looking nothing like Linkletter), and Mary Vivian Pearce as Diane's mother. The parents are upset over the daughter's drug use and behavior, but Diane just wants to be herself. After being slapped by her mother, Diane runs up to her room, while the father calls her a "disgusting slut." Diane, in despair, then falls out of her window and dies, while her parents plead, "So please come back to us. We love you. Call collect."

Anyone who has viewed *Multiple Maniacs* will recognize that the film's setting is Waters's apartment. Shot in one day in October 1969, the film proved that the equipment worked, and although Waters dismisses the film as just a test, he did get a certain amount of mileage out of it for showings, both with his own features and with other films (where it played as a short subject before films like *Reefer Madness*).

The short films helped Waters to learn the craft, with each one being a step forward in his career as a filmmaker. With the 1960s coming close to an end, it was now time to take the next step: a full-length film. It would be everything dreamed of, and yet not quite the success Waters wanted it to be.

7

A Gutter Film

The Making of *Mondo Trasho*

If someone is having a festival of my stuff, I always tell them, 'Make *Mondo Trasho* the hardest one to see, because if you've never seen any of my work and go see that first, you ain't coming back.'

—John Waters to John G. Ives.

Plot

A young woman named The Bombshell (Mary Vivian Pearce) takes a bus to the park to feed the roaches. Approached by a groveling man (John Leisenring) who is fascinated by her feet, the woman goes with him into the woods, where he sucks on her toes (shrimping) and she fantasizes about being Cinderella.

Meanwhile, Divine (Divine) is driving down the road when she sees a hitch-hiker (Mark Isherwood) who is dismissive of her. Divine imagines the hitch-hiker naked, leading to her being distracted and hitting The Bombshell. With The Bombshell in a coma, Divine drags her to the car and drives off. Divine shoplifts clothing and steals shoes from a homeless woman in an alley, changing The Bombshell into the new outfit in a laundromat.

While at the laundromat, the Virgin Mary (Margie Skidmore) appears to Divine. Divine pleads for help and the Virgin Mary assists with a wheelchair provided by her assistant (Lizzy Temple Black). Divine wheels The Bombshell back to the car, only to find a man (Bob Walsh) stealing it. Now on foot, Divine pushes the wheelchair with The Bombshell in it. They soon stumble upon an escaped asylum patient (Mink Stole). When men from the asylum appear, they grab all three and take them back to the asylum, whereupon the patient does

VHS box art for *Mondo Trasho* (1969), which has never been released on home video in any other official form due to music licensing issues.

a topless tap dance for all the other patients before finally being suffocated with a bag and attacked by some of the others.

The Virgin Mary reappears. Her assistant gives The Bombshell—who is still comatose—a fur coat and Divine a knife to escape along with the patients. Divine takes The Bombshell to an insane, drug-addled doctor (David Lochary). He cuts off The Bombshell's feet and replaces them with monster feet.

In the waiting room, Divine is interviewed by a newspaperman and photographed as she poses, until the arrival of the police, who start beating Divine. The doctor's assistant (Pat Moran) steals The Bombshell's fur coat, and a gun and knife fight occurs. The doctor, his assistant, Divine, and the now-awake Bombshell escape the mayhem, but Divine has been severely injured. They drive off together, only stopping so that the doctor can try to kidnap a girl (Trish Waters), but he fails.

Divine and The Bombshell are pushed out of the car along a road and the pair struggle to get to a nearby farm, where Divine crawls through a pigsty and dies. The Virgin Mary appears again to have her assistant put flowers on Divine's body as The Bombshell stumbles away.

Bewildered, The Bombshell soon discovers that if she clicks her monster feet together, they will transport her back into the city. She finds only misery there, as she is hassled by a gang of men and then by two women who gossip openly about her appearance. Clicking her heels again, The Bombshell disappears and the two surprised gossips walk away, still complaining about her looks.

Claims to Condemnation

In this section, the movie is reviewed for elements that would have led to the Legion of Decency giving the film a C rating.

- Mocking religion with the Virgin Mary supplying rather silly assistance to those in need
- Drug use by the doctor and his assistant
- Nudity (female topless and one man's backside)
- Woman being molested, possibly killed
- Shrimping
- Surgical abomination
- Minor transgressions: vomiting, shoplifting, attempted kidnapping, pulling a knife on a cop, and irresponsible driving. Also robbing the cabbie. The cabbie, on the other hand, scores with heaven for his willingness to get the wheelchair from the trunk even after being robbed by Divine.

Additional Cast and Crew

Bob Skidmore is the chicken executioner at the beginning of the film. Margie Skidmore plays both the Virgin Mary and the woman shocked in the laundromat. Marina Melin and Susan Lowe play asylum inmates. Bob Walsh not only steals Divine's car but later moons The Bombshell near the end of the film. (Too bad they couldn't get the same car that is stolen for the shot.) Speaking of which, Divine has his first dual role, playing not only Divine but also one of the male hooligans in the car bothering The Bombshell late in the film. John Waters does a voice-over as the newspaper reporter, while Rick Morrow appears as the photographer. Mink Stole appears three times: as the homeless woman who gets her shoes stolen by Divine, as the tap-dancing asylum patient, and at the end of the film as one of the two gossipy women talking about The Bombshell. The other older woman is Mimi Lochary, who was David Lochary's mother. David Lochary dubs her voice. David Lochary also did Divine's makeup and worked as a production assistant with Bob Skidmore.

Production

The summer of 1968 saw Waters in Provincetown, writing in longhand ideas for his first full-length film. Waters still was at a point where he was not set to do a lot of dialogue scenes, so he mostly concentrated on the visuals and plotting of a silent movie and did some snippets of dialogue and a soundtrack of music after filming was completed. "I think it was in my head, and I knew what we were going to shoot every day," Waters told John Ives, "but whether I ever wrote the whole thing down, I don't know . . . I think I just told them, 'Okay, today we're gonna—' and everybody basically wore the same costumes through the whole thing."

The film's title came from exploitation documentary films of the time period—such as *Mondo Cane, Mondo Freudo,* and many others—which claim to be factual documentation of bizarre lifestyles but commonly appear to be fake footage of people doing odd things for the camera, with usually at least one half-naked woman appearing at some point. The title itself led to the very first sequence in the film—the man dressed as a medieval executioner who beheads several live chickens that then scramble around without their heads before dying. It was an intentionally shocking start to the film and the first time Waters has chickens killed for his films. Waters would joke about it in 1982 with Scott MacDonald, saying, "I'm shocked when I look at it now; especially because he kept missing!" A few years later to John Ives, he would tone the joking down a bit: "I'm shocked that I ever filmed that. That's the most hideous thing I ever filmed." Unlike in *Pink Flamingos,* where the cast and crew cooked and ate the chickens used, they did not do so with the ones in *Mondo Trasho,* and Waters went on to say, "I was trying to do a joke on *Mondo Cane* . . . but it's something I'm a little ashamed of, because it was really cruel. I just can't look at it when it comes on."

The Dreamlanders all returned to Baltimore and worked for free, using their own clothing or costumes that were found or stolen from elsewhere. Sets were the backstreets, alleys, and laundromats of the city, with many spots used without permission. Thus, everything was on the cheap, with the real money going into the camera, film, and processing. Looking to cover costs, Waters turned to his father, who offered him $2,500 as a loan to make the film. (Waters typically bounces back and forth between $2,000 and $2,500 as the budget for the film, but, as Waters nearly always says, his budget was doubled for *Multiple Maniacs*, and that film cost $5,000, so $2,500 is probably correct.) Waters had discovered that there was no way a regular theater or drive-in could or would show his 8 mm productions, so the jump to a better format was due. Waters used a 16 mm camera but still filmed without sound; instead, he and some of the other Dreamlanders would record the soundtrack later and then have it added to the optical soundtrack of the 16 mm film at Quality Film Lab, with the help of Pete Garey. "This man at the Quality Film Lab in Baltimore knew I didn't have money," Waters told Scott MacDonald, "and he would give me pointers." Waters was still attempting to synch up sound afterward with his visuals, but at least this way, the soundtrack would be forever matched to the picture, with no chance of the two going out of sync.

Waters filled the film with musical material from his own record collection. This made for whimsical pairings, such as Divine driving in her car with "The Girl Can't Help It" playing on the soundtrack, or the group entering the asylum to the sounds of "We're Off to See the Wizard" from *The Wizard of Oz*. On the other hand, viewers have to put up with hearing "Riot in Cell Block 9" by the Robins, "Get a Job" by the Silhouettes, "Blue Moon" by the Marcels, and other snippets of songs multiple times. The use of such songs also led to the main reason the film has only limited official release on videotape and has never been released on DVD or Blu-ray—licensing issues with the music makes the film cost-prohibitive due to the amount of money that would need to change hands in order for the film to be released. Instead, there is an underground market for the film, typically a DVD burn of the videotape release that came out in the 1990s.

Filming was done on the weekend and off-days and squeezed in whenever there was a chance to get the principals together to film a little more. "We called it a gutter film because it really was filmed in gutters, alleys, laundromats," Waters told Scott MacDonald. "We'd go to laundromats because they had neon lighting so we wouldn't need lights. After we got arrested, we were always looking over our shoulders. We were so paranoid; we'd jump out of the car, film the scene and leave."

Yes, about that arrest.

On November 3, 1968, Waters and several other cast members went to an area of Johns Hopkins University to film the early scenes of Mary Vivian Pearce being shrimped and the car accident with Divine. As part of the script, Divine is driving a car when she fantasizes that a hitchhiker is nude, causing her to not see The Bombshell come from out of the woods, leading to Divine hitting The Bombshell.

Mark Isherwood plays the hitchhiker and at one point he appears on-camera with his back to the camera, supposedly nude. Waters, in an interview with *Variety* on November 13, 1968, said that Isherwood was not completely nude in the scene, but was wearing "the theatrical equivalent of a fig leaf" over his crotch. This coincides with the November 13, 1968, report in the *Baltimore Sun*, which stated that Isherwood "was said to have posed with his buttocks exposed during a filming sequence." Mink Stole, in an interview with Avclub.com, also pointed out, "Mark was fully clothed and he had a robe on between takes." Waters and the others had not gotten permission to even film on campus, let alone told them what they would be filming.

Graduate students at a nearby dormitory could see the filming and called the campus police. A fifty-five-year-old campus security officer came down to witness the filming and then went to call the police. "With Divine in drag, a nude guy, the rest of the cast, and the camera equipment, we sped off in the Cadillac Eldorado convertible, trying to escape," Waters told Scott MacDonald. The security guard had gotten the license plate of the car Waters was in and—according to one version of the story—the police caught up with everyone but Divine, who was in another car. Names and addresses were taken, and an arrest warrant was issued for Isherwood the following day. Four other members of the crew were picked up for the misdemeanor charge of "participating in indecent exposure" as well: Waters, Mink Stole, David Lochary, and Mary Vivian Pearce. Waters told Scott MacDonald, "We were all in a paddy wagon, and looking back on it, it was fun, but at the time . . . ." It could have been worse for Waters, as he told John Ives: "I had a huge hunk of gold hash in my pocket and I talked the cops into, 'Can I go up to my room and just get one thing?' Luckily they said yes, and I ditched the thing." Divine raced home and stayed out of sight for the duration, avoiding charges. The group elected the person with the smoothest voice, David Lochary, to try to get the charges dismissed, but his patience was also the worst of the group and he did more to antagonize the police rather than help. This would finally escalate into the police reporting to the press in February 1969 that Lochary's middle name was "Gaylord" (actually, it was Crawford), and this was noted as such in the newspaper article that appeared even though the *Baltimore Sun* had known his middle initial was C when reporting about the "crime" a few months before. (Worse yet, the February article in the *Baltimore Sun* misspelled his last name as "Lcohary" and then printed his name twice instead of listing Mink Stole's name.)

Judge Howard L. Aaron was given the case and told the *Baltimore Sun* that he had been "boning up on obscenity laws" since the week before, but he then had to surrender jurisdiction on the case when the defense attorney, Fred E. Weisgal of the American Civil Liberties Union (ACLU), requested that a grand jury hear the case. "Just when I get a good case," the judge told the newspaper. "All I ever get is riff-raff." Stole would laugh about it later to Avclub.com, saying: "The judge thought he had *Tropic of Cancer*. He thought he had cracked this major porno. We were just kids making this movie." The charges were dropped by the state in early February 1969 and the subsequent judge, Solomon Liss, dismissed the case by reading a poem about it being best to disrobe behind closed doors. Waters offered the judge two "freebie" tickets to the premiere of the show on March 14, 1969, but the judge stated that "if the film is as bad as some underground movies he has seen in New York, he would not be anxious to see it."

The publicity helped the film, with the criminal case getting a front-page mention in *Variety* as well as newspapers. Even so, Waters was still promoting his films on his own and in the very specific areas of Baltimore and New York, so the film's notoriety was limited. The criminal charge did cause Mink Stole problems later on, as she mentioned in the same interview: "Years and years later, when I wanted to get my real-estate license, it was held up. They only write down that you've been arrested, they don't write down the disposition of the case, which was dismissed, and they didn't have the records from [1968] in Baltimore. It held me up with the FBI for a while."

As to filming Divine's death scene, the gang simply drove until they found a farm, hopped out, and filmed the sequence with Pearce, Divine, and the others as Divine wallows through the pigsty and "dies." Waters would later report that there was smoke coming from the chimney of the farmhouse nearby, so obviously people were home while they were filming, but the owners never came out and Waters and the others never bothered the farmer, so everyone was left wondering what the other thought of the whole situation. Waters was especially happy to get the shot of the one pig mounting the other, suggesting years later that to get such a shot with professional trainers and animals would have cost thousands of dollars.

Waters designed Divine's gold Capri pants and halter top, which they had only one of and was missing an elastic belt for the waistline, "The whole outfit had become quite funky by the end of the film," Waters mentioned in *Shock Value*. "The tailor who made the costume wasn't that good, so Divine's capri pants never were tight enough. You can see him struggling to pull his pants up throughout the entire film." The only other main expense for the film was the pair of monster feet Pearce wears near the end of the film, which were "dollar-ninety-eight monster feet from a joke shop," Waters told John Ives. To Waters, the feet were significant to the plot of the film because although the mad doctor gives The Bombshell the monster feet, they do bring her happiness in the magical ability to get away from the ugliness of people that bother her in the end. Waters would admit to John Ives, however, that the Bombshell never rises above the taunts she receives at the end of the film and that he could have done more there to make the point, saying: "She should have put a pair of heels on those feet. You know? And walked happily on. That is what it was about."

Release

Beyond having a brief scare due to the indecent exposure rap, the cast and crew saw the filming go smoothly. Par Moran, Mink Stole, David Lochary, and Divine then joined Waters to record dialogue to be inserted into the soundtrack at various points in the film—specifically, when Divine is with the Virgin Mary and, at the end of the film, when Stole and Lochary play the disgusted women. Waters then edited the film in preparation for its premiere in mid-March.

Mondo Trasho premiered March 14, 1969, at the Emmanuel Episcopal Church and played on March 15 and 16 for nine shows. Waters then attempted to "four-wall" the film himself, getting it next played twice a night for a week at the Beaux Art in St. Petersburg, Florida, in April 1969. Showings followed at the Museum of Art in Santa Barbara in June 1969; the Cinema Kenmore Square in Boston in July; the Art Cinema in

Provincetown in August 1969 (the bookstore where Waters worked allowed him to put up a display for the film in their window); the U-P Screen in New York City; and at Bard College in Annandale-On-Hudson, New York, in September. After that, Waters was back in Baltimore to work on his follow-up film, *Multiple Maniacs*, only to then tour with *Mondo Trasho* in February at the Cinematheque 16 in Los Angeles (many of the same films in this series also played in Glens Falls, New York, in June 1970) as part of an underground film festival, and then in Philadelphia for a week in February 1970. There was also a short run of the film in Toronto somewhere in early 1970 as well.

Reviews, when available, were positive, probably because comedy was such a rarity when it came to underground films. As Waters mentions in *Shock Value*, *Variety* called it "a very amusing satire on films that exploit sex, violence and steaminess." The *Los Angeles Free Press* called Divine "undoubtedly some sort of a discovery." The biggest delight to Waters was Pauline Kael's review of Fellini's *Satyricon* in the *New Yorker*, which she called "Fellini's *Mondo Trasho*."

The traveling involved in four-walling the movie in small theaters paid off, with Waters being able to pay back the $2,500 loan from his father. Later in 1970, Waters would push *Mondo Trasho* again, along with his next movie, and it would be this two-film catalogue that would lead to needed exposure in other parts of the country, as will be discussed in Chapter 8.

In the videocassette revolution of the 1980s, *Mondo Trasho* was released by a company called Cinema Group Home Video in 1987. Cinema Group Home Video also released videocassettes of *Multiple Maniacs*, *Female Trouble*, and *Desperate Living*. (*Pink Flamingos* had already been released by Wizard Video in 1981, while *Polyester* would be released by Thorn EMI / HBO Video in 1983.) As mentioned earlier in this chapter, because of issues related to music rights, the film has never been released on DVD, so the videocassette release is the only official home-video version available.

Waters has since looked back on the film itself as probably his worst. "I cringe. It's completely overexposed. I mean, believe me, this was no choice in style. I didn't know what I was doing," Waters told *BOMB* magazine in 2004. Waters also criticized the length of the film to John Ives in 1992, saying: "*Mondo Trasho* is ninety minutes long; it should have been twenty. It's got twenty minutes of good footage in it. It takes [The Bombshell] an hour to get to the bus." Waters has even had second thoughts about the film being available for people to see, as he told Jack Stevenson: "Every once in a while I'm tempted to take it out of distribution. But … what the hell—it's already out there. And there are parts of it I like."

The experiment with 16 mm film and an optical soundtrack had worked out for Waters, with the film paying for itself over the course of several months in 1969. Now it was time to move up another step.

8

And George Figgs as Jesus Christ

The Making of *Multiple Maniacs*

[Criterion] asked if I wanted to keep it exactly as is, with every mistake in there. I said, 'Are you kidding me? I never purposely had mistakes in there! I don't want the splice marks to show, I don't want the dirt in the lens! Make it look good!'

—John Waters to the *Guardian* about Criterion restoring *Multiple Maniacs*

Plot

Lady Divine (Divine) and Mr. David (David Lochary) run a bizarre travelling sideshow called the Cavalcade of Perversions, with Mr. David as the emcee. It's a free show to see various "acts against God and nature, acts that by their mere existence would make any decent person recoil in disgust." Inside the main tent are various performers whose acts include licking bicycle seats, homosexual kissing, eating vomit, and building pyramids while semi-nude.

The show is actually an elaborate ploy to entice squares into the tent in order to rob them. It is only at this point in the "show" that Lady Divine appears, with a gun, and kills one of the spectators (Margie Skidmore) when she mouths off to Lady Divine. The group leaves the victims behind and then splits up the take before going their separate ways. Lady Divine walks off with her assistant Ricky (Rick Morrow) and mentions that she is getting fed up with the Cavalcade and threatens to kill everyone the next time they pull such a job.

Meanwhile, Mr. David, who is in a relationship with Lady Divine, is having an affair with Bonnie (Mary Vivian Pearce), who is an oversexed idiot and obsessed with Mr. David. He offers to meet her at Pete's later to discuss their situation and then leaves with Lady Divine and Ricky. They go back to their apartment, which they share with Lady Divine's daughter, Cookie (Cookie Mueller). Mr. David notices that Lady Divine has been getting a bit crazed the past few times they have performed with the Cavalcade, and the murder of one of the victims that day has him considering leaving her after six years. Lady Divine threatens to tell the police about Mr. David's involvement with a certain incident in California and drops Sharon Tate's name. Mr. David is mortified, although he has no recollection of the event.

Mr. David leaves to meet up with Bonnie, only for the bartender, Edith (Edith Massey), to call Lady Divine and rat him out to her. Lady Divine leaves the apartment to confront Mr. David, whereupon she is attacked by one of the Cavalcade workers, Susie (Susan Lowe), and a bearded man in a dress (Howard Gruber). Divine then sees the Infant of Prague (Michael Renner Jr.) who guides her to a church (St. Michael and St. Patrick Catholic Church). She goes in and is seduced by Mink (Mink Stole), a religious fetishist, who proceeds to give Divine a "Rosary job" while Divine fantasizes about Jesus turning hot dog buns and a fish into Wonder Bread and cans of tuna and then being crucified.

In a room upstairs from Pete's, Mr. David and Bonnie discuss Lady Divine and decide that she needs to die and that Bonnie should pull the trigger on the gun. Lady Divine walks with Mink, and the pair decides to kill Mr. David. Mr. David and Bonnie arrive back at the apartment first, with Mr. David getting into an argument with Ricky and Cookie. As Cookie attempts to leave, Bonnie panics and shoots Cookie in the face, killing her. It is at this point that Mr. David notices a newspaper stating that the criminals who killed Sharon Tate had been caught, and therefore he was innocent the entire time.

The pair tie up Ricky and put him, along with the dead Cookie, behind the couch just as Lady Divine and Mink appear. Bonnie hesitates just long enough with the gun to allow Divine to stab her multiple times and kill her. She then kills Mr. Davis, rips out his heart, and eats it. Near the brink of insanity, Divine plans an assault on a number of celebrities and their families. It is then that Ricky attempts to make his way out from behind the couch and Mink shoots him dead by accident. Angry, Divine kills Mink and then notices the dead body of her daughter, Cookie.

Truly insane, Lady Divine slips into a swimsuit and a fur coat and lies on the couch, whereupon a giant lobster, Lobstora, appears out of nowhere and

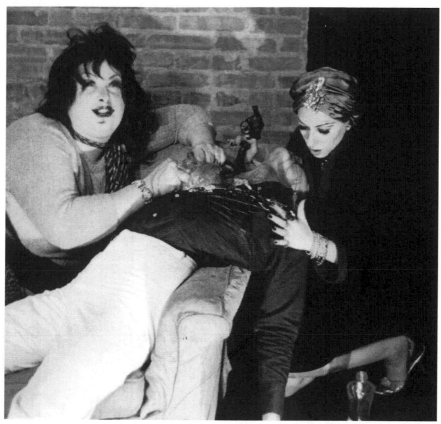

Divine (Divine) is ready to begin chowing down on the heart of Mr. David (David Lochary) while Mink (Mink Stole) looks on in *Multiple Maniacs*.

rapes her. Divine, foaming at the mouth, goes on a rampage through the city, smashing cars and scaring the townspeople, until the National Guard arrives and kills her, ending her era of terror.

Claims to Condemnation

- Blasphemy on multiple occasions, including the "rosary job," the man shooting up at the altar, and the sacrilegious "Passion Play"
- Drug use on-camera
- Nudity (female topless and one man's backside [in this case, Divine) Homosexual kissing, indications of sexual relations outside of marriage, insinuations of sexual fetishes of various sorts
- Minor transgressions: vomiting on-camera, murder, robbery, disrespect to authority

Additional Cast and Crew

This was the first Dreamland film to feature Edith Massey, Paul Swift, and Cookie Mueller, and the first film to feature work from Vincent Peranio (more about each of them in Chapter 2). Many of the Dreamland regulars appeared as both members of the Cavalcade and as patrons. It was the last film to have David Lochary performing makeup for Divine. (Van Smith would take over on the next film.) It's also the only Waters film where Lochary plays a part that is anywhere near being sympathetic; in every other film he portrayed evil men initiating plots against others.

Production

Having repaid the loan from his father for *Mondo Trasho*, Waters, in the fall of 1969, asked him for $5,000 to cover the cost of his new movie, *Multiple Maniacs*. It was Waters's first full script—written on a yellow legal pad while he was working the summer of 1969 at the bookstore in Provincetown and then photocopied on a ditto machine so that Waters could give out pages to each of the cast. Waters was able to get a single-system 16 mm camera, commonly used for news footage. It was handy and gave Waters the ability for the first time to have natural sound with his actors on film, but there is an issue with using this type of camera: the soundtrack needs to run slightly ahead of the picture in order to match up when projected. This makes editing such a film—especially with primitive editing equipment—hard. Thus, longer takes are required, which is why, when viewing the film, the camera tends to stay locked in place while the actors say two to three pages of dialogue without a cut. It wasn't a style; it was a necessity. This also explains why new shots sometimes look like the actors freeze in place before saying their lines—it was needed in order to make sure the dialogue would not be cut off when splicing a film together.

Because Waters knew that the actors would need time to learn their lines, he initiated readings at his place a few days before the weekend filming so that people would know what to say. Mink Stole, in the Criterion DVD collection, mentioned that Waters would also act out all the parts and wanted the actors to do them exactly as he did. She also was upset when she appeared with smudged lipstick on her face after Divine kisses her in one scene.

Waters's response to her about it was dismissing, as he said, "If that's going to bother you, you're in the wrong business." "I was tyrannical," Waters told *AnOther Magazine*. "I had to be because we had to get it made and we only had so many days." Because of the indecent exposure there were several scenes shot around the house belonging to Waters's parents. "There wasn't even such a thing as a film permit, so we just ran out there and shot it like *Cecil B. DeMented* did," Waters said in the same interview. "That's why I shot the Cavalcade of Perversions scenes on my parents' front lawn, which is kind of bizarre when you think about it. They never really came down to look, but they were always supportive." The scene where Divine goes insane and smashes in the windows of a car (a scene that Waters thought should have been cut down, as he said to the *Guardian*, "Does Divine have to break *every* window in the car?") was shot in the driveway of his parents' house as well. On that occasion, Waters's mother came down to see how the filming was going. "My mother met Divine there when we were shooting the scene where she's in a bloody bathing suit and was smashing the car's windshield,"

Mink (Mink Stole) and Divine (Divine) discuss their joint plans in *Multiple Maniacs*.

Waters said in an interview with *Rolling Stone*. "Divine was so nervous to meet my mother that he took the wig off. Then he was a man in a woman's bathing suit covered with blood, which made it worse."

The most notorious shot in the Cavalcade of Perversions scene is that of the puke-eater, which was performed by a man that Waters still refuses to mention by name, as he hasn't seen the actor in years. For those curious, the vomit was actually creamed corn, which "works very well as puke," as Waters remarked to *Rolling Stone*. The car Mr. David, Lady Divine, and Ricky used to make the getaway from the Cavalcade was Lochary's white Cadillac convertible. "It barely ran," Waters told *AnOther Magazine*, "and while we were shooting the scene, it died. So we pushed it into the parking lot of a project in the worst neighborhood and got out and just left it there. Divine had to get out in drag, while the others were holding guns, right in this project—not the most friendly place for a white person to be in this part of town." Waters reflects in his DVD commentary for Criterion that the phone number Mr. David gives out was Waters's own phone number at the time.

As Waters had only one light to use when filming indoor scenes, most of the indoor scenes take place in the living room of his apartment, looking much the same as seen in *The Diane Linkletter Story*, filmed soon before production started on *Multiple Maniacs*. Only the living room is used in the movie—although we see Divine at one point heading up the stairs as if to get to Cookie's room. The posters on the wall in Cookie's room match those in the corner of the living room which is seen prominently near the end of the film. This means that instead of moving the camera equipment to another room, they simply turned the camera to the right, moved furniture out of the way, threw a mattress on the floor and made it "Cookie's bedroom."

Lobstora, as mentioned in Chapter 2, was a creation of Vincent Peranio and his brother that cost a total of $37.50. It was based on a large lobster that was seen in postcards for Cape Cod, which Waters—in the middle of an LSD trip—thought would be funny to have attacking people in a film. Peranio was happy with the work on the prop, although he was a bit embarrassed when he realized that the lobster left a leg behind when moving out of frame. Waters kept the prop for years before finally discarding it into the ocean when he realized he had no room for it at his place.

Earlier in the same scene, Divine rips out the heart of Mr. David and takes a bite out of it on-camera. This was achieved with a cow's heart and intestines that Waters had gotten from a butcher and "kept in [his] refrigerator for two days" before filming. Under the hot light, the heart quickly became disgusting, but Divine went through the act. "That was the trainer wheels for eating shit," Waters joked to the *Guardian*.

The scene in the church was actually filmed in a church. Several churches at the time were left-leaning and politically motivated, and it was not uncommon for churches to allow "subversive" political groups to meet

The artwork for the DVD and Blu-ray reissue of *Multiple Maniacs* (1970).

in such sanctuaries. Waters had a friend who knew the priest at a church that said okay to them filming there. Waters knew it was going to be a bit tricky to film, however. To *AnOther Magazine*, he said, "I knew I was never going to be allowed back in that church once [the priest] found out what we shot in there!" "My friend, who was a hippie and a political activist," Waters told the *Guardian*, "he went in there and talked to the priest about Vietnam and stuff while we shot the scene." Waters also got the footage of the man shooting up at the altar while there. "The priest then came to the premiere," Waters told the *Guardian*. "I felt really bad for him because he was almost crying. To this day, I have never told where that church is. I'm not so sure I completely remember anymore." Waters has gone on record to suggest that he is even shocked by the scene, and mentioned that when showing it to a young audience, they hung their heads in disbelief. "I think, how did I get away with this? How did any of this happen?" he said to the *Guardian*. In the director's commentary on the Criterion DVD as Mink is shown wiping the rosary clean after having pulled it out of Divine—an effect actually done with chocolate—Waters comments, "Now this is especially hideous. There's no possible reason that this shot is in the movie."

Another questionable element was that of the Sharon Tate murder tied into the storyline, with Divine implicating Mr. David in the crime. When filming had started, the investigation was still ongoing as to who murdered Sharon Tate and five others on August 8, 1969. The victims had been found with the word "pig" written in blood on the front door (which is why Divine spells out this word to Mr. David when taunting him). It was only at the beginning of December 1969 that the news broke that the murders had been done by members of the "Manson Family." "When we shot this," Waters mentions in the DVD commentary for the film, "they had not caught Charles Manson. Nobody knew who he was at all or anything about it." As the filming on *Multiple Maniacs* was wrapping up at the beginning of December, the headlines that the perpetrators had been caught began to appear. "The night right before we finished, they caught Manson," Waters told *Rolling Stone*. "So I had to put that in [Mr. David finding out he was not the killer] because I knew it didn't make sense. Even then, nobody knew who those people were. We didn't know that story was going to turn into what it became." As fate would have it, Waters would later become friends with a couple of the people who had participated in crimes for Manson, and the following film, *Pink Flamingos*, would be dedicated to three of the members, while a model helicopter made by another would appear at the beginning of *Female Trouble*.

Release

The filming went from late October through the first week of December. As it was a new process for Waters to edit the film, it was not until April 10, 1970, that the film premiered at the First Unitarian Church on Franklin Street. The movie ran for nine performances through April 12. The First Unitarian had been suggested to Waters as an alternate "premiere site" when the Emmanuel Church he had used the past decided they had "risked their necks enough for 'art,'" as Waters writes in *Shock Value*. Lou Cedrone of the *Baltimore Evening Sun* in his review said, "Waters's first 'talkie' is also his first 'sickie.'" Once the film reached the city, the *Los Angeles Free Press* raved about the film, saying, "You have never, and I mean never, seen any movie remotely like *Multiple Maniacs*," and compared the film to Tod Browning's *Freaks*.

Luck was on Waters's side with the film coming out when it did, as a movement had started in various cities around the country—more specifically various "college towns" around the country—where young people were wanting to see more offbeat films in a type of party atmosphere. A chain of theaters called the Art Theater Guild was running into issues because many of their theaters were devolving from showing "art films" to skin-flicks and then to pornography as the 1970s crept into view. The problem was there needed to be some reason to support the theaters' reason for being called "art" theaters. Mike Getz, a relative of the owner of the guild, came up with the idea of distributing underground films and cult movies (like the aforementioned *Freaks*) under the title of "Underground Cinema 12," which was based on an earlier concept he was involved with called "Movies 'Round Midnight" that played in the Los Angeles area in the early 1960s. The films were shown as midnight movies on the weekend—a concept that would wildly catch on in the 1970s, especially in cities with big college campuses. As the 1970s rolled along, it was not unusual to see young people and even high-school kids waiting in line to go into the theaters to see films like *Flaming Creatures*, *Pink Flamingos*, *El Topo*, and others. Getz would get many of these films to show, and the "Underground Cinema 12" was popular from 1967 to 1977.

Getz had heard about *Multiple Maniacs* and offered a deal to Waters. "I gave him a print for forty weeks, and I got a dollar a minute every time they played," Waters told John Ives. "It was great; I got ninety dollars a week. Ninety dollars then was maybe like five hundred today." This led to Waters heading out to Los Angeles with David Lochary for the premiere of the film (and so Waters could attend the Charles Manson trial, which was commencing at the time). Yet the "Underground Cinema 12" was only around in about seventeen cities, and Waters knew that there were plenty of places that were not showing the film. "No one would distribute it, so I went around the country with it in my car," Waters told *SFGate* in 2016. "I'd go to whatever the weirdest art theater was, and say 'Can I rent your theater?' and I'd four-wall it." This would lead to the successful showings of *Multiple Maniacs* and *Mondo Trasho* in San Francisco that are discussed in Chapter 3. Waters stayed in San Francisco for several months before finally heading back to Baltimore to work on his next film in 1971.

Not all attempts to get the film seen worked as well. A print sent to Canada had been intercepted by the Ontario Board of Censors, and when Waters asked for the print back, he was told that the board had burned it. Closer to home, the film premiered at a church in Baltimore in 1970 and played a few times at Corner Theater in July 1971 and later in 1974, but it didn't have a commercial run in Baltimore until 1981 due to the Maryland Board of Censors refusing to grant permission when reviewing the film in 1971.

It was not the first run-in with Baltimore's own Mary Avara, the head of the Maryland Board of Censors, but as it turns out, it would be the last film that Waters would end up having to send through the board when it came to their attention in 1981. When *Multiple Maniacs* had first been released, Waters knew what a fight he would have with censor board of the state—a board that many states used to have but slowly disappeared as the country turned to the ratings system of the MPAA, and especially after home video was becoming the norm in the early 1980s. What was the point of paying taxpayers' dollars to support a group that ultimately could not stop any film from being seen by people if they could rent or buy it on video in a few months anyway?

Still, the Maryland Board of Censors had been a thorn in Waters's side, and Waters had given Avara headaches since the release of *Pink Flamingos*. Waters's response in 1981 to all the hassles Avara would give him in the 1970s was, "Every time Mary Avara hassles me, she puts money in my pocket." Avara's thought on Waters in 1997 to the *Baltimore Sun* was, "I wanted to throw him out the window!" And that mutual dislike blossomed for many years until her death in 2000, whereupon Waters's quote to the *Baltimore Sun* was, "My sympathy to her family and friends. But beyond that, for the first time in my life, no comment."

Waters had known there would be issues with his earlier films, but *Multiple Maniacs* and the films before that were still raw enough that he was happy just to get them played in exhibits in Maryland where it wouldn't face the board's ire. Meanwhile, both *Multiple Maniacs* and *Mondo Trasho* could play in theaters pretty much everywhere else in the world without questions. Yet, even as the board was facing extinction by June 1981, Avara still refused to allow the nearly twelve-year-old *Multiple Maniacs* to be seen in the state in commercial theaters—specifically the Charles Theater, where it was to be shown at midnight on January 9, 1981.

In the summer of 1980, the owner of the theater submitted the film for approval for a showcase that fall, and the board subsequently rejected it, due to the "parody of Christ's death" but also for Divine being raped by an obviously cartoonish giant lobster. Avara was also offended by the "rosary job" scene in the church, telling the *Baltimore Sun*, "I tried to move heaven and earth not to release that film," and went on to say that even if the board did close in June 1981 she would "work for free" to stop it from being seen. Waters, on the other hand, couldn't see what harm the film could do to audiences at that point, as he told the *Baltimore Sun*, "When they see *Multiple Maniacs*, they know they aren't going to be getting a film like *9 to 5*."

The film was sent to Circuit Court Judge Joseph H. H. Kaplan to review the banning. His response to the film was that "the court's eyes were assaulted," and he went on to state that the film was "horrendous, sickening, revolting … most distasteful," and "obnoxious, but not legally obscene." The ruling allowed the film to be seen in October that year at the Key Theater in College Park and then finally at the Charles on January 9, 1981.

The film would be released in 1987 by Cinema Group Home Video and then later in 1994 by another company called Raven Video. The film was released on DVD and Blu-ray by Criterion on March 21, 2017, with interviews from cast members, an audio commentary, a movie trailer, a short documentary, and with the film cleaned-up by Janus Films for showing in theaters in 2016, prior to its release by Criterion. The film used for the new release had been Waters's personal copy of the film, which he had put into a closet for twenty years and then in an attic that sometimes had temperatures up over 100 degrees Fahrenheit. When *Rolling Stone* asked if he just didn't care what happened to the print, he admitted that he didn't because, the attic "was the best place to put it." He continued: "Let me tell you something: Those Kodak reversal films last. Paul Morrissey told me the same thing; he shot a lot of Warhol movies on that too. My films didn't fade. *Cleopatra* did."

There was a sense of irony knowing that Janus Films had made the new print of the film for distribution to theaters. "The most amazing thing is that it's done by Janus Films, the ones who did early Bergman in American and Godard and Truffaut, so it's kind of funny," Waters reflected in 2017 to *AnOther Magazine*. "It looks like a bad John Cassavetes movie now. It looks better than it has ever looked but it doesn't look too good, you know, so you don't have to worry. I'm so happy that it has been rehabilitated and released."

Looking back on the film in the introduction of his script book—*Hairspray, Female Trouble, and Multiple Maniacs: Three MORE Screenplays by John Waters*—Waters reflected, "Ingmar Bergman was right. The 'silence' of the dead is sometimes so deafening." The first film that really showcased a lot of the Dreamlanders is also a reminder of how many have died: Divine, David Lochary, Cookie Mueller, Edith Massey, Paul Swift, Howard Gruber, Paul Landis, and most recently Rick Morrow. Even Lobstora is long gone, tossed into the bay when it had outlived its usefulness.

But for the moment in 1970 through 1971, there were fun days ahead for Waters and the gang as they built on the success of his first two full-length films. Finally, he had films that were playing theaters, and one with proper dialogue. Now would come the time to go up another notch and do color.

And make the most infamous/famous film of his career.

9

Like a Septic Tank Explosion

The Making of *Pink Flamingos*

> I don't think it's my best movie, but God knows the day I die it will be in the first paragraph of my obituary.
>
> —John Waters discussing *Pink Flamingos* with Steve Appleford in 2007.

Plot

The Narrator, Mr. Jay (John Waters), introduces the audience to the trailer home of Babs Johnson, alias Divine, "the filthiest person alive." She lives there with her son, Crackers (Danny Mills); a companion named Cotton (Mary Vivan Pearce); and her mother, Miss Edie (Edith Massey), who lives in her crib in the trailer. Miss Edie's only interests are eggs and the man who brings them, the Egg Man (Paul Swift).

Across town lives Raymond and Connie Marble, who want the title of "filthiest people alive" and hate Divine. The Marbles run a business, one of many illegal practices, where they kidnap young women, have their servant Channing (Channing Wilroy) impregnate them through "artificial insemination" using a syringe, and then sell the resulting babies to lesbian couples for $5,000.

The Marbles hire Cookie (Cookie Mueller) to date Crackers and find out details about Divine's life. Crackers takes Cookie out to his shed behind the trailer, forcing her to have sex with him and a confused—and soon headless—chicken, while Cotton watches. It is rough on Cookie but beneficial to the Marbles, as Cookie soon contacts them with information on "Babs," including the address of her trailer.

The Marbles commence with their plan to prove to Divine that they are filthier than her by sending her a "bowel movement" with a birthday card staking their claim to the title. The Marbles feel momentarily triumphant, but they soon are disturbed and angered when they discover Channing dressing as and talking as Connie (and momentarily Raymond) while reciting things they had said earlier in their bedroom. They lock him in a closet in the house and leave to check out Divine's trailer.

The surprise gift isn't going to spoil Divine's birthday party at the trailer, and there is further good news when the Egg Man—who, like Miss Edie, has an obsession with eggs—asks Miss Edie to marry him. Divine has her birthday party with all her degenerate guests who provide entertainment, including a man with a "singing asshole." The Marbles witness the party from a distance and are disgusted. They call the police and report the party, but the party guest ambush the cops and eat them. As such, the party ends well, and concludes with the Egg Man taking Miss Edie away in a wheelbarrow to marry her.

Babs (Divine) greets a new morning outside of her trailer.

The narrator announces that Divine has found out about the Marbles's scheme and, with the Marbles out (including Raymond being shocked by a person who exposes themselves to him while in the park), Crackers and Divine break into their house and lick everything in sight. The two get so excited in their work that they begin to have sex but then hear Channing in the locked closet and go to investigate. Channing tells them about the girls in the basement and they drag him down to them. They release the girls and give Channing to them, who castrate him before killing him.

Meanwhile, the Marbles go to Divine's trailer and set it on fire. As the trailer goes up in flames, they proclaim their title as the filthiest people alive. They arrive back at their house, only to discover that the furniture is rejecting them—pushing them off like ejector seats in a James Bond movie—due to the licking done by Divine and Crackers. Worried about the girls, they find Channing's dead body. Returning upstairs, they run into Divine, Crackers, and Cotton, who gag and tie them up then take them out to the woods for a press conference and trial. The Marbles are found guilty of "assholeism" and are tarred, feathered, and shot dead.

After the press leave, unsure they can even use the story, the trio decide to move to Boise, Idaho. As they head off, the narrator announces that what the audience is about to see is real and proves that Divine is the filthiest actress in the world. They follow a dog into an alley and, once it has taken a dump, Divine reaches down and scoops up the pile and pops it into her mouth. She then smiles and winks to the camera in the ending to end all endings of a film.

Claims to Condemnation

- Rape
- Masturbation
- Incest
- Bestiality
- Shrimping (once again)
- Murder
- Nudity (female and male frontal nudity [the first Waters film to feature male genitalia])
- Cannibalism
- Minor transgressions: shoplifting, public defecation, kidnapping, cross-dressing (by Channing and the Marbles), and disrespecting authority

Additional Cast and Crew

The film has a dedication at the beginning: "For Sadie, Katie, and Les, February 1972." These were the aliases given to three members of the Charles Manson Family: Susan Atkins, Patricia Krenwinkle, and Leslie Van Houten. Van Houten would later become friends with Waters, and he would write about her in his book *Role Models*. In that same book, he admits he treated the Manson murders in this film and in others before and after as a means to shock the audience "in a jokey, smart-ass way ... without the slightest feeling for the victims' families or the lives of the brainwashed Manson killer kids who were also victims in this sad and terrible case."

There were not many firsts or lasts in *Pink Flamingos* for the cast and crew, as many of those who worked on *Multiple Maniacs* came back to work on *Pink Flamingos*. The film marks the first appearance of Elizabeth Coffey, who was halfway through a sex-change operation when Waters decided he needed someone who could shock the Raymond character when he exposes himself in the park midway through the film. According to Waters in 1973, Coffey completed the procedure about three weeks after filming her scene in *Pink Flamingos*. Coffey returned, post-operation, in *Female Trouble* as Earnestine, Divine's lover in prison.

This is the only appearance of Danny Mills in a Waters film. Mills dated Mary Vivian Pearce for a time and even moved with her and Waters to a place in New Orleans. He and Pearce eventually broke up, and both Waters and Pearce in later interviews mentioned that Mills ended up in prison for a time due to his involvement with a LSD drug ring. He never made another movie after *Pink Flamingos* and passed away in January 2017.

Pat Moran returns to the front of the camera but only briefly appears as Patty Hitler in the birthday party scene. More was filmed of her—she's the gossip that tells Divine about the Marbles, which the narrator speaks of—but Waters cut her main scene out of the film.

This was the first film to have Van Smith's involvement for Divine's costumes and makeup. The makeup for Divine is an extension of that Smith used for Divine for his appearances in San Francisco when promoting *Multiple Maniacs* and *Mondo Trasho*.

Max Mueller, Cookie's baby son, appears as Noodles, the baby given to the lesbian couple early in the film. According to Waters in *Shock Value*, Noodles was the name that Cookie wanted to give her son when he was born, but the hospital refused. Instead, the name was used for his character in the film.

As for the man with the "singing asshole"? The man had evidently developed the ability to manipulate his anus early in life—once even showing his ability to his parents as a kid—and, after seeing some of Waters's earlier films, thought it might be something that could be included in one of his movies. Calling Waters, the man auditioned at Waters's house and was invited to perform the feat for the birthday party scene in *Pink Flamingos*. The man would only do it on film if there weren't many people around, especially women, and only after drinking heavily. "I remember doing the whole thing with the singing asshole," Waters told John Ives. "We shot him one day with no one there and then filmed the people watching and applauding empty space." The man also asked that Waters never reveal his name, although he did later seek some recognition from it, as Waters told Avclub. com: "He went to the re-release 25 years later—he's like 50 years old—and he sat in the theater. When his scene came on, he would look over at the person next to him and whisper, 'That's me.' People would be really uptight, because what could you say when you're sitting there in the theater and the guy with the sphincter is right next to you? And he just did it on his own, which I thought was really a good star appearance."

Production

One thing is for sure—after 1974, rarely has the term "pink flamingos" been used without referencing this movie.

Waters first came up with the idea for *Pink Flamingos* while driving cross-country with David Lochary to four-wall his earlier films in 1970s. "I became obsessed with all the sleazy trailer parks that marred the countryside along the highways and tried to imagine how awful trailer life must be," Waters reported in *Shock Value*. "I realized that if I could somehow create a mobile home even tackier and cheaper than the ones I had seen, I would have the perfect setting for Divine and family."

Getting the money together was easy—Waters turned to his father, who was willing to loan his son $10,000 to make the film. Waters, in an interview with *Interview* magazine in 1973, stated that part of the money was used to buy himself a car, while in *Shock Value* he mentioned that they went over-budget by $2,000, which is why Waters sometimes refers to the film as costing $10,000 and other times $12,000. Even locating a trailer was not difficult. "It cost $100," Waters told *Interview*. "It was a burnout. I got it at a junk place and there had been two explosions in it, and there were only two walls and no ceiling."

Finding a location for the trailer was harder, however. Still stinging from the indecent exposure arrest during *Mondo Trasho*, Waters wanted to place the trailer in an area where he could be undisturbed by bystanders and the police. As it turns out, Bob Adams, a friend who also went by the name of the Psychedelic Pig, was taking care of a house owned by someone else that sat on a 200-acre farm at 14620 Philpot Road in Phoenix (located in northern Baltimore County). Overgrown with trees and brush, the farm was hard to see from the road, making it ideal to privately film the movie. A day's hacking through the rough made a path from the house—where Adams was living with others—to an area where Divine's trailer could be placed for filming. Adams agreed to let everyone film there, not realizing that eventually the trailer would be burned down. Although Adams would also serve as a soundman on the film, he took off the day of the fire and went to New Jersey so he could "reserve deniability" if anything went wrong. "When I saw the scene on film," Adams told the *Baltimore Sun* in 1999, "I almost passed out. The whole woods could have burned down. I would have been in big trouble." Waters too worried about the fire, as he told *Interview*: "It was winter and it was very dry, it was a woods and everything was so dry, and it was a huge fire. They used five gallons of kerosene, and when it was burning it looked as if it were getting out of control, and I was picturing like *Bambi*, you know, animals all running out of these woods on fire, but thank God it didn't spread, because it really was raging."

Even with the spot available, there were still problems with the location filming. A tow truck refused to move the trailer to the desired location, and it took two separate attempts by farmers with tractors and the help of everyone on the farm to move the trailer to the spot. The trailer was a wreck even before sustaining more damage in the move, but Vincent Peranio managed to pull it together—even using cardboard at one point—to make the trailer somewhat presentable. (Besides, it was supposed to look like a dump anyway, so damaged goods were fine for the film.) The other issue was that the house was still a good distance away from the filming, so the cast and crew typically were stuck out in twenty-five-degree weather the winter of 1971, shooting in the trailer, with only one movie light "with a mile-long extension cord running to the house" and not much else. This is one reason why the breath of the performers can be seen so often in the film when scenes take place in the trailer—especially cut scenes (later included in the twentieth-fifth anniversary version of the film).

The house on the farm does appear in the film, although only its basement. The scenes showing the women in the dungeon were filmed in the basement of the farm house rather than at the location where the Marbles's house was, which was Waters's home that he shared with Mink Stole on 3900 Greenmount Avenue in Baltimore. The cast and crew enjoyed working in Waters's place due to central air ("Babs," in the deleted scenes, may have hated it, but the people working on the film certainly didn't), working bathrooms, and adequate lighting. The only issue about the location for Waters was having his furniture dismantled so that the chair and couch could be shown "rejecting" the Marbles when they sat on them.

Other locations used in the film were the post office at 601 East Homestead Street, where the Marbles sent their "birthday gift" to Divine; North Howard Street, where Divine struts down the street to "The Girl Can't Help It"; and Charlcote House at 15 Charlcote Place, where Divine goes to the bathroom. The most famous location in the film is the final one—the alley off of Tyson Street—just a block from the Drinkery that Divine, Crackers, and Cotton walk by when they see the dog. Yes, that dog (which, according to Waters in a 2012 interview with KPBS, belonged to Pat Moran).

The scene would become the best known of Waters's career and of Divine's as well, although both got sick of discussing it by the mid-1970s. "*Pink Flamingos* gave [Divine] incredible notoriety, which is sometimes very, very hard for an actor," Waters told John Ives. "At the end, he joked about it with me, but underneath it all he was very wary about it, because twenty years later that was still the first question they always asked him."

The episode is covered in some respects in Chapter 3, which details how Divine first mentioned the idea of eating dog feces on-camera as early as 1971 in interviews for *Multiple Maniacs*. As time went on, Waters talked with Divine and decided that it would be the ending to the next movie, even if the script had not been completed at the time filming commenced. Divine agreed to do it, although he did have some health concerns about doing it, even if it meant he could spit it out immediately after filming. (In fact, he spits it out immediately while the camera was rolling, as can be seen in the movie.)

Waters has referred to witnessing Divine's call to the hospital about his concerns, but Cookie Mueller also wrote about the incident in an article that may more accurately represent what occurred. While Waters was filming elsewhere, Divine, Van Smith, Mueller, Lochary, Stole, and Pearce were

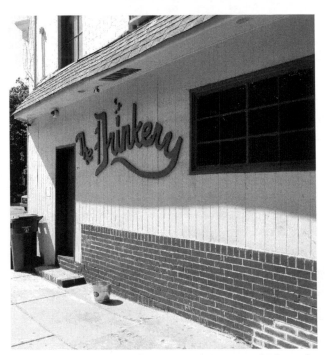

The Drinkery, a tavern still in existence in 2019, which can be seen briefly as Babs, Cotton, and Crackers spy the dog that will lead to the moment everyone remembers from this film.

discussing what could happen to Divine. Smith suggested that Divine call the pediatrics department at Johns Hopkins, which Divine did, telling the doctor, "My son just accidentally ate some dog feces. What's going to happen to him?" The doctor assured Divine that the worst that could happen was that there was a possibility that the child could end up with tapeworms. Or as everyone later would joke in a scream, "THE WHITE WORM!"

There were some discussions of cutting away when the dog relieved itself and replacing the feces with something else, but Waters turned down the idea. "Everybody would know we replaced the real shit for fake," He told Mueller. "Divine's gotta scoop it right up still warm off the street." Divine at least requested that the dog be fed steak for a few days in order to make the results somewhat more pleasant.

Unsurprisingly, with all the ruckus and people staring and following it around, the dog did not immediately poop on cue on the day they filmed the scene, and eventually the dog had to be given an enema in order to get anything before daylight was gone. Finally, the dog went and Waters anxiously called for Divine to dive into frame and get the job done. Waters reported in *Shock Value* that Danny Mills and Mary Vivian Pearce had to run away from the filming for fear of laughing on-camera. Divine's response, according to Waters, was to mumble, "Now I know I'm insane," before rushing to rinse out his mouth.

Speaking of animals, there was also the scene were Crackers forces the live chicken in between himself and Cookie when having sex. Waters always jokes that since chickens get killed all the time, why was this any worse? "I think we made the chicken's life better," Waters stated in a documentary on the twenty-fifth anniversary edition of *Pink Flamingos*. "It got to be in a movie, it got fucked, and then right after filming the next take, the cast ate the chicken." When discussing the scene with *Interview* magazine in 1973, Waters stated that thirteen chickens died for fame, with Danny Mills cutting the throats of each in order to complete the footage needed. It should be pointed out that none of the chickens were actually sexually molested, only put in between Danny and Cookie, and all were eaten. "[Danny] said that he wouldn't mind doing it if he could eat them, and he ate all of them, every chicken we killed in the movie he ate, 'cause he said he wasn't going to do it for some 'warped entertainment value' but if he could eat them, he'd kill them." Mueller got the worst of it, having to put up with headless chickens that were still alive and clawing at her naked skin. Mueller, in her article about the making of the film collected in her book, *Ask Dr. Mueller*, went on to state that she felt sorry for the chickens until later that night when all of the dead birds were cooked for the cast and crew to eat, and then they were just delicious.

The close-up "artificial insemination" scene—where Channing inserts a syringe into a woman—was done with a stand-in for the actress in the scene, as she refused to do it, which the other women in the cast agreed with. "We would all eat shit, catch on fire, fuck chickens, but wouldn't do close-up crotch shots," Mueller wrote. "There has to be a line drawn somewhere."

One thing that wasn't faked, as many fans know, is that of the present the Marbles sent to Divine, which turned out to be a "bowel movement." The night before filming the scene, Waters pulled Divine aside and asked, "Would you shit in a box and giftwrap it?" Divine did just that, and the reaction from Mills and Pearce once they opened it was more real than acting, due to the smell. To Waters, it proved how much of a "trooper" Divine was. "I can't imagine ever saying that to Kathleen Turner," Waters joked to the *Guardian*.

Other lines were drawn as well. In one scene, Mink was to be caught lying and, with the chant of "liar, liar, pants on fire" being said, another character—probably Divine—was to set her Mink's hair on fire. When first asked by Waters, Stole agreed, but she began to balk when time came to do it. "Here is what was going to happen," Stole told *Dirty Mag* in 2011. "I was going to be sitting in a chair, and somebody was going to light a match to my head, while somebody else would be ready with a bucket of water—none of these people were professional stunt people by the way! And I wasn't supposed to react." Stole had bleached her hair white and then used pink ink in it to give it its color for the film, so her hair was already brittle and "flimsy," making it sound even more dangerous to her. The final straw was when she discovered Divine would be eating dog feces at the end of the film. "Nobody would have remembered anyhow," Stole went on to say in the same interview about setting her hair on fire. "I could have been bald for the rest of my life for a completely forgettable moment!" Waters had bought Stole a wig to wear after the fire, and Stole remembered Waters being upset over the money he spent on the wig that was no longer needed. Stole, however, did take the wig to wear over her real hair for her day job. It never fit correctly, and Stole even tried wearing it backward—a suggestion from David Lochary—to little better use.

In later years, Waters had second thoughts of the fellatio scene between Divine and Danny Mills, as he told John Ives. "They knew each other and they were friends, so it was a little embarrassing." The idea was to parody *Deep Throat*, the pornographic film featuring fellatio, but as time has gone on, people do not get the reference, and it tends to simply make people uncomfortable. "It's the one scene I do regret from *Pink Flamingos*. If I had my way, it would be cut out. But I can't do that because people would think the film was censored."

Another stunt suggested and turned down was one where Cookie was to have been discovered living in her mom's house by Cotton and Crackers. A sledgehammer was to smash through a television set that was turned on during the scene. Mueller refused to do the scene after being told by experts that doing such a stunt would cause the television set to explode. Eventually the scene shot ended up not being used anyway, so it became a moot point.

The script—still handwritten by Waters at that point in his film career and not even completed before filming began—appears in Waters's book *Trash Trio*, but Waters has stated that the script reproduced there follows the finished film and does not include scenes that were dropped before or after filming. Waters has gone on record as saying that at least a half hour of footage was cut from the film before being released. (He sometimes has estimated the amount to be closer to an hour.) For the twenty-fifth anniversary release of *Pink Flamingos*, in theaters and then later on DVD by New Line, Waters located close to ten minutes of footage shot but not used for the film. This footage was added after the ending of the film for viewers, with Waters introducing each little segment. Included are:

- Divine and Cotton waking up in the countryside and feeling refreshed.
- Divine dictating her autobiography, "Being Divine."
- Channing trying to weasel out of impregnating the kidnapped women, with Connie Marble suggesting the method we see him use in the film.
- Connie wondering why Raymond has left her with the "asshole servants."
- Crackers bringing his chicken to Divine to cook, now that he's done with it. He also shows her the issue of *Midnight* with her on the cover as "the Filthiest Person Alive!" and an FBI Wanted poster for Divine. (Divine mentions that one of the aliases on the Wanted Poster is "Glen Milstead." When Waters reproduced the wanted poster in *Shock Value*, Glen's last name is censored.)
- Miss Edie introducing one egg to another egg in her crib, before eating one.
- Raymond and Connie discussing Divine's trailer home and the misery of living in the woods, with animals "fucking and shitting right out in the open." (Raymond is carrying a tire with him that would lead to a sequence where a tire swing was left at the trailer with a note saying

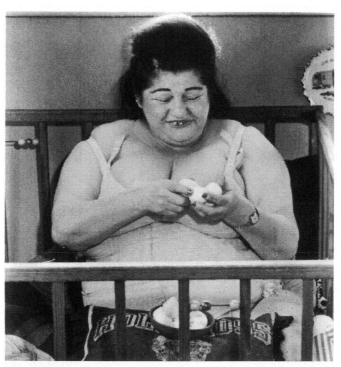

Edie (Edith Massey) loves her eggs, which leads to true happiness for her in *Pink Flamingos*.

"Swing on this a while, baboon!" Waters discussed the tire swing in *Shock Value*, but it is not included in the deleted footage.)

■ Raymond and Connie tying up Miss Edie and smearing eggs all over her in their assault of Divine's trailer, which was the second part of their plan. Note that in the film Connie tells Raymond to commence with part one and then later part three, with no part two having been done.

■ Patty Hitler (Pat Moran) gossiping with Divine about the Marbles.

■ Divine returning to the trailer to find what the Marbles had done to Miss Edie. (Waters, in his introduction, points out that Edith is missing her baby bonnet in the shot, which conflicts with Divine's dialogue).

■ Cotton running to Divine after finding boll weevils in her hair. Both are slightly nude at the time.

■ Cotton and Crackers going to Cookie's house and killing her and her mother. They then profess their love for each other, leading to Crackers saying one of the most questionable affectionate labels to ever be given to another person. (Even Waters, in the narrative for the clip, wonders what he was thinking.)

■ Cotton and Crackers returning one of Cookie's ears to Divine in triumph. Divine eats it. (It's clear that this scene was shot at the same time as the one where they find Miss Edie after her assault, with everyone still in the same positions.)

■ Divine and Crackers touching, rubbing, and feeling everything in Connie's office.

■ Raymond and Connie arriving back at their house, with Connie still raving about Channing's body having touched her clothes.

■ Divine cutting Connie's hair while tied to the tree at the end of the film (since Mink Stole nixed having her hair set on fire).

■ Cotton, Crackers, and Divine skipping along and singing "We are the Filthiest People Alive" in pig Latin.

■ A scene that is known to have been filmed but not included in the additional footage of the twenty-fifth anniversary edition was one featuring Mink Stole in a parody of a scene from *Snow White*. At one point, Connie was to look into a mirror and ask "who is the filthiest person alive." A face appears in the mirror—the owner of the limo used in the film—to tell her that she is the filthiest person alive.

Filming was scheduled to take five months, starting in the fall of 1971, with the cast and crew working on weekends. Along with the $2,000 of additional costs, the filming took an additional month to complete due to issues with defective equipment and the cold. "We would shoot whole days on *Pink Flamingos*," Waters remembered to John Ives, "and it wouldn't turn out, because I didn't know what I was doing. The film jammed and came back with big scratches down the middle of it." Editing took weeks—with the footage having a time delay between edits in the film, as was also experienced with *Multiple Maniacs*—leading to stalled actions and long takes. "I didn't have an editing machine," Waters continued in the same interview, "so I would edit it and then put it back through the projector to look at the cut. Can you imagine? With no work print. To this day I don't know how that's possible." Finally, the film was ready in February 1972 for its March opening.

Release

The film premiered on March 17 at the University of Baltimore, bringing with it an attempt to make it as much like a real movie premiere as possible. The *Baltimore Sun* covered the event, claiming: "Four hundred people and one dog watched the ninety minutes of occasionally entertaining absurdity on film. The dog looked as though he enjoyed it." Television cameras were there from the closed-circuit channel the university had, recording the event, which featured most of the cast with the exception of Divine, who was out in San Francisco at the Palace Theater.

The film was promoted with the line, "An exercise in poor taste," and would appear next at the Corner Theater (891 North Howard Street, not far from where Divine struts in the film) on March 30 through April 1 for four showings. Waters, confident that the film was his best yet and grabbed hold of audiences, went to Robert Shaye, the head of New Line Cinema, to see if the company would distribute the film for him. New Line was started in 1967 and was a distributor of comedies and horror films that were made by small regional companies. Waters had previously gone to them with *Multiple Maniacs* but was turned down due to the film being in black and white (another reason why Waters switched to color with *Pink Flamingos*, as many theaters refused to run new films that were in that format unless there was a major push behind it from a studio [for example, *The Last Picture Show* in 1971 from Columbia and *Young Frankenstein* from 20th Century Fox could get away with such a thing, but not an unknown with a minor distributor]). When Waters turned up with *Pink Flamingos*, Shaye acquired the rights to the film under the new "young-oriented" subsidiary distribution title of

Saliva Films. (Saliva released only five films before being absorbed back into New Line: *Pink Flamingos, Female Trouble, Desperate Living, The Best of the New York Erotic Film Festival (1973)* and *Sextoons* (1975), which was a collection of sex-oriented animation.)

The problem was that New Line didn't know what to do with the film. It wasn't really pornography, although it had the chicken scene and the one brief fellatio bit at the Marbles house; it wasn't really a horror film; and some, no doubt, wondered if it was a comedy. They were unsure how to promote the film, and it lingered on the shelf at the distributor. Waters went back to San Francisco for a bit and then down to New Orleans with Pearce and Mills to live, unsure what would happen to his movie. Late in 1972, Waters found out that New Line had sent the film to Boston to have its first commercial run through the distributor at a gay porno theater called South Station Cinema.

According to Waters in *Shock Value*, he and the cast were "furious," and he went on to say, "David Lochary went to spy and reported that 'there was more action in the bathrooms than in the theater.'" Waters returned to Baltimore and begged New Line to give the movie a chance in an art-house atmosphere. Waters had learned from earlier experiences of four-walling his films to drive-ins and grindhouses that the audiences who wanted pure smut would tune out of the film, but those who knew movie genres and were looking for something more would find something to like in his films. "I went insane," Waters told the *Washington Post* in 1997. "It's not that I was against gay porno theaters, it just that *Pink Flamingos* always did terrible in real exploitation theaters. Surrealism and irony are the things the exploitation audience hates—they know you're making fun of them."

The Elgin Cinema by 1973 had earned a name for itself for their "midnight movies," which first started in 1970 with *El Topo*. Done in a similar fashion to the earlier Underground Cinema 12, the Elgin steered their programming to recent art films and oddball programming, including a Saturday night marathon that was typically from "Midnight til Dawn" and could be anything from a number of comedy shorts and Marx Brothers movies to art films. In late February, Waters contacted the theater about showing *Pink Flamingos*, and the management at the Elgin agreed to give it a one-night showing on March 2, 1973. "John was the one who got it in the midnight shows at the Elgin," Sara Risher of New Line Cinema told John Ives. "He worked a lot on his own on that; it was his idea to hand out flyers and all that." The ad in the March 1, 1973, issue of *Village Voice* announced what was supposed to be a one-off showing of *Pink Flamingo* (with the "s" missing at the end of the title), with the tagline "A Trip Thru Decadence." (Saturday's midnight shows were all twelve chapters of the serial *The Return of Captain Marvel*, plus twenty cartoons, to give an idea of the programming at the Elgin Cinema then.)

Waters drove "through a blizzard" to David Lochary's New York loft, and they began hitting the phones, calling friends and calling in favors to get the 600-seat theater filled. The theater was half full, which was enough to convince the Elgin staff to try it again the subsequent Friday. By the time Waters's twenty-seventh birthday approached in April, the film was doing so well that the Elgin began showing it every weeknight at midnight, and it would continue playing at the Elgin for a total of forty-eight weeks. "I knew if it would work anywhere, it was there," Waters told the *Baltimore Sun* in 1986. "Because at that period of time, *El Topo* had just closed. It was the only place that had this built-in audience." Within a week, Waters heard from the Cannes Film Festival. "Bang. Rightly or wrongly, you can never be completely successful unless it happens in New York."

The movie began to pick up steam from there, slowing rolling out to other parts of the country, like Philadelphia in October 1973 (where it played

Danny Mills, who played Crackers in *Pink Flamingos*, with Divine. Their scene together late in the film was to parody the then-popular *Deep Throat* film, and turned out to be one Waters would later regret.

for years), and becoming stronger in 1974 in places like Detroit, Louisville, and Los Angeles—which only helped to promote Waters's follow-up, *Female Trouble*, in 1974. Early runs of the show even featured "Pink Phlegm-ingo Barf Bags" for audience members, connecting it to the gimmicks that would have made William Castle proud. Reviews were confused to say the least, with one of Waters's favorites being from Susan Stark of the *Detroit Free Press*, who in 1975 said the film was "like a septic tank explosion, it has to be seen to be believed." *Variety* in December 1974 described the film as such: "Dregs of Human Perversity. Draws weirdo element. Monstrous." Vincent Canby of the *New York Times* panned the film, going so far as to suggest Waters had received "faulty toilet training." Kevin Thomas of the *Los Angeles Times*, however, said: "As we're being liberated by our laughter, we're made aware how much more easily we can be offended by actually quite harmless scatological excesses than by the realistic depictions of bloodshed and brutality which are routine—and which are markedly absent from this movie." Positive—if a bit heavy-handed—stuff for the film.

Still, after the release of the film, many were ready to believe the worse, which both helped and hurt the image of the film and Waters over time. A February 5, 1975, item planted in *Variety* to help promote *Female Trouble* said that Waters was looking for someone to commit suicide in his next movie for $500,000, which certainly had people wondering if Waters was a monster behind the camera. No matter what was said, however, the film did remarkably well on the Midnight Movie run, staying in Philadelphia for over a hundred weeks and in Los Angeles for four years, among other strongholds in the country, making it one of the biggest successes of such cult films besides *The Rocky Horror Picture Show*. Within a couple of years, the film that had cost $12,000 to make had made back over $2 million, with Waters and certain members of the cast and crew earning twenty-five percent of the profits, which Waters stated in *Shock Value* had been paid to him honestly by New Line. Waters would make this arrangement with his "main eight people" to received twenty-five percent of "every movie up to *Polyester*," as Waters told John Ives. "I mail checks four times a year. Sometimes it's fifty bucks, sometimes it's a thousand—if there was a video deal, or something." (It should be noted that Robert Maier in his book *Low Budget Hell* suggests that this twenty-five-percent arrangement was for movies from *Pink Flamingos* and before, which contradicts Waters.)

The film was exhibited at the 1976 Cannes Film Festival, where it was picked up by several countries. Some banned the film outright—Switzerland

and, until the 1980s, Australia and Norway—while Waters in a 1982 interview stated it was also banned in France. The film was never sent to the British Board of Film Censors and instead played in private clubs for a couple of decades, even after the original film was released for a short time in the United Kingdom. The BBFC did pass the film uncut in 2008, but it was never seen that way commercially until 2014 in Britain. The Japanese release was uncut but with the obligatory optical circles that obscured pubic hair, for which Waters would remark made the film look even dirtier than it actually was when the audience followed the "bouncing balls." There were other problems as well—the film was busted in Hicksville, New York (on Long Island), which Waters reflected on, stating, "We discovered that it was cheaper to plead guilty and just pay the $5,000 fine." In January 1985 the film was seized by authorities in from the Valley Art Theater in Tempe, Arizona, for reasons of obscenity, but it eventually played the theater in July 1997. In 1990, after the success of *Hairspray*, a couple rented *Pink Flamingos* in Orlando, Florida, at a video store and were so shocked that they complained to vice agents with the Metropolitan Bureau of Investigation, who sent a fourteen-year-old girl to rent the video, thus being able to bust the store on "charges of distributing obscene material to minors." There were a handful of other cases like it as well, which Waters reflected as being hard to find in his favor, as featured in an interview in the book *Hollywood V. Hard Core*. "When you show these films in a courtroom at 10:00 a.m. to a jury who have never met . . . believe me it's frightening. They see it completely out of context. When audiences go to see that movie, they know what they're getting—they to go laugh, they go to be outraged. But with the jury, they don't know if they're getting a burglary case or what, and they then suddenly get *Pink Flamingos*. And it looks really weird in a courtroom."

Although the Baltimore Censor Board was briefly discussed in the previous chapter, it would be *Pink Flamingos* that would lead to Waters first facing the wrath of Mary Avara. She and the board had stopped a showing of the film on the University of Baltimore campus in September 1973, even though it had premiered there a year and a half before. The board's objection was that the film lacked their approval, and they insisted that the scene with the chicken, the fellatio, and the artificial insemination all be cut. Avara was frustrated, however, that nothing could be done about Divine's act with the dog feces at the end of the movie. "They didn't have that on the books, so they couldn't bust it because the Supreme Court hadn't ruled whether it was obscene to eat dog shit," Waters told John Ives. So the film went out with the ending even though Avara wanted it cut. (Admittedly, Waters has stated a few times over the years that he could understand wanting to cut the artificial insemination shot, calling it the ugliest image in the film.)

The film was picked by The Museum of Modern Art to be part of their 1976 "Salute to American Humor," for which Waters has suggested should be

The most famous pose in one of the most infamous films of all time, *Pink Flamingos* (1972).

a good reason to no longer have the film face censorship board. Nevertheless, when *Pink Flamingos* was set to be rereleased in a twenty-fifth anniversary edition that was to play in movie theaters, it was decided to make sure that the Motion Picture Association of America got to see it to give it a rating. This was in particular deemed a necessity after the 1990 Orlando obscenity case, where people got the idea that John Waters made "fun, quaint little comedies" like *Hairspray*. "I loved the idea of the ratings board having to sit down to watch it," Waters told the *Washington Post* at the time. "Talk about an endless screening! It's as rude as it ever was, maybe ruder because of the political correctness issue." The MPAA gave the film an NC-17 rating, stating that it contained "extreme perversities shown in an explicit way."

The film had initially been released on VHS in the United States by Wizard Video in 1981 and then by Harmony Vision in 1982. The twenty-fifth anniversary version, with extras mentioned earlier in the chapter, came out on VHS and DVD in July 1997 from New Line, then in a two-for with *Female Trouble* in 2001, and finally in a seven-movie collection called *Very Crudely Yours* in 2005. It also has appeared on cable television uncut. "It's on the Sundance Channel uncut," Waters exclaimed to Screenanarchy.com in 2007, "which is just shocking to me actually. In some cities that's regular cable. The Directors Guild called and asked if they could blurb a blowjob scene and I said yes, but they forgot to!"

In 2014, more than forty years after making the original movie, Waters returned to the film by creating a seventy-four-minute video remake of the movie, *Kiddie Flamingos*, which had the script rewritten and done as a table-read with children (many of whom were children or grandchildren of friends). "I rewrote the script of *Pink Flamingos* to make it G-rated," Waters told Vice.com. "I took everything out, but really it's the same script. It's just a battle of filth, but there's no sex or violence. So if you know the movie, it's even more perverse." The film was showcased in his 2015 art show, *Beverly Hill John*, but Waters has stated that he does not consider it to be a part of his filmography.

At this point in his career, Waters is probably right in his assumption that his obituary will target *Pink Flamingos* within the first paragraph, although it'll probably be the headline used if not within the first sentence itself. It does make one curious about the Academy Awards or TCM farewell reel for whatever year his death will unfortunately occur, just to see if they'll show slow-motion footage of Divine picking up dog feces. Yet, there certainly is no mistake that *Pink Flamingos* was the film that pushed Waters from being a struggling underground filmmaker to a bankable commodity. With its success, Waters was able to find backers for his next movie, while New Line picked up distribution rights to his two earlier films, *Mondo Trasho* and *Multiple Maniacs*, which allowed Waters to no longer worry about attempting to four-wall his movies and even allowed him to quit his job at the bookstore in Provincetown and concentrate strictly on his movie career.

The downside was that the film was completed in 1972 and took quite a while to show a return. By the time things began to turn for the better, 1974 was coming into view, and it was time to start working on a new movie. Waters already had an idea in mind by that point, as he told *Interview* magazine: "I'd like to do a biography of someone from their teenage years when they grow up and get the gas chamber." With that simple outline, Waters would build one of his best-remembered movies, *Female Trouble*.

10

Cha-Cha Heels

The Making of *Female Trouble*

> Where do these people come from? Where do they go when the sun goes down? Isn't there a law or something?
>
> —Rex Reed in his review of *Female Trouble*

Plot

The film documents the life and times of Dawn Davenport (Divine) through different phases:

"1960: Youth": Davenport is in high school with her friends Concetta (Cookie Mueller) and Chicklette (Susan Walsh). It's Christmas and all Dawn can think about is the cha-cha heels she wants from her parents. When they don't get her the right shoes on Christmas Day, Dawn knocks over the Christmas tree onto her mother and runs out of the house. She gets picked up by a scummy man, Earl Peterson (Divine), who takes her to a dump, and they have sex on a dirty mattress, where Dawn steals his wallet.

Time passes. Dawn is pregnant, and Earl refuses to have anything to do with her. She has the baby alone in her shabby hovel.

"1961–1967: Career Girl": Davenport works as a waitress and a go-go girl while raising her daughter, Taffy (Hilary Taylor). Dawn and her high school friends work as a gang in rolling drunks for additional cash.

"1968: Early Criminal": Taffy is becoming disobedient, and Dawn doesn't know what to do other than abuse her. Her friends take her to the Lipstick Beauty Salon, where "you have to audition to get your hair done." She meets Gator (Michael Potter), who lives next door with his Aunt Ida (Edith Massey), a nasty woman who we find out doesn't like eggs. Gator is a beautician at the Lipstick Beauty Salon and straight, which upsets his aunt, who wants him to "turn nellie" and start dating boys. When he takes up with Dawn, a life-spanning feud with Ida begins.

The Lipstick Beauty Salon is run by Donald and Donna Dasher (David Lochary and Mary Vivian Pearce), who take a special shine to Dawn. Dawn and Gator soon marry.

"1969: Married Life": Life isn't very sweet for the newlyweds, with Gator cheating on Dawn and Ida ramping up the feud.

"1974: Five Years Later": Taffy (who, as Waters states in his script book,

Dawn in her see-through wedding gown from *Female Trouble*.

is "now played by twenty-six-year-old Mink Stole") is looking pretty bad for what should be a fourteen-year-old. Thinking of divorcing Gator, Dawn goes to the beauty shop and is invited to meet with the Dashers. They want Dawn to be part of a "beauty experiment" where she models for them as she performs crimes that "tickle our fancy." Dawn accepts their offer as long as they fire Gator, which they agree to do. Gator decides to move to Detroit to work in the auto industry, cementing his heterosexuality and infuriating Ida. Gator stops by to give Dawn a going-away present of a punch in the face.

Dawn begins her modeling career with the Dashers by smashing a chair on Taffy's back after she ruins dinner. Ida arrives and splashes acid in Dawn's face, which is terrific for the Dashers. When the bandages are taken off, Dawn's face is covered with scar tissue, which the Dashers convince her only enhances her beauty. They dress up her place, and when she feels fatigued they shoot her up with liquid eyeliner. of The Dashers are so pleased that they present Dawn with Ida, trapped inside a giant birdcage. Dawn celebrates by cutting off Ida's left hand while Donald Dasher snaps photos.

The excitement soon ebbs, however, with the arrival of Taffy, who finds out from Dawn that her father is Earl. Taffy goes to visit him only to stab him to death when he tries to molest her. She returns home and gets Ida a hook and then runs off to join the Hare Krishna people "downtown" after fighting with Dawn. She returns home to release Ida while Dawn is preparing her first show at a club. Taffy arrives backstage and is strangled to death by Dawn, while Donald Dasher takes pictures. Dawn then goes out to perform for the crowd, and the performance involves a trampoline, a crib, fish, and finally a gun. She asks who wants to die for art, and when an audience member (Vincent Peranio) stands up, she shoots him dead and begins firing into the panicked crowd.

The Dashers give themselves up to the police immediately, pleading that Dawn had forced them to join her in her criminal activities. Dawn is finally caught after a dragnet with dogs commences, and she is put on trial. The Dashers and Ida are witnesses against Dawn, helping to send her directly to the electric chair.

In prison, Dawn makes out with Earnestine (Elizabeth Coffey) and signs an autograph for Cheryl (Marina Melin) before her execution. She sees her upcoming death in the chair as the fulfillment of her career. She gives an acceptance speech as she is strapped to the chair, telling everyone—and us in the audience—that she loves "every fucking one of you!" as the switch is pulled.

Claims to Condemnation

- Murder
- Nudity (female and male genitalia)
- Child abuse
- Homosexual kissing
- Minor transgressions: Disrespect to authorities, vomiting, smoking in school, eating a meatball sub in class

Additional Cast and Crew

George Hulse, who appears as the high school teacher, will appear as the doctor Mole threatens in *Desperate Living* and as the high school principal that calls Francine in *Polyester*. (He also appears briefly in *Cecil B. DeMented*.) Roland Hertz, who plays Dawn's father, appears as Muffy's husband in *Desperate Living*. Sally Albaugh, who is seen briefly getting her hair done in the beauty salon (she's the one saying that she won't bring her six-year-old into the salon), was Divine's double for the scene in which Dawn and Earl have sex. Albaugh also appears in *Desperate Living* as one of the hags. Al Strapelli, who plays the judge at the trial, returns in *Desperate Living* as Peggy's doctor at the beginning of the movie. Pat Moran appears briefly as one of the prisoners near the end of the film. Divine sings the theme song to the film, which has lyrics by Waters and uses music written by original Jefferson Airplane bassist Bob Harvey for an earlier song of his called "Black Velvet Soul."

Some firsts and lasts: This was the first and last time Mary Vivian Pearce plays a major antagonist in any of Waters's films, and she does well in the role. It was the first of two times that Edith Massey plays a "bad guy" in a Waters film. It was the first appearance of George Stover in a Waters movie and the second and last appearance of David Lochary's mother, Mimi, in one of his films (she plays a jurist). The film would be the last appearance of David Lochary in a Waters movie. Charles Roggero was hired to edit the film with Waters, making it the first time that Waters had someone helping in that capacity on one of his movies. (Roggero will work in the same capacity on *Desperate Living*, *Polyester*, and *Hairspray*.) This was also the first film that used Christine Mason as a hair stylist—a role she would perform on each subsequent Waters movie up through *Cry-Baby*. She also appears as the prison bailiff who breaks up Dawn and Earnestine near the end of the movie. Mason passed away in 1999.

Robert Maier did sound for the film. It'll be the first of five films that he would work on for Waters, including doing sound and being a unit manager on *Desperate Living*, a line producer and production manager on *Polyester*, a line producer on *Hairspray*, and a location manager on *Cry-Baby*.

Production

As Waters states in *Shock Value*, there was a ready-made problem with any follow-up to *Pink Flamingos*: "I knew that if I tried to top the shit-eating scene in *Pink Flamingos*, I'd end up being seventy years old and making films about people eating designer colostomy bags." It was while visiting a notorious prisoner in San Quentin in 1973 that Waters came up with the idea for his next film.

As with *Pink Flamingos*, *Female Trouble* also opens with a dedication. And as with that movie, this one was also dedicated to a member of the Manson Family: Charles Watson, who was one of the main instigators behind the murders of Sharon Tate and others on August 9, 1969. Waters became friends with Watson and visited him in prison. While visiting Watson and seeing all the people lined up to visit "celebrity criminals" like Timothy Leary in the visiting room, Waters hit upon the idea of a film dealing with crime as beauty. As mentioned in an earlier chapter, this is also a focus of Jean Genet's novel *Our Lady of the Flowers*, so the idea may have been percolating in Waters's head for a time. Waters also attributed the idea to that of the trials he had gone to where there were people who attended as if going to concerts to see their favorite artists. No matter where it came from, as per *Shock Value*, Watson—who would reform in prison and become a born-again Christian— thought the concept was insane. Nevertheless, Watson sent Waters a wooden helicopter he made in prison, which Water used in the opening credits to the film under the dedication to Watson.

Waters envisioned Divine in the lead role, looking much like a woman who had appeared in a photograph by artist Diane Arbus. "It's a picture of a woman holding a drooling baby with her blue-collar husband, and she looks exactly like Divine in *Female Trouble*," Waters told the *Toledo Blade* in 2015. It was also one of the first Waters films besides *Multiple Maniacs* where Divine's character has no redeeming qualities to her. Even in *Pink Flamingos*, Divine—wearing her blue leotard like some type of bizarre superhero— jumps in to save the two girls in the basement dungeon. That said, it was the first of Waters's films in which none of the character can be redeemed; Taffy is so irritating and such a nitwit that it is impossible to even feel sorry for her. "Most people in my films are rotten people—they're not nice or sympathetic characters. Especially in *Female Trouble*, I don't think there is any person in the whole movie that has a decent bone in their body," Waters said to Bill George and Martin Falck. Meanwhile, the Dashers, with their comeuppance of Dawn, almost feel like karmic retribution for Lady Divine's execution of Mr. David and Bonnie back in *Multiple Maniacs*.

Yet, when John Ives pointed out that there was a lot of damage done to everyone in *Female Trouble*, Waters disagreed to a point: "It has a happy ending because she died famous, which is all she cared about. So the electric

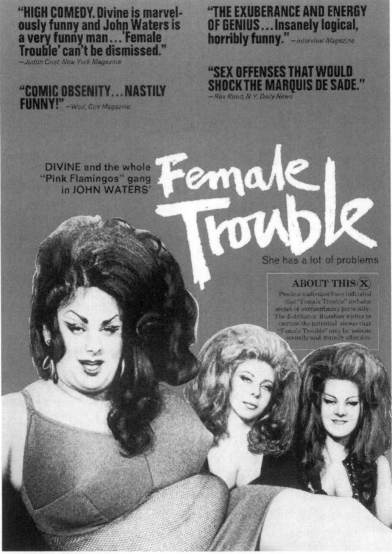

Divine takes over as Dawn Davenport in *Female Trouble* (1974). Behind Dawn are her two former schoolmates, Chicklette Friar (Susan Walsh) and Concetta (Cookie Mueller).

chair is a very happy ending." Later in the same interview, Waters explored the idea a bit more: "She had this horrible blue-collar, white-trash life until these beauticians paid attention to her and turned her into a star, even though it was worse than what she had before. That's what that movie was about, that notoriety and fame are really the same."

Waters worked on the script while the push was ongoing for *Pink Flamingos*, thus upsetting the usual rhythm of writing in the summer in Provincetown and filming in the fall in Baltimore, which had worked so well with his three previous films. Besides, Waters was about to venture into new territory, with his father refusing to invest in his next film. On the other hand, his father also didn't want to be paid back from the last film. "They paid for *Pink Flamingos*," Waters told Michael Guilen in 2007, "and I started to pay them back and he said, 'Look, you didn't go to college. Don't pay me back. Put it all into the next movie and don't ask me again.'"

With those funds, Waters had a starting point to work toward a bigger-budget film—with the initial title of *Rotten Face, Rotten Mind*—but then dropped the title when he foresaw critics reviewing the film as "Rotten Movie." Instead, he went with a phrase given to him by Cookie Mueller, as discussed in Chapter 2. With the growing success of *Pink Flamingos*, Waters was able to borrow money from Jim McKenzie, who ran a cinematheque at the University of Maryland, and a friend with some ready cash, Jimmy Hutzler, to put together a budget of $25,000. (As with *Pink Flamingos*, Waters sometimes adds $2,000 to the budget amount, and is sometimes quoted as saying *Female Trouble* was made for $27,000.) Ironically, while he no longer had to hustle his films from one theater to another, he still had to be a salesman in pitching the films to people in order to get money to make the films—a process that he was not thrilled with but would continue to do for most of his subsequent films. At least there was the bonus of knowing that New Line was ready to negotiate on distribution rights once Waters finished the film under their Saliva Films brand. (New Line was still very much a distribution company for movies at the time, and it would only begin producing films in 1977, with *Polyester* being the first film the company produced with Waters.)

With money in the door, location scouting and set building were next:

- The set for Dawn's home was done in an abandoned and condemned apartment above "a friend's store," as Waters put it in *Shock Value*.
- The Poly Technic Institute building at 200 East North Street was used for Dawn's high school.

- Dawn's family home at the beginning of the movie was at 104 Othoridge Road in Lutherville, where the actor playing Dawn's father shouted so loudly and so often as Divine ran from the house in several takes that neighbors thought a family dispute was going on.
- The outside of Earl's shabby dwelling is located at 1516 Mill Race Road, although the interiors seen in the movie were part of a set.
- Dawn's first job as a waitress was at the Little Tavern at 519 East 25th Street, just down the block from where Waters had been living at the time. The Little Tavern was also where Waters got to first become friends with Cookie Mueller after she won the contest for dinner there at the *Mondo Trasho* premiere. (The location is now a pizza place.)
- Waters's apartment at 315 East 25th Street was used for the Dashers' place, but most of their scenes take place at the beauty salon at 112 East Patapsco Avenue, which was a functioning salon at the time, although it is now a church. As Waters reported in *Shock Value*, the film crew accidentally caused pipes to burst in the salon on the next-to-last day of filming, leading to water damage that Waters had to pay for before the owner allowed him to finish filming in the salon.
- There was also a return to Tyson Street—where Divine followed the dog in *Pink Flamingos*—for the brief scene of Dawn and her gang attacking the drunk man, and West Baltimore Street for Dawn's strut down the street.
- The pastor, whose name has disappeared in history, of a church that has never been named, agreed to let Waters film the wedding scene at his church, staying in his office in order to avoid the commotion, especially once he saw Divine in the see-through wedding gown. Years later, the pastor's wife contacted Waters to use him as a witness in divorce proceedings with the pastor, but when Waters made it clear that no money changed hands, that the movie wasn't a "porno," and that he'd be happy to be a witness for the pastor, the summons was dropped.
- The theater where Dawn sees who wants to die for art was located at 8223 Frederick Road in Ellicott City, Maryland. The marquee still stands, but the theater is long gone. The nightclub act in the film is much like that of the one Waters wrote for Divine, which he did in San Francisco when at the Palace Theater. "He ripped telephone books in half, he threw fish, he did all that," Waters told John Ives in 1992. "We did the act other places too, like at colleges. We always had a stolen cop uniform we'd bring with

us, and get some hippie to play the cop. At the end of the act, the fake cop would come on stage and Divine would kill him."

■ No mention of locations would be complete without mentioning the prison used in the final scene, which was and is a functioning prison. Waters was surprised when the warden of the Baltimore City Jail, Gordon Kamka, agreed to let him film the death-row sequence there, "as long as you bring Divine." (*Shock Value*) The crew brought in their own electric chair, which worried some prisoners, as well as Divine, who began to think that Waters would "send a few volts" through the chair in order to enhance his performance. Waters had to prove the chair was not connected to anything before Divine would continue with the scene.

For the film, a 16 mm color camera was used along with a Nagra audio-tape recorder, which was a common device to use for sound recordings on films, as it can be synched-up to the filming, allowing for more freedom with the sound during editing. The film was also a first for Waters in having more than one movie light for scenes, allowing for more internal scenes to be shot, whereas even with *Pink Flamingos*, many scenes were filmed outside using natural light. There was still the tendency to hesitate at the beginning of each cut because of the sound, but this would be the last Waters film to show that hesitation. Filming equipment came by way of LeRoy Morais, who was the head of the film department at the University of Maryland Baltimore County (UMBC) campus, and Yochen Breitenstein, who was a film adviser. Waters was allowed to use the UMBC equipment as long as students were permitted to help with the film, but as Robert Maier reports in his book, many students didn't want to be up at seven o'clock on a Saturday morning with nothing to eat or drink in cramped quarters, so there was not much participation by the students. There were also rumblings about Waters's usage of equipment being so frequent that one student complained to the dean about not being able to make their own films because "someone was making a porno movie with the campus's equipment."

In December 1973, Pat Moran had placed a "help wanted" ad in the *Baltimore Sun*, which read "Now Casting for unedrground [sic] horror film," with a time and a number to call. Casting would continue into March 1974, as the filmmaker was looking for "actors & actresses—forty to sixty yrs. old," undoubtedly for the authoritative roles in the film. "They're all my closest friends," Waters told the *Baltimore Sun* regarding the people playing the oddballs in his films, versus hiring "straight people." "We get these off-the-wall types. We're looking for Marcus Welby and Donna Reed."

Beyond the "singing asshole" moment in *Pink Flamingos*, *Female Trouble* was the first Waters film to have scenes shot out of order. Two scenes in particular were filmed out of sequence due to nature: Divine needing to grow his hair out for the role of Earl, and Susan Lowe giving birth to a baby for the "birth of Taffy" sequence.

In the film, Divine makes four appearances as Earl—first, driving by to pick up Dawn; next, at the dump where they have sex; then, a scene with Earl working in a shop; and finally the death scene where Taffy kills him after barfing all over her. This was the second time Divine played a dual role in one of Waters's movies—he had a brief role playing someone very much like Earl at the end of Mondo Trasho—but it was a first for having dialogue. Earl, of course, has sex with Dawn on a dirty mattress in a dump, which allowed Earl's later comment that Dawn should "go fuck yourself" to be literally true. This was the last scene to be shot with Divine as Earl, and it was filmed in an actual dump where garbage men were working outside of frame. Sally Albaugh (who sometimes went by her married name of Sally Turner) was dressed as Dawn for the first part of filming, and then Divine was whisked off to Van Smith to have his head and face shaved and made up as Dawn, while Turner was dressed "in drag" as Earl. The crew then returned to film the scene to get Divine as Dawn. "The garbage men were there, just, like looking," Waters told John Ives. "And then they were more shocked when we came back two hours later with Divine in a complete other outfit dressed as a woman."

As filming began, Susan Lowe was pregnant and agreed for Waters to use her baby, once it was born, for the birth scene in the movie. After giving birth to her son, Susan brought her young daughter and her mother-in-law to the filming of the scene. The grandmother was none too thrilled to see her new grandchild being covered in fake blood and shoved up Divine's dress with a prophylactic full of liver (to substitute for the umbilical cord). When Susan's daughter freaked out over Divine handling the baby, the grandmother took the children away as quickly as possible. The shot had been completed, however, so what was needed had been accomplished.

The other family-related shock came years later when Waters's mother and father finally attended a showing of the film and saw the sequence where Dawn tips the Christmas tree over on her mother. "Which happened to my grandmother, kinda," Waters told *Citybeat* in 2004, "the tree fell over on her. But I fully exaggerated it. I wasn't there when it happened, but I heard my parents talking about it." Imagine their surprise when a long-ago story was incorporated into their son's movie.

According to Robert Maier in his book, in the scene where Taffy goes to visit her father, the footage of Earl's sore-covered penis that appears in the film was not that of Divine but rather Pat Moran's husband, Chuck Yeaton, with Van Smith doing the makeup job to make it look as bad as possible. Elsewhere, Waters and Divine tried an ipecac in order to have real vomit for the scene when Earl throws up on Taffy, but Divine was unable to throw up even with the ipecac, and fake vomit was used as done before and since in Waters's films. There was also to have been a close-up of the Dashers giving Dawn her injection of liquid eyeliner, and a nurse arrived to do the injection of saline for the filming, but the results did not look convincing and were never used.

Robert Maier states that filming completed before Christmas 1973, but this contradicts an interview with Waters from December 11, 1973, in the *Baltimore Sun*, in which he discusses the film and admits that he was still unsure if Dawn's execution would be by gas chamber or electric chair. There is also the "help wanted" ad from March 1974 that suggests filming was not completed until the spring of 1974. Waters edited the film for several months in 1974 at the UMBC campus from a work-print of the film—the first time Waters had the cash flow and equipment to do such a thing. Known to have been filmed but cut from the movie was a scene where Dawn, Concetta, and Chicklette cut the tips of their fingers in order to mingle the blood and "seal a pact" between them. According to Waters, one of the actresses involved cut her fingers so deep that she passed out after

Dawn has finally figured out that she's been a sap, in the trial scene of *Female Trouble*.

the take. By May 1974, Waters suggested to the *Philadelphia Inquirer* that he had hopes to premiere the film in late July, but it would take a touch longer before the public saw his film, and for those in Baltimore it would be even longer until they saw it in an uncensored form.

Release

The film premiered at the University of Baltimore on October 11–13, 1974, for nine sold-out showings. The promotion for the film used the tagline "She had a lot of problems." Waters reported in *Shock Value*, "I made back a substantial part of the budget even before New Line began distributing the film nationally." This version of the film on 16 mm film ran ninety-two minutes. When New Line made the decision to enhance the 16 mm print to 35 mm (typically referred to as "blow up a film") for viewing in bigger (and better) theaters, the film was cropped by three minutes. Removed was a quick sequence with Sally Albaugh as a salon patron who doesn't want her hairdresser around her six-year-old, and a longer one of Dawn hiding out in the woods and attempting to escape by crossing a river. The river-crossing was done by Divine in the middle of the winter in a lightweight outfit, and with the river having a strong current, so Divine was upset about seeing the scene cut from the 35

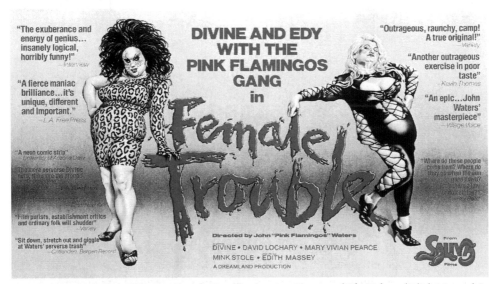

Poster artwork used to advertise *Female Trouble*, showing Dawn and Ida Nelson (Edith Massey) in their most outrageous looks from the movie.

mm version. In Europe, the film was released at ninety-seven minutes, five minutes more than its initial 16 mm release, and contained the aforementioned scenes with Turner at the salon and Dawn crossing the river. It is this ninety-seven-minute long version that was released on DVD by New Line in a double set with *Pink Flamingos* in 2001 and has become known as the preferred version by fans. (The earlier ninety-two-minute version was first released on VHS by Wizard Video in 1982 and then by Cinema Group Home Video in 1987 before New Line released it again in 2001.) Additional footage includes:

- Dawn telling the receptionist at the salon that she is planning to divorce Gator.
- Dawn giving Taffy the address of her father.
- Earl spending a bit more time on his sandwich before Taffy arrives.
- Aunt Ida and Taffy talking more when Ida makes her escape.
- More footage of Dawn in prison with her cellmates.
- Ending credits and a reprise of the theme song.

The 35 mm print of the film premiered at the New York Theatre on the Upper West Side of Manhattan on November 16, 1974. It next appeared at the RKO on 59th Street on the Upper East Side on February 12, 1975. Judith Crist reviewed the film and stated, "It's as amateurish, inept, gross, vulgar, and low camp as the raunch genre can get—and yet dammit, it can't be dismissed." Vincent Canby, who had hated *Pink Flamingos*, felt no better about *Female Trouble*, stating: "Waters makes the fatal mistake of attempting to explain his mini-minded drag show on the grounds it's really where America is at. Silly pretensions of that sort, openly admitted, are a wooden stake through the heart of bad taste, which survives only by being heedless." The film began being filtered out to other parts of the country in summer 1975. (It opened in Los Angeles on July 30, 1975, for example.) Some areas received the film in the fall of 1975, while a release in Philadelphia for Easter, promised by Waters, didn't happen, and the film was only finally released there in November 1975, more than a year after its premiere at the University of Baltimore.

Waters had a special showing of the film during all these other openings around the country when he returned to the Baltimore City Jail on March 14, 1974, to show the inmates the film. Waters explained in *Shock Value* that the inmates were silent until Dawn knocks over the Christmas tree onto her mother. "The audience went wild, and I knew I had won their hearts."

The only part of the film the "captive" audience didn't enjoy was the ending, as the death penalty had been reinstated the day before. Still, there was applause after the movie ended and one convicted murderer, after the movie was over, told Waters, "Hey, brother, you ought to show this film down at Clifton T. Perkins Hospital for the criminally insane. I think they'd like it better."

The film was released with a self-imposed X rating—a rating which, due to the female and male genitalia on display, probably would have been handed down to the film anyway. Many of the ads released had a statement within them telling people that the film had "scenes of extraordinary perversity which may be seen as morally and sexually offensive." The film went to Cannes and was picked up for release in other countries, facing far less censorship problems than in Maryland. (The BBFC asked for Earl's penis to be edited out, as that was their only concern.) Mary Avara was still at the Maryland State Censor Board, and Waters arrived to see that the board was viewing his film alongside *Flesh Gordon* and an 8 mm peepshow loop. Footage where Dawn and Gator are having sex was asked to be cut because of a "vagina shot," even though it was Divine wearing her "cheater" (a strap-on fake vagina with fake pubic hair), but Waters was able to argue with the board about the cut. However, the scene where Gator has a woman sitting on him was deemed to be cunnilingus and therefore forbidden. To Waters, the board advised, "She can sit there, but can't move" (even though nothing can be seen and there is not actual contact). When Waters finally agreed, Avara handed him scissors and told him to make the cut right then and there on the "thousand-dollar print" he planned to use for the University of Baltimore premiere in October 1974—the print that, according to Waters in *Shock Value*, was "now marred with an ugly splice and irritating sound jump." To add insult to injury, he then had to pay a sixteen dollar fee for having to badly cut his own film just to please the board. "I think it was done just out of spite—to cut one second out of a film," Waters told Bill George and Martin Falck in 1974. "What is that second going to do? Make people rush out and murder someone?"

At that point he decided it was a battle he was never to lose again.

11

Backwards Day

The Making of *Desperate Living*

My hometown newspaper, the *Baltimore Sun*, wrote an editorial about me and they headlined it 'The Prince of Puke.' And my mother read it and she looked at me a little sadly and she shook her head and said, 'Somehow, when your father and I were raising you, we didn't really have it in mind that we were raising you to be the Prince of Puke.'

—John Waters, while promoting *Desperate Living* to the *Tampa Tribune*

Plot

Released from a sanitarium far too early, Peggy Gravel (Mink Stole) is in the finishing stages of a nervous breakdown in her home. When her husband, Bosley (George Stover), tries to give her a shot to calm her, she assaults him and screams for their housekeeper, Grizelda (Jean Hill). Grizelda attacks Bosley, suffocating him to death by sitting on him.

Now on the run, Peggy and Grizelda drive off, wanted by the police. They are stopped by a cop (Turkey Joe), but it turns out he'll let them go on to a place called Mortville if they give him their panties and deep kisses. Satisfied, he lets them go on without the car, and the pair soon arrive in the bizarre town of Mortville, which is a mix of rickety sheds and cheap fairy-tale landmarks, including a castle in the distance. The area is policed by a group of male hustlers in leather. They meet Mole (Susan Lowe), who offers them a shed in the back in exchange for a lottery ticket Grizelda had stolen from Bosley earlier.

Peggy and Grizelda are introduced to Mole's girlfriend, Muffy (Liz Renay), and Mole admits that she is a man trapped in a woman's body. The conversation is cut short by goons arriving to arrest Peggy and Grizelda. In the paddy wagon,

Grizelda makes a pass at Peggy, but Peggy rebuffs her. The two are dragged into the castle to meet Queen Carlotta (Edith Massey), who forces them to eat live roaches. After executing a prisoner in front of them, the Queen tells the pair what to expect in Mortville and then sends them off to wear clothes that suit them as "trash."

The Queen is told that Princess Coo-Coo (Mary Vivian Pearce) has returned to the castle after spending time with Herbert (George Figgs), the garbage man of the nudist colony in Mortville. The Queen forbids her to leave the castle until her fortieth birthday. The Queen then retires to her chamber, where she has Wilson (Ed Peranio) "rob her safety deposit box," as it were.

Peggy and Grizelda return to Mole's shack in their new outfits. After getting Peggy to settle down, Muffy and Mole tell their stories of how they ended up in Mortville. In a flashback, Muffy is a suburban mother who finds out that her high-as-a-kite babysitter (Pirie Woods) has put her baby in the refrigerator. The baby is safe, but Muffy is furious, drowns the sitter in a bowl of dog food, and then drives off with her drunken husband (Roland Hertz) stuck in the driver's-side car door. Mole's story shows her as a wrestler back in the 1960s. She goes berserk in the ring, gorging out an eyeball of her opponent, Big Jimmy Dong (H. C. Kliemisch), killing him and then strangling the referee. The two couples then fight about the lottery ticket before going to their respective beds, where each couple has sex.

The next morning comes with the Queen announcing that it is Backwards Day, and everyone must wear their clothes the wrong way around and walk backward for tourists. At the castle, the Queen is informed that the Princess has escaped during the night. She gets on her royal cot and has her goons take her out to find the Princess, issuing that Herbert is to be shot dead on sight.

Mole, Muffy, Peggy, and Grizelda head to the nudist colony, where they meet Shina (Marina Melin). Coo-Coo soon arrives and asks to see Herbert, only for the goons to shoot him dead when they are reunited. The group rush out and head to Flipper's Bar, run by Flipper (Cookie Mueller). Peggy and Grizelda leave after Peggy is attacked in the restroom, while Mole and Muffy find out that they won $1,000 in the lottery and are finalists in the big prize. Coo-Coo drags the dead body of Herbert away to the shed that Peggy and Grizelda use.

Outside, they run into the Queen, who parades down the street yelling insults at the people. Mole, fed up, hits the Queen with a mudball.

Peggy Gravel (Mink Stole) is getting a mouthful from Mole McHenry (Susan Lowe), while Grizelda Brown (Jean Hill) looks on in a late scene from *Desperate Living*.

Meanwhile, Grizelda and Peggy arrive back at their shed and find Coo-Coo there. Peggy flips out and screams for the goons. Grizelda tries to fight the men off and in the process the shed collapses on her, killing her. The surviving goons drag Coo-Coo away.

After some spanking of a nude goon named Grogan (Steve Butow), the Queen decides she will poison the population with rabies for Mole having thrown a mudball at her. Just then, Coo-Coo and Peggy are brought to the Queen in dog cages. They are released from their cages and Coo-Coo attacks the Queen, who has Coo-Coo gang-raped by the goons. Peggy begs to be made the new princess, and the Queen decides to give her a trial run by having Peggy spread rabies to everyone in town. Peggy agrees.

Having won the money in the lottery, Mole goes to Baltimore and has sex-realignment surgery after threatening the surgeon with a knife. She returns with her new member sewn in place, but Muffy is horrified and asks Mole to cut it off. Mole does so and throws it out into the streets where a dog eats it. Muffy then sews up the gaping wound.

Peggy, now dressed as the wicked queen of *Snow White*, makes the rabies potion and gives Coo-Coo a shot of the potion before she is thrown out of the castle. Mole and the others find Coo-Coo and agree to help her kill the Queen. The women assault the castle and enter the royal chamber. Coo-Coo bites the Queen on the leg, and Mole kills Peggy by shooting her with a gun up her behind. They then kill the Queen, cook her, and present her to the happy people of Mortville, who dance in the street while Coo-Coo finally dies of rabies. And with the Queen having been infected with rabies by Coo-Coo, everyone in town will soon die of rabies after eating her. But ... uh ... let's stick with the happy ending and not dwell on that part.

Claims to Condemnation

- Murder
- Homosexuality
- Rape
- Nudity (female and male genitalia)
- Cannibalism
- Minor transgressions: disrespect to authority, vomiting, naked pogoing.

Additional Cast and Crew

This movie marks the first appearance of Jean Hill, who would go on to play a small but memorable role in *Polyester* and appear briefly in *A Dirty Shame*. Brook Yeaton, Pat Moran's son, appears as Bosley Jr. (with the stage name of Brook Blake). Paul Swift makes his last appearance in a Waters film as Mr. Paul, while Pat Moran sneaks in as the bathroom pervert.

This is the first time Waters has a "star" appear in his film, with Liz Renay (1926–2007) playing Muffy. Renay was a stripper who had become famous for being the girlfriend of mobster Mickey Cohen and refusing to rat on him, leading to a three-year prison term on Terminal Island in California. She wrote her autobiography, *My Face for the World to See*, while in prison, and it was this book that brought her to Waters's attention. Waters went to Los Angeles and took Renay to dinner at the Brown Derby to entice her into being in the movie. Renay was an exhibitionist in many ways, volunteering to get naked even when not requested. It is her breasts seen in the "glory holes" in the bathroom stall that Peggy enters at one point in the movie, and she had no issue with having roaches crawl over her body in one scene. Her only stipulation to Waters before filming was that she would not perform sex acts on-camera, which Waters knew wouldn't be an issue. She was signed for $10,000 plus expenses for three weeks of work in January 1977. From all

A posed picture of Mole McHenry (Susan Lowe) and Muffy St. Jacques (Liz Renay) from *Desperate Living*. Liz Renay was Waters's first true celebrity guest star in one of his films.

accounts, Renay was a trooper who was fine doing whatever was needed during the filming. There were only three issues she had: the food, which she called worse than prison food; Mole cooking the rat, which also repulsed her; and the dialogue in the scene where Muffy is sewing Mole back together after the castration. Renay did not want to say Muffy's line telling Mole that she would "eat it like old times," as it reminded her too much of prison incidents she had seen with other prisoners. Waters finally talked her into it, but, as he reported in *Shock Value*, "I can still tell every time I watch this scene that she is mortified."

The film was the first for Waters to not feature Divine since the days of *Roman Candles*. Waters had written the part of Mole for Divine, but Divine was contractually obligated with *Women Behind Bars* in New York, and later London, at the time. "I wrote the lead part for Divine," Waters told the *Guardian* in 2007, "but he couldn't do it because he was doing a stage play at the time. And I realized then that if you write the part for one person and they can't do it . . . then what?" The role instead went to Susan Lowe, and it would be her biggest role in a Waters movie. Several longtime actors on Waters's movies appeared as goons: Channing Wilroy, Steve Parker, Chuck Yeaton (Pat's husband), David Klein, and Peter Koper (who owned the farm where Mortville was built).

There was some mild controversy as to the lack of David Lochary's involvement in the film, as *Shock Value* implied—although never implicitly stated—that Lochary had died before filming completed on *Desperate Living*. This is not correct, as filming wrapped by March 1977 and Lochary died four months later in July 1977. Yet, it all comes down to semantics: Waters positioned his paragraph about Lochary's death in the middle of discussing his cast for *Desperate Living*, when it should have gone elsewhere in the text. Waters did have a point to make in saying that he had not decided to use Lochary again due to his angel dust habit, but when one considers the film made, there is the question as to what part he would have played anyway. There simply is not a part in the film that would have suited Lochary's personality—all of the male parts are small, and none have any of the charming evil that Lochary could bring to a character. To have inserted Lochary would have meant adding a role unnecessary to the film.

Robert Maier, who had jumped in as the sound man on *Female Trouble* when there were issues with the original man hired, was bumped up to production manager on *Desperate Living*. Dave Insley also returned from the previous film to do lighting on the new one. Waters hired Chris Lobingier and Alan Yarus to write music for the film, which Waters requested be done in a "cheesy *Dr. Zhivago*-type score." Charles Roggero once again contributed to the editing with Waters, while Van Smith and Vincent Peranio returned to work behind the scenes on designs of both costumes and settings, respectively.

Production

As mentioned previously, Waters now had a distributor, New Line, who was happy to help push his films out to the public. The problem for Waters was that it would be 1977 before they looked into producing their own movies (the first being *Stunts*, directed by Mark Lester) and three years after that before they produced more. For now, even with their commitment to distribute, Waters had to find the money to actually make his next picture on his own.

Fortunately for him, *Pink Flamingos* had gained momentum in various theaters around the country and was still going strong at the time. *Female Trouble* may have performed to a lesser degree of *Pink Flamingos*, but it made a profit and was still circulating, as were Waters's earlier films here and there (sometimes even in double-bills). Waters has stated that he used what money he made by that point on *Pink Flamingos* and *Female Trouble*—about $30,000—and put it back into the next project. The goal was to make a film for $50,000, although that would eventually rise to $65,000, and Robert Maier once again came back to help budget the film with Waters. Waters then formed Charm City Productions, a limited partnership, and went looking for investors.

James McKenzie, a university professor who had helped raise funds for *Female Trouble* anonymously, contributed. William Platt, whom Waters refers to in *Shock Value* as "a one-time camp counselor of mine who was now an eccentric environmental activist," contributed money and helped out with video on the new film. The third partner was David Spencer, who, as Waters mentioned in interviews, was "an heir" who had money. For this, all three got their names listed as associate producers on the film. When a writer for the *Morning News* in Wilmington, Delaware, asked the owner of the Rondo Center Theater in town how Platt got such a prestigious title on the film, the owner quipped, "Put up two-thirds of the money."

Waters began working on ideas for the movie in the year before writing the script, which he started on during one of his usual summer pilgrimages to Provincetown and then finished up in Baltimore as fall approached in 1976. "I wrote *Desperate Living* about the worst community you could live in. It wasn't Provincetown, but it was certainly about living in an eccentric small town," Waters said to Gerald Peary in 1997. With financial support in good order, the Dreamlanders began working on details, such as casting, sets, and location shooting, for months before filming began. "This time," Waters told the *Baltimore Sun* as filming was wrapping up in March 1977, "we set out to do a lot more than in the other films. It was impossible to do it all, but you push on almost to where you collapse. You get close to that point and you go some more."

Ironically enough, it was the one script of his from which he allowed one of the cast to improvise. The scene in question was where Peggy prepared the rabies potion in the caldron. "John said, 'I didn't write anything for this scene so just make something up,' and I was like, 'WHAT?! I don't know how to do that, I never did that," Stole told *Dirty Mag.* "I obviously had to though, when Peggy Gravel was concocting her rabies potion she says something like 'a pinch of bat, a touch of rat,' I made those lines up."

Waters had been able to find a farm to build the city of Mortville on a twenty-six-acre piece of farmland that belonged to Peter Koper and Laurel

Douglas at at 4545 Gross Mill Road in Hampstead, which they agreed to let Waters use as long as "every trace of Mortville would vanish when the filming was completed." Waters, in *Shock Value*, went on to say, "They realized, as it was designed, they would have to drive right through the main street of Mortville to get to their own house on top of the hill, and they wanted a guarantee that this would only be a temporary situation." Vincent Peranio then spent weeks working with a crew going through dumps and demolition sites to find material to help build a shantytown, and, for a total cost of $7,000, they built a fake castle out of plywood at the end of a one-block area built on the farm.

Pat Moran bought a wanted ad in the August 29, 1976, edition of the *Baltimore Sun*, which stated, "Now casting for low budget horror movie. Parts open—blk. Actress over 200 lbs, beefy too, character roles & others." Two hundred women responded to the ad, according to the *Baltimore Sun* in March 1977, but Waters was introduced to Jean Hill elsewhere and picked her for the role needed. Meanwhile, during the filming, Pat Moran was in charge of rounding up extras to appear as citizens of Mortville. "I call between 50 and 125 people," Moran told the *Baltimore Sun*, "and maybe 25 to 35 show up. The extras have to fit a certain description, preferably fat or thin. The problem is you wind up with so many of your peers, people in the same age bracket, and you want them to look like they're not your friends."

One concern of filming, which took place between November 1976 and January 1977 on a farm in the middle of nowhere, was the cold. To the *Baltimore Sun*, Waters's said, "People get exhausted. Working in the summer under hot lights would be terribly unpleasant." According to Waters in *Shock Value*, Moran would rent a school bus and pick up extras outside of Massey's thrift shop at six o'clock in the morning and would not return them from the farm until late at night. "I was against the Mortville extras providing their own transportation because I knew that if they had their own cars they would escape before I had finished shooting for the day." William Platt also would drag in some extras, and while all added to the look of Mortville, many in the cast and the crew refused to drive out with them, as a number were drug addicts shooting up or people in an alcoholic stupor that would urinate on themselves while being driven over to the farm. It was even worse for those filming as nudists, who had to strip down to nothing in thirty-degree weather in mid-November. They managed to do so long enough to complete the shots before being covered in a blanket, although one older extra refused the blanket in order to happily show himself to any of the women on the set.

Before the first week at the farm was up, the farmhouse was off-limits to everyone after the heavy use of the toilet caused the septic tank to back up into the house and cause problems in the land nearby. Only the main cast who needed facilities in order to dress and be made-up for their parts were allowed there, so the extras and the crew had to suffer in temperatures that were rarely above forty degrees. There was little food available as well, and a well-intended daily supply of chili soon grew tiresome and was abandoned after one lunch made several people sick. Instead, a run to a nearby pizza shop tended to be the only option. Outdoor filming also presented an issue when flooding came through the area, causing some of Mortville to float away, but fortunately the castle was safe and everything was retrievable for what filming was still needed. There were some concerns when Susan Lowe, as Mole, had to lean out of an upper window of the castle to announce the death of the Queen, as it involved her standing precariously on a ladder that had been leaned up against the facsimile, which made people wonder if the whole thing would come crashing down, but it fortunately remained standing during the filming.

The only other exteriors needed for the film were that of Peggy's house at the beginning of the film, which was done with a return to the house of Waters's parents and his mother's bedroom. There was also the Johns Hopkins filming, where Mole goes for her realignment surgery—easily done on campus—and Mole cashing in the lottery ticket at 1001 St. Paul Street. Everything else occurred on the farm or in a large warehouse loft in Fell's Point that was converted into the new Dreamland Studios. The loft had plenty of space for all the interior shooting needed for the film (besides that of Peggy's bedroom at the beginning, which was shot in the house). The only problem was that it was an old building so close to the road that filming typically had to take place during stop-lights at the corner below. The loft was freezing cold as well, but at least the cast and crew were in the city and could find occasional relief.

Desperate Living was the last film Waters shot on 16 mm film (and it was later blown up to 35 mm by New Line for release to theaters). It was his first film, however, to employ a director of photography, Tom Loizeaux, who worked with Robert Maier at Maryland Public Television at the time. Waters was at first hesitant about such a chance, as he had always done such a role on other films, but, as he told John Ives, "They weaned me away from that—correctly, God knows—in *Desperate Living*." At one point, the 16 mm camera froze up and Loizeaux and Maier borrowed one without permission from the television station for a weekend shoot, which got them an off-the-record reprimand. Otherwise, filming went as well as expected under such conditions.

The title sequence with the rat being eaten from the lovely dinnerware was done with an actual cooked rat (surprising, as the footage could have easily been filmed without cooking the rat, but it was done for authenticity). Unsurprisingly, no one wanted to use their own oven to cook the rat, and Waters was not going to do so either. Instead, Vincent Peranio and the title designer, Alan Rose, sneaked into the house of someone they didn't like and cooked the rat while the person was out. "Believe me," Waters told the *Guardian* years later, "you'll never get the smell out of an oven. You cook a rat and it's the worst smell you've ever smelled in your life. You can clean that oven twenty times and it's still going to have that lingering odor of burnt rat!"

Peggy was scripted to run over a dog at one point early in the film, and to achieve this, Waters bought a dead dog from a "veterinary hospital where they did experiments" to use in the scene, thawing it out at Susan Lowe's place before use. Mink Stole was driving the car in-character but had a hard time resisting the urge to miss the dead dog in the street and continued to swerve to avoid it when shooting occurred. Once the gag was completed, it was Waters's responsibility to get rid of it. "I felt like one of the Moors Murderers and was worried a cop would see me disposing of the 'body,' spot blood in my trunk and start asking a lot of nosey questions."

There were some concerns on the parts of Jean Hill and Mink Stole when it came to the scene where their characters were force-fed roaches while handcuffed in front of the queen. Waters, stating that he must be getting conservative in his old age, agreed to only use live roaches in the close-ups of the bowl holding them but then substitute them for raisins when the "roaches" were fed to them.

There was more apprehension about the scene where Muffy returns to her home and finds her child (listed as being played by an obviously scared Damien Overholser) inside the refrigerator. "I had to convince my friends with kids that there would be no danger of suffocation," Waters said in *Shock Value*. "I'd get the cameras rolling, somebody would put the child in the fridge, and I'd call 'Action!' Liz Renay, who played the mother, would rush in, open the door, and snatch the child to safety." Unfortunately, the crew did not expect for the child to grab hold of the egg shelves inside the door once inside, and on the first take, the child nearly fell headfirst to the floor when the door was open. A second take occurred, and in the film you can see that the little boy did the same thing, with Renay catching him quickly enough to let the take be the one to use instead of attempting a third try—much to the relief of the child's mother.

The only issues with the actors came by way of Massey, who was having difficulty in remembering all the lines that she had to say as the Queen. "It was hard for her," Mink Stole reported in the *Dirty Mag* interview. "Because she didn't even know what she was saying half the time, and she would try so hard!" It would sometimes take twenty takes to get the dialogue out of Massey, but finally the work was in the can.

With filming completed in mid-January, Waters and Charles Roggero worked to edit the film over ten weeks in preparation for its premiere.

Release

Waters, Moran, Chuck Yeaton, and Chuck's brother Roger went around Baltimore stapling flyers to poles, walls, and fences for the movie's premiere at the University of Baltimore's Langsdale Auditorium on March 27–29, 1977. Robert Maier, in his accounting in his book, states that there were no problems with the Maryland censor board for *Desperate Living*, which seems a tad unusual considering some of the antics in the film. Waters's *Shock Value* presents a different story: not wanting a repeat of the situation that occurred with *Female Trouble*, Waters claims he had a lawyer familiar with censorship issues with him when he went to the board. When cuts were demanded and Waters refused to make changes, an assistant to the state's attorney general watched the movie to resolve the issue. After seeing the movie, he told Waters, "They really hate your films, you know. But bad taste isn't illegal," and allowed the censor seal for the movie without any cuts.

Avoiding their complaints about the film left Waters relieved, but only momentarily. As it turns out, a backlash came from unexpected quarters when Waters found himself and the film a target of feminist and gay groups who found the movie insulting to lesbians. Further, it appeared to them that Waters had taken the name of his new movie from a Baltimore-based lesbian newsletter with the same name and used it for a film that showed lesbians as a joke to be mocked. A protest at the Orson Welles Theater in Boston even led to the cancellation of the film appearing at the theater. "Gay papers really came down on me," Waters told Scott MacDonald. A showing of the film was halted because of protests. Others joined in the attack as well, including Kevin Thomas of the *Los Angeles Times*, who commented that "Waters's acute sense of the absurd ends up being a vicious attack on lesbians." Waters was amazed and infuriated by the accusation and has never quite let it go. "First of all," Waters asked in *Shock Value*, "I wondered, what makes lesbians immune from satire? I didn't notice them bitching about my other films,

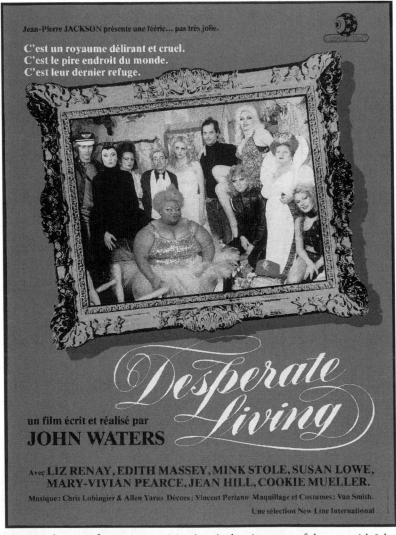

The French poster for *Desperate Living* (1977), showing most of the cast with John Waters.

where I made fun of gay men, drag queens, heterosexual families, and even grandmothers .... Second, what kind of name was *Desperate Living* for a gay newsletter? It seems an odd choice of words to promote a lifestyle, and the very title seemed to invite lampooning."

In defending his actions, Waters possibly clarified why there was resentment: Waters is a gay man who couldn't hold aspects of that culture sacred, as expected by members of any group that feels persecuted. Yet Waters had made clear over the years that he had little patience for the idea of people being self-segregating themselves and "circling the wagons" to protect their perceived culture. Gay culture was something he was a part of, but it did not mean he had to prove anything by being gay. "I'm a film director," Waters told James Grant in 1994 when asked about being a gay film director. "Gay is an adjective that I certainly am, but I don't know that it's my first one. I think if you're just a gay filmmaker, you get pigeonholed just like if you say, I'm a black filmmaker, I'm a Spanish filmmaker, I'm a whatever."

Besides, although there has always been the assumption made about Waters's sexual preference, it was never something that he actively sought to build his career on, as he told Michelangelo Signorile in an interview:

> I was on the cover of some magazine called *Gay News* or *Gay Times*—I don't remember what it was—in 1972, but not because I came out—but because it was the only magazine to ask me to be on the cover. And a lot of magazines, including *The Advocate*, did an interview and said, 'The most out director,' but they never had the nerve to ask me if I was gay. They thought it was—like my parents—it was something worse than gay. So a lot of people never asked if I was gay because they were afraid I'd say, 'No, I'm a necrophiliac'—which, even that, that's just fear of performance.

The negative response that he received at the time of *Desperate Living* may have something to do with his inclination in later years to not discuss personal politics—such as working to have gay marriage made legal in the United States—in interviews unless pressed. This was similar to his feelings on if he has to belong to a certain group, as evidenced in his attitude toward gay or straight barrooms, and several times he has talked about being more comfortable in places where the crowd was a mix of people of different sexual orientations rather than only gay or straight. "I still like sexual confusion. If I would go to a gay bar, the person I would like wouldn't hang out in gay bars either. They would be one of the four lunatics in a hipster bar,"

Waters told Jonathan Valania. To Waters, the point wasn't to make fun of a culture but instead to make fun of human beings doing what they do no matter who they are. Fortunately, over time, such anger toward the film has dissipated, with members of gay culture having embraced the movie and with it even being cited as an early work in gay cinema. "*Desperate Living* is brought by gay women's groups to colleges all the time to raise money, so things change," Waters told Pat Sherman in 2005.

The film opened in New York on October 14, 1977, more than six months after its premiere in Baltimore, with Waters appearing at the D. W. Griffith Theater that night to answer questions about the movie. The movie poster and the original newspaper ad—which appeared without issue in the

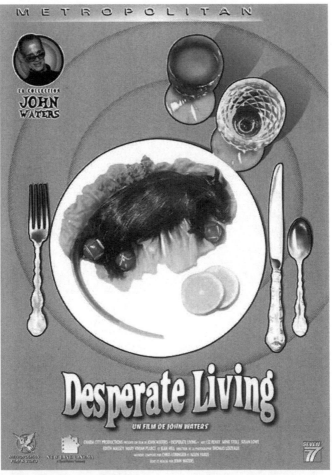

A later French poster for *Desperate Living* showing a stylized version of the original "rat dinner" poster.

October 17, 1977, edition of *Village Voice*—picture a re-creation of the opening title's image—that of the rat served on a fancy dining plate—with the tagline, "It isn't very pretty . . . ." Flyers for the movie that went up in New York had this image, which caused a ruckus when the student helpers posting the flyers would put them up without permission, which was not appreciated when it occurred on the windows and doors of restaurants.

The *New York Times* refused to run the ad with the cooked rat, and in most cities the film was advertised without any image beyond the title. A substitute ad of Liz Renay screaming was used in its place for The *New York Times*. (Subsequent issues of the *Village Voice* used this version of the ad as well.) A press showing of the film found the critic for *Good Housekeeping* walking out after ten minutes and The *New York Times* dismissing it by saying, "This one takes the cake." Waters makes mention in *Shock Value* that Tom Allen of the *Village Voice* said the movie "had to be seen to be believed" but failed to mention that Allen went on say: "[Waters is] an austerely economical director who is figuratively comparable to Bresson. His troupe are beautiful ogres because they collaborate in absolute harmony with his ends and are, therefore, not exploited. To paraphrase Rex Reed, Where else would these people go when the sun goes down?"

The film did not reach LA until November 18, 1977, and only ran for a week. In other areas of the country, such as Detroit and Miami (which didn't get the film until January 1978), the film was pushed as a midnight movie, but that definition was already starting to fade away in late 1977 and early 1978—certainly on the east and west coasts. Middle America stuck with midnight movies until the early 1980s, but video broke the camel's back on the concept of getting together with friends and going to an offbeat movie in a theater. What was the point when one could easily just rent a movie or even see it on HBO or another cable network?

The video version of the film was first released in 1985 by Continental Video with a cover showing Liz Renay surrounded by the goons. The back cover shows a very good color shot of Pat Moran from the film, which is of note because she is essentially an extra in the film itself. The film was later reissued in 1987 by Cinema Group Home Video with a cover that is more in line with the plot—that of Mole and Muffy looking at the camera. The back cover shows Liz Renay in two photos—one being the photo used for the alternate movie poster of Renay screaming, and the other of her with the goons, as seen on the front cover of the Continental Video version. The film was first released on DVD in 2001 by New Line and was paired with *Polyester*. It was released on its own by Warner Archive Collection in 2017.

The film was picked up in other countries, although it was edited somewhat for Italy, and it did play across the United States, but it was not the success of Waters's last two films. "All my films made money except for *Desperate Living*, which has almost broken even," Waters told the *Chicago Tribune* in 1984. By 1992, Waters would tell John Ives that the film had finally begun to make money.

Waters has also admitted that there is a dark edge to the film that may have had something to do with its slow return. Waters told Jack Stevenson: "I like it … but, ah, I think it's the least joyous. And I wrote in the screenplay book that really maybe it's a film to watch if you're crashing from a glue high." When asked about Divine not being in it, Waters said: "It's easy for me to think that was some of the problem of it, because there is something not very joyous about it. Maybe I was in a bad mood when I wrote it."

12

The Wonders of Odorama

The Making of *Polyester*

I think you can shock people in ways that aren't quite so obvious. You can be a little more subtle about it.

> —John Waters to David Shute in 1981 on having former teenage heartthrob Tab Hunter play love scenes with Divine in *Polyester*

Plot

After an introduction to the Odorama process by Dr. Arnold Quackenshaw (Rick Breitenfeld)—where we learn we must scratch the number on the Odorama card when a number appears onscreen—the movie's story begins.

Francine Fishpaw (Divine) is a suburban woman, with a very sensitive nose, living in a suburban nightmare. Her husband, Elmer (David Samson) runs a porno theater that he happily promotes, embarrassing her; her son, Dexter (Ken King), is a huffer who gets his kicks stomping on women's feet; her mother treats her like a servant; and her daughter, Lu-Lu (Mary Garlinton), is flunking out of school, two months pregnant, and out of control. There is only so much heartache a woman can take, after all. Even her dog, Bonkers, hates her.

The only ray of sunshine in her life is that of Cuddles Kovinsky (Edith Massey), Francine's former maid who recently received an inheritance and has a chauffeur, Heintz, driving her around. Cuddles joins Francine to catch Elmer red-handed with his mistress, Sandra (Mink Stole), at a local hotel. Elmer is happy to grant her a divorce and begins hassling Francine with obscene phone calls and pranks, crumbling her resolve even further, and she begins drinking heavily. Soon enough, Dexter is arrested as the foot-stomper, bringing additional shame to Francine, while Lu-Lu faces the horrors of a home for unwed mothers. Finally, a Halloween prank by Lu-Lu's boyfriend, Bo-Bo, goes wrong, leading to the grandmother being shot by Bo-Bo, Bo-Bo dying (shot by the grandmother), Lu-Lu trying to commit suicide, and the dog hanging itself.

The initial movie poster for *Polyester* (1981), which pushed Odorama, the smelling gimmick used for the film.

Having reached bottom, the family begins to rebound. Lu-Lu has a miscarriage but returns to the houes as a peaceful macramé-making hippie, while Dexter is reformed and uses his fetish as an outlet for his artwork. Best of all, Francine finds true love with Todd Tomorrow, a man she had seen fleetingly and finally gets to know at a horrible auto accident.

Things are going well until one night when Elmer and Sandra sneak into the house in order to kill Francine. At the same time, Todd and the grandmother out themselves to Francine as working together to drive Francine insane so they can sell off the house and the children and go away together. In the following confusion, Sandra accidentally kills Elmer, Lu-Lu strangles Sandra, and Heintz, with Cuddles in his car, kills both Todd and the grandmother. The bad guys are dead and the world is smelling fresh as Francine heads back into the house with her loving family.

Claims to Condemnation

- Blasphemy, with the title of the porn film being "My Burning Bush" ("at 2, 4, 6, 8, and 10")
- Drug use on-camera (huffing)
- Murder
- Surprisingly, there is no nudity in the film with the exception of some out-of-focus photos on the walls of Elmer's office. Nor much in the way of profanity.
- Sexual relations outside of marriage; insinuation of sexual practices outside of heterosexual norms (foot fetish, although in a rather odd form)
- Minor transgressions: vomiting, robbery, and disrespect to authority (the nuns)

Additional Cast and Crew

David Samson, who plays Elmer, would return in *Hairspray* as an WZZT official. Mary Garlington (Lu-Lu) would never make another movie with Waters, but she did model 1950s-style clothing with Susan Lowe in a photo layout for the *Baltimore Sun* in 1983.

Stiv Bators (1949–1990), who plays Bo-Bo, was the lead singer of the Dead Boys and later the Lords of the New Church. Waters met Bators on a talk show in Baltimore and asked him to be in the film. "I liked the idea that he

Todd Tomorrow (Tab Hunter) and Francine Fishpaw (Divine) in a quiet romantic moment from *Polyester*.

Dexter Fishpaw (Ken King) is having a relapse—a scene filmed but then cut from *Polyester*, leaving the movie with a discrepancy when Dexter turns up without an eyebrow late in the film.

was a lunatic, but in real life isn't one," Waters said in an interview with *Exploitation Retrospect* in 1986. Waters mentioned in the director's commentary and in his one-man show that when Bator died from a brain injury due to a traffic accident, Bator's girlfriend told Waters that she snorted some of his ashes to feel "closer to him."

This was the last Waters film to feature longtime Dreamlanders Cookie Mueller and Marina Melin, both of whom play victims of the foot-stomper in the film. (Susan Lowe also plays the first victim seen in the film.) It was also the last film Waters made with Edith Massey, who returned to playing a sweetheart of a character after playing nasty ones in both *Female Trouble* and *Desperate Living*. Massey never did learn the art of saying her lines properly but was loved by one and all anyway. "She did nail some of her lines deliciously," Waters told Screenanarchy.com, "but you can ask Mink; sometimes, 'Take 38!' You can hear her in 'Purr, purr, Francine.' I would say, 'It's "Poor Francine,"' but she couldn't say it because of her teeth."

It was also the first of Waters's films to have Mary Vivian Pearce in a cameo—she plays one of the hellish nuns at the home for the unwed mothers—rather than in a larger costarring role. The other nun was played by Sharon Niesp, who also appeared as Shotsie, Flipper's jealous girlfriend in *Desperate Living*, and as the bouncer at the Pelt Room in *Pecker*.

It is also the last Waters movie to feature Divine as the star. Divine would only appear in one more film for Waters, *Hairspray*, in a strong but secondary role as Tracey's mother. *Polyester* is also the first film since *Mondo Trasho* where Divine plays a woman who isn't in control and is sympathetic. (Okay, perhaps Divine isn't that sympathetic in *Mondo Trasho*, but her character did go through the film trying to help the woman she nearly killed with her car.) Divine relished playing the role, knowing he was getting typecast to always play vicious women in movies or on stage. "I like to think of this movie as my *Mildred Pierce*," Divine told the *Advocate* at the time of filming. "In every other film, Crawford was venomous, but suddenly in *Mildred Pierce* everyone was mean to her."

Dr. Arnold Quackenshaw, the "Prominent Ear, Nose and Throat Specialist" who introduced the film, was played by Rick Breitenfeld, the director of Maryland Public Broadcasting at the time. He was a last-minute replacement for a New York actor who Waters had hired and who bailed on the production the morning of his scene. Frantic to find a replacement in order to avoid a $2,000 loss for the day's planned shooting, Waters took the recommendation of a friend and called Breitenfeld. "He said as long as he wasn't going to be mortified he'd do it," Waters told Claude Thomas Brooks. "I assured him he wasn't and he agreed. He was a thousand times better than the actor we had [planned to use]." Rick Breitenfeld died in September 2018 from cancer at the age of eighty-seven.

Waters initially tried to get his old crush, Dagmar (see Chapter 1), to come out of retirement in order to play the nasty grandmother in the film. "I tracked her down when she was about eighty," Waters told *Index Magazine*, "and went to visit her and tried to get her to play the grandmother in *Polyester*. And she wouldn't, but I loved that I met her and went there." Instead, Joni Ruth White, who had appeared in minor non-sex-related roles in the porn films *Babe* (1981) and *Wanda Whips Wall Street* (1982), and later appeared in the cult films *Smithereens* (1982) and *Street Trash* (1987), took on the role of the grandmother, La Rue.

Production

In a November 11, 1977, interview for *Desperate Living*, Waters was already talking about "Smell-O-Vision"—"My next movie is going to have an R rating. It's going to be a love story, and I hope to do it in Smell-O-Vision," he told the *Tampa Tribune*. A month earlier in an article for *SoHo Weekly*, he mentioned it as well, stating that he wanted Annette Funicello to star. Ultimately, however, he began work in 1977 on two scripts—one a parody of Hollywood love stories and the other a more "commercial" script idea he had that needed a fifteen-year-old girl "with experience and pimples," but more about that one in the next chapter. "Overall," he told the *Tampa Tribune*, "I'd like to get away from the X-rated stuff and make movies that are a lot less gross. Otherwise, I just paint myself in a corner. But on the other hand, I don't want to make *Benji* either."

That was all in 1977. It would be 1980 before *Polyester* began filming on September 1, 1980. "It took three years to raise the money for *Polyester*," Waters told Scott MacDonald. "That's the worst part of filmmaking, the part I hate. It's the most depressing part; you feel like a used car salesman, and you go around with your synopsis and talk to people, some of whom you don't even know—they're just rich." By May 1979, Waters, again working with Bob Maier, had a budget together for the new film, estimated at $160,000. Waters was able to raise a little over $50,000 himself while at Cannes in 1979, when he received word that Michael White, who had produced *The Rocky*

Horror Picture Show, wanted to pitch in on the production. With the financial backing of White, New Line Cinema agreed to step in and cover the rest of the cost. By the time the film was completed, the budget ended up at $320,000 (ironically, double the initial budget amount, thereby fitting in with his "doubling" budgets, although not quite in the traditional way where it was based on the budget of his last film). New Line had stipulations for the money, however: the film had to be R-rated (which was fine by Waters, as mentioned earlier in this chapter), use professional music, be filmed with a 35 mm camera, bring Divine back, and find a costar with a recognizable name. Waters was agreeable on all counts. He did find the contract sent to him by New Line funny, however: "I had [a morals clause] with *Polyester*," Waters told James Grant. "New Line had just never taken it out from the standard [contract]. So I called New Line, because it said that I couldn't make a movie that would offend the community. I said, 'Are you kidding? That's what you pay me to do!'"

New Line was on board in 1979, and for the first time, Waters began working on rewrites to one of his scripts. "When writing *Polyester* in Provincetown," Waters recalled to Gerald Peary, "I'd go every day next door to Dennis Dermody's house and we'd watch the 'normal' family on *Father Knows Best*. That's how I was raised. In the *Polyester* script, I tried to subvert it." For those who knew of Waters's love of Douglas Sirk, it was obvious that Waters was looking to parody the epic crisis of suburbia that Sirk brought to the screen in films like *All That Heaven Allows*. (See how often mirrors in

One version of the Odorama card given to theatergoers when they came to see *Polyester*, which was a scratch-and-sniff card that corresponded with numbers that blinked on the screen at certain points during the film.

Francine's house are used—a staple of Sirk's work.) There were also the overly dramatic romantic movies—like *An Unmarried Woman* and others—that became a genre of their own in the late 1970s to make fun of.

Meanwhile, Sara Risher at New Line was trying to make Waters's dream of Smell-O-Vision into reality. A film from 1960 called *Scent of Mystery* used Smell-O-Vision as a gimmick by having odors pumped into theaters at specific points in the film, but it was considered a disaster as the smells took time to reach theater patrons and were thus out of synch with what was being depicted in the scenes. There were attempts to have the smells come out of the seats themselves, but it didn't always work right or the smells were too faint. Also, there was no way to disperse the older odors before newer ones were added, thus turning the theaters into foul-smelling places that had people gasping for air.

Instead, it was decided that *Polyester* would use a scratch-and-sniff card, to be called Odorama, which would be handed to patrons when they entered the theater. The 3M Company agreed to make two million cards for the film, which Risher told them would be "a wholesome family movie." Speaking to John Ives, Risher continued: "I couldn't tell them I wanted fart smells; I had to say I needed rotten eggs or something. When we were finished with the movie, they came to New York to see it, and we never heard from them again. I'm sure they were mortified." The smell of the cards, even before being scratched, could be a bit much to take, as Waters remembered to Claude Thomas Brooks in 1982: "Some of the trucks in New York that were to deliver 500,000 cards refused to do it because of the smell."

The cost? According to Dr. Quackenshaw at the beginning of the film, the cards cost "millions of dollars." However, in reality, the cards cost "a couple of hundred thousand dollars," as per Waters in interviews at the time. Development of the cards was around $35,000, but New Line found that it was the cost of printing and shipping the cards to theaters that they had greatly underestimated. The idea was to "ship x amount to a theater, and have them ship back what they don't need, then send the unneeded ones to the next theater." The problem was that theaters have always been notoriously lazy and cheap when it came to returning promotional material to the studios—it's the main reason so many posters and other items used for movies have found their way into the hands of collectors instead of going back to the studio to be destroyed. New Line would send 2,000 to 3,000 cards to a theater for a week's showing of the film, and when they asked for the cards back, the theater would say they had been destroyed or had gotten lost. This may very well have been true, although many cards worked their way into the collectors' marketplace over the years. And have theaters pay for them? That wasn't going to happen, especially when the movie was being promoted everywhere as having these cards—it would be the studio that would look bad, as the theaters could simply say that they never got the cards. So new cards had to be sent out, and thus what looked to be a cheap gimmick became a rather expensive one for the studio in the end.

Waters was thrilled at audiences' reactions to the cards at the theaters. As he mentioned to the *Guardian*, "The first time I saw everybody scratching and sniffing, I thought, 'Oh, it works!'" He also found their reactions entertaining, as he told Scott MacDonald: "You see the skunk and then the number comes on and you think, 'Oh, no!' But like you paid to get in, so you go ahead and scratch. At least you know you have the choice: you don't have to scratch." As each of the ninety prints of the film made their way across the country, cards for the patrons went with them. When the film aired at theaters in more recent years, the cards were recreated; for a showing at the Edinburgh International Film Festival in June 2011, the cards were made by AromaCo of Wallingford in Oxfordshire, United Kingdom. According to Waters in an interview with the *Guardian* in 1998, original cards from the movie's first run sell for $150–$200 each, although the eventual glut of other versions, even bootleg ones, have brought the price back down a bit over the years. "I've seen some from third world countries," Waters continued in the *Guardian* interview, "where the numbers are crooked because they were put on by hand—it's so depressing!"

The smells used for the theatrical release were:

1. Rose: Dr. Quackenshaw demonstrates the card while smelling a real rose.
2. Flatulence: Elmer passes gas in bed.
3. Airplane glue: Lu-Lu and Bo-Bo are huffing glue in his car.
4. Pizza: Elmer pranks Francine with multiple pizza deliveries.
5. Gasoline: The grandmother gives Francine what appears to be an alcoholic drink, but it turns out to be gasoline.
6. Skunk: A skunk appears when Francine and Cuddles go on a picnic.
7. Natural gas: Francine finds Lu-Lu passed out with her head in the oven.
8. Leather upholstery: Francine smells the upholstery in Todd's car.
9. Dirty shoes: Todd and the grandmother force Francine to smell dirty shoes.
10. Air freshener: With all the bad guys dead, Francine is given air freshener to clear the air.

In June 2003, Paramount released an animated movie based on two cable network Nickelodeon series, *Rugrats* and *The Wild Thornberrys*, called *Rugrats Go Wild*. As a tie-in to the movie, people could go Burger King or Blockbuster and get scratch-and-sniff cards to use in the film, much like in *Polyester*. In fact, Paramount even used the same name for the cards, Odorama, which bothered Waters. As it turns out, New Line had failed to renew the copyright on the name, so it was fair use. One smell was even the same between the two movies: dirty shoes.

Getting Divine wasn't hard, once the money was right. New Line's initial offer to Divine was a flat fee of $5,000. Divine was already talking to John about the role by that point and was inclined to sign when his manager, Bernard Jay, stopped him. As it turns out, Jay had by chance run into Michael White, who was enthusiastic about helping to get *Polyester* made and confessed to doing so namely so he could see Divine in another movie. Knowing that one of the main backers was important for the budget, Jay knew New Line was at least going to listen to their offer and negotiate. Cutting it close to the start of filming in August 1980, Jay requested that Divine be given a fee of $15,000, two percent of the profits, confirmed dates for filming with overtime if it went over, and first star billing above the title. New Line readily agreed and things appeared to be set, but then Divine failed to pass his physical for the film. A $300,000 insurance policy was issued to cover Divine in case his health failed while filming the movie.

There was another insurance concern as well, which went back to the Odorama cards. "The insurance people at New Line were concerned about us distributing Odorama scratch cards for *Polyester*," Waters told the *Hollywood Reporter*. "'What if someone eats one?' they asked. So I called an intern over and said, 'You want to get ahead in the film industry, here, eat one of these.' He chewed it up and they waited a while to make sure nothing terrible happened, and then said, 'OK, we're fine, go ahead.'"

In comparison, negotiations with Tab Hunter (1931–2018) were easier. Hunter had made his name as an actor in the mid-1950s and usually was categorized as a teenage heartthrob, who gradually moved to appearing in summer stock and dinner theater by the 1970s. Both Divine and Waters liked him as an actor, and Waters decided to contact Hunter about the role of Todd Tomorrow in the movie. Hunter liked the script and Hunter told Waters, "Let me wear burgundy polyester." Waters told Hunter that the "leading lady" was a man, but Hunter blew off the news, having more interest in playing a part that was different and fun than concerns about his movie star past. "I have to give Tab Hunter a lot of credit for that because he really had some nerve to make that movie then and he did a great job," Waters told Screenanarchy.com in 2007. "People couldn't believe that Tab had done this and actually kissed Divine in the movie and everything. They wouldn't even show pictures of Divine and Tab together embracing in the magazines."

Waters did have one request for Hunter: "I called him and I said, 'Don't watch *Pink Flamingos,'* because I thought if he saw that, he never would come." Hunter was paid $10,000 for ten days of work on the film, but there was an additional catch—the film was non-union. If Hunter was still part of SAG, he either would not be able to be in it or would cause all the other actors to have to be paid union scale, which would have wiped out the budget. Hunter didn't care, however; he said he was in for the film anyway and arrived to film his part with no issues besides Divine being thrown by working with him. "He was really professional with Divine and the only time I saw Divine nervous was the night before when he knew Tab Hunter was coming the next day and he had to slow dance with him. That was the first scene we filmed: Cuddles's debutante party," Waters told Screenanarchy. com. Hunter enjoyed working with Divine and Waters so much that when he began work on his 1985 movie *Lust in the Dust*, he attempted to get Waters to direct and offered roles to Divine and Edith Massey. (Waters declined and Massey passed away before filming could begin.)

Other roles were done in a more traditional way for Waters—Pat Moran paying for a wanted ad in the *Baltimore Sun*. The ad was the first to not state the upcoming movie was a horror film, but it would also be the last ad Moran would place in the *Baltimore Sun* for one of Waters's movies. The ad stated: "NOW CASTING FOR John Waters film. Parts open—Teenage bad girl and bad boy, Paunchy father, glamorous grandmother & many others."

The movie was a number of firsts for Waters behind the camera. It was the first to be shot in 35 mm (instead of 16 mm and then blown up to 35 mm); the first to be shot in a continuous schedule through the weeks rather than on weekends; and the first to use a video system for Waters to watch all the filming. "I'm right on the set. But I generally watch the actual shot on the TV screen with earphones," he told John Ives. "It was the first time I ever knew about it, or I would have demanded it all along." It was also the first film by Waters that took advantage of product placement, with the company getting cases of Tuborg Beer, Pepsi, Oreos, and other items in trade for placement in the film. Robert Maier says in his book that they got so much stuff that they had a yard sale to make some money for the film and sold off most of the beer to local bars for half price.

Filming started on September 1, 1980, and ran for a total of thirty-one days, finishing at the beginning of November. The first day's shooting involved the aerial shot of the Fishpaw's house, which was done with a helicopter that made one pass successfully and then had an emergency landing on a golf course a short distance away when engine problems developed. The house at 538 Heavitree Hill in Severna Park was rented for two months for $1,000 and was completely refurnished for the movie. Most of the neighbors had no issues with the filming, but one did threaten to sue for a variety of reasons—mostly because the filming was becoming an irritant, although newspaper reports stated a neighbor was upset over a "lesbian scene" shot for the film (which turned out to be a scene of Divine hugging Massey while in character). Tempers were soon calmed and things went smoothly for the rest of the filming. One main location for filming was that of the White Gables Motel at 8781 Veterans Highway in Millersville, Maryland, for the scenes of Elmer and Sandra being caught by Francine. Todd's drive-in was actually the Edmondson Drive-In in Cantonsville, Maryland, which was demolished in 1991.

The car wreck scene where Francine meets Todd caused issues with passersby who thought the accident was real, including at least one person who went into hysterics when they saw the head in the road. Speaking of realism, Jean Hill got so into her role that she actually bit into a tire when she was only supposed to fake biting into it. She ended up losing a front tooth in the process.

After filming was completed, Waters once again worked with Charles Roggero on editing the film. As Bob Maier mentions on his website in a post from March 2012, "Waters was fanatical that his films not exceed ninety minutes. He thought that comedy could not hold an audience longer than that." At least two scenes that were filmed are known to be cut (as photos of their filming exist). The first scene is when Francine tries to sneak past the press at her house by going out the back door. She instead runs into an angry mob of reporters, including George Stover and Steve Yeager, who pin one of her arms back so they can get pictures of her. The other scene deals with Dexter having a relapse after returning home and shaving one eyebrow off. This explains why Dexter suddenly is missing an eyebrow in the final scenes of the movie, and a photo still was issued showing Ken King with the electric razor in his hand taking off the eyebrow.

The entire cast of *Polyester* with director John Waters outside the home used in the film. The staging of the shot is an obvious attempt to pose the cast as happily walking arm in arm, as was so common for publicity photos for films back in the 1950s.

Composer Michael Kamen (1948–2003)—who had worked on New Line's first production, *Stunts*, in 1977—was brought in by New Line to produce a proper score for the film for a total of $10,000. While preparing for his work on the film, Robert Maier met Chris Stein of the band Blondie. At the time, Blondie was a very popular band, with stunningly beautiful Debbie Harry as the lead singer. Maier, sensing a chance for a musical coup for the film, asked Stein if he and Harry would write some material for the film. Stein was immediately committed to the idea, as at the time he was looking to get into scoring films and saw this as a foot in the door. Unfortunately for the film, Harry was contractually unable to sing lead vocals on a song for the movie, but she did contribute three songs and sang backup vocals on one. The three songs were:

- "Polyester": Written by Christ Stein and Deborah Harry. Sung by Tab Hunter.
- "Be My Daddy Baby (Lu-Lu's Theme)": Written by Deborah Harry and Michael Kamen. Sung by Michael Kamen, with backing vocals by Deborah Harry.
- "The Best Thing (Love Song)": Written by Deborah Harry and Michael Kamen. Sung by Bill Murray.

As can be seen, Stein may have been pursued, but Harry contributed a bit more to the film. As for Kamen, he worked with other rock musicians before and since the film, so although he would have rather done the score on his own, it was a situation he was used to being in. Kamen would go on to write scores for films such as *The Dead Zone, Die Hard, Brazil, The Iron Giant*, and *X-Men*, among many others. At first, Waters was a bit peeved about the addition of Stein and Harry, not because of them but because Maier brought the suggestion to New Line, who mandated their material, making Waters feel that he was not in control of his own project. Bill Murray, who had just left *Saturday Night Live* and had just enjoyed huge success in *Meatballs* (1979) and *Stripes* (1981), was a friend of Stein and Harry and sang the vocals for free, which New Line saw as another great investment for the film. Waters would work with Harry again in his next film, *Hairspray*.

Release

Polyester premiered at the Charles in Baltimore on May 15, 1981, and ran until May 28 of that year. It was then officially released throughout New York and New Jersey on May 29, with fifty prints going to theaters in the area. With the fad of "midnight movies" in its final stages, *Polyester* was the first film from Waters that was to run in most parts of the country as a normal feature with multiple showings each day rather than midnight shows on Fridays and Saturdays. The movie would open in Connecticut and Maryland in June and then in North Dakota, South Dakota, and Ohio in August. The premiere in Los Angeles occurred on September 11, 1981, which was also when it popped up in Chicago. It was still popping up in new locations in the United States as late as November 1981, with showings in Rochester, New York. After that, the film would make some rounds at a midnight show or a double feature with one of Waters's earlier films.

The film had a poster with artwork showing Francine holding out a trashcan and a toilet. Collected around these two items was a variety of objects, many of which were items on the scratch-and-sniff cards. Waters reportedly hated the artwork, but it was too late to make changes. When the film was released in some other countries, some posters showed Divine reclining in Tab Hunter's arms, while others showed Francine checking her foot while getting ready for the day, as seen in the beginning of the film. The tagline used on the poster and in the trailer shown in theaters was "Filmed in Odorama—Smelling Is Believing," while the French poster added "You have to ~~see it~~ smell it." The UK movie poster used the tagline, "It'll Blow Your Nose!" The US movie trailer also had the additional tagline, "The Movie that Rips the Pants off Suburbia!"

One final first: *Polyester* was the first Waters film not to face censorship issues when presented to the censorship board in Maryland. Nor did it face any resistance anywhere else in the country. In looking at the film today, some may even wonder how it managed to get an R rating consider there is no nudity or much in the way of profanity in the film.

The movie would be released on videocassette in 1983 by Thorn EMI / HBO Video with a cover showing Divine again in the clutches of Tab Hunter (albeit a different photo than the one used on some movie posters). It was released as part of a double-feature collection on DVD by New Line in 2001, paired with *Desperate Living* and with an Odorama card attached inside the box for use during the film. It would be released again in 2004 as a single DVD with another version of the Odorama card.

Critical response was positive for the most part: *Variety* called the film "a fitfully amusing comedy of not so ordinary people." The *Hollywood Reporter* claimed it was "a funny film which still may be found totally tasteless by many." A reviewer for the *Cincinnati Enquirer* found the combination of the movie with the Odorama card "an experience well worth the money and the labor." *Time* magazine had one of the most positive of reviews, with the reviewer calling Odorama "a wondrous screen gimmick" and claiming the movie in general offered "more honest laughs than *Airplane*." However, that very sense of being toned down upset some of Waters's longtime fans, who felt that Waters was selling out. Waters had gotten used to that line of talk over the years, as he told The *Florida Times-Union* in 2017: "There were some after *Pink Flamingos*, even *Female Trouble*, that said I had sold out, because I guess, what was the next thing you could have done, a snuff movie? I guess they were mad it wasn't a snuff movie." Waters reflected on this further in a 2000 interview with Jamie Painter Young: "When I started, the first thing I ever wanted to do was a successful beatnik movie. Then I wanted to make underground movies, and they didn't have them anymore. Then midnight movies—they didn't have them anymore. Then independent movies. Then Hollywood copied them. Then I made weird Hollywood movies."

With the film out and doing fine in its run, Waters began looking ahead to his next movie, telling multiple sources that it would be a movie where Divine would play triplets, "two women and a man." He would abandon that idea quickly enough and instead concentrate on a sequel to *Pink Flamingos* that he would not abandon until after the death of Edith Massey in late 1984. (See Chapter 20 for more details.)

Instead, he would finally fall back on the "commercial" idea he had back in 1977 about a fifteen-year-old girl with pimples. It would be another six years before that idea would finally make it into theaters.

13

Killing People or Eating

Working at the Patuxent Institution

I think it's ironic that I should get a paycheck from the state of Maryland to rehabilitate criminals by showing them my films.

—John Waters to the *Baltimore Sun*, February 3, 1985

At this point, it should be no surprise to readers that Waters has spent a lifetime attracted to crime and criminals, considering his past interest in attending trials and also considering his interviews, articles, and even friendships with certain "celebrity" criminals. Crime, in some manner, has been the focus of nearly all of his films. (Only *Hairspray* and *Pecker* avoid major criminal activities of one sort or another.) "I discovered I actually enjoyed the company of criminals," Waters told the *Baltimore Sun* in the mid-1980s. "Not because I approved of what they did, but because they fascinated me. I was interested in the difference between them and me. I believe we could all be murderers; what interests me is why some lose that control for that one minute."

This fascination brought about his working with criminals in prison, thanks to a longtime friendship with Havey G. Alexander, a man he first met back in 1964 in the same alley behind the bar where he had become friends with Pat Moran and Maelcum Soul.

Alexander (1935–2012) was a writer and scholar of film, teaching film at the University of Baltimore as well as founding the Baltimore Film Festival. "I first got to know him in 1964 at Martick's," Waters told the *Baltimore Sun* in 2012. "They wouldn't let me in, but I got to know him behind Martick's back in the alley. Harvey was an eccentric intellectual and a real bohemian, but always very friendly. He was a film fanatic." Alexander would later showcase Waters's early films at the university's film festivals, including *The Diane Linkletter Story* in 1970 and *Pink Flamingos* in 1972.

By the early 1980s, Alexander was teaching an English class at the maximum security Patuxent Institution in Jessup, Maryland. The institution first opened in 1955 as housing not for "career criminals"—those who had fallen into a life of crime—but typically for those who had perpetrated one violent crime and were under psychological care. (Waters told NPR in 2009, "It wasn't for people that pled insanity but it was for people that maybe should've.") The focus was thus on trying to motivate the prisoners toward bettering their mental and social chances in the outside world if released.

Knowing of Alexander's work at the institution, Waters offered to be a guest teacher at one of his classes in the spring of 1983. Knowing how well *Female Trouble* had gone over with the prisoners at the Baltimore County Jail in 1974, Waters brought the movie to show to the inmates at the Patuxent Institution, where he was shocked to discover that the inmates looked like a class found at a junior college rather than rough, tough inmates. The showing of the film went over as well as it had in 1974 at the county jail, and Waters—with the help of Alexander—petitioned the warden, Norma Gluckstern, to teach writing and acting classes with a number of prisoners who requested such a class. As Waters points out in *Crackpot*, the warden looked over the list of prisoners and remarked that many were there for the "most heinous of crimes" even though many of them had the highest IQs.

Teaching a class once or twice a week during a four-year period, Waters would arrive with one of his films and a projector to show it. Then he would discuss aspects of writing or his films, he would do improv—anything to reach the prisoners. "I tried to be a good teacher," Waters told Becky Fritter in 2008, "and motivate my students to write well and participate. We screened a lot of films, like *Pink Flamingos*. We did a lot of improv, and I feel like it was a success overall and that I was a good teacher." Waters has remarked in a few places that the showing of *Pink Flamingos* was an event in itself, as the final scene were Divine eats dog feces sent all the African-American prisoners out of their seats and running from the room. Other films shown were *The Evil Dead*, *Fat City*, *Wiseblood*, *Freaks*, and *Even Dwarfs Started Small*.

One aspect of the class was having the prisoners do improvisations in which they played characters that were different from themselves. Writing was also expected, and the students worked on screenplays, including a group project called *Reckless Eyeballs* (also known as *Rotten Apples*). Waters also introduced them to the ways of low-budget filmmaking. "I'm talking serious low budget, we shot the films in the camera with no editing," Waters told Becky Fritter. "We'd do a take, and wait for a song to come on the radio to use as a soundtrack. There were no costumes, just whatever the students could grab. The bikers played the girls, the black people played the rich people, and the white people played the servants. Everything was backwards."

While Waters at times worried if he was doing it more for himself rather than the students, it did seem to help some of the men to find an outlet, other than crime, for their anger and frustration. Waters mentioned to the *Baltimore Sun* in 1985: "I tell them, 'The next time you want to murder someone, don't do it, write about it, paint it, make a film about it. These films are my crimes and I get paid for it.'" Over time, the prisoners began to trust him, and Waters felt that he did help some of them progress. Even so, he did recall one student who talked about his rehabilitation while eating lunch with Waters, but when someone saw the empty plate in front of him and asked him if he was finished, he replied, "What? ... Killing people or eating?"

Although there were no complaints about the program, after four years the institution decided to stop it. Waters has run into some of his former students outside of prison over the years, however, at book signings and elsewhere. Some have done better than others. "One of my best students got out after serving twenty-nine years and he's doing very well," Waters told NPR. "Another got out and killed two more people. Although it's impossible to tell who's going to behave a certain way, and I had no say in their sentences whatsoever, maybe it's better that way, because I was certainly surprised at the one who did get out and killed more people. He was actually in *Serial Mom*."

The classes came at a good time for Waters as well. His script for a *Pink Flamingos* sequel, covered more in-depth in a later chapter, had gotten nowhere in the 1980s and, with Edith Massey's death in October 1984, had fallen apart. Instead, his focus began turning back to memories of his youth, leading him back to the dance show he used to watch as a teenager. With the demise of the classes at the institution, Waters began to throw himself into his new script, which would eventually become a film in 1988 and would, for some of his fans, eclipse the impact he made with *Pink Flamingos*.

14

How to Tease

The Making of *Hairspray*

> I want to sneak all my most humorous pernicious ideas into the most mainstream thing I could possibly do. To make a Hollywood movie that's at the same time a John Waters movie.
>
> —John Waters to the *Baltimore Sun*, October 5, 1986

Plot

The year is 1962 and the place is *The Corny Collins Show* at WZZT in Baltimore. The program is a local dance show in the city, much like *American Bandstand*, but with local teenage dancers—called the council—who have their own fans. Corny (Shawn Thompson) hosts the program, with his trusted assistant Tammy (Mink Stole) keeping the kids in line. The head dance couple on the program is the easygoing Link (Michael St. Gerard) and the stuck-up Amber (Colleen Fitzpatrick).

While the kids who dance on the show are arriving to get ready for that day's episode, Tracy Turnblad (Ricki Lake) races home from school with her best friend, Penny Pingleton (Leslie Ann Powers), to watch the show. Tracy lives with her father, Wilbur (Jerry Stiller), and mother, Edna (Divine), above her father's joke shop, the Hardy-Har. Edna is devoted to her daughter, and while she doesn't understand Tracy's fascination for *The Corny Collins Show* and the music being played, she accepts it. Penny's mother, Prudence (Jo Ann Havrilla), thinks it's the gateway to crime and Hell, however, and is angry with Penny for not obeying her every whim.

Amber's dominating mother, Velma Von Tussle (Debbie Harry), forces Amber to practice the dances and does not like the idea that songs by black artists are picked on the show for the dances. Meanwhile, her father, Franklin Von Tussle (Sonny Bono), is opening a "whites only" amusement park and needs Amber to push his flyers at the dances around town that the members of the council attend to help promote the show.

Tracy and Penny go to a hop that night at the VFW, where they discover that two black kids who came to dance are turned away at the door. They go in anyway and Tracy soon is dancing the Madison between Link and Amber. At the hop with Corny is also Motormouth Maybelle (Ruth Brown), who hosts the television program once a month for "Negro Day," and she judges a dance competition that ends up being between Amber and Tracy with their partners. Tracy wins the applause of the others and the hatred of Amber, who doesn't like not being number one. Many of the other kids seem to like Tracy, however, and Corny invites her to come down to the station the next day for tryouts for a spot as a dancer on the show.

Penny and Tracy try out with another girl, Nadine (Dawn Hill), who is excellent as a dancer and had been on the program during its once-a-month "Negro Day" episodes, but because she is black, many of the council just laugh her off for trying to integrate the "regular" show. Even with their dismissive attitude, however, Corny and his assistant, Tammy, give knowing looks to each other and appreciate Nadine's attempt to break through. It is clear that both of them would be happy to have the program integrated if

Divine as Edna Turnblad in *Hairspray*, his last role for John Waters. Waters had originally envisioned Divine playing both Edna and daughter Tracy, but by the time production was to commence, it was decided that Ricki Lake should play the younger role instead.

possible. When Amber starts making remarks about Tracy's appearance, Corny calls her out and tells her she is off the program that day for being out of line.

Soon after, Penny runs to Tracy's home and has her parents watch the next episode of *The Corny Collins Show*, in which Tracy appears as one of the dancers, having obviously won the tryouts. Amber may have been mad before, but she's livid when Tracy picks Link for the "Ladies' Choice" dance. Tracy gets an immediate offer to model clothes for Hefty Hideaway, a clothing store "for the ample woman," from the owner, Mr. Pinky (Alan J. Wendl), which she accepts with the help of Edna. The two then get a makeover.

Things may appear to be looking up, but trouble is brewing at school, where Amber begins to spread rumors about Tracy, while Tracy runs into problems because of her "ratted up" hair and ends up in the special education class. There she meets Motormouth's son, Seaweed (Clayton Prince), and introduces him to Penny. Soon enough, Penny becomes smitten by Seaweed, just as Link asks Tracy to go steady.

Link takes Tracy and Penny to Motormouth's record store, where several kids are dancing up a storm. Penny's mother follows her and freaks out that her daughter is in a predominately African-American neighborhood and dancing with Seaweed. A few days later, Penny and Seaweed take L'il Inez, Seaweed's sister, to "Pre-Teen Day" on the show, but the security refuse to let them in because the show is segregated. When Tracy hears about this, she goes with Link to protest with the trio outside the studio, leading to Amber's mom asking Edna if Tracy is "mulatto" and Edna shaking Velma violently. Corny and Tammy argue with a WZZT official (David Samson) and station owner Arvin Hodgepile (Divine) about letting the little girl in, but they refuse.

That night, Link, Penny, and Tracy join Seaweed at a dance hosted by Motormouth and featuring Toussaint McCall singing his hit "Nothing Takes the Place of You" (which was actually recorded in 1967, so it's an anachronism in the film). The two couples go to an alley to make out, but they are interrupted by Tracy's parents, who have been looking for them. The four make a run for it and find shelter in a beatnik couple's place (the couple is played by Ric Ocasek and Pia Zadora) but soon leave in fear of possible drug use. Back on the streets, the parents of Tracy and Penny corner them. Penny's parents have a quack psychiatrist, Dr. Fredrickson (John Waters), with them, and they drag Penny away, promising to make her "all better."

The next day is the big *Corny Collins Show* at the grand opening of Tilted Acres, an amusement park owned by Amber's father. There is a protest outside of the park, as the park is segregated, which is fine with the television station owner, who is there and monitoring things to make sure Collins doesn't try to sneak in "one black face on the air." Going on the air, Collins introduces Tracy and Amber as the top contenders in the Miss Auto Show contest. Both introduce dances on the show, with Amber doing the Limbo Rock and Tracy doing the Waddle. Right after Amber declares, on the air, that Tracy has roaches, a white supremacist outside the park lights a cherry bomb, panic breaks out, and a riot ensues. Collins, Tammy, and Link are all hurt, while Tracy is dragged away by the police for trying to defend Link.

At Penny's place, she desperately tries to straighten her hair like a beatnik as creepy Dr. Fredrickson uses his hypnosis wheel and a futuristic cattle prod to get Penny not to like Seaweed any longer. A bandaged Seaweed arrives and breaks her out of her room. Meanwhile, at the Montrose Reformatory for Girls, Tracy is also straightening her hair and sees Link on television at the hospital, pledging his love for her.

At the Auto Show the next day, the governor opens the exhibition and is met with opposition from Tracy's family and others who want Tracy released from the reformatory. When the governor arrives back at his mansion, Motormouth and L'il Inez handcuff themselves to the governor and demand Tracy be released. Back at

Franklin Von Tussle (Sonny Bono) goes terrorist with the help of Velma (Debbie Harry). Bono was happy to be in the film, although he jokingly told Waters that he expected that once he left the room, "thirty people were going to run in and eat dog shit."

the Auto Show, Amber's parents have snuck in a bomb, hidden in Amber's mother's hairdo, and plan to use it at the show if Amber doesn't win the Miss Auto Show competition. The station owner tells everyone on the show being filmed at the Auto Show that Tracy won the contest, but since she is in reform school, the honors went to Amber. Amber announces that she will do a new dance called The Roach in honor of Tracy.

The governor pardons Tracy. She leaves the reform school and arrives while Amber is still doing The Roach. The crowd—no longer segregated—follows Tracy to the dance area in front of the cameras and begins to dance, thus integrating the show. Collins is so happy that he hugs and kisses his assistant Tammy, to her surprise. As Amber's parents scream at Amber to leave with them, Tracy comes back out wearing a new dress—pink and covered with drawings of roaches—from Hefty Hideaway. As everyone in the room begins to do The Bug (done by acting as if covered in bugs), the bomb goes off in Velma's hair, sending her hair flying across the room and onto Amber's face. With Amber's parents being arrested and Amber struggling to get the hair off her head, Tracy takes her rightful place on the throne. Her first proclamation? "Let's dance."

Claims to Condemnation

- Minor transgressions: vomit, lewd dancing, possible drug use, mild profanity. Some, sadly, would probably still protest interracial dating and dancing.

Additional Cast and Crew

Waters originally envisioned the Von Tussles' mother and daughter with Joey Heatherton and Pia Zadora playing the respective roles. Heatherton passed on the offer but would finally appear in Waters's next film, *Cry-Baby*. Zadora bailed on the role of Amber, mostly because she didn't like the part. "He wanted me to play the prom queen, but I was on tour," Zadora told John Ives. "I didn't really want to play the prom queen, anyway; I wanted to do something a little more mature and sophisticated. So I said, 'I'd love to, but I can't because I'm on tour.'" Zadora did agree to play a cameo in the film if Waters could squeeze her in between tour dates in Philadelphia and Washington,

D.C., which Waters readily set up. Zadora had no idea what her part would be and went into filming her scene as a beatnik without any preparation.

Ric Ocasek, who has had a musical career as both a solo artist and as a member of the rock band the Cars, makes his only appearance in a Waters movie, playing the other beatnik with Zadora. Rumors circulated in late 1987 that Waters would be directing the Car's music video for their single "You Are the Girl," with Divine appearing, but nothing came of it.

In an interview with James Grant in 1994, Waters remembered talking with others for the mother and daughter Van Tussle roles who turned him down, including Mamie Van Doren, who "said that she deserved better than Divine," and Lisa Marie Presley. Stockard Channing also turned down a role, but it is unclear what part she would have played. Instead, Colleen Fitzpatrick played Amber, "the queen." Fitzpatrick was a professional dancer who turned sixteen at the time of the production. She would go on to begin a recording career—first with a band called Eve's Plum, which released two albums between 1993 and 1995, and as Vitamin C, a stage name under which she recorded an album entitled *Vitamin C* in 1999, which reached Platinum level in sales. She presently works as Vice President of Music for the children's cable network Nickelodeon.

The two competing families of *Hairspray*: the Turnblads, played by Jerry Stiller, Ricki Lake, and Divine, versus the Von Tussles, played by Debbie Harry, Colleen Fitzpatrick, and Sonny Bono.

Debbie Harry returned for her second and last film with Waters, this time in front of the camera as Velma Von Tussle. Sonny Bono was a bit of a surprise to some fans, considering Bono was known as a conservative Republican who was seriously looking to run for political office, which seemed contrary to Waters's personality. However, Bono fit the bill for the part, was a well-remembered name, could act, and was easygoing. "He was great," Waters told Screenanarchy.com. "He kept saying that he thought I was going to trick him; as soon as he'd leave the room—thirty people were going to run in and eat dog shit. He'd keep saying, 'Is there some scene you haven't told me that's in this movie?'" Bono, Harry, and Jerry Stiller were the first celebrities besides Divine to be announced for the film, with Harry announced in May and Bono and Stiller announced in early June.

Ruth Brown (1928–2006) was a singer-songwriter known for her work in rhythm and blues, as well as soul music. In the 1970s, she began doing some acting roles, which naturally led her to a project such as *Hairspray*, although some conflict did take place. "At first," Brown told the *Chicago Tribune* in April 1988, "John Waters and I had our differences. I didn't like dressing up in a crazy blond wig. But Divine, God bless him, mediated between us. He put his arm around me and said, 'Don't worry, Ruth. For every fan that you lose there are two more that you'll win.' And it's true. This film has brought Ruth Brown to a whole new generation."

Her character of Motormouth was based on a real-life disc jockey from the era, Paul Johnson, professionally known as Fat Daddy. "In Baltimore, Fat Daddy was the biggest disc jockey on WSID and hosted [the monthly] 'Negro Day' on *The Buddy Deane Show*," Waters said to the *Washington Post* in December 2004. "Fat Daddy's real name was Paul Johnson, and he wore a long cloak and an Imperial margarine crown." Waters would later hunt down Fat Daddy's recording of "Fat Daddy (Is Santa Claus)" for his compilation album *A John Waters Christmas*. "He saved my life in high school, just listening to him every day on WSID."

Divine was initially to perform in the roles of Tracy and Edna. However, New Line was hesitant to have Divine as a teenager making out with a sixteen-year-old boy in the film. Waters was also uncertain, and it is clear from earlier interviews going back to the initial days of even thinking of the project that Waters visualized the movie with a real teenage girl rather than Divine. Fortunately, according to Bernard Jay in his book on Divine, Divine wasn't feeling like he was right for the part of Tracy either and elected to take the part of Edna alone. Jay, as Divine's manager, knew that Divine rarely read anything else in a script other than his own part and probably did not know of the part of the station owner. Jay brought it to Divine's attention and then asked if Divine could do that role as well in order to get another male part on his CV to help with future roles. Everyone was amicable to the suggestion.

With that out of the way, the production still had to find someone to play Tracy, who they eventually found with Ricki Lake, a young local singer and dancer who had done little in the way of acting. "I was terrified about who was going to play Tracy," Waters told *Film Journal*, "because if you don't like her you won't like the movie. Ricki was almost like Tracy for real. And she was never uptight about being fat. She said she hated that the only roles offered to her were sensitive, unhappy fat girls—she was sick of playing them." Lake looked back on the film in 2016 and agreed with Waters's assessment to *People* magazine: "She is so much who I was in my teens, so much of my persona. I watch the film, and it was just me dressed in clothes from 1962."

Lake at first found herself at odds with Divine, who—even though he knew it made little sense—saw Lake as a bit of a usurper to his position in Waters's films (perhaps understandably so, as it was the first time in quite a while that Divine was not the star of one of Waters's films). The ice was broken when Divine saw that Lake was not used to wearing heels, and he began marching her up and down to get her used to wearing them in a manner that looked appealing. Lake found filming such hard work that she began to lose weight, which forced her to eat more in order to regain the weight needed for her look in the film. Divine was happy to help her out in eating, coming up to Lake and saying, "C'mon, Ricki, let's go eat a roast! Let's go eat a pie!"

This was the first film featuring Alan J. Wendl, who plays Mr. Pinky, and would go on to appear in every one of Waters's films after this. It is also the first appearance of Rosemary Knower, who plays Mrs. Shipley, the special ed teacher, and Doug Roberts, who plays Paddy Pingleton, Penny's father. They'll both skip *Cry-Baby* but will appear in every Waters film after that.

Of the old Dreamlanders, Mink Stole has the rare chance to play a positive character in one of Waters's films, portraying Corny's assistant, Tammy. Susan Lowe pops up briefly as an angry mom who hits her daughter with her purse after leaving the principal's office. Mary Vivian Pearce has one line as a mother of a youngster telling Seaweed and Penny that they're holding up the line on "Pre-Teen Day." George Stover also turns up as one of the policemen at the Governor's mansion, as does Chuck Yeaton and Peter Koper (who had loaned Waters his farm for *Desperate Living*).

One later Dreamlander who would have been perfect for the film but is missing is that of Jean Hill. Waters had written a small role for her—most probably Nadine's mother in the cut scene where Penny and Seaweed are

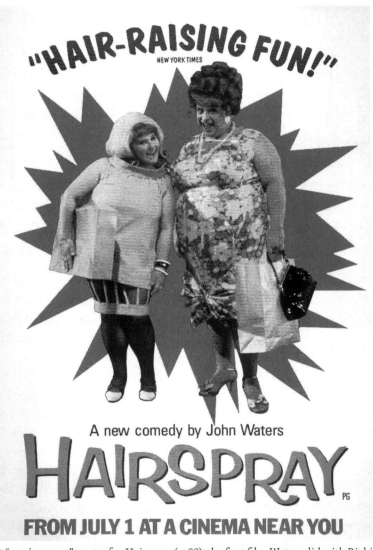

A "coming soon" poster for *Hairspray* (1988), the first film Waters did with Ricki Lake and the last with Divine. Divine helped teach Ricki how to walk in heels and keep the pounds on when Lake began losing weight during the filming.

hiding out in Nadine's basement—but Hill was unable to appear due to health reasons. She will return in *A Dirty Shame*.

While Waters had done voice-over work before and after *Hairspray*, the film would be the only time he appears on-camera in one of his films besides a brief cameo in *Serial Mom* as a reporter.

Production

Waters tried—stupidly tried, as he has frequently said in later years—to get *Flamingos Forever* off the ground after filming *Polyester*. (See Chapter 20 for more details.) As 1985 came around, he finally saw the light and realized that the project was never going to happen, and if he wanted to get back into making movies, he had better come up with something quickly. That brought him back to an old script idea dealing with memories of his youth about the heydays of *The Buddy Deane Show*, a local Baltimore dance program of the late 1950s and early 1960s. It was a show he loved so much that he wrote about it and interviewed former cast members of the show for his book *Crackpot*. Mixed in with those happy memories was the knowledge that there was segregation occurring in the city, which kept people of different races from mixing together. "I really wanted to bring that in because nobody makes comedies about that subject—it's really a touchy subject," Waters told Kevin Lally in 1988. "But all that stuff did happen. To ignore that would be untruthful about that period—they just didn't have blacks on those shows. It's a very unpleasant subject, an embarrassing subject for the people who are from that period."

Waters went first to New Line Cinema with the project and, surprisingly, was turned down. Not wanting to give up on it, Waters developed a ten-minute pitch for the film and went to the studios and possible other backers. "I would startle them by just jumping up and doing the Watusi or something, just show them the dance, and they would look at me all embarrassed. But you have to pitch a movie, you know?" he told the *Guardian*. Eventually, Waters found a potential backer, but two months into pre-production, the backer sold the project back to New Line Cinema, who agreed to a $2 million budget for the film in May 1987. Product placement by Pepsi, as in *Polyester*, once again helped cover some of the budget.

One major upside to the film was that there was now enough money to do things above the board and bring in the unions. Actors belonging to SAG, who had experience playing roles on-camera, replaced friends and neighbors that usually played roles in Waters's earlier films. The crew was also made up of all professionals and things could be done in a manner that didn't depend on some amateurs learning to use ancient equipment on a moment's notice. However, there was a downside. "The more money you have, the harder it is, because there's more people, more pressure," Waters told the *Morning Call* while filming was going on in 1987. "You have to deal with producers. When I made those old movies, they were home movies, basically. I just went out into a field and made it. The crew was one other person."

As standard, Pat Moran began looking for actors for several of the roles, and although there would be no "help wanted" ad for this film like Waters's films from the 1970s, Moran did get the auditions mentioned in the *Baltimore Sun* a couple of times. Auditions for young people to play members of the Corny Collins Council occurred in April 1987, followed by auditions for extras in May.

The music budget for the film was originally set at $150,000, but New Line agreed to increase that amount to closer to $450,000 in order to get music rights for the real songs of the period rather than have an original soundtrack created for the film. The only original song was the theme song, which was cowritten and performed by Rachel Sweet; all others were songs written around the time period of when the film takes place.

Filming began on June 1, 1987, at the Dorney Park and Wild Water Kingdom in Allentown, Pennsylvania—a rare excursion outside of the Baltimore area for Waters. This was where the scenes for the Tilted Acres amusement park were shot, as Dorney Park had enough old-fashion rides that with some clever shooting it could look like it came out of 1962. This scene also involved the many extras needed for the riot scene in the park and thus allowed the crew to get the biggest scene for the film out of the way first (besides filming on the one day of the week the park was closed—Monday). Some additional filming happened on the Tuesday as well, thanks to weather issues the first day. A sequence shot where Motormouth chases the Van Tussles onto a bumper-car ride and repeatedly rams them featured one of the original Buddy Deane dancers, Mary Lou Barber, and took most of a day to film. The cast and crew then spent time riding a few of the rides in the closed park to finish out their last day there.

The first week of filming also involved interior scenes shot at Perry Hall High School at 4601 Ebenezer Road in Nottingham, Maryland, where Tracy is reprimanded and sent to "special ed" class because of her hair. (The crew would return at a later date for a couple more days of filming after school ended for the year.) Exterior high school scenes for the dodgeball game occurred at Mergenthaler Vocational Technical Senior High School at 3500 Hilen Road in Baltimore. Other locations were:

- Tracy's home and the location of the Hardy-Har were located at 100 N. Luzeme Avenue, Baltimore.
- The Von Tussles lived at 209 S. Clinton Avenue, Baltimore.
- Hefty Hideaway was, at the time, Stella's Bridal, located at 3309 Eastern Avenue, Baltimore.
- Just a skip away from Stella's was the El Dorado Beauty Academy at 3301 Eastern Avenue, Baltimore, where Edna and Tracy get their makeover after visiting Hefty Hideaway.
- The Baltimore County Jail at 222 Courthouse Court in Towson was used as the Montrose Reformatory for Girls.
- The house used for the governor's mansion is located at 514 East Seminary Avenue in Towson.
- The film's television station WZZT was located at 1140 E. Cold Spring Lane in Baltimore. This was also the home of Flitet 3 Studios, which did many local commercials, making it the perfect place for filming interiors of the set for *The Corny Collins Show*. The location was also used for some soundstage work in the film *Cecil B. DeMented*.

Filming concluded on July 24, 1987, and there was a wrap party at Hopkins Glass House that evening. That same day, the *Baltimore Sun* contained a garage sale ad at Pier 1 on Clinton Street, where the production was selling off "props used in the making of John Waters's movie *Hairspray*." Included in the sale were 1950s-era furniture, clothing, and antiques, as well as the "car of the future" that Amber rides around in near the end of the film.

Editing started soon after, and for the first time on one of his films, Waters was not 100 percent hands-on for the editing. "I told him we didn't have time for that," *Hairspray* producer Rachel Talalay told John Ives after the process. "That the editor would edit the film and he would look at their assembly." Janice Hampton, who would edit Waters's next three movies, was brought on board to do the editing for Waters. "Editors had to wean all that stuff away from me," Waters admitted to John Ives. "In the beginning I just did it myself. And it was hard to edit—there weren't a lot of choices in *Pink Flamingos* because of the single system. The choices were: 'Do I cut this out or not?'"

As always, Waters made it a priority to keep the film around ninety minutes in length. To do that, he had to cut several scenes as well as prune the film's material. Waters has typically released book-form versions of his scripts that are edited to match that of the films, but, surprisingly, for the release of his 2005 book *Hairspray, Female Trouble, and Multiple Maniacs: Three MORE Screenplays by John Waters*, the script for *Hairspray* appears complete and includes scenes and dialogue cut from the film. The cut scenes include:

- Amber does an ad on *The Corny Collins Show* for Tilted Acres, telling everyone that its grand opening will be June 1 (ironically, the same month and day filming started on *Hairspray*).
- A scene in which Tracy is forced to not only work in her father's store but made to be the victim of several gag gifts (joy buzzer, whoopee cushion). When customers arrive, Tracy does the same to them, making them leave in tears. She demands money from the last customer, causing him to run in fear. "Thanks for not buying anything!" she shouts as the scene closes. This scene, a favorite of Jerry Stiller, was shot at the real store Hardy-Har was based on. It was only when seeing the completed film with an audience that Stiller realized the scene had been cut from the film. Looking at it, it was probably cut because it makes Tracy's parents seem rather unsympathetic and shows a nasty streak to Tracy that isn't really there anywhere else in the film. (Ricki Lake does get to say the "Thanks for not buying anything" line in *Serial Mom* when a woman leaves without a purchase at her swap meet table.)
- After the dance where Tracy wins the contest with Fender, she is making out with him in the parking lot when Amber and Link come by. Link is about to get into a fight with some gang members when Tracy saves him with her can of hairspray, spraying it in the faces of the attackers.
- Tracy shows off her hickey that she got from Fender the next day at school. She mentions allowing Fender to dry-hump her leg so he wouldn't have "blue balls." Having Amber see her the night before ties into Amber telling her classmates about her being nude in a car, which does appear in the film. She's lying, of course, but she does have a real incident to stretch the truth from. The script has her going on to say that Tracy is a nymphomaniac, however.
- Tracy skips school to be ready for the audition that day, and she shoplifts shoes when a snooty shop owner tells her that the store doesn't have anything in her size. Looking for a place to "hang low," she breaks into

Amber's house to dye her hair blonde. She snoops through Amber's things while doing so. While the scene does explain how Tracy suddenly appears with her hair partially blonde, and even presents her shoplifting sympathetically, it still could have been a turnoff for the general audience, so this scene was, as Waters states in his book, "wisely cut out of the final product."

- The reaction shots of the kids being grossed out by Amber making out with the singer on Pre-Teen Day were cut, as they simply didn't work the way Waters had planned.

- When Tracy is picked up by her folks in the "bad neighborhood," Edna tries to lecture her and instead gets a lecture from Tracy about being as racist as the others. She threatens to run away to Mississippi to be a freedom fighter but is stopped. The scene does show why her parents switch their attitude and become members of the NAACP soon after.

- A sequence filmed but cut showed a roach crawling out of Tracy's hair when she is introducing The Waddle at the amusement park. (So in this context, Amber wasn't simply being a jerk, there really was a roach in Tracy's hair.) The scene was cut when Bob Shaye of New Line saw it and said to Waters, "What is this? A [Luis] Buñuel film?" (See Chapter 5 for more details on this director.)

- A sequence shot at the amusement park where Motormouth chases down the Von Tussles on the bumper-car ride took most of a day to film and was ultimately cut.

- Nadine returns to the film at this point when Seaweed and Penny arrive at her house to hide after Penny breaks out of her house. Nadine is hardly happy to see them, especially as "hairhoppers" like Penny are supposed to have roaches in their hair. When Nadine's mother sees Penny, she immediately reaches for the roach spray and blinds both Seaweed and Penny with it as they stumble away from the house.

- Dance sequences were dropped as well, including ones for "The Push 'n' Kick" and "The Stupidity." At least "The Madison" made it in to the film, which was only proper, as the dance really did originate in Baltimore.

Release

Waters had hoped for the film to get a PG-13 rating in order to allow more people to see the film. He was surprised when it got a PG. "I made a family movie," Waters told the *Baltimore Sun* in 2000. "It was a PG—a shock. I remember when it got a PG rating; I wanted to commit suicide." After years of fighting censors over shots of fake vaginas and chicken deaths, Waters had made a film that anyone could see. To some of his older fans, this reeked of selling out, but Waters looked to the film as being even more rebellious than his earlier ones. "Subversive, to me," he told Jamie Painter Young, "is the fact that *Hairspray* became one of the best-selling videos for children's birthday parties and it starred a drag queen. That's subversive."

Initial hopes were to release the film in January 1988, and as it was, the film did get a sneak preview at the Wiltern Theatre in Los Angeles on January 17, 1988, with additional showings on January 21 and 23. The movie had a second sneak preview at the Miami Film Festival in Fort Lauderdale, Florida, on February 7, 1988. The official premiere of the film took place on February 16 at the Senator in Baltimore, and it was a televised extravaganza featuring Divine, Waters, Moran, and cast members. The film played in Baltimore a few times over the next week and a half before the film was released coast to coast on February 26, 1988. Such a nationwide opening was a first for Waters, who had seen all his previous films pop up in regional release through distribution methods of his own or through those of others.

The poster for the film showed only the legs of two dancers, along with the tagline "1962 ... JFK was in the White House ... John Glenn was in orbit ... Cadillacs had fins ... Beehives were in ... And girls really knew how to tease!" This was subsequently replaced with a number of snippets from the many positive reviews for the film. To Waters's surprise, no one seemed to care either way about the film's positive statements about integration and the Civil Rights movement, nor its occasional—albeit very mild—digs at the actions of certain protestors at the time. "Nobody was ever offended by that," Waters told John Ives. "I don't think I got one review in the whole world that was offended by that. [Making fun of] the sacred cow wasn't as strong as I thought, which is probably one of the reasons for its success." The film opened in nearly eighty theaters across the country, and with the positive reviews and strong ticket sales, it appeared that Waters had made a film that was to be remembered as a happy experience for all.

Then Divine died a little over a week after the film was released. "*Hairspray* had been out a week," Waters told Screenanarchy.com, "and so it ruined the joy of that because we had just done a press tour through the whole country. Everybody had news footage of us laughing and then they'd cut to the funeral. Who wants to see *that* movie?" Further damage came when New Line decided to bump the number of theaters showing the film to over two hundred on March 11; this was a huge jump in theaters when the film probably would have done better had it been slowly released across the country, building interest by word-of-mouth.

RCA/Columbia Pictures released the movie on videocassette in 1989, followed by a re-release in 1996 by New Line. 2002 saw the film released by New Line on DVD, while a Blu-ray edition occurred in 2014.

The film overall was deemed a success, even with those hiccups, and would make over $8 million on a budget of $2 million. From this, Waters would have studios suddenly after him for his next film after years of being dismissed. Things were in motion for Waters to do another pet project, *Hatchet Face*, but *Hairspray* would eventually find a life of its own in the early 2000s.

Broadway

In January 1990 it was announced that producer Scott Rudin had obtained the rights to develop a stage show based on *Hairspray*. "This has been in the works for a long time," Waters told the *Baltimore Sun*, "and I think it has all the elements for a great musical. What we need is a fifteen-year-old Ethel Merman to play the lead." Then . . . nothing. According to a May 8, 2002, article in the *Baltimore Sun*, "Rudin let the rights lapse, and *Hairspray* seemed to have fizzled out."

Margo Lion had already established herself as a successful independent Broadway producer by the time she considered turning *Hairspray* into a musical. She produced the two-part *Angels in America* for Broadway in 1993 and was behind the successful musical *Jelly's Last Jam* in 1992, among others, but had just come off the demise of a musical called *Triumph of Love* in early 1998 when she happened upon a showing of *Hairspray* on television. She had dismissed the film when seeing it in 1988 but now had second thoughts while watching it on television. "I couldn't figure out what it was about," Lion told the *New York Times* in 2002. "I realized I had been very square in 1988. Halfway through, I literally said: 'Yes, this is it. I found it.'"

"It combines all the things I love," Lion told the *Baltimore Sun* in 2000. "A wonderful comedy that has kind of a delicious and fresh style and it also is a story that's about something, which is the push for integration in Baltimore." Speaking with the *New York Times*, Lion recounted meeting with Waters, when she promised, "I will always try and honor your voice. I will not make a generic Broadway show." She then handed him a cassette tape that had four songs for the proposed musical, with Nathan Lane singing the part of Edna Turnblad. "And I have that tape," Waters told the *Fort Myers News-Press*. "I guess that's a collector's item, right?" Waters soon agreed to the production.

Lion had prepared by bringing in Marc Shaiman to work on the music. Shaiman had begun his career working with Bette Midler back in 1979 and had been a regular contributor to *Saturday Night Live* in the 1980s. He had also written music for such films as *South Park: Bigger, Longer & Uncut* and

The soundtrack album for the 2016 live network broadcast of the musical version of *Hairspray*. The Broadway musical would run for over six years before being turned into a movie musical of its own in 2007.

Team America: World Police, making him a strong candidate for irreverent musical material in the show. Soon enough lyricist Scott Wittman joined him to write on the project as well. The book for the musical was initially given to Mark O'Donnell, and then Thomas Meehan, who, fresh off the success of writing the book for Mel Brooks's *The Producers*, came in to help punch up the dialogue a bit.

Previews began on July 18, 2002, on a production budget of $10.5 million. Cast in the musical was Harvey Fierstein as Edna, Marissa Jaret Winokur as Tracy, Laura Bell Bundy as Amber, Kerry Butler as Penny, Dick Latessa as Wilbur Turnblad, and Mary Bond Davis as Motormouth Maybelle. By the time the musical opened on August 15, 2002, there were already ticket sales of $2 million—strong signs that the production would be a success.

Hairspray would run on Broadway until January 4, 2009. It would go on to win eight Tony Awards out of twelve nominations at the 2003 ceremonies. The awards it won were:

- Best Musical
- Best Book of a Musical: Mark O'Donnell and Thomas Meehan
- Best Original Score: Marc Shaiman and Scott Wittman
- Best Actor in a Musical: Harvey Fierstein
- Best Actress in a Musical: Marissa Jaret Winokur
- Best Features Actor in a Musical: Dick Latessa
- Best Costume Design: William Ivey Long
- Best Direction of a Musical: Jack O'Brien

The musical also won ten Drama Desk Awards in 2003, including awards in many of the same categories as it won for the Tonys.

As is understandable for a live production, some of the storyline and positioning of scenes had to change to accommodate there simply not being enough time and space to do everything that appears in the film. The audience is first introduced to Tracy in the first song, "Good Morning Baltimore," only for the film to switch immediately to the filming of an episode of *The Corny Collins Show*. Other changes include:

- Velma Von Tussle, Amber's mother, is now the television station manager.
- Tammy is now one of the dancers rather than Collins's assistant.
- The program is getting ready for a national broadcast on June 6, when Miss Teenage Hairspray 1962 will be crowned.
- It is announced that one of the girl dancers will have to leave the show "for nine months," so auditions will be done the next day at the station.

- Tracy meets Seaweed in detention before joining the dancers on the show.
- Spritzer—a new character—is the president of Ultra Clutch, the hairspray sponsor for the program.
- Velma, Amber, and Edna—rather than Penny's mom—break in on the party at the record store.
- Tracy plans to have Motormouth and her daughter appear on the "mother-daughter" episode of the show, thus bringing integration into the program. Link refuses to join them and all the protestors are arrested at the show.
- Wilbur has to mortgage the Har-De-Har Hut to bail out everyone, while Mr. Pinky drops Tracy as his model for her radical ideas.
- Seaweed and Link break Tracy and Penny of jail and get ready for the Miss Teeange Hairpray contest the next day.
- The invasion of the show is a success, with Spritzer calling Velma a genius and giving her a job promoting hair products "for women of color." It's a positive ending for all, with even Penny's mother being happy for Penny.

While the musical would end on Broadway in 2009, national and local productions continue, sometimes to the confusion of Waters. "I thought, great, when this gets done in schools, finally the fat girl and the drag queen can get a part," Waters told the *Baltimore Sun* in 2013. "But it's not true. What's so funny now is that it's politically correct. Now the skinny black girl plays Tracy. I love it. It's so postmodern." There was also a movie adaptation of the musical adaptation of the original dance movie, which came out in 2007.

Movie Musical

When New Line Cinema saw how well the Broadway musical was doing, and that a similar musical version of a movie—*The Producers*—was being made into a film, it was only logical for New Line to do the same. New Line hired Craig Zadan and Neil Meron, who have done updated versions of other musicals, mostly for television, such as *Gypsy* (1993), *Annie* (1999), *The Music Man* (2003), and the theatrical production of *Chicago* (2002). Mark O'Donnell and Thomas Meehan were brought in to write the script but were replaced with Leslie Dixon, who had written *Outrageous Fortune* (1987) and adaptations of *Freaky Friday* (2003) and *The Heartbreak Kid* (2007). Adam Shankman, a choreographer who had moved into directing with *The Wedding Planner* in 2001, was brought in to direct and help coordinate with the others what changes were needed for the film.

While it is easy to joke that it was an adaptation of an adaptation, that is essentially what occurred here—the production team looked to avoid remaking the original film and instead took what was there of the musical and turned it into a traditional musical film. This meant making changes to the plot, just as the musical had made changes from the original film.

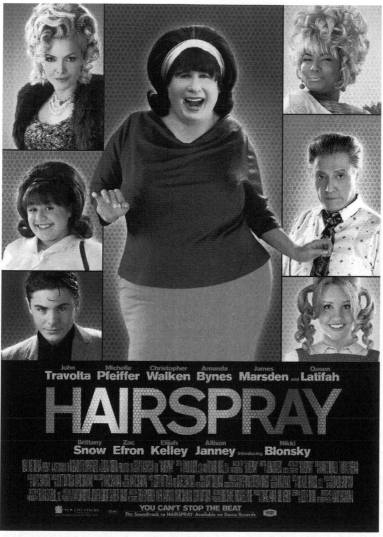

Movie poster for the 2007 movie adaptation of the 2002 Broadway musical adaptation of the 1988 original film of *Hairspray*.

The cast in the film included John Travolta as Edna, Christopher Walken as Wilbur, Michelle Pfeiffer as Velma Von Tussle, Amada Bynes as Penny, Queen Latifah as Motormouth Maybelle, James Marsden as Corny Collins, Brittany Snow as Amber, Zac Efron as Link, Elijah Kelley as Seaweed, and newcomer Nikki Blonsky as Tracy.

John Waters makes a cameo as the flasher seen in the opening number, and Jerry Stiller returns to play Mr. Pinky in the new version of the story. Ricki Lake appears briefly as a William Morris Talent Agent, while Harvey Fierstein has a brief vocal cameo in the ending credits song, "Mama, I'm a Big Girl Now."

Songs were changed and some were dropped for the new storyline to work as a film. As mentioned above, "Mama, I'm a Big Girl Now" was moved from its position early in the beginning of the story to the the ending credits, mostly because it was decided that it did not advance the plot and was too complicated to film without making it look hokey. Interestingly, the version used in the film features vocals from Ricki Lake, Marissa Jaret Winokur, Nikki Blonsky—the Tracys from the two films and the Broadway production—along with Harvey Fierstein, the original Broadway Edna, and John Travolta.

"Cooties," performed by Amber, is turned into an instrumental, although a version is heard in the end credits as well. Since in the film version Tracy does not go to jail, there was no need for "The Big Dollhouse," while "Velma's Revenge" and the reprise of "Good Morning Baltimore" were dropped to keep the pace of the film moving.

Two new songs were added for the film: "Ladies' Choice" and "Come So Far (Got So Far to Go)." A third called "I Can Wait" was for Tracy to sing while locked in the basement but was subsequently dropped as well.

Other changes include:

- Tracy in school waiting to get home to watch the show, rather than first showing the kids in the show first before moving on to Tracy after her introductory song "Good Morning Baltimore."

- Link first talking to Tracy in detention instead of at a dance afterwards.
- Tracy sings "I Can Hear the Bells" after this meeting, making it later than where it appears originally in the musical.
- "It Takes Two" is moved to right after "The Nicest Kids in Town" near the beginning of the film, instead of after Tracy becoming a member of the council.

- Negro Day is shown in the film, unlike the 1988 film and Broadway show. This brings the best improvement in the 2007 version, as it allows a pointed take on how white performers appropriated songs done by black performers to make them "safe" and saleable to white kids.
- Velma and Amber meet Edna and Tracy in a diner and nasty words are said.
- Link goes with Tracy to detention and gets invited to the record shop before "Run and Tell That!" rather than having the dodgeball scene. Little Inez's portion of the song takes place outside of school rather than at the record store. (For close readers, the name "L'il" was changed to "Little" in the 2007 film.)
- Velma makes a pass at Wilbur in order to cause trouble between him and Edna. This is the biggest change in the story, which ultimately leads back to Wilbur and Edna singing "You're Timeless to Me" but wipes out the protest and Tracy going to jail as in the first movie and Broadway show.
- "I Know Where I've Been" is moved in front of "Without Love"
- Tracy escapes the police and makes it to Penny's basement, but Penny's mother locks Tracy in the basement and ties up Penny in her room. Seaweed and friends help them escape during "Without Love"
- "Cooties" is dropped (appearing only in the ending credits and not in the story itself).
- Tracy's entrance is different in the final show, along with that of Edna.
- Little Inez is named the winner rather than Tracy.
- Velma is fired instead of given a bigger, better job.
- Edna gets a final wild dance.

Filming was done in Toronto and Hamilton, Ontario, which Waters found ironic. "It was weird going to Canada and seeing a $75 million version of my movie," Waters told *Baltimore* magazine in 2007 while describing a budget that was thirty times what he spent to make the original movie. "It was weird seeing Highlandtown built in Canada. Seeing the fake Baltimore always makes me laugh. It looks like Essex, in a way. And that's all right, because Essex and Highlandtown are the same world. It looked pretty good to me."

The film had sneak preview presentations in theaters during May 2007 and was then released in theaters on July 20, 2007. It received mostly enthusiastic reviews, although some, such as the *New Yorker*, took issue with the number of changes made to the musical for the new film, while a few questioned having to use John Travolta for a role that Harvey Fierstein played quite well on Broadway. Salon.com begrudgingly gave a thumb's up to the film but raised concerns that a plot which was so crazy in the original and Broadway production seemed to have been tamed to help audiences and lost something in doing so. One can say they knew what they were doing, however, as the film made just over $200 million worldwide.

And still one more nationally seen version to go.

Hairspray Live!

There was a time many years ago where having live broadcasts of musicals on television was the norm. Fans of Waters should know that, especially given his fascination with the television broadcast of *Peter Pan* done back in the 1950s and repeated for many years after. Back in 2013, NBC decided to do such a spectacular again, with a live broadcast of *The Sound of Music*. That production went over so well that NBC did so again the next year with *Peter Pan* and then the following year with *The Wiz*. When it came time to find a new musical to use in 2016, the network went with *Hairspray*.

The musical was adapted for television by Harvey Fierstein, who had played Edna in the original Broadway production and would play her again in the NBC telecast. His version of the show was very much like that of the Broadway show, with only one song cut, "The Big Dollhouse"; two songs from the 2007 movie added, "Ladies' Choice" and "Come So Far (Got So Far to Go)"; and some minor trimming to Tracy's jail scene to eliminate a minor subplot about Wilbur mortgaging the joke shop. Some fans of the 2007 musical version were upset to see the live version not match that of the 2007 film, but the NBC version is actually much closer and truer to the spirit of the Broadway production.

A national search was done to find a new Tracy and the eighteen-year-old newcomer Maddie Baillio. Both Ricki Lake and Marissa Jaret Winokur appeared as workers for Mr. Pinky as an acknowledgement of past Tracys for *Hairspray*. Martin Short—known for working on Broadway in various comedic and musical parts—played Wilbur Turnblad. Kristin Chenoweth played Velma; Garret Clayton played Link; Ariana Grande was Penny; Jennifer Hudson was Motormouth Maybelle; Cove Cameron was Amber; Ephraim Sykes was Seaweed; Derek Hough was Corny Collins; and Shahadi Wright Joseph was Little Inez.

Also appearing were Andrea Martin—Martin Short's alumni from *SCTV*—as Prudy Pingleton, Rosie O'Donnell as the gym teacher, and

Sean Hayes as Mr. Pinky. Paul C. Vogt, who plays Mr. Spritzer in the show, replaced Harvey Fierstein as Edna on Broadway for a time.

Over nine million viewers watched the live event, making it the most-viewed program of the night. It was released to streaming channels and on DVD on December 20, 2016, and then repeated on NBC on December 27, 2016. Reviews were kind, with *Variety* stating that it was the best musical attempted by NBC up to that time. The broadcast won three Emmy Awards: Outstanding Hairstyling for a Multi-Camera Series or Special; Outstanding Production Design for a Variety, Nonfiction, Event, or Award Special; and Outstanding Technical Direction, Camerawork, Video Control for a Limited Series, Movie, or Special.

Other Spin-offs

For years, New Line Cinema was after Waters to write a follow-up. "We begged him to do a sequel to *Hairspray* about the late sixties," Sara Risher told John Ives. "We offered him carte blanche, but he doesn't want to do it." There was an attempt by Waters in the late 1980s, as per his book *Crackpot*, to write a pilot for a television series, but nothing happened beyond that stage. Then in 2009, after the success of the 2007 musical film, New Line came back asking again, and this time Waters wrote one called *White Lipstick*, which was one of the alternate names Waters thought of calling *Hairspray* when working on it in the 1980s. "It is about when the real sixties hit and [*The Corny Collins Show*] isn't popular anymore. It's the new hip coming in—which really happened. So you know, the black kids want to have their own version of the show—they don't want to have to share with the white people."

Other plotlines that Waters discussed for the sequel included Link pretending to be British to help his singing career—and having pimples on his forehead under the Beatles wig that sing to him—and Little Inez turning into an Angela Davis radical. Meanwhile, there were rumors that the script finds Tracy still famous but being ridiculed because of her weight, while Edna has slimmed to the point that Wilbur has lost interest in her. "We never got to the songs," Waters told Broadwayworld.com. "In the script, I just described what the songs should be, but it was just a development deal. I mean, Marc and Scott really laughed when they read it, but I don't think the producers themselves did."

In 2013, talks of turning *Hairspray* into a weekly musical series began. "It's the gift that keeps on giving," Waters was heard saying by the *Hollywood Reporter*. "I got paid to write a sequel, *White Lipstick*, which never happened, and a television series, which still might. But I just want to keep on with it until we get to *Hairspray on Ice*."

Which, with the way *Hairspray* has done over the years, may still be a possibility.

15

Take the Kids

The Making of *Cry-Baby*

I thought I could trick them in with Johnny Depp. But they smelled a rat: me.

—John Waters to the *New York Times* on why moviegoers
did not go to the theaters to see *Cry-Baby*

Plot

In 1954 Baltimore, Allison Vernon-Williams (Amy Locane) is infatuated with Wade "Cry-Baby" Walker (Johnny Depp) and his gang of "drapes" ("greasers," "teddy boys," kids from the wrong side of the tracks who relish it). Allison is a "square" (uptight, right-wing . . . white) and knows it is trouble to mess with a drape, but she's finding it hard to resist the smoldering charms of Cry-Baby.

Included in his friends:

- Mona "Hatchet-Face" Malnorowski (Kim McGuire), whose parents (Troy Donahue and Mink Stole) sell cigarettes to kids for a penny a piece (six for a nickel) outside of school. As the casting notes for Hatchet-Face states, she has a great figure and a face that is "unusual."
- Milton Hackett (Darren E. Burrows), a rough kid and Hatchet-Face's boyfriend. His parents (Joe Dallesandro and Joey Heatherton) are religious fanatics, with his mother falling under spells of speaking in tongues.
- Wanda Woodward (Traci Lords), with parents (Patricia Hearst and David Nelson) so obliviously square that they've managed to warp themselves around to be hated by other squares and accepted by drapes. Wanda tries hard to rebel, taking on the role of a sexpot, even though secretly she's a good girl (casting notes state that she's actually a virgin). She is being

hassled by a photographer named Toe-Joe Jackson (Alan J. Wendl), who wants to take "nudie-cutie" pictures of her.

■ Pepper Walker (Ricki Lake), Cry-Baby's sister. She's pregnant with her third child. Pepper and Cry-Baby's grandparents, Ramona Rickettes (Susan Tyrrell) and Belvedere Rickettes (Iggy Pop), take care of Pepper's two kids, Snare-Drum (Jonathan Benya) and Susie-Q (Jessica Raskin). The Rickettes run the Turkey Point Swim Club and do a little stealing on the side.

Allison is dating Baldwin (Stephen Mailer), a super-square whose family has bad blood with the Walkers. She lives with her grandmother, Mrs. Vernon-Williams (Polly Bergen), who doesn't like her talking with the drapes.

Cry-Baby, meanwhile, is having issues with a girl, Lenora Frigid (Kim Webb), who isn't Cry-Baby's style ("He likes them bad, not cheap") but is stalking him at Turkey Point, where he sings at the "Jukebox Jamboree" with his gang. Cry-Baby's grandparents are so proud of him that they buy him a motorcycle, which he takes to the charm school where Allison is singing, and he invites her out to Turkey Point. Before Allison can reply, Baldwin sucker punches Cry-Baby, but that only drives Allison to Cry-Baby, and she leaves with him on his bike.

At Turkey Point, Allison is accepted by his gang and given a makeover in the drape image. Later, as they make out, Allison finds out that both of Cry-Baby's parents died in the electric chair, and so he does something rotten every day in their honor and cries a single, salty tear for them.

Baldwin and his square friends go out to Turkey Point, vandalizing the cars and setting Cry-Baby's motorcycle on fire. The squares beat up on the drapes and attempt to wreck the place, while Lenora tells Allison that she's pregnant with Cry-Baby's baby. Although the squares caused all the damage and violence, it is the drapes who are arrested and taken to court.

The judge (Robert Walsh), smitten by Mrs. Vernon-Williams, agrees to let Allison go with her supervision, but the others are not so fortunate: Pepper's two children are sent to an orphanage to find "God-fearing parents"; the Rickettes are fined $2,000; and Cry-Baby is sent to the Maryland Training School for Boys for "rampant juvenile delinquency." Outside of court, Lenora manages to persuade the press that she is engaged to Cry-Baby, which makes it into the morning paper and onto the radio.

The next day, it appears the squares are having a parade in honor of destroying Turkey Point, but it's actually a march to a new thing called a "theme park," the Enchanted Forest. Allison, believing the news about Lenora, tells the press she "spits on his tears." Cry-Baby hears the news and has to be subdued with a fire hose at the training school. An escape attempt by Cry-Baby leaves him without his pants, filthy, and right in line to get his hair cut at the school.

Elsewhere, Wanda finds out that her parents is sending her away that afternoon to Sweden as part of an exchange program. She leaves home and is picked up by Toe-Joe, who promises to drive her to the theme park. Hatchet-Face and Milton steal a helicopter in hopes of rescuing Cry-Baby but only barely escape capture themselves. The Rickettes and Pepper steal the children back from the Chatterbox Orphanage and take off for the theme park as well.

At the park, Allison is singing "Mr. Sandman" with Baldwin and his friends, but it is clear she is finding them much creepier than any of the drapes, and she notices that Baldwin is making eyes with Lenora, who has decided to be a square. She also notices that Cry-Baby's family and friends are in disguise and nearby in the park as she finishes the song. Belvedere

Cry-Baby's gang (*left to right*): Hatchet-Face (Kim McGuire), Milton (Darren E. Burrows), Wanda (Traci Lords), Cry-Baby (Johnny Depp), and Pepper (Ricki Lake).

Rickettes swings her away from the stage and they all ask her to go save Cry-Baby because "he needs you." Mrs. Vernon-Williams tells Allison to "pick the man who loves you the most."

Allison soon is outside the training school, crooning a song, and convincing the judge to let Cry-Baby out, right before he has his head shaved. Cry-Baby is released in a ceremony, but Baldwin announces that his grandfather pulled the switch on Cry-Baby's father, "and every Christmas he tells the story and we just laugh." Cry-Baby challenges Baldwin to a game of chicken with each on the top of their cars. Pepper gives birth in Cry-Baby's car as the game commences. Baldwin's car turns first and goes straight into a chicken coop, making Cry-Baby the winner. As the movie ends, Allison flies through the air and into Cry-Baby's lap, while all the gang looks on with a single tear running down their cheek.

Claims to Condemnation

- Minor transgressions: disrespect to authority, French-kissing, baby born out of wedlock, vomiting (if you include the deleted scenes).

Additional Cast and Crew

This was the only film Waters made with Johnny Depp, who had done small roles in a few films up to this point, such as *A Nightmare on Elm Street* (1984) and *Platoon* (1986), until he got the role of Officer Tom Hanson on *21 Jump Street*, the early cop-series hit from Fox. Being on the program helped get Depp noticed and advanced his career, but it also slotted the young actor into a teenage hunk persona in his private life of which he had little use. In archival footage shown in the DVD documentary *It Came from Baltimore*, Depp describes why he did the film: "One of the big reasons why I decided to do *Cry-Baby*, aside from the fact that John is one of my heroes in film … [was because] it was a chance to really make fun of the image that had been shoved down America's throats by the company that I work for." Depp, in the documentary, also suggested that because of his role in *Cry-Baby*, Tim Burton took interest in him for *Edward Scissorhands*, which opened up his career even further and allowed him to move on to bigger films. He signed on for the film in February 1989. Some voiced concerns when Depp was arrested for assaulting a hotel security guard the second week of March, but Waters blew it off at the time. "I thought it was great," Waters told the *Baltimore Sun*. "I left a message on his [answering] machine saying, 'What? Are you promoting the film already?'"

Printed in the March 12, 1989, edition of the *Baltimore Sun* was an audition notice: "Needed is a twenty-year-old actress to play the lead role of Hatchet-Face, a 1950s juvenile delinquent and member of Johnny Depp's gang. Must have an unusual face and a good figure." Kim McGuire did not submit a photo for an audition, however. Instead, she had sent in her photo to the casting director of the film *Reversal of Fortune*, which was being cast at the time, and they passed her photo off to Moran and Waters, who called her in for Hatchet-Face and gave her the part. She would return for a cameo in *Serial Mom* as a stage diver.

The *Baltimore Sun* featured a long article on March 13, 1989, about the casting process for extras, with over 800 people waiting in line in groups of ten to audition and show if they "look great and can move well and have confidence in themselves without trying too hard," Waters told the paper at the time. Also with him were Pat Moran, Greg Mason, and producer Rachel Talalay.

Other actors joined in March and early April, with Patricia Hearst getting the most headlines—even more than rock performer Iggy Pop (Waters met him at a dinner party and suggested the film to him), Polly Bergen, or Traci Lords, the last having been in the news often at the time. Lords was still struggling to get her career in general audience films moving and stated in the DVD documentary *It Came from Baltimore* that she got physically ill before auditioning for the film. Moran and Waters, on the other hand, were sympathetic. To them, Lords was essentially a kid that was being portrayed by the press and the public as some type of evil mastermind in a situation that was not of her own doing, and they felt she needed a break. (See Chapter 2 for more details on that and the cast's and crew's actions when working with her on this movie.) "It feels good to be playing somebody young," Lords told the *Baltimore Sun* during filming, "because I never got to be young. For me, it was like going back to a period of life I never really had. It gave me a chance to be sixteen, to be young and stupid. I was old and stupid. I was never sixteen."

Ricki Lake came back for her second film with Waters, as did Alan J. Wendl, who played Toe-Joe Jackson, and Kim Webb, who was Carmelita, one of the dancers on *The Corny Collins Show*. Darren D. Burrows auditioned for Waters on March 26, 1989, which was Easter Sunday, and got the part of

Milton. Stephen Mailer in the DVD documentary mentioned that his brother Michael had been asked by Mink Stole to audition for *Polyester*, but his mother refused to let him be in a movie for Waters, which gave Stephen a good reason to audition for *Cry-Baby* when given the chance.

There were other familiar names of those that joined the cast. "I guess you could call some of it stunt-casting," Waters admitted to Steve Appleford in 2007. "I love Joe Dallesandro and Joey Heatherton, but all of them

A promotional still for *Cry-Baby* (1990) made sure to mention the numerous cameos in the film, including (*starting top left*) Patricia Hearst, David Nelson, Joey Heatherton, Joe Dallesandro, Willem Dafoe, Mink Stole, and Troy Donahue.

together was part of the *Mad, Mad, Mad World* takeoff I was trying to do."
This was the first film Waters did with Patricia Hearst, who would return
for all of Waters's remaining films. Susan Tyrrell (1945–2012) was a well-
known actress and partier, who had appeared in *Andy Warhol's Bad* and
was nominated for an Academy Award for Best Supporting Actress in 1973
for *Fat City* (1973). David Nelson was the son of Ozzie and Harriet Nelson.
Joe Dallesandro had made his name first by posing nude for photos for photographer Bob Mizer and then began appearing in films for Andy Warhol,
which led to eventually crossing over to general films and television. Joey
Heatherton is a singer-actress that had been in the news a bit back in the
1980s for a handful of arrests involving robbery and assault. (The charges
were either eventually dropped or she was acquitted.) William Dafoe also
makes a cameo appearance in the training school scene.

Troy Donahue (1936–2001) also faced some rough patches, although
mostly in the late 1960s and into the 1970s. He had been a popular actor
in films and was usually mentioned in the same group of actors like Tab
Hunter, who were "teenage heartthrobs." In fact, that connection was so
common that even people on the film had thought he had already made
a film with Waters a few years before. Even Waters wasn't immune, as
Donahue told the *Baltimore Sun* with a laugh in November 1989: "In the last
shot of the film, he did it—John called me Tab."

Of the Dreamlanders, Mink Stole appeared as the chain-smoking, iron-
lung-wearing mother of Hatchet-Face, while Mary Vivian Pearce turned up
as a mother at a picnic scene. Susan Lowe popped up as a parent in the night
court scene. Channing Wilroy helped as a musical consultant on the film,
while Vincent Peranio, Van Smith, and Pat Moran did their usual jobs.

This was the last film Robert Maier worked on with Waters. Maier had
worked in some type of production capacity on each Waters film since *Female
Trouble* and worked to secure locations for *Cry-Baby*. A rift would develop
between Maier and Waters even before filming began, and Maier would later
write a book, *Low Budget Hell: Making Underground Movies with John Waters*,
which was not received well by some people around John Waters.

All of that would be in the future, however. "It was wild, those days,"
Waters said in the *It Came from Baltimore* documentary. "That was the wild-
est movie I've ever made for partying, because think of it: Johnny Depp, Traci
Lords, Susan Tyrrell—hardly a shrinking violet—Iggy Pop—totally sober,
completely clean, with Susan Tyrrell—Ricki Lake, Patricia Hearst, David

Nelson." Looking out over the players at lunchtime, Waters would get a kick out of seeing people like Patricia Hearst and David Nelson eating together.

Production

Back in 1985, Waters was working on a script called *Hatchet Face*, which he described to the *Santa Fe New Mexican* as "a comedy about one woman's multi-level beauty problems." That script would slowly evolve into *Cry-Baby*, which centered more on the drapes vs. squares concept than he had originally planned.

Waters has always been fascinated with people who were "bad seeds"— kids from the "wrong side of the railroad tracks" who usually ended up becoming juvenile delinquents. In the Baltimore area of the 1950s they were called "Drapes" (or "Drapettes" for girl members), and there would be other names for them there and elsewhere, but whatever they were called, they were obviously kids that were bad news. It is an obsession that goes back to his youth. "I remember the first drape I saw," Waters told the *Boston Globe* in 1990. "My parents took me to a bowling alley, and this drape was so great. He played 'The Joker' over and over, driving my parents insane." Waters also had etched on his memory that of Carolyn Wells, a fourteen-year-old drapette who was found half naked and dead from a skull fracture, which was major news when Waters was eight years old. In *It Came from Baltimore*, Waters said, "They used to tell you at school, 'This is what happens to drapette girls.' You know, that hung out with a fast crowd, 'cause she did. She was fourteen and hung around with boys that stole cars, and hooked school."

The image of drapes was further pushed by the rock and roll films of the 1950s and early 1960s, with guys in leather jackets and white T-shirts hitting on the sweet, innocent girls. Drapes were sometimes even the troubled hero, like James Dean in *Rebel without a Cause*, Marlon Brando in *The Wild Ones*, or Elvis in his early films. It is that "Hollywood" creation of the image that was an influence on the look of *Cry-Baby* as well, especially the low-budget films that played mostly at the drive-ins back in the 1950s."I rented a whole bunch of those when I was writing *Cry-Baby*," Waters told the *San Francisco Weekly* in April, 1990, "and took the clichés from them. The main thing I wanted to do was to make a movie that would have been shocking in 1954—which, of course, would be a comedy today. I couldn't have shown *Cry-Baby* in 1954; it would have been too weird." It took seven to nine months of research before Waters began working on the script.

In the pitch for the movie, Waters wanted to showcase the look of the drapes, but he had an issue, which he described in *It Came from Baltimore*. "The only really great drape pictures I had were in a very famous book of gay '50s photographs by Bob Mizer, who discovered Joe Dallesandro ... I couldn't show them [the book] because it's my first studio movie—they'll think, 'Oh, great, you're gonna make a movie about naked boy juvenile delinquents.' So I showed them the pictures that weren't naked." Included in the photos were street toughs and one in particular that matches the image of Iggy Pop in the wash basin seen in the film. "I couldn't show them what was on the next page."

Problems with pictures may have been a concern, but getting into the studio to pitch wasn't. "This was the only time ever that every studio wanted to make my next movie," Waters mentions in *It Came from Baltimore*. "*Hairspray* had come out. It was a success. Everyone thought it was a bigger hit than it was. There was a bidding war—that has never happened to me before or since." Eventually Imagine Film Entertainment, founded by Ron Howard and Brian Grazer, agreed to produce the film for Universal Studios, making it their first film of the new decade and one of four films made by the production company for Universal that year (along with *Opportunity Knocks*, *Kindergarten Cop*, and *Problem Child*). The film's original budget was $8 million,

The original movie poster for *Cry-Baby* (1990), the only film project Waters did that he did not have to hustle to pitch to a studio, thanks to the success of his 1988 film, *Hairspray*.

then $9 million, and finally $12 million—quite a jump from the $2.5 million budget of *Hairspray* just two years before. Waters would continue to refine the script, stating at the time of filming he did three to five drafts. (In the DVD documentary he claims it was a total of seven drafts.)

Along with being brought into a major studio like Universal and Imagine, and with the infusion of so much money, came the intrusion of Hollywood people. Although it was filmed in Baltimore with over forty crew members, there were many more that joined from Los Angeles—Maier noted in his book that many seemed to have second jobs as owners of Subway sandwich stores and were constantly calling long-distance to manage their stores while working on the film in Baltimore. Decisions were made on both coasts as well, although Waters had control of the project as long as things went smoothly. According to a *Baltimore Sun* report from June of that year, each day's filming cost $70,000. In the past, Waters used to mumble "Dollar, dollar, dollar" while trying to motivate people on his set, which changed to "Thousands, thousands, thousands" on *Cry-Baby*. "But at least it's no longer money that I borrowed. It's money that someone put up," he told the *Baltimore Sun.*

Rehearsals took place at Waters's house. Amy Locane, who was still underage at the time, went to the first rehearsal with her mother, and she felt odd having to get on the floor with Johnny Depp and act the make-out scene with him while her mother watched. Filming then began on April 17 and was supposed to continue until June 30, but it ran an extra week due to rain delays.

Ten days were spent in Sykesville, Maryland, a location that was picked out by Robert Maier due to its 1950s-style streets, downtown area, and homes. This area can mostly be seen in the sequence where Baldwin bunny-hops the marching band down the street to Allison's place, which was filmed on May 20. A stunt with two men flying through a window of the second floor of the Wade H. Warfield Building and through the roof of a Studebaker Commander convertible was filmed as well, although the stunt did not make it into the film. The city was also the location for the Chatterbox Orphanage, which is actually a Presbyterian church at 7314 Spout Hill Road, but due to rain the two days needed for filming the sequence occurred on July 1 and 2 during the week of pick-ups.

Other locations where filming took place were:

- The high school is Franklin Middle School at 10 Cockneys Mill Road in Reisterstown, Maryland.

- The RSVP Charm School is actually Cloisters Castle at 10440 Falls Avenue, Lutherville, Maryland.
- The police station is the police station at 1620 Edison Highway in Baltimore.
- The Enchanted Forest theme park is at 10040 Baltimore National Pike in Ellicott City, Maryland.
- Wanda stomps out of a house and begins hitchhiking at the 3000 block of Milford Road in Milford, Maryland.
- The training school where the women strut in for visiting hours is located at the "long abandoned" Cottage C of Spring Grove State Hospital in Catonsville, Maryland.

Rain may have caused a lot of delay, but the worst part according to Waters was the Chicken Race, as he told John Ives:

> I had to sit in that fucking car for a week. One whole week. Every day. They only actually drove a short distance, and we had to get up to speed to make it with this big camera trucking thirty people around and mikes and everything. Then cut. And you had to drive all the way around and start over to get the next ten seconds of film. In both cars. They then had to move the car, and in each lap all the cars in the background are set to be going by like in a cartoon going past the same car. So it took forever.

Many of the extras had never danced professionally. More importantly, Johnny Depp may have come from a musical background, but he knew he couldn't dance. Choreographer Lori Eastside was brought in to teach everyone some dance steps for the musical numbers. (Eastside would choreograph several other films before becoming a casting director for extras on several films.) One dance number cut from the film, "Chicken," which occurs during the battle of the bands near the end of the film, nearly ended in a fight. Depp, in character, was supposed to occasionally act aggressively to Stephen Mailer as Baldwin while "Chicken" was performed. When it got to the end of the song, when Mailer has to bend over at one point, Depp—too into playing the role—kicked him hard in the rear, leading to the two starting to square off for a real fight before Waters stepped in between the two.

The mood between cast and crew appears from reports to have been pretty up. There was some tension, however, when the extras dancing together in the Turkey Point scene were told right before filming that they would be required to French-kiss their partner "with lots of tongue action."

Fortunately, those who were paired up played along and got to know each other in a new way very quickly.

Filming in the Baltimore area was completed during the first week of July, and then Waters went to Los Angeles to shoot a week of retakes, work with editor Janice Hampton, who had edited *Hairspray*, and assist with the music recorded for the film. While *Hairspray* was full of music, there was only one original song in the film; *Cry-Baby*, on the other hand, was a mixture of original rockabilly songs and re-recorded songs with altered lyrics (done by Waters and Rachel Sweet). Becky Mancuso and Tim Sexton were brought in as music supervisors, and two original songs by former Blasters member Dave Alvin were recorded for the movie: "King Cry Baby" (cowritten with Doc Pomus) and "High School Hellcats." Although Depp can sing and gave tapes of his work to Waters and the producers, it was decided to have James Intveld (also of the Blasters) sing the songs for Depp. Amy Locane's voice was replaced by Rachel Sweet in the film as well. Timothy B. Schmit of the Eagles and Poco played on "Sh Boom" and "Mister Sandman," while Al Kooper produced three of the updated tracks for the movie.

Editing the film took time. Waters stated in the DVD documentary: "We had to get a PG-13 for the movie; that was in my contract. And that was a nightmare." One gag in particular that was affected by the needed rating occurred in the courtroom scene when Wanda tells her mother to get her "the fuck out of here," Wanda's mother thinks it's "silly teenage slang" and asks the judge if they can take Wanda "the fuck home." The problem was that you could only get away with saying "fuck" once in a PG-13 movie, and the gag involved saying it three times. So in order to get the PG-13 rating, the first two times were censored with a bleep on the soundtrack, which actually make the joke cuter in a way, as it seems like even the movie itself is offended by the word. Having Patty Hearst, as Wanda's mom, be the only person that gets to actually say the word makes it funnier as well. Alas, the bleeps were taken out of the director's cut that was eventually released on DVD.

That special edition director's cut DVD includes some additional footage, uncensored bleeps, and a little over six minutes of extra running time. The website Movie-censorship.com gives a concise breakdown of what was added to the director's cut:

- The scene where we meet Hatchet-Face's mother and father selling cigarettes to the students can only be seen in the director's cut.
- Allison seeing Cry-Baby for the first time after school, and Cry-Baby spitting out the match he chews.

- Toe-Joe talking to the woman in the bikini on his car starts with some dialogue not heard in the theatrical version.
- Allison's song "A Teenage Prayer" is interrupted at the Charm School by an air-raid siren, and Baldwin kisses Allison under the table while they wait out the air-raid.
- There are several dances observed at the Jukebox Jamboree while Cry-Baby and Allison ride over on Cry-Baby's bike.
- At the courthouse, Wanda's parents happily play cards with each other (and happily allow each other to cheat while doing so). When Allison is brought in, her grandmother tells her to fix her hair.
- The courtroom scene also features the uncensored "fuck" gag, the Rickettes talking about Cry-Baby's music, and Mrs. Vernon-Williams awkwardly showing she is not ashamed of her daughter being with "negroes" at Turkey Point.
- As Baldwin leads the dance down the street, he and his friends spot the Rickettes with Pepper, and they all start throwing tomatoes at them.
- Arriving at Allison's place, Baldwin and his friends tease Allison by singing a version of "The Naughty Lady of Shady Lane."
- After rescuing the kids from Chatterbox Orphanage, the Rickettes make their escape with Snare-Drum driving.

The director's cut DVD also includes a section of scenes cut from the film before release and not included in the director's cut version of the film:

- A child contortionist in the Charm School talent show. In the DVD documentary included, it is told that Waters wanted such a child contortionist for the film, but after filming the scene with "Little Ruth," her scene was cut. (Probably because it may look a little strange, but the kid is so cute, you can't hate it, and audiences were supposed to find the people at the charm school snobby). Unfortunately, no one told Ruth or her family, and when they came to the premiere they watched only to discover she was not in the film, which mortified Waters and Moran when they found out.
- Toe-Joe begins to drive Wanda to his photography studio. She tries to escape the car, but discovers there is no door handle.
- Milton gets sick in the helicopter and then throws up on the judge outside of the Chatterbox Orphanage just as the Rickettes and Pepper arrive to steal back the kids. "We had a vomit scene," Waters told *BAM* in 1990, "but we cut it. Not because of any studio pressure, but because it was too confusing—not the actual puking, but where they puked."

- At Toe-Joe's photography studio, Lenora is there posing. Wanda, forced to pose for Toe-Joe, realizes that Lenora has been lying about being pregnant (a plot point never established otherwise in the film). There are a few shirtless men and other women there posing. Toe-Joe then announces that they will all be posing for photos that day where they "go all the way." All but Lenora rebel, with Wanda frantically telling everyone that she's never done anything and is still a virgin. The scene fades out at that point, but it is clear she and the others escape.
- Mrs. Vernon-Williams announces the battle of the band at Turkey Point, and Baldwin's group sings "Chicken."

The film was tested by Universal in suburban areas in the fall of 1989 and then changes were requested for the film. Waters felt some of the testing could help the film but got uncomfortable when testing went on much longer than he felt necessary, as he told John Ives: "The first two tests are good, and after that it isn't good. We changed some things in *Cry-Baby* and I have no idea today if it helped or hurt." The one positive for Waters was being given a chance to fix things he couldn't see as errors until the film got in front of an audience. "Never before had I had the chance to see something that didn't work in one of my films and go back and change it." By February, the film was complete and one way or another was going to be seen soon enough by the public.

Release

Talk at the time of the film's completion was that *Cry-Baby* would be released in early 1990. In March 1990 came word that the film would premiere at the Santa Barbara International Film Festival on March 10, but Universal pulled the film from the festival the day before it was to be shown. Instead, the world premiere of the film was held on March 14, 1990, at the Senator in Baltimore. Most of the cast arrived for the showing, but there were signs that things were not going to be quite as much fun as the filming had been. Photographers followed many of the cast into the after-party, including a few who followed Traci Lords into the women's restroom, and others who hounded Johnny Depp and his date, Winona Ryder, to the point that security had to intervene.

The film was released on April 6, 1990, across the country in over 1,000 theaters. It was the most exposure that any of Waters's films ever got at one time, which may have been perpetuating a mistake that New Line had made when they oversaturated the market for *Hairspray* two years before. While Waters was happy to see one of his movies playing in parts of the country that had never seen one of his films in a theater, the need for audiences to see the film was softer than hoped for. Waters saw the writing on the wall immediately. "On opening night, when I walked into the Waverly Theater—which has always been sort of my home for my movies in New York—and there were two empty seats, I knew it was not going to work. They should have turned away a hundred people," he said to John Ives.

Ticket sales were slow and reviews were also uneven. Andy Seiler of the *Central New Jersey Home News* called the film "half-baked and unoriginal" and "a must-see for Waters fans and '50s rock enthusiasts" but "probably a must-miss for everyone else." Jack Garner of the Gannett News Service said: "Waters seems to be trying to walk the line between his sick cult camp comedies of earlier years and his mainstream hit, and [the film] falls, instead, between the cracks." On the other hand, Gene Siskel of the *Chicago Tribune* called it "a winner in the end" and gave it three stars. Roger Ebert also liked the movie, calling it a "passable imitation of a 1950s teenage exploitation movie."

By the time the movie had completed its run in theaters, it had only made a little more than $8 million—$4 million less than what it cost to make. Waters felt some of the blame came from what audiences expected of him at the time. "The difference was that it did not have Divine as a reference point, which there was nothing I could do about. The heroes were too normal for a John Waters movie," he said to John Ives. Sara Risher, on the other hand, told Ives: "The reason *Hairspray* worked—and *Cry-Baby* didn't—was that [Waters] had a very vulnerable protagonist in *Hairspray*, someone everybody could relate to and care about. In *Cry-Baby*, I don't think we felt for any of the characters in that same way." Yet Waters found that the film did remarkably well in Australia and in Europe, especially in Paris, where there was an appreciation of the juvenile delinquent films Waters was lampooning, and perhaps this was the reason it did not do well in America—viewers, especially young viewers, hadn't seen those films nor had any interest in them.

Although there was disappointment with the returns on the film, the film has discovered its own cult following once it was released on video, which has helped the studio slowly make back its investment in it. The film was first released on VHS by MCA-Universal in September 1990, followed by rerelease in 1998, the DVD special edition in 2005, and then on Blu-ray in

2014. Making money or not, the film did lead to a special moment for Waters when it became an official selection at the Cannes Film Festival, where the film was given a standing ovation. As he told John Ives: "Standing at the top of that red carpet and turning around with eight million paparazzi, with Pat and Ricki Lake and Rachel Talalay, my producer, it was a huge high to me. That was a fantasy that I wanted since I was fourteen."

Broadway

"Everybody thinks *Hairspray* was my musical, 'cause it's a big Broadway musical now. That was my dance movie. This was my musical, and there is talk now of this being a Broadway musical. I'm in the opening stages about that now." Waters stated this in the DVD documentary that came with the 2005 DVD director's cut. As could be expected, when it was clear how well *Hairspray* was doing as a Broadway musical, it was understandable that the movie Waters thought *was* a musical would soon hit Broadway as well.

When putting together *Hairspray*, it was pointed out in interviews that Margo Lion was a rarity in being a solo producer of Broadway shows at a time where mostly corporations were the producers to help cover costs. Case in point: several such groups—like the Universal Pictures Stage Productions and the Pelican Group—were just some of the producers listed for *Cry-Baby* when it finally reached Broadway.

Brought into the writing of the show were Mark O'Donnell and Thomas Meehan from *Hairspray*, who worked on the book, and Adam Schlesinger and David Javerbaum, who worked on the music. Schlesinger wrote the title track to the film *That Thing You Do!* and had worked several times with David Javerbaum on comedy music for the Tony Awards—his work also resulted in winning an Emmy Award for the song "It's Not Just for Gays Anymore," sung by Neil Patrick Harris at the sixty-fifth Tony Awards. In July 2006, two staged readings of the proposed new musical were done for investors with the hope of obtaining $10 million dollars to get the musical ready for out-of-town engagements at the 5th Avenue Theatre in Seattle in February 2007.

Instead, the show finally came together in 2007, with announcements in February 2007 that the musical would do its out-of town engagements at the La Jolla Playhouse in San Diego, California, from October 30 through December 16, 2007. The start date then changed to November 18, 2007.

The beginning of the "Please, Mr. Jailer" dance number from *Cry-Baby* (1990). After the success of *Hairspray* on Broadway, it seemed like a natural adaptation for the stage.

The plot of the Broadway show is similar to the film but, as could be expected, was changed to fit the format of the stage (so car races and burning motorcycles were out). Cry-Baby's real name was changed from Wade Walker to Milton Hackett. Cry-Baby wants to compete in a singing contest being organized by Mrs. Vernon-Williams, although nearly everyone is skeptical of him being in it. A fight breaks out and Cry-Baby is arrested. Allison organizes an effort to free Cry-Baby, eventually succeeding, but then is told that a girl is pregnant and that Cry-Baby is the father. Allison goes back to her former boyfriend, Baldwin. He and Cry-Baby have a chicken fight, which Cry-Baby wins. Everything ends happily.

The cast is toned down a bit, with Cry-Baby's gang just the girls, while Dupree—the African-American character who in the film buys a muffler—is bumped up to a major supporting character in the musical. Some of the songs are fun and do stay in the spirit of the Waters film, such as "Baby Baby Baby Baby (Baby Baby Baby)" and "The Anti-Polio Picnic," but many have pointed out that Waters's film was parodying a movie genre that had already in many ways been done onstage in shows like *Grease*. Thus, ticket-buyers were slow to respond to the show, even if *Hairspray* was a success.

The show was directed by Mark Brokaw, with choreography by Rob Ashford. It starred James Snyder as Cry-Baby and Elizabeth Stanley as Allison. The musical moved to the Marquis Theatre on Broadway on March 15, 2008, and then opened on April 24, 2008. Running only sixty-eight performances after forty-five previews, the show ended on June 22, 2008, after weak box-office results and critical reviews.

The show has now since moved on to community theater, where it has seen some positive response. It still has a life of its own but obviously showed that not every film Waters made would be workable as a Broadway show. "Once *Cry-Baby* didn't work, I think my Broadway career ended," Waters told Randy Shulman in 2009. "If *Cry-Baby* had been successful, I think *Serial Mom* would have been next. But I think *Serial Mom* would be a better television show, like a weekly series where mom kills the political correctness."

Speaking of which . . .

16

Fashion Has Changed

The Making of *Serial Mom*

It's the infamy of crime which has really always fascinated me. Much more than the crime itself. That's what *Serial Mom* is about.

—John Waters to James Grant

Plot

May 14, 1993. Detectives arrive at the Sutphins home in the suburbs to discuss obscene phone calls and letters sent to their neighbor, Dottie Hinkle (Mink Stole). Beverly Sutphin (Kathleen Turner) pleads wide-eyed innocence, while her husband Eugene (Sam Waterston) is clueless. After their son, Chip (Matthew Lillard), goes to his job at the video store, their daughter, Misty (Ricki Lake), heads to school, and Eugene goes to his job as a dentist, Beverly sends harassing phone calls to Dottie for having once unknowingly taken a store parking space Beverly had planned to use.

Beverly goes to a meeting with Chip's math teacher, Paul Stubbins (John Badila), who is concerned about Chip's preoccupation with horror movies. He suggests that Beverly did something wrong with Chip's upbringing, which leads to her running the teacher down in the parking lot and backing over him to make sure he's dead. A student, Lu-Ann Hodges (Kim Swann), sees her and is soon on the news talking about it, which Beverly happens to see. The police are suspicious of Beverly, and Chip's friend Scotty (Justin Whalin) doesn't win points by jokingly suggesting that Beverly killed Mr. Stubbins.

The next day, the detectives show Eugene the number of books about killing and killers that Beverly has been buying. Meanwhile, Misty is upset that her

The Sutphins family in *Serial Mom* (1994), who look like a sweet, alternate-universe version of the Fishpaws from *Polyester* (1981), although they turn out to be even more dangerous to hang around.

(possible) boyfriend, Carl (Lonnie Horsey), had stood her up for the swap meet, where she has a table. Beverly tries to make her feel better, but then she spots Carl at the swap meet with his girlfriend (Traci Lords). In a dark mood, Beverly follows Carl into the men's room and kills him with a fireplace poker that her friend Rosemary (Mary Jo Catlett) had just purchased at the swap meet. Beverly is once again seen at the scene of a crime, and Rosemary discovers blood on the poker and Beverly's shoes.

At the house, Eugene discovers Beverly's scrapbook on serial killers, a signed photo from Richard Speck, and an audio tape to Beverly from Ted Bundy (John Waters). Misty also suspects her and tells Chip, leading them all to have a very unsettling dinner with Beverly that night. Chip tries to get her to talk by mentioning that Scotty thinks she is the killer. Beverly laughs and then excuses herself from the table, going to the garage and taking off in the car. The family, sure she is heading to Scotty's, drive over to Scotty's place only to discover him masturbating in his room.

Beverly has actually gone over to the home of Ralph Sterner (Doug Roberts), who had a toothache earlier that day, forcing Eugene to cancel an outing with Beverly. She kills him and his wife, Betty (Kathy Fannon), and returns home before the family does. The police try to arrest her in church, but Chip and his girlfriend, Birdie (Patricia Dunnock), help her escape. They hide her at the video store where Chip works, but when a customer returns a tape without having rewound it, Beverly hunts the woman (Patsy Grady Abrams) down and kills her with a leg of lamb while "Tomorrow" from *Annie* plays. Scotty sees her and Beverly chases him, first on foot with a knife and then in various cars. Scotty tries to hide in a club where the band Camel Lips (L7) is playing. Beverly burns him alive in front of the cheering crowd, killing him, just as the police arrive. The confused Beverly is handcuffed and taken away, as everyone chants, "Serial mom!"

In October of the same year, Beverly has her trial. Beverly represents herself and manages to be acquitted of all charges, while her family cashes in with memorabilia and other opportunities that come with fame. Near the end of the trial, Suzanne Somers (Suzanne Somers) arrives to watch the proceedings for a television movie she is to make in which she will be playing Beverly. It appears that being a serial killer has done more positive things for her family than otherwise.

After the trial, Beverly tracks down a juror (Patricia Hearst) who wore white after Labor Day. Although the juror pleads with Beverly that "fashion has changed," Beverly kills her with the receiver of a pay phone. As Suzanne Somers annoys Beverly, the body of the juror is found.

Claims to Condemnation

- Minor transgressions: murder, masturbation, mild female nudity, language.

Additional Cast and Crew

Rumors flew for a time that many different women—including Glenn Close, Julie Andrews, Meryl Streep, and Roseanne Barr—were considered for the lead role in *Serial Mom*, but this had more to do with the pitch to different studios than what Waters intended. "It was originally developed at Columbia," Waters told Undertheradarmag.com in 2017, "and I went to a couple different places and each time it would switch executives, they would have their own ideas of who they think was going to make money, and you know they were all wrong. They all think that this person will open this movie in this country, and if that were true every movie would be a hit, wouldn't it?"

Of the rumored names, Susan Sarandon is known to have been in serious discussions and came close to taking the lead role, as she told Ryan Murphy of the *Los Angeles Times* in late December 1992: "I would love to do a comedy. [Waters and I] had a number of lunches together and I liked him very much. I thought the script really hit upon some funny things and some interesting points of society, in terms of what's happening." Negotiations failed either because sources say she was priced out of their range at the time, or—as Sarandon told Murphy—she didn't want to start work on the film as early as the planned March 1993 starting date.

Instead, Kathleen Turner signed on for the film in late January 1993 for filming to start on April 12 in Baltimore. It was a lucky break for the production, as initially, when the film was to be done at Columbia, Turner would have been impossible to get; once it moved to Savoy and the budget jumped, things fell into place. "When this film was with other studios," Waters told

Beverly Sutphin (Kathleen Turner) in a classic pose for the film *Serial Mom* (1994).

James Grant, "we did not have the budget to hire Kathleen. But when we did, she was my No. 1 choice, believe me."

Turner, in the commentary for the DVD release of the film, said that she initially stopped reading the script when it got to the murder of Carl and pulling out his liver (which in the film is an obvious parody of a similar scene shown earlier in the film from H. Gordon Lewis's *Blood Feast*). Nevertheless, she picked up the script again and continued to read to the point that she called Waters and told him that she was curious about how Waters would shoot such scenes. Waters, on the same commentary, took the train to New York and was at Turner's place within five hours to discuss the script, eventually winning Turner over. Many of the long-timers and newcomers that worked on *Serial Mom* were at first timid around Turner, who had at that point been perceived as being very standoffish and very serious, but they discovered a woman who was willing to jump in and do what was needed to get the film done. Matthew Lillard, in the DVD documentary for the film, talked about being impressed by Turner turning up on day one and knowing the names of everybody in the cast and crew, which Turner told him was a necessity on any film.

Besides the surprise announcement of Turner in the film, there were also eyebrows raised over Waters getting Sam Waterston, who saw his status skyrocket with the 1984 film *The Killing Field* and who appeared in two well-remembered Woody Allen films, *Hannah and Her Sisters* (1986) and *Crimes and Misdemeanors* (1989). That Waters was able to get Waterston—especially when Waters was seen as a director who filled his films with "pop culture references"—had some people wondering what Waters had in mind. Waters knew there would be that disconnect on the part of some audience members. "Most surprising is to get Sam Waterston or people you would never expect to be in a John Waters movie," Waters told Steve Appleford. "I try to get the best actors I can get. My main direction is to never wink at the camera, to say every ludicrous line as if you believe every word of it."

That evasion of "winking" threw off Mink Stole, who has a major supporting role in the film as neighbor Dottie Hinkle. "The one thing John kept telling me over and over again was that we weren't making a movie like we used to. He kept telling me to pull the emotion down, to make it smaller," Mink Stole told the *Detroit Free Press*. "It got to the point where I feared I might be invisible."

Ricki Lake returned for her third film in a row with Waters. She was about to begin work on her daily talk show—one that lasted for several years and was aimed at the teenage and college market—and had lost weight in between *Cry-Baby* and *Serial Mom*. When asked by Gail Shister of the Knight Ridder Newspapers if that would make any difference to how she is used in the film, Waters shrugged off the question: "She's a major part of my life. I don't care if she weighs 300 pounds or 100 pounds. I've had very good luck with big girls. Ricki looks good either way."

Other returning cast members from *Cry-Baby* were Traci Lords, in a meaty cameo as Carl's girlfriend, and Kim McGuire, as a stage-diver at the Camel Lips show. Susan Lowe, as a courtroom groupie, and Mary Vivian Pearce, as a book buyer, made their usual appearances in the film.

This was the first appearance of Scott Morgan, who played Detective Pike. He'll appear in all three of Waters's remaining films, as will Tim Caggiano (Marvin Pickles) and Patsy Grady Abrams (Mrs. Jenson). John Badila (Mr. Stubbins) and Stan Brandorff (Judge) return in *Pecker*. Richard Pelzman, who plays the doorman who recognized "Serial Mom" at the nightclub, returns in *A Dirty Shame* as "Paw Paw."

Serial Mom was an early picture for Matthew Lillard, who has had a very productive career since, and is probably still known for his role in the first *Scream* film (1996) and his continuing work as Shaggy in *Scooby Doo*, both in front of the camera and as a voice actor. Mary Jo Catlett, who appeared in small roles a few times on the television series *M*A*S*H*, plays Rosemary, the neighbor who is ignorant of recycling. Waters states in the director's commentary for the film that the character of Rosemary would have been the part Divine would have played if he had lived. "Now, the script would've been different. It would've been a different part, but I imagine that would've been Divine's role."

Besides the surprising, but intentional, cameo of Suzanne Somers is the appearance of actress Bess Armstrong as Eugene's dental nurse. Armstrong, a Baltimore native, is the wife of producer John Fiedler, and she'll pop up again in a bigger role in Waters's next film, *Pecker*.

Appearing as the band Camel Lips was the all-female band L7, a name which Waters points out in the director's commentary as meaning "square," while the interviewer on the commentary also points out that it's a sexual term used in much the same way as "69." In the film, they perform the song "Gas Chamber," which was written by the band with John Waters's contributions to the lyrics. As suggested by the name of this make-believe band, the band members were given padded pants to wear to accentuate their crotches, which—in the hot environment of a nightclub in summer—became uncomfortable as filming went on.

The March 21, 1993, edition of the *Baltimore Sun* announced that Waters and company were looking for extras for the film. That process didn't get nearly the coverage as it had for *Hairspray* and *Cry-Baby* in the *Baltimore Sun* this time around, however.

Production

Looking toward a new script, Waters took his fascination with the celebrity of crime and marveled at how people could so easily go from being "normal" to killing others. Waters also pointed to his work with prisoners in the 1980s as being a reference for his thinking when writing the movie as well. By June 1992, announcements appeared in newspapers that Waters was working on a script for Columbia called *Serial Mom*, and it was to be about a mother who is a serial killer. The pitch went over so well that Waters hadn't even left the building before he was told about it being green-lit. "We left the office," Waters told the *Guardian*, "and we were waiting by the elevator and this executive came out and said—and this is a great, true Hollywood story for

The band L7 appeared in *Serial Mom* (1994) as Camel Lips, a stage act that required rather uncomfortable outfits for the band members.

me—'Can you write this movie in three months?' And he said, 'Don't go to any more meetings; don't fuck with us, and it's a yes.' And I thought, 'God, you know, that's when Hollywood's great, when something like that happens. You run for your life then; never ask why; just get out of town!'"

Then things changed at the studio, as Waters told the *Baltimore Sun*: "[Columbia] loved the script; they accepted the script right away. In fact, writing the script was the best part. But then it got involved in politics. All the people I worked for were replaced and suddenly I was working with all new people. It was complete torture." The film went into a turnaround and various studios picked over the pitch by Waters before passing. During that time of finding a studio, Waters attended pitch meetings with John Fiedler, a producer who had a handful of small films released by that point but who was a Hollywood regular, which Waters felt, as per his comments on the DVD commentary track, helped get them in the door at the studios more so than if it had just been Waters alone. Fiedler would return to produce Waters's next two films after *Serial Mom* as well.

Finally, in February 1993, the announcement came that the film had moved to Savoy Pictures Entertainment, which was, at the time, a new company that was made up of executives previously with Columbia and bank-rolled by two other companies. Waters's film was on the list of three films to be made to kick off the company—the others being *Shadowlands*, a film by Richard Attenborough starring Anthony Hopkins and Debra Winger, and *A Bronx Tale*, which starred Robert De Niro and was his directorial debut. Savoy Films produced fewer than thirty movies that were either art films or action/comedies that bordered on being art films, mostly all of which had low box office returns, before folding in 1998.

Budgeted at $13 million, *Serial Mom* was produced by John Fiedler and Mark Tarlov, who both also produced *Pecker*. "I know that sounds ridiculous compared to my first films," Waters told J. T. Leroy in 2000, "but my [later films] are all done with full unions, the Screen Actors Guild and the teamsters. They are made just like regular Hollywood movies." Filming went smoothly, starting on April 12, 1993, and continuing until June 14, 1993. (Ricki Lake would immediately leave after the wrap party on that night in order to be in New York the next day to begin production of her talk show). The first week of shooting included the scenes at the high school where the math teacher is killed, which was filmed at Towson High School at 69 Cedar Avenue, Towson, Maryland. (This was the very school where Divine spent years being beaten-up, although newspaper reports at the time of filming merely stated that Waters had friends who went there while growing up rather than the sordid details that could have gone with it.)

Beverly's house is located at 600 Lake Drive in Towson, although the interiors of her house were all done on a studio set. The only interior filmed inside the house was that of the scene where Dottie spots Beverly outside her window and destroys the Fabergé egg belonging to Rosemary. This made it appear to be Dottie's house, although it was actually the same house used for the exteriors of Beverly's home. The exterior of Dottie's house—where she is stabbing at the flowers in her yard—is at 618 Lake Drive.

Chip worked at a video store that was located at 400 W. Cold Spring Lane in Baltimore, and it was an actual video store called Video Americain that lasted more than twenty more years after the film before finally closing. Hammerjack's was also a real nightclub, located at 1101 South Howard Street off of I-395. It was torn down to make room for a stadium in 1997.

The church where Beverly is nearly apprehended is the Church of the Good Shepherd at 1401 Carrollton Avenue in Towson. The film completed filming between June 4 and June 14 with the trial sequence, which was shot at the Baltimore County Courthouse, at 400 Washington Avenue in Baltimore.

During filming, Waters hosted a Q&A with Turner at a special screening of her film *House of Cards* on June 9, 1993. There was also a special moment during filming when Turner asked if she could bring her friend, Supreme Court Justice Sandra Day O'Connor, to the courthouse for a visit. Several people were awestruck by meeting the justice, only to find that she was just as impressed in meeting Patricia Hearst, who was there to film her part as Juror #8. Also of note during filming was Waters telling Sam Waterston—after filming the scene where Eugene finds Beverly's scrapbook—that the Christmas card in the scrapbook was a hand-painted card made by serial killer John Wayne Gacy.

The program *Entertainment Tonight* ran a short "sneak preview" of one scene from the film during the weekend of August 13, 1993. There were initial talks of releasing the film in February 1994, which got pushed back to April of that year—first to April 8 and then finally to April 15, 1994—just two days after when initial filming began in 1993. Savoy then began to get cold feet about the film. "When [the studio executives] finally saw it, they'd freak out, even though it was the exact script that I'd said I was going to make," Waters told Austin Trunick in 2017. Soon, Savoy requested that Waters change the ending of the movie to suit the tastes of those who attended test screenings. In 1994, Liz Smith interviewed Turner about Savoy Pictures wanting to change the ending to the film. "Both John and I have refused. Savoy says it's 'too John Waters'—well what the heck do they think a John Waters movie is? I believe the way we filmed it works and I have confidence in that. If they touch it, they are going to violate the whole thing." The *Detroit Free Press*, on April 10, 1994, stated that Waters "beat back efforts by Savoy to have him shoot a new ending for *Serial Mom*, which concludes on a decidedly malevolent, mean-spirited note."

"I don't complain," Waters would reflect in the interview with Austin Trunick in 2017. "I don't name any executives, because the movie's still out there and it's still playing. A couple of them are dead, so they can't defend themselves ... But, if I had done what they had wanted me to [do], we wouldn't be discussing it today. It would have failed twice; it would have failed later in life when these movies do find success."

Release

The film premiered at the Senator in Baltimore on April 6, 1994, and its showing was tied in with a fundraiser for AIDS Action Baltimore, which raised $59,000. The premiere was originally to have been held on March 18, 1994, but it got pushed to the later date in order to get it closer to when the film would be released nationwide. It would be the last film of Waters's to be open in theaters across the country on the same date when it opened on April 15, 1994. After this, his subsequent films would go back to regional release over several weeks.

There were positive reviews for the film at the time. Peter Travers at the *Rolling Stone* gave the film four stars, saying, "Waters dishes out enough subversive wit in *Serial Mom* to keep you memorably entertained." Others, like Roger Ebert, took issue with the tone of the film, with Ebert elaborating that Turner played the role in a way that he felt made Beverly "sick crazy" instead of "funny crazy," and he criticized the multiple times she's railroaded into killing people because others tell her to, thus making her pathetic instead of someone we as the audience can root for in her crimes. Other critics pointed out that a 1993 HBO movie—*The Positively True Adventures of the Alleged Texas Cheerleader-Murdering Mom*, which was based on a true story about a woman who attempted to have a teenager killed because she stood in the way of her daughter's success as a cheerleader—covered the same type of material in a more upbeat fashion.

The film would quickly sour at the box office, earning only $7.8 million after costing $13 million (some sources say $13.5 million) to make. It would be the second box-office disappointment in a row for Waters, but time has told a different story. First released on VHS by Warner Home Video in May 1998, then later on DVD in May 2008, and finally on Blu-ray in May 2017, the film found its audience with fans who did not see the film when it originally came out to theaters in 1994. The movie is now considered among fans to be one of Waters's best films, and it has been a big seller on the video market, with many pointing out that Waters's take on celebrity trials and murders has come to pass. Waters's subject matter was especially ironic given that the film was theatrically released into theaters just two months before the

Autographed copy of the Blu-ray special edition of *Serial Mom*.

infamous murders connected with O. J. Simpson that would lead to a media circus over his trial. Waters has since remarked that it is the one movie of his that fans of both his earlier works and later ones seem to all like.

But in 1994 all of that was still in the future. With the film not doing well at the box office after the studio requested changes that were not made, it was obvious that Savoy was not going to be making another film with Waters. Waters now was in a position where he had to come up with a new idea for a movie that would be needed to be sent through the same pitch process he had to go through for *Serial Mom*.

He had a script idea in mind, and it finally would get made. It's just that it would have to wait a few years while he made another movie instead.

17

Full of Grace

The Making of *Pecker*

They're just traditions in Baltimore and nowhere else: pit beef and "teabagging."

—John Waters to Gerald Peary on the two most
memorable elements of *Pecker*

Plot

Pecker (Edward Furlong) is an eighteen-year-old man who works at a sandwich shop, the Sub Pit, while still living at home with his eccentric family. Pecker is his nickname due to his lack of interest in eating. His main passions are his girlfriend, Shelly (Christina Ricci), who obsessively runs a laundromat, and taking photos of everyone and everything around him.

Pecker's mom (Mary Kay Place) runs a thrift shop that caters to people with little money, while his father (Mark Joy) runs a nearby bar. Business is slow at the bar due to a lesbian strip club across the street called the Pelt Room, where the strippers show pubic hair. His grandmother (Jean Schertler) runs a "pit beef"—roast beef cooked for hours and then sliced into sandwiches—stand outside of the house and has a ventriloquist doll of the Virgin Mary that says "Full of Grace" (although she doesn't appear to realize that she's the one manipulating the doll/statue and when it says this). His sister, Tina (Martha Plimpton), works the bar at the Fudge Palace, a gay strip club, where all the strippers are straight but where no "teabagging" (slapping genitals on someone's forehead) is allowed. Or it's at least frowned upon.

Pecker has a show of his photos at the Sub Pit, where he meets Rorey Wheeler (Lili Taylor), who has an art gallery in New York City. Rorey loves a

Philly's Best at 1101 West 36th Street, located in the Hampden area of Baltimore, stood in as the Sub Pit, the sub shop where Pecker works and shows off his artwork at the beginning of *Pecker*.

picture of "the pubic hair of a stripper" and buys it for thirty dollars, and she offers to have a showing of Pecker's work at her gallery. Since he just got fired from his job at the Sub Pit—for displaying a picture of "the pubic hair of a stripper"—he is happy with the sale and okays the show.

The show goes well for Pecker, although Shelly is unhappy being around people who go to dry cleaners instead of laundromats. Tina causes problems for being forthright in calling a man a "mary," as she would in her job at the gay bar. At the dinner to celebrate the art show, Shelly begins to stress out over being away from her laundromat, fearing her customers are already "pissing in the dryers" because she's not there. In addition, Pecker's mom invites two homeless people who were standing outside the gallery to the dinner, which rubs people the wrong way. Also Pecker's little sister—Little Chrissy (Lauren Hulsey), who will only eat candy—is freaked out by the fancy dinner, and her actions gets the attention of the Baltimore City Child Protection Services (CPS).

Back in Baltimore, the paper has the news, and with it comes word that the family's house was robbed by a man who "didn't get paid for" a picture that Pecker had taken of him. All that is stolen is the TV, the VCR, cookies, a clock radio, an electric shaver, and Tina's Liza Minelli CDs, but nothing of Pecker's was touched. Still, even with news that another show is being lined up for him in New York, Pecker is starting to feel that he has caused problems for everyone instead of helping them or doing what he really wants to do with his photos, which is simply to display them without the fame that is quickly being attached to him.

The next morning, an issue of *Artforum* arrives, showing Pecker's grandmother and the Virgin Mary on the cover, but that bit of brightness is dimmed when Dr. Deborah Klompas (Bess Armstrong, in a part that reeks of Mink Stole) of CPS arrives and demands they put Little Chrissy on Ritalin. Pecker tries to take pictures, but with his instant celebrity status, people are refusing to be "used" by him in his photographs, and another person plans to sue him for using her picture without her consent. Pecker's best friend Matt (Brendan Sexton III) gets caught shoplifting because he's been seen in the photos doing so, making his life and career a failure. Meanwhile, the *Village Voice* referred to Shelly as a "stain goddess," and she begins to get obscene phone calls at her laundromat.

Little Chrissy is soon a zombie on Ritalin, Shelly is refusing to talk to Pecker, and people are trying to remake his mom into somebody for fashion photographs. Even the workers at the Pelt Room are being arrested for having shown "bush" in their stripping, thanks to Pecker's photos of one of the strippers doing her act. And Pecker's grandmother faces a backlash when women who come to see the Virgin Mary speak notice that the grandmother is moving her mouth, making her a heretic in their eyes. With that, the Virgin Mary no longer speaks, "ruining" the "miracle."

Even the Fudge Factory is facing problems, as Pecker's photos make it appear that everyone should go there for "teabagging." The owner only wants gay customers and never wanted teabagging there anyway, so he is livid enough to not let any of the straights in until they pony up some cash. Unfortunately, the first older couple inside the Fudge Factory find their son dancing (although he protests that it's just his trade and that he's not gay). Tina is fired, and although Pecker protests, he can't stop himself from taking a picture of Tina's grief over losing her dream job of announcing the strippers at the club.

The only one who seems to be enjoying Pecker's newfound fame is Rorey, who is working as Pecker's agent. She sends him a top-of-the-line camera to use. Pecker continues to take photos, but they are meaningless to him. In his basement to give him a check and talk over his next show, Rorey makes a move on Pecker and he reciprocates, only for Shelly to catch him in the act and photograph him. Rorey is sorry to cause Shelly any pain, but admits that she was really wanting to have a nice boyfriend for once. This just puts more pressure on Pecker, who feels like what he has done has ruined everyone's life.

Pecker wants his life back. He refuses to do the new show at the Whitney that Rorey had planned and instead, with his money, hires Matt to work for him. Shelly attempts to escape Pecker in a voting booth during Election Day, but Pecker sneaks his way into her booth. Shelly doesn't understand art, but Pecker tells her that art can be found everywhere, even in her job dealing with dirty clothes all day. She begins to see what he means and they reconcile, having sex in the voting booth.

Sometime later, the bar Pecker's dad owns is transformed into Pecker's Place, which is a combination thrift shop/bar/strip club/art gallery allowing everyone a place to do what they do best. Further, instead of a busload of people going to New York to see Pecker's art in a gallery, a group of patrons arrive by bus outside of Pecker's Place to see his work. The locals get in for free, but the out-of-towners have to pay. The Whitney crowd who drove in are stunned and embarrassed to see that they are the subjects of his new

Pecker (Edward Furlong) taking pictures of his girlfriend Shelly (Christina Ricci) at the laundromat she manages during the happy, early days of Pecker's art career.

work. Soon they realize that their snootiness can't compare with people actually being people, and they join in the fun at Pecker's Place. Rorey has found a new talent to push—a blind photographer—and Little Chrissy is off the medication and sugar ... although she's now gobbling vegetables like no tomorrow.

Soon people are happy, drinking, and stripping in the club, leading to some more teabagging, while the Virgin Mary returns, this time talking through the doll without any assistance. Everyone cheers Pecker and "the end of irony." Asked what he plans to do next, Pecker gives it some thought and suggests that he may try to make a movie.

Claims to Condemnation

- A ventriloquist doll based on the Virgin Mary.
- Full frontal female nudity.
- Minor transgressions: shoplifting, mild teabagging.

Additional Cast and Crew

At the time of filming, Waters joked to the *Baltimore Sun* about the number of actors in his films that would not be considered your normal cast for a John Waters movie, saying, "It's practically a Woody Allen cast."

Waters picked Edward Furlong for the title role based on the number of "intense kind of brooding kids" he played in films ever since his role in *Terminator2*, where he played the young John Connor. "Eddie understood the part. Completely," Waters stated at a press conference for the movie at the *1998 Toronto Film Festival*. "I just had to talk him into believing that he had a great smile."

He had also been following Christina Ricci's career when he asked her to audition for the role of Shelly. "I interviewed her right on that couch—it's not a casting couch," Waters told Gerald Peary. "Ricki Lake for *Hairspray* and she were the same. They read with no direction from me, and it was exactly the way I'd been playing the parts in my head. They just got it!" Van Smith reported to the *Baltimore Sun* that Ricci was in tears when she realized how she would look in the film, with Waters responding, "Tell her everybody looks bad in my movies."

Martha Plimpton was an early choice to play Pecker's sister Tina. In more than one interview at the time, Waters voiced the opinion that if anyone were to make a movie about Cookie Mueller, Plimpton should play the part. Plimpton was surprised to get the role, as she told Jenny Peters of the *Daily Times*: "I never really thought I fit into that world. So it was surprising to me, and thrilling, obviously that he would believe that I could do that." Plimpton went on to say in the same interview that she feared Waters would be a director looking for people to improvise and giving them "free rein to do anything," an idea she found "sort of paralyzing." However, like those who have worked with Waters, Plimpton learned that this wasn't the case, saying: "He is probably one of the most specific directors I've ever worked with. He knows exactly what he wants at every given moment. He has no time for phony baloney sort of pretense."

Brendan Sexton III, who plays Matt, had previous appeared in Todd Solondz's *Welcome to the Dollhouse* (1995) and many small and large roles since. Lili Taylor usually appeared in dramatic roles and would appear in the movie *Four Rooms* with Alicia Witt, who will be a costar in Waters's next film, *Cecil B. DeMented*.

The *Boston Globe*, in October 1997, stated that Ricki Lake would be appearing in *Pecker* and that she had made changes in her talk show schedule so she could take the train to Baltimore two days a week and film her role. As she, Taylor, Plimpton, and Ricci were all listed in early promotional material about the film, it is difficult to imagine what role she would have played in the film. Lake will return in the subsequent Waters film, *Cecil B. DeMented*.

Mink Stole was living in Los Angeles at the time of filming but flew in to film her scene as the Precinct Captain (and, a rarity, to play a character who isn't evil in some fashion ... maybe a little uptight, but hardly evil). "When we had big premieres of *Pecker*, her name got the biggest applause of anyone in all three cities," Waters told the *Guardian*. "It was great for me, because it showed that people have grown up with my movies and have grown old with her." Also appearing of the old school were Susan Lowe as a hairdresser, Channing Wilroy as a neighbor, and Mary Vivian Pearce as a homophobic woman. The film even saw the return of Bob Skidmore in the role he was born to play—a deliveryman.

Pecker saw the first appearance of Joyce Flick Wendl (Alan J. Wendl's wife in real life) as the street person hanging outside the gallery when Pecker has his first New York show. She'll return in Waters's last two films. With her in the scene is Liam Hughes as the "Wild Man of 22nd Street." Hughes will return in *A Dirty Shame* as the "Coffee Sex Addict." Jean Schertler, who plays Pecker's grandmother, also returns in *A Dirty Shame* as a grandmother on a bus.

The stripper T-Bone, who appears in male drag near the end of the picture, is played by Mo Fischer, a well-known "drag king" whom Waters interviewed for *Grand Street Magazine* in 1997. Her drag king character's name is Mo B. Dick. The character of T-Bone was based on Zorro—a stripper Waters had seen as a teenager and wrote about in his book *Role Models*—who would come out naked and angrily yelled at the men, "What the fuck are you looking at?"

The blonde on the bus who gets a little freaked out by Matt is Stacey Kiebler, born in Baltimore County, who would go on to become a Nitro Girl on the wrestling program WCW and later a wrestler for another wrestling company, WWE.

Production

Serial Mom is remembered today as a very popular DVD to both rent and buy, but it did poorly at the box office. With the one-two punch, Waters was looking for another studio for a script he had called *Cecil B. DeMented*. When interest proved to be lacking, Waters turned his attention to an idea of the art world and how fame can sometimes not be what everyone wants it to be like. Pecker is a young man who takes photos and is looking for people to like them—hence the show he advertises with flyers at the sub store—but isn't seeing what the art fans in New York see in them. "Pecker's pictures, to be successful, have to be taken out of context and looked at with irony," Waters told *Entertainment Today* in 1998. "I don't think that's wrong—I collect modern photography, and I have pictures of people I don't know who look ugly hanging in my house. But I just always wonder what the people in the pictures think later, especially if the photograph becomes famous. And it's never famous because of them; it's famous because of the photographer."

Although Pecker is a kid who picks up a camera that he doesn't know how to work and makes art by using his friends and family—who all tolerate his interest—Waters never saw the character as being a version of himself. Perhaps a glorified "wishful thinking" type of version of himself, but not how he would have acted, as he wanted that fame and knew he could handle it. "It wasn't corruptive at all to me," he continued to *Entertainment Today*. "I was wanting people to notice my movies. I wanted the New York world to discover them. It wasn't like Pecker."

Potential backers were given a ten-page treatment and an ad campaign, but it was not quite the quick sale that *Serial Mom* had been. "Once when I was pitching *Pecker*," Waters told the *Guardian*, "I mentioned teabagging and this guy's face just dropped, and he screamed, 'what did you say?' and I just knew we didn't have the movie at the time."

The movie poster for *Pecker* (1998), with Edward Furlong as Pecker, an artist who does not want to be a star.

Eventually, Waters landed with Fine Line, who agreed to make the film at half of the cost of *Serial Mom*. "Pecker is cheap, $6.5 million," Waters told Gerald Peary at the time. "When lately has someone made a full union movie at that price with Teamsters, IA, etc., and, well, all those actors?" The only roadblock was that of the MPAA, who had flagged the title of the movie as being an issue. Waters, flashing back to his fights with the Maryland Board of Censors, saw red. "My lawyers had a list of titles to show them like *Shaft, Free Willy, In & Out*, and I gave a little speech saying, 'Pecker might be vulgar, but it's not an obscene word.' And 'This is a movie about someone who wants his good name back. And in this case the good name is Pecker!'" As Waters told Peary, the MPAA came back telling Waters that they were fine with the title but added, "We saw your title and had to flag it."

Filming started on October 21, 1997, in Hampden—an area of Baltimore that now has a thriving art community running through most of the shops in the main drag, called "the Avenue"—and the location of Atomic Books, where Waters has all his mail sent. The sub shop where Pecker worked is actually Philly's Best at 1101 West 36th Street, and is still there. The building where the Pelt Room was, at 3851 Falls Road, has been remodeled and is now a restaurant. The Spin and Grin at 3401 Keswick Road is a salon, while Pecker's house at 3842 Quarry Avenue burned down several years ago. Finally, the place where people go to vote, among other things, was at St. Luke's Evangelical Lutheran Church at Chestnut Avenue and West 36th Street.

Filming moved along without incident, which was somewhat disappointing to Vincent Peranio, who admitted that he missed the old days, while telling the *Baltimore Sun*, "I love the grittiness of the first films, the surprise and the shock. I think some of the films get a little too nice, a little too sweet." Of course, he readily admitted that the only way they were going to continue making movies was to make them for bigger audiences, so the changes had to come, but he would lament those old days many times in interviews since.

The filming of the rats humping in the trashcan was done with the help of a veterinarian and a gimmick trashcan that allowed people to hold the rats in place and shake them. "In the last take, they kept doing it and they wouldn't stop," Waters told the *Guardian*. "And I was sitting by the monitor and there was no sound, so I was joking, 'Fuck me, baby,' and then I look over and the veterinarian's seven-year-old daughter was standing there." When the hairdresser on the set tried to pet one of the rats immediately afterward, the rat bit him, sending him to the hospital with a story about being bitten by a rat while filming it having sex. "The nurse laughed right in his face," Waters reminisced.

It wasn't his only odd encounter with children on the movie. As Waters was filming the police raid on the Pelt Room, school was letting out and a school bus full of young kids watched as the demonstrators in the street shouted, "We want bush! We want bush!"

The scene where Matt is shoplifting and then requests a job application is straight out of Waters's past. Waters once frequented a store he shoplifted at so often that when he did request a job application, he later returned to find that they were considering hiring him, which scared him off from ever returning to the store.

For the final bar scene, in which Patricia Hearst gets up on the bar and begins to dance in her slip, there were no problems from Hearst. Speaking at the Toronto Film Festival in 1998, Waters said: "She brought her own slip to make sure she had the right one. I was never gonna ask her to do anything that I thought she would be uncomfortable doing. To be honest, when she came to Baltimore for this, she walked into my living room and said, 'How's this?' And she unzipped the dress she had on and I went, 'Fine, you've got the part.'"

All the photographs that were done by Pecker were actually photographed by Chuck Shacochis with an old Nikon camera belonging to Waters, which did cause some minor delays in filming. "They were taken on the last walk-through rehearsal, just before the first take. Because they had to be in the scene I was shooting," Waters said at the Toronto Film Festival. "The whole film had to be scheduled around those pictures. And since we didn't have access to the location before that day, we had to fake it, the scenes weren't blocked. So it was very complicated."

Filming completed on December 3, 1997, with plans for the film to be released in the second half of 1998. Former Police guitarist and accomplished composer Stewart Coopeland wrote the score for the film, including two songs cowritten by Waters: "Straight Boys" and "Don't Drop the Soap (For Anyone Else but Me)." The film would be the last Waters film for Janice Hampton as the editor.

Release

The film premiered at the Senator on September 16, 1998, with the *Baltimore Sun* holding a contest for people to take pictures for submission to the newspaper, whereupon John Waters would pick several to put on display in the lobby of the Senator Theatre for the night of the premiere. Winners got to attend the premiere as well as get autographed copies of the movie poster.

The film was officially released on September 25, 1998, and began moving through regions of the country over the next few months. The movie was a first for Waters, in that there are no bad guys in the film—even Lili Taylor's character, Rorey, is not out to hurt anyone, she's just trying to do the best for Pecker and sees him as a catch as a boyfriend. Every other Waters film has bad people trying to treat others poorly—sometimes there are even levels of badness, like in *Pink Flamingos*, when we root for people we would dislike in other movies because there are even worse people than them in the film. *Pecker* is uncommon for that reason—everyone seems to be happy working out their issues and being together, even if at first they feel somewhat awkward about it.

Reviews were overall positive. Michael O'Sullivan of the *Washington Post* called it a "screwball hymn of praise to old-fashioned family values." Robert Ebert, who traditionally has shown little patience for Waters, did not care for it, feeling the film full of missed opportunities for shock value, when Waters preferred to go for laughs. Many critics found the gentle nature of the film so unlike what they were used to from Waters that they felt a bit put out over it, which may have been a shock to them in a way as well.

The film cost only $6.5 million to make but made back only $2.3 million in theaters. The film appeared on VHS by New Line Home Video in July 1999 and then as a double-set DVD combo with *Hairspray* by New Line in 2001. Warner Brothers released it as a single disc in June 2005.

It would be four years until Waters made another movie. On the upside, at least it was a film based on a script he had been wanting to make for quite some time.

18

DeMented Forever

The Making of *Cecil B. DeMented*

Cecil B. DeMented is more, to me, a parody of me if I were humor impaired and was going to become a film terrorist.

—John Waters to James Egan

Plot

Honey Whitlock (Melanie Griffith) is a popular, but airheaded, Hollywood movie star who is in Baltimore to promote her new movie, *Some Kind of Happiness*, at the Senator. As the film goes along, we learn that she's actually on the skids: she's made a number of box-office duds, has an ex-husband who happily goes on a talk show to gossip about her, and has to deal with the public opinion that she's a hack. She doesn't help her image by being dismissive of others on the way to the film's charity premiere, forcing her assistant, Libby (Ricki Lake), to make a fool out of herself with the hotel staff, and being extremely rude with the help at the hotel.

Also hiding behind an image of innocence is that of the staff at the Senator, who turn out to be a group of cinematic terrorists called the "Sprocket Holes," whose leader is crazed underground filmmaker Cecil B. DeMented (Stephen Dorff). They appear to all be happy, clean-cut workers at the theater, but as the ceremony gets closer to beginning, the audience sees that they all have guns and bombs hidden away in the theater and are communicating through walkie-talkies and other surveillance equipment. With each other they share coded messages that are famous but bastardized rebellious quotes mixed with movie jargon.

After an opening speech by Sylvia Mallory (Mink Stole) at the Senator—which involves Sylvia turning down the oxygen to a young boy on stage who had begun being obnoxious—Whitlock comes onstage to introduce the film. She has just barely begun when the Sprocket Holes take over the stage, exploding small bombs and starting a fire in order to create chaos in the theater as they kidnap Whitlock and shove her into the trunk of the limo waiting outside. In the ruckus, Sylvia falls over dead of a heart attack, the first victim of the terrorist group's actions.

Melanie Griffith as Honey Whitlock in *Cecil B. DeMented* (2000).

The group dives into the limo and they drive to the decaying remnants of a theater called the Hippodrome, where the group plans to make their underground film of "Ultimate Reality." The movie, *Raving Beauty*, is to star Whitlock, with the terrorists working either in front of or behind the camera. It is inside the theater that Whitlock's blindfold is taken off and DeMented introduces himself. He has a tattoo on his arm that shows the name of famous director Otto Preminger. He introduces the rest of the terrorist crew, each of whom is marked with a tattoo of another director and has made a vow of celibacy until they get their film made; in other words, they're horny. The crew members are:

- Cherish (Alicia Witt): Whitlock's costar in the planned film. The tattoo on her thigh says "Andy Warhol." She is a known porn actress who has played a parody of Whitlock's characters in several porn films, such as in her new film, *Some Kind of Horniness*. (Her porno seen at the theater later in the film, where her character is on her bed writing in her diary, is reminiscent of the Whitlock film playing at the drive-in when Whitlock's character is in bed writing in her diary.) She is to play Whitlock's daughter in the movie. Cherish later rants about suppressed memories of her entire family, including grandma, having sex with her one Christmas—a story that everyone else in the group has heard far too many times and obviously believe is not true.

- Lyle (Adrian Grenier): Whitlock's leading man in the planned film. The tattoo above his left nipple reads, "Hershell Gordon Lewis." He spends his time so high on drugs that he won't even really feel it when he is shot in the forehead later in the movie. Even so, he manages to say his lines without difficulty with just a prompt. He is to play the owner of a theater showing a Pasolini Festival in the movie. (It should be noted that Lyle looks like he could be Howard Gruber's son.)

- Pam (Erika Auchterlonie): Director of photography. Her tattoo on her arm says "Sam Peckinpah."

- Chardonnay (Zenzele Uzoma): Sound. The tattoo on her torso says "Spike Lee."

- Lewis (Lawrence Gillard Jr.): Art director. The tattoos on his fingers spell out "David Lynch."

- Fidget (Eric Barry): Wardrobe. The tattoo on his chest says "William Castle." He has parents (Patricia Hearst and Mark Joy) who want him back and assume that the movies he watched as a kid turned him into a terrorist. He's undecided if he wants to remain with the group.

- Raven (Maggie Gyllenhaal): Makeup and resident Satanist. Her tattoo near the nape of her neck reads "Kenneth Anger." She punches Whitlock in the face because Satan just told her Whitlock "needed more color."
- Rodney (Jack Noseworthy): Hair. The tattoo on his bicep reads "Almodovar" (for director Pedro Almodovar). He plans to change Whitlock's hair color to platinum and hates roots. He's straight but wishes he were gay for the sake of Petie.
- Petie (Michael Shannon): Driver. His tattoo is "Fassbinder" (for Rainer Werner Fassbinder). He is heartbroken that Rodney cannot love him back in a physical way.
- Dinah (Harry Dodge): Producer. Their tattoo reads "Sam Fuller." It is Dinah's money that is paying for the movie.

The next day, Whitlock is given her new hair color, makeup, and outfit for first day of filming. She drives the crew to agony with her walk-through rehearsal of the first scripted scene—where her character and two others decide to stage a revolution against mainstream cinema. However, once the camera is rolling, she gives an excellent professional performance. Nevertheless, she thinks the concept is idiotic and states, "Ask anyone in any country and they'll tell you that Hollywood makes the best movies in the world." DeMented ignores the comment and tells her that they plan to move on with his vision—filming in real places with real people and real terror.

The first outside scene takes place at a strip mall theater, where people are watching an extended director's cut of *Patch Adams*—a movie made longer when "the first one was long enough!" They terrorize the weeping audience and cause them to scatter. Whitlock is unhappy with it but is begrudgingly happy with the news reports showing people praising her. Meanwhile, the Maryland Film Commission is staging a live conference and oyster luncheon to promote movie productions in Baltimore. While watching the conference, DeMented has "a vision" and sends the group out to the conference to stage another part of the film.

DeMented gives Whitlock a gun to use in her role, and she jumps off a building, lands by the podium, and shoots one of the attendees. She knows that the gun is real, but DeMented swears to her that it's loaded with blanks. When she fires the gun, she is pleased to find that DeMented was not lying and that the person she "shot" is okay (the guy who is "shot" is happy as well). That euphoric moment is over quickly as the police arrive and a gun-fight takes place. Rodney is killed, and DeMented is wounded in the crossfire. Whitlock gives herself up but is roughly handed by the police, so when

DeMented and the others follow, Whitlock is happy to see them and readily escapes the police when DeMented shoots out a front tire, forcing the police car to smash into the ticket booth of the Grand Theatre.

It is there that the terrorists run into an angry mob of family-moviegoers. The mob gives chase, forcing the Sprocket Holes to seek help in the Patterson Theater, where a group of action movie fans watching a kung-fu film hold off the angry family-picture fans. Back at the Hippodrome, Whitlock is allowed to walk around on her own without restraints, having now joined the others. Everyone is being branded; Fidget is reluctant, as is Whitlock, but both soon join in.

The Sprocket Holes next invade the studio where a sequel for *Forrest Gump—Gump Again—*is being filmed, with Kevin Nealon playing Forrest. The terrorists disrupt the filming, but a number of teamsters begin shooting at them on the set, shooting Lyle in the forehead and hitting DeMented in the shoulder. Pam and Fidget are both hit, and then Dinah takes two hits square in the chest. Those of the group who are still alive, including the wounded, take off, with the teamsters in pursuit. They manage to make it on foot to the Apex, where an "All Anal Evening Starring Cherish" festival is going on. With Cherish driving them on, the men in the audience singled-handedly drive away the incredibly grossed-out teamsters, and the Sprocket Holes head off for their final assault.

The Bengies Drive-In is having a triple-feature show of Honey Whitlock films, including a look-a-like contest and free wanted posters for each car. DeMented, seriously wounded, incites the drive-in audience, and the terrorists climb to the top of the snack bar. Fidget's and DeMented's parents try to talk them down, but it is of little use. In a final act against Hollywood Cinema, Whitlock is filmed setting her hair on fire.

The film is finished, and so is the patience of the police, as sharpshooters begin to pick off members of the Sprocket Holes, starting with Pam. The Sprocket Holes are anxious as well—now that the film is done, they can finally have sex, and they begin to go at it on the roof of the snack bar—with Raven and Petie finding groupies in the crowd for pairing off. Cherish is next to be shot by the police, dying instantly while having sex with DeMented.

As DeMented creates a diversion by setting himself on fire and throwing himself off the roof of the snack bar, the other remaining living members escape with the film and newfound members to join the cause, while Fidget winds up back with his parents. Whitlock is captured, and as the crowd either jeers or cheers her, she walks dreamlike, as if at a premiere, waving and blowing kisses to the crowd as she makes her way to the paddy wagon and jail.

Claims to Condemnation

- Bestiality
- Drug use on-camera
- Depiction of masturbation
- Indication of sexual relations, both heterosexual and homosexual, outside of marriage.
- Minor transgressions: vomiting, murder, robbery, disrespect for authority, making fun of *Patch Adams*.

Additional Cast and Crew

An ad for auditions appeared in the *Baltimore Sun* on September 20, 1999, stating that the movie would be "shot entirely on location in Baltimore, beginning the first week of October." Approximately sixty speaking roles were open, and young people in particular—"teenagers through early twenties"—were sought. "No experience is necessary, and no face is wrong."

Melanie Griffith is a popular actress who had been in movies since the 1970s, with Arthur Penn's *Night Moves* being one of the first really big films for her. The 1980s were an important period for her, with such films as *Body Double* (1984), *Something Wild* (1986), and *Working Girl* (1988). Waters had acted with Griffith in a brief scene in *Something Wild* (see Chapter 23 for more details), and liked her performance in Larry Clark's *Another Day in Paradise* (1998). "I thought she might do it," Waters told Avclub.com. "She was an A-list star, but in that film, she allowed herself to be very different from the usual ingénue." Knowing that her husband at the time, Antonio Banderas, had worked with Pedro Almodovar, convinced Waters that Banderas may be helpful in persuading her to take on the role as well, which was the case. Waters mentioned at the time that Griffith had to leave the production at one point to shoot advertising for Revlon cosmetics—a look very much counter to her makeup in the film.

Stephen Dorff had been spending a certain amount of time performing in films such as *S.F.W.* (1994), *I Shot Andy Warhol* (1996), and *Blade* (1998) when he took on the role of Cecil B. DeMented. Alicia Witt had made her film

Stephen Dorff as the "cinematic terrorist" Cecil B. DeMented.

debut as Alia Atreides in David Lynch's *Dune* (1984) and then appeared in such films as *Bodies, Rest & Motion* (1993) and *Mr. Holland's Opus* (1995). Adrian Grenier would later become better known as Vincent Chase on the series *Entourage*. Lawrence Gilliard, Jr. would later be a regular on the series *The Wire* and has bounced between television and movies since. Maggie Gyllenhaal would appear in *Donnie Darko* in 2001 alongside her brother Jake Gyllenhaal. One of her bigger films was 2008's *The Dark Knight*, in which she played Rachel Dawes. Jack Noseworthy has been in a number of films, including as the brattish Eric in *The Brady Bunch Movie* (1995) and was also in *S.F.W.*

Michael Shannon has had a very successful career after this film, moving on to such films as *Bug* (2004) and *Take Shelter* (2011). He appeared as a regular on HBO's *Boardwalk Empire* (2010–2014) and played General Zod in *Man of Steel*. Considering how often he has played men smoldering on the end of a breakdown, it is interesting to see him in something a bit lighter, if not less chaotic. Eric M. Barry has produced films for the Nickelodeon series *Crashletes* (2016–2017). Zenzele Uzoma is listed on Imdb.com as having finished a film called *Flimsy Company*. (2018).

Ricki Lake appears in a small role as Whitlock's assistant. "It's a really nice part," Lake told Lydia Martin of Knight Ridder Newspapers. "It's a small part, but I can't play the part he actually wrote for me. I work the whole time and so I'm not available." She'll make a very brief appearance in Waters's next film as well. There is little information on Erika Auchterlonie other than that she made an appearance in an episode of *Homicide: Life on the Streets* in 1997.

Finally, of the Sprocket Holes, there is Harry Dodge, who was credited in the film as Harriet Dodge. Dodge is an artist and writer from out of San Francisco and is presently a faculty member at the California Institute of the Arts.

Waters told Jaime Painter Young that they did have one other actress in mind for a role in the film, but there was an issue with the script: "We had one actress that was cast as one of the Sprocket Holes and then read the script and said, 'Morally, I find this reprehensible.' Oh! That shocked me!"

Of the regulars, there was Mink Stole, who at the time of *Pink Flamingos* had been asked to set her hair on fire "for art" (a part of the *Cecil B. DeMented* script that didn't get past her). Susan Lowe and Mary Vivian Pearce appear as family-film mothers. Alan Wendl appears as the security guard at the filming of *Gump Again* and his wife Joyce is the woman throwing up in the "Movies in the Mall" theater. Channing Wilroy is also seen briefly in the filming of *Gump Again*. It did not escape anyone's notice that Patricia Hearst was appearing in a film about an affluent woman being kidnapped and forced into crimes against her will, and Waters pointedly mentioned that he avoided drawing arrows to the link in the film, saying that there was no chance that Hearst would wear a beret, hold a gun, rob a bank, etc.

Production

In the production notes on the DVD released, Waters talks about seeing an article about him that was titled *"Cecil B. DeMented."* He laughed but it got his mind rolling on an idea for his next script. "I thought, 'Well, people always refer to me as a cult director; suppose I really was a cult director?' In the true sense of the word, like a director that would appear in a trailer and say to his fans, 'Send me money. Go commit crimes.' And the audience would do it in real life. Commit suicide for celluloid. That kind of scary tribute."

There was also a personal agenda for him as he was becoming known for films that were not the edgy type of material expected from him by the fans who loved *Pink Flamingos* and *Desperate Living*. In his own way, he was still being subversive, but people seemed to also clamor for more antisocial actions in his movies. Films like *There's Something About Mary*, *Scary Movie 1–5*, and others pushed the envelope when it came to gross-out humor but typically didn't do it in a clever or funny way. "I'm making fun of myself," Waters told Ben Nuckols. "What is an edge anymore? Do you have to die? Is that the only thing left, now that everyone's hip, every critic is hip, and everything I used to do twenty years ago is on TV?"

Waters finished the *Cecil* script after completing *Serial Mom*, but the proposed deal he had with French producer Yves Attal (probably best remembered for the Liv Tyler film *Stealing Beauty* in 1996) and UGC Images fell apart in 1997. Waters moved on to getting a deal for his *Pecker* script and only returned to the older idea after filming of that movie was completed.

In May 1999, *Variety* accounted that Waters had signed with Studio Canal Plus—a French production company that was slowly beginning to make American productions. The budget was set for $9.3 million, an increase from *Pecker* of nearly $3 million, but it involved a story with explosions, effects, and action sequences—a far cry from just needing to pay for *Pecker*'s talking Virgin Mary. Distributor Artisan came on board in the summer of 2000 to help distribute the film to theaters (and eventually on DVD).

The film, done under Icecap Productions, commenced filming on October 4, 1999, after first being announced to start earlier in September. Many of the locations for filming took place at theaters that Waters went to while growing up in Baltimore.

- The Senator Theatre at 5904 York Road has been the home of many premieres for Waters's films over the years. It is used for the location of the premiere Whitlock is attending in the film. An ad in the *Baltimore Sun* appeared on Sunday, October 17, 1999, to announce that the theater would be closed from October 18 through October 21 in order to film the opening scene of the film.
- The Hippodrome at 12 North Eutaw Street was really in poor condition at the time filming was done at it to show DeMented's hideout. It has been restored since then.
- The interiors of the Sprocket Hole's hideout were not filmed at the Hippodrome, however, but at the Century, just a few blocks away at 18 West Lexington Street.
- The "Movies in the Mall" strip mall theater, where the Sprocket Holes interrupt a showing of the director's cut of *Patch Adams*, was the Beltway

Movies 6 at the time of filming and is still in operation as the Horizon Cinema 6 at 7660 Belair Road in Fullerton, Maryland.

- After fleeing the attack on the Maryland Film Commission—which was filmed outside the National Aquarium at 501 East Pratt Street—the Sprocket Holes end up outside of the Grand Theatre, which was located at 508 South Conkling Street.
- They make a break for it to go inside the Patterson Theater at 3134 Eastern Avenue, which was roughly a quarter of a mile away rather than just around the block as it appears in the film.
- The escape from the teamsters occurs at the Apex Audit Cinema at 3417 Eastern Boulevard. Just like the Senator before it, the Apex had an ad in the *Baltimore Sun* to announce they would be closing on October 26 and 27 for the filming of the scene.

The Hippodrome in downtown Baltimore, where Cecil and the gang hide out *Cecil B. DeMented* (2000).

John Waters with Melanie Griffith in the Hippodrome in downtown Baltimore.

- The movie concludes at the Bengies Drive-In at 3417 Eastern Boulevard in Middle River.

Filming was completed on November 19, 1999, with editing done by Jeffrey Wolf, who would go on to do Waters's *A Dirty Shame* in 2004. The opening theme song, "Opening Credit Theme," was written by Moby, who told the *Los Angeles Times* in January 2000, "I've had to turn a lot of offers down in order to focus on my own records, but since [Waters] has been a hero of mine since I was fourteen, I had to say yes." Waters co-wrote the songs "Bankable Bitch," "No Budget," and "DeMented Forever." The film was ready in early 2000 for its premiere in May as an official festival entry at the Cannes Film Festival.

Release

The movie made its American premiere at the Senator on August 2, 2000, and then was released slowly across the country starting on August 11, 2000. A charity auction for the Prisoner Aid Association took place for a week started August 12, 2000, with props and costumes from the film going up for bidding.

Reviews were mixed and the box office was a disappointment at only $2 million, with some suggesting that that Waters was no longer shocking in the way that critics—although not the fans—expected him to be. The film would be the first Waters film to be released simultaneously on DVD and VHS in January 2001.

While the film did not do well, is has been fondly remembered by fans, and Waters was later asked what would have happened to the characters after the movie. "What I think would happen is that Cecil really wouldn't be dead," Waters told J. T. Leroy. "He would be severely burned like the person in *Mask*, and he would go to Paris and become a French director and would have to be saved by his cult. The two black kids would become very rich from the footage, which they'd sell to 20/20. And certainly Melanie Griffith's character, Honey Whitlock, would have pleaded insanity, maybe even have been convicted, but for a short amount of time. It would be very good for her career, and she would be back working with all of the best of the new young independent film directors!" A deservedly happy ending for the berserk filmmakers. Maybe not so much for the people they killed along the way, but one can't have everything.

In real life, things were not looking quite as good for Waters's next project, which he already knew would be centered on sex addicts. The film would face controversy and would seemingly be the last picture Waters will make—but if he had to go out, it might as well be with the biggest bang possible.

19

Let's Go Sexing

The Making of *A Dirty Shame*

> I'm glad this next movie of mine isn't about violence. A comedy about sex ought to be fairly safe.
>
> —Waters to Jack Garner in 2001 on his high hopes for *A Dirty Shame*

Plot

Sylvia (Tracey Ullman) is an uptight woman who lives with her husband, Vaughn (Chris Isaak). Their daughter, Caprice (Selma Blair), a.k.a. Ursula Udders, a very large breasted woman, is a compulsive exhibitionist and needs to be locked in her room in order for her to be kept under control. Sylvia drives to work and sees multiple cases of weird sexual happenings, such as an elderly couple passionately kissing at a bus stop, a pantless man moving his garbage can around the house, and a group of big, hairy gay men—known as bears— moving into a house down the street.

After her car runs out of gas on a busy street, Sylvia gets hit in the head by the handle of a lawnmower. A mechanic and "sexual healer" named Ray Ray (Johnny Knoxville) sees this and helps her back into her car, telling her that the head injury has now made her a sex addict. He performs a "service" on her and gives her his card. Before leaving, Ray Ray gave mouth-to-mouth resuscitation to a squirrel that had been hit by a truck (the same truck with the lawn mower in the back that had struck Sylvia) and brings it back to life.

Sylvia gets to work, a convenience store run by her mother, Big Ethel (Suzanne Shepherd), who is repulsed by the sexual antics that seem to be surging in the area. Big Ethel is friends with Marge (Mink Stole), who agrees to help Ethel with a "Hartford Road for Decency" meeting that night to discuss the wickedness happening around them. Vaughn arrives at the convenience store to work as well, but when Sylvia offers to have sex, they drive home. Yet, they can't make it to the house and instead have sex in the car, which is witnessed by several people as it turns out.

At the meeting, there are a few holdouts who don't see anything wrong with the number of sexual incidents happening in the neighborhood, but it is upsetting to many who have been called "neuters" by those who have been converted to being "sex addicts." At a retirement home where Vaughn's mother lives, Sylvia begins to hallucinate sexual activities all around her, and she ends doing a version of the "Hokey-Pokey" by squatting on a water bottle and picking it up, sending everyone out of the room. Her mother hears about the incident later and cannot believe it.

Later that night, Sylvia goes on a sexual rampage, stealing clothes and makeup and looking for a good time. She ends up at Ray Ray's shop, where she meets fellow head-injury victims who have become sexual addicts:

- Loose Linda (Jewel Orem), who has had sex with the entire Hartford Road Police Department.
- Paw Paw (Richard Pelzman), who likes cunnilingus.
- Dingy Dave (James Ransome), a mysophiliac who loves dirt.

Sylvia (Tracey Ullman) is out on the prowl as a newly converted sex addict in *A Dirty Shame*.

- Officer Alvin (Alan Wendl), who is into age regression and "intensely eroticizes being an infant."
- Betty and Wendell Doggett (Susan Allenback and Paul DeBoy), who are into threesomes.
- Warren the Mailman (Jonas Grey), who enjoys exhibitionism.
- Papa, Mama, and Baby Bear (David Moretti, David Dunham, and Jeffrey Auerbach), who are the big, hairy gay men seen earlier in the film.
- Messy Melinda (Susan Rome), who is into Sploshing, which is a sexual attraction to food.
- Fat Fuck Frank (Wes Johnson), who likes large breasts.

Ray Ray announces that Sylvia is his twelfth disciple (which shows Ray Ray can't count, as there were already twelve before Sylvia turned up, but anyway . . .) and that the group will go forth to discover a new sexual act. They go their separate ways for "sexing" while Vaughn is out looking for Sylvia. Sylvia lets her daughter out, and they go to a bar called Holiday House together, where Caprice strips for the crowd while Sylvia has a biker perform cunnilingus on her. Ethel and Vaughn arrive and capture Caprice, while Sylvia is hit on the head by a bottle and is in shock over what she is doing.

Doctor Arlington (David DeBoy) arrives at Sylvia's house, force-feeds Prozac to Caprice, and convinces everyone to go to a meeting for former sex addicts. Meanwhile, frisky squirrels in the attic cause part of the ceiling to fall on Caprice, which in turn causes her breasts to deflate and inflate. At the meeting they meet various other sex addicts trying to control their urges, but Ray Ray comes in with his apostles and disrupts the meeting, leading to an orgy. Sylvia is converted back to an addict, but Ray Ray is slipped Prozac and goes into a sexual coma.

As the neuters hold a protest in the streets, the addicts begin to riot. Families begin to desert the city as the townspeople go crazy one way or another. At his shop, Ray Ray is brought back to sexual life with the help of a popper and begins to levitate. It is "astral-orgasm, reaching an out-of-body state through sexual arousal." Caprice is finally hit on the head again and is back to being an addict. Soon everyone is going at it, and Ethel and Vaughn are on the run, with even the trees and plants looking to have sex.

Elsewhere, David Hasselhoff is on a flight, and a block of waste drops from the plane on to Vaughn's head, changing him as well. Vaughn joins the others, while Ethel dies, only for Ray Ray to bring her back to life in a hearse.

She is changed as well and gets ready to have sex with the men who came to pick her up in the hearse.

As everyone headbutts each other as part of a sexual act, people begin to levitate. Ray Ray arises above them all and, in the final moment of the film, climaxes from his head.

Claims to Condemnation

- Masturbation.
- Various sexual practices too numerous to mention.
- Nudity (female and male genitalia).
- Minor transgressions: doing the Hokey-Pokey, improper use of a water bottle.

Additional Cast and Crew

Johnny Knoxville was already known to Waters for the *Jackass* series and was Waters's date to the premiere of *Hairspray*. (See chapter 23 for more details on Waters's involvement with *Jackass*.) "I courted Johnny for a couple of years even before we made it. We would have lunch and I would show him bear magazines," Waters mentioned in the documentary included on the DVD release of the film. Knoxville jumped at the chance, as he told the *Baltimore Sun*: "I would do anything. I don't even need to see a script. To be in his film, especially a naughty, NC-17 John Waters film—what else could a girl want?"

Tracy Ullman had made a very strong career for herself as a comedian in movies and television, which at first kept Waters away from her as he tended to not want such actors in his film because they "rely on their shtick." But he was convinced to send the script her way. Ullman was hesitant about the role until her husband convinced her that it was time she did something a bit controversial. As per the documentary on the DVD, Ullman's twelve-year-old son saw the script and forbade his mother to make the movie until he heard that Johnny Knoxville was going to be costarring with her in it. Thus, the family was happy with the project, and Ullman joined the cast in August 2003.

Selma Blair said she was game to try the role and was surprised at how tight of a ship Waters ran during filming. "If you don't put the period in the right place, he knows it," Blair told the *Baltimore Sun*, noting that she could sometimes see Waters mouthing the lines along with the cast as they were filming.

Chris Isaak is a musician who has acted in a number of films and had his own television comedy series on Showtime from 2001 to 2004. In the DVD documentary, it is mentioned that Isaak, at the wrap party, sang along with a karaoke machine that featured one of his own songs, and most of the women of the cast and crew gathered around to hear him sing.

Early reports about the filming in *Variety* stated that Paul Giamatti was cast for the film, but his name dropped off the cast credits as filming commenced. There is no indication of what role he would have played in the film, as Johnny Knoxville and Chris Isaak were already cast for the film as well.

Susan Allenbach is Waters's assistant and also played the role of Betty Doggett, who appears completely nude at one point in the movie. Doggett agreed to do the part before finding that out, however, and went back and forth on if she would appear in the film or not. "I've got children, I've got parents that are still alive . . . So I kind of ran it by all of them, and my kids thought it was funny, and my parents kind of laughed. And most of my girlfriends who are my age, my middle-aged girlfriends, were all like, 'Do it, do it, do it.'"

Jackie Hoffman got the role of Dora based on Waters seeing her in the Broadway musical version of *Hairspray*.

Suzanne Shepherd agreed to the role of Big Ethel without knowing what the film was about. She arrived for her wardrobe fitting after having read the script on the train to Baltimore and was in tears of embarrassment over the role. "I really thought I was going to have a heart attack," Shepherd admitted in the DVD documentary. "I started to shake and cry and thought, 'What in the world am I—I can't be in this movie!'" Knoxville and Ullman attempted to console her but did not get far before Shepherd saw Selma Blair wearing the prosthetics for Caprice's huge breasts. "I thought, 'How did I end up in this? This is like Gomorrah!'"

A read-through at Waters's house soon after helped Shepherd feel better, but Blair seemed to pounce on Shepherd's concerns, egging her on with sexual terms in the script and telling Shepherd that she would be participating in various ones in the film. Waters tried to keep Blair quiet, but her attitude was, "What? She should know." Shepherd went home, determined to not be in the film, but her husband convinced her otherwise and even wrote a song for her about the situation. Shepherd relented and in the DVD documentary stated that she never had more fun than when she was working on the movie.

Jean Hill in the DVD documentary admitted that she never read the script beyond her own dialogue, and was surprised to discover after the fact that the movie was about sex addicts. "I thought I was getting away from all that," she laughed.

In the same documentary, David Dunham, Dave Moretti, and Jeffrey Auerbach discuss being bears (or rather, two bears and a cub) in real life. They also felt that being bears did not make them fetishists or sex addicts in real life, but was greatly exaggerated—as with most everything else in the film.

Michael Gabel, who plays the mailman in the movie, was already cast to appear as Iago in the Baltimore Shakespeare Festival production of *Othello*. This caused some issues with the festival, and Waters mentions in the DVD documentary that he got a rather angry letter from the festival about losing an actor for his film. Gabel, in the documentary, mentioned that he also got the chance to appear as Howie Newsome, the milkman, in a production of *Our Town* and was able to arrange his filming schedule so he could do both—film as the lecherous mailman during the day and then perform on stage as Howie Newsome at night, which was a bit confusing to the actor at times.

Sascha Wolhandler, an extra playing one of the sex addicts in the convenience store near the end of the film, got her foot broken during filming when the "young boy-toy" (as she called him in a *Baltimore Sun* article at the time) who was going at it with her tripped and dropped a knee on her foot. She told the newspaper that she arrived at the ER and told someone, "That's the last time I play a sex addict in a movie and have a twenty-five-year-old stud fall on me."

Ricki Lake appears in a cameo as herself on her television talk show early in the film. Mink Stole, Patricia Hearst, Scott Morgan, Channing Wilroy, Rosemary Knower, Jewel Orem, Richard Pelzman, Alan Wendl, Joyce Flick Wendl, Gwendolyn Briley-Strand, Kate Kiley, Patsy Grady Abrams, Doug Roberts, Jean Schertler, Michael Willis, Frederick Strother, Liam Hughes, Steve Mack, Don Hewitt, Bob Adams, Michael Ahl, Tim Caggiano, Angela Calo, Paul M. Clary, Gino Colbert, Susan Duvall, Rick Kain, and George Figgs as an unidentified "Neuter" all made return appearances from earlier Waters movies to appear in *A Dirty Shame*.

Of the crew, returning was Pat Moran, Mark Ordesky, and Ann Ruark in producer roles, with Moran casting as well. Jeffrey Wolf returned as editor.

Vincent Peranio returned for production design, Susan Kessel for set decorations, and Van Smith for costume designs. Gina W. Bae, Anne Marie Izner-Preston, Amanda Johnson, and Cheryl "Pickles" Kinion returned to help with makeup. Howard "Hep" Preston also came back to do hair. Many, many others in other production roles had come back for Waters's 2004 film as well.

Production

Waters began talking about the script in 2001, describing it as a movie about blue-collar sex addicts. Although Waters felt that sex was silly in its own way, and our unease about the topic needed mocking, he also wanted to present the other side: that maybe it's okay for us to not always try to be liberal in our thinking about other people's fetishes. To Jenny Stewart, Waters said: "My suggestion for the ad campaign for this movie was going to be 'Can tolerance go too far?' If you can just see both sides of things sometimes, it makes a big difference, you know? For example, some of these fetish groups. As much as I'm for the freedom of people, they have no sense of humor about

Caprice, a.k.a. Ursula Udders (Selma Blair). The "nude breasts" prosthetic was worn as a vest by Blair, covering her completely, although people still had difficulty in not staring during the filming, especially when the character was "naked."

it, and that to me is shocking. How can you be a pickle top and not laugh about it? Or even say it with a straight face?"

While working on the script, Waters attempted to come up with phrases that were obviously slang for something but would sound innocent enough to pass the censors. "By the fact that the trailer was approved for PG audiences, when she says in it, 'I feel like yodeling in the canyon'—they didn't know what that meant, obviously."

The project took some time finding a home, especially after the lackluster results for *Cecil B. DeMented*, but eventually was sought by Christine Vachon of Killer Films and Ted Hope of This Is That production company in June 2003. A budget of $15 million was put together, with Fine Line signing on for worldwide rights to the film in September 2003. Filming was to begin September 15, 2003, but it was postponed due to Hurricane Floyd, which passed through the area that week. Instead, filming began the following week on September 22.

The day the production was to film the scene at the nursing home, where Sylvia picks up the bottle, was also Ullman's first day filming. Earlier in the day, Waters and Ullman met up at a 7-11 convenience store with prop masters Brooke Yeaton and Jeff Gordon to see if the special effect would work. The effect was done with a magnet in Ullman's underwear and another magnet in the lid of the bottled water, so that when she squatted over it, the bottle latched on to the underwear, giving the appearance needed for the scene.

The group decided to try it out right there in the 7-11 parking lot, not realizing that a group of workers at a gas stations across the street had been watching "and their mouths were just wide open," as Waters told Jenny Stewart in 2005. "Tracey went into the 7-11 to get something and some guy came up to her and said, 'Would you like to have sex? I have a really large penis.' She screamed, because she thought it was a setup, but it wasn't at all. And that just happened to be her first day in Baltimore!"

Special effects were needed for the film, including the need to turn trees and shrubs into pornographic images. The trees with breasts and crotches were done with a variety of equipment on real trees in the Harford Road neighborhood where filming took place. Packing wrap was used to cover the trees up during the day in order to avoid any of the neighbors complaining about them. Effects work was also needed for Selma Blair's character's huge breasts, which were created by Tony Gardner. Three versions were made, each for a different need, with a special one made for the dancing scene at Holiday House that occurs midway through the film. The breasts were lightweight in order to give Blair the least amount of discomfort possible and were strapped to her with makeup used to cover up where the seams were and to make them look as real as possible under the lights. As the prosthetic worked like a vest over Blair's body, she would walk around forgetting that the breasts were showing, as it always felt she was wearing clothes anyway. Waters admitted that it was difficult to not look at the breasts while trying to film, and Blair said that school-age girls who visited the set with others would sometimes ask her if "they hurt," thinking they were real.

The footage of old nudie films and the birthing shot were taken from films collected by the company Something Weird, which released oddball, hard-to-find films, including old nudie and sexploitation films on video, DVD, and Blu-ray. Waters gave the company a list of topics from such films that were needed for A Dirty Shame, and clips were then put together for use in the movie.

Filming locations for the movie were:

- Sylvia's house at 2905 Pinewood Avenue, Baltimore, Maryland.
- The Bears Home at 3046 Pinewood Avenue, Baltimore, Maryland.
- The Park and Pay convenience store at 7501 Harford Road, Baltimore, Maryland.
- Ray Ray's shop, which is actually an oil-change shop at 4620 Harford Road, Baltimore, Maryland.
- Holiday House at 6427 Harford Road, Baltimore, Maryland.

Filming was completed at the beginning of November 2003, with editing to follow. The objective was to have the film ready for the Cannes Film Festival in May 2004 and then release the film in mid-summer throughout the country, but the studio decided that the film was not quite ready and the appearance at the Cannes Film Festival was cancelled. Furthermore, the MPAA had looked at the film and decided to give it the rating of NC-17 in May 2004.

The rating of NC-17 was created in 1990 as a means for the MPAA to give a film a rating that did not designate it as pornography. The X rating had killed certain films over the years, as the public had associated it with porn for so long that newspapers would refuse to run ads for such films in the more conservative 2000s. So the rating of NC-17 was a way to say that a film was adult in nature but not necessarily pornography (albeit, such films do tend to have some graphic sexual scenes in them).

The problem was that several newspapers treated advertising for such films the same as they had with X-rated ones and refused to run ads for them. More importantly, Blockbuster and other video-store rental chains—which were huge at the time—refused to carry NC-17 movies as well. Chain stores such as Walmart were the same way. Thus, an NC-17 rating had a huge potential of killing off sales at the box office and later on video. As pointed out in the DVD documentary as well, Johnny Knoxville had a huge teenage audience at the time, and they would not be able to see a NC-17 movie, so that was an additional issue. Nevertheless, the MPAA told Waters that they gave up trying to say what needed to be changed for the film to get an R rating after ten minutes, deciding instead to go with NC-17 without any notes for "pervasive sexual content."

"I think it's fair," Waters reflected on the rating in the DVD documentary. "The MPAA said there's nothing the matter with an NC-17 rating. They're technically right, but they should use their lobbying power—which they have, big lobbying power—to go to Blockbuster, to go to Walmart, places that will not accept or sell NC-17 movies and make those corporate people change their mind. That is their duty, of the MPAA, if they want this rating to be real. If they want it so when every time in the trades—when it says I got an NC-17, it doesn't say 'slapped' with an NC-17 rating. If it was a fine rating, it wouldn't say 'slapped.'"

Release

The film premiered at the Senator in Baltimore on September 14, 2004, and started showing for general audiences on September 17. On September 24, 2004, the film opened at 133 screens and moved through the country over the next few months. Reviews, as with the past few films from Waters, were somewhat mixed, although there were plenty of positive reviews, including the *Los Angeles Times*, the *Village Voice*, and *Rolling Stone*.

As required by his contract with New Line, Waters needed to present them with an edit of the film that would generate an R rating from the MPAA. This version, typically referred to as the "Neutered Version," was released with the approval description of "For pervasive strong crude sexual content, including fetishes." Why this version would have a longer description that sounds more threatening than the NC-17's "For pervasive sexual content" is anyone's guess.

The R-rated version of the film has various dialogue changes to avoid even mild profanity—such a numerous proclamations of "Jesus Christ" being changed to "Judas Priest" (heard as early as when Sylvia realizes she left her keys in the bathroom at the beginning of the film), while "Fat Fuck Frank" becomes "Fat Freak Frank." There are also a few gag-lines that are cut as well,

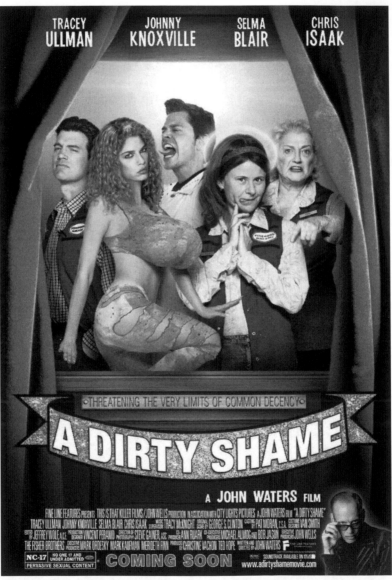

The "coming soon" poster for Waters's 2004 film, *A Dirty Shame*, which manages to get Waters's image into the poster.

such as Ray Ray asking his apostles for a volunteer to help Sylvia with her "cunnilingus bottom."

Alternate camera shots and even obvious digital blurring are also used in the R-rated version to avoid showing suggestive actions and nudity in the film as well, even when it obviously wasn't necessary. For example, the man carrying around his trashcan without pants in the NC-17 version wears diaper-like underwear in the R version, even though all that could be seen in the original was his behind, which would not have resulted in even a PG-13 for most films.

Some of the major changes:

- Vaughn in the bathroom is showed in close-up rather than from further away to avoid showing that he was masturbating.
- Sylvia and Vaughn have less dialogue about the mailman's mail to their daughter, and the scene fades out before Vaughn is shown reaching down to perform a sex act on Sylvia in the car.
- The nursing home orderly who humps a trashcan and the doctor who humps the wheelchair are only shown in a medium shot.
- The other orderly, who appears with full-frontal nudity, is wearing underwear in the R-rated version.
- Sylvia squatting on the bottle and picking it up between her legs is missing from the R-rated version.
- Betty and her husband have the same dialogue when talking to Vaughn, but both appear clothed in the R-rated version, while the NC-17 version has them with full-frontal nudity.
- Caprice takes off her top at Holiday House in the NC-17 version, but keeps her top on in the R-rated version.
- There is more indication of the biker performing a sex act on Sylvia in Holiday House in the NC-17 version, whereas it is simply implied in the R-rated version.
- Squirrels actually are shown mating in the attic in the NC-17 version.
- Mr. Pay Day describes his actions in the NC-17 version.
- The popper bottle is blurred out in the R-rated version.
- The trees and bushes that look obscene (because, well, they are) are missing in the R-rated version.
- The snake in Ray Ray's pants is not seen in the R-rated version.
- The "climax" of the film, as can be expected, is actually gorier in the R-rated version, with Ray Ray's head exploding rather than shooting out a stream that eventually lands on the camera lens.

Johnny Knoxville as Ray Ray in *A Dirty Shame* (2004). Knoxville was "attached to star" in Waters's planned follow-up, *Fruitcake*, for several years, but the project never found a studio.

Surprisingly, there is a third version of the film which has turned up as well and for a time was available on streaming channels such as Amazon and Netflix. It is listed as the R-rated version, but it's actually a mishmash of both the R-rated version and the NC-17 one, which I'll call the "neutered-curious" version for sake of clarity. We still see both female and male full-frontal nudity in the neutered-curious version, and even the over-the-top final "climax" to the film is there. However, all the dialogue matches that of the R-rated version, making the visuals even more bizarre in a way. Sylvia wanting to go "funin' after lunch" and "Fat Freak Frank" wanting to see "ta-tas" while there is still full frontal nudity seems like the ratings board was asleep at the wheel.

No matter what version of the film appeared in theater, the restrictions facing the film through advertising held the film back. In the end, the movie made only close to $2 million on a $15 million budget. It was another small box-office return on one of Waters's films, and the signs were all there as to how it would now be even harder to get another movie made. "I'm having a hard time getting my movie made right now because *A Dirty Shame* didn't do well because it was rated NC-17," Waters told Steve Appleford. "And there's no independent video shops anymore, and all the chains won't carry NC-17 movies. It's worse now, because I have to fight liberal censors, not stupid ones. And they're much more lethal."

As with other later Waters films, *A Dirty Shame* has eventually found its audience and is slowly making money. Ironically, the NC-17 version has no problem being shown as a streaming offer from companies such as Amazon. com and others, while video stores who refused the movie have all become dinosaurs. One could say that *A Dirty Shame* outlasted its critics, and in an age allowing us to become more aware of fetishes thanks to the internet, the movie speaks more clearly today than it did when it was made.

One way *A Dirty Shame* was worth it was when Waters took actress-writer-director Jeanne Moreau (1928–2017) with him to the French premiere of the film, which he described to Randy Shulman in 2009: "We're sitting there watching this movie and I thought, 'What is she going to think about it?' And it was over and I just was nervous and I said, 'We had a lot of censorship problems,' and she said, 'Why, darling? It was pure poetry.' And I said, 'Well, no one's ever called it that before.' That's one of the highlights of my life, Jeanne Moreau saying that to me."

20

Nobody Would Give Me the Money

The Lost Projects

"It's a terribly wonderful children's Christmas adventure called *Fruitcake*. That's about all I can say about it, because after you do something, you have to talk about it the rest of your life. Before you do it, it's like a girl saying, 'I'm almost pregnant.'"

—John Waters speaking to the Associated Press
in 2007 about a film project never completed

Waters have been very successful over the years working on a number of projects, be it books, art, or—of course—his movies. Nevertheless, no matter what he produces at the moment, those who interview him naturally want to look ahead.

Waters, being a private person in many ways, usually balks at such questions. Not that he doesn't have something in mind—for example, as seen in the chapter on *Polyester*—but he has a hesitation of speaking of anything he is considering as if he may "jinx" it. There's nothing unusual about that; many of us do that when looking ahead to something we want to do, and creative types are more susceptible than most to notions of karma and superstitions when it comes to future projects. Besides, if Hollywood teaches you one thing, no matter how many people say they are interested in a film idea you have, it doesn't mean that it will happen until you're actually filming it . . . and in some cases, not even until it literally is on a screen being shown to audiences.

So Waters usually begs off when asked about what movie he plans to do next, and he almost always admits that he is being tight-lipped because he doesn't want to "jinx" it (a rare superstitious side to a man who has little patience for superstitions). Yet, there have been occasions where he has either commented on projects he'd like to do, ones that went bust in years past, and some that took on other forms over time.

Divine as Triplets

In 1982, while still promoting *Polyester*, Waters mentioned to Scott MacDonald an idea he had for his next film: "I'm going to start writing soon. I want to do it with Divine as triplets. You know, have scenes where they talk and everything. My production manager said he's going to quit if I do that." This is obviously an extension of the dual roles that Divine had played in *Female Trouble* and *Multiple Manaics*, as well as one discussed in Chapter 14 where Waters originally envisioned Divine playing the role of Tracy and her mother in *Hairspray*. Instead, Waters turned to a project that he would attempt to get made for years before finally abandoning it—*Flamingos Forever*.

Flamingos Forever

Certainly the most famous of Waters's projects that never got off the ground, mostly because Waters finally had his proposed script published in his book *Trash Trio—Three Screenplays by John Waters* in 1988. Mentions of the project, including its title, first appeared around August 1983, when Waters discussed it with the *Baltimore Sun*: "Sequels have become a genre all by themselves. I want to bring together all the most popular people who have been in all my films for it. Of course, what I'd really like to make is something like *Divine Meets Francis the Talking Mule*, but no producer in his right mind would ever give me the money for it." According to Robert Maier's book, *Low Budget Hell*, the script was finished in 1983, and Maier offered to budget the proposed film at $600,000 (which, as done with his films before it, was effectively doubling the previous film's budget).

Waters's comments to the *Baltimore Sun* about the film being a means to gather together some of the "most popular people" into one film certainly matches a script that reads like a collection of favorite past moments in Waters's films—especially *Pink Flamingos* itself. "It's a satire on Hollywood sequels," Waters told the *Chicago Tribune* in 1984. "It tells what happens when Divine and Edie return to Baltimore and become cult-like figures. It will be more Fellini than X-rated, an exploitation film for the art moviehouses."

To summarize: Divine returns to Baltimore after years of living in Boise, Idaho, where she is met by a group of her followers who have tattooed "F" on their heads. She returns with Cotton II, Crackers II, her young son/grandson (since Crackers II is the father), Miss Edie, and Duane, who likes to dress up in girls' clothing. Upon returning, they face the fury of Vera Venniger, who is the sister of Connie Marble (who, as we learn in the script, is burning in Hell because of Divine). Vera is married to Wilbur, a mortician who does cheap funerals and is a necrophiliac. They kidnap children, hook them on heroin, and force them to cause trouble in the area.

Vera and Wilbur devise to create a scandal for Divine by locating her parents, the cleanest people in the world, and then dropping a bomb on her. Divine saves the children from the Vennigers with the help of Velveeta Jones, a "400-pound black woman," but the Vennigers seemingly kill Divine with their bomb. At her funeral, however, Divine rises from her coffin to extract her revenge on Vera with the help of the children. The script ends with Divine and family riding a giant dog turd (like how Aladdin rides his magic carpet in *Thief of Baghdad*) into the sky to their next destination, Cape Canaveral.

There's more to the script than just the synopsis above, including finding out the real name of Divine's character, but that's for buyers of Waters's book to find out. Although the script is very much a revised version of *Pink Flamingos* (even down to a standing execution of the bad guy), it was also sillier and would have satisfied Waters's wish to make a film that was not X-rated. It is interesting to note that some elements from the script eventually made their way into future Waters movies. The first is the use of young children as lovable delinquents, as seen later in *Cry-Baby*, but other moments from the script are stronger. This includes the groupies who follow their leader, much like those who followed Cecil in *Cecil B. DeMented* and the apostles who follow Ray Ray in *A Dirty Shame*; the "Hokey-Pokey" dance that gets more manic as it proceeds, as seen in *A Dirty Shame*; and the ability for Divine to perform "miracles"—including special effects used to show lasers shooting from her body—much like Ray Ray does in *A Dirty Shame*.

Mink Stole had read the script and was committed to return for what would have been a cameo as Connie Marble. Edith Massey was also on board, although she never could remember the name of the script correctly, commonly referring to it as "Forever Flamingos." Waters believed that Pearce would return in some role, although it was obvious that Cotton II was written to possibly be someone else. Waters also stated in interviews that he didn't think he'd be able to get Danny Mills for Crackers, however, so he was probably planning on recasting both parts anyway. Of course, it is obvious that Velveeta Jones was to be played by Jean Hill, and others working in Baltimore would have returned for the sequel as well.

The main issue was that of Divine, who had been working in clubs with his live act for a few years by that point and had gotten two movie roles in 1985 that were independent of Waters, both of which were major steps forward for Divine's acting career: the co-starring role in Paul Bartel and Tab Hunter's *Lust in the Dust*, and a role as a male bad guy in Alan Rudolph's *Trouble in Mind*. At last, Divine was starting to see light at the end of the feces-eating tunnel he has had to live with for years, but it looked like Waters was asking him to remind the world where he started. "Divine didn't want to do *Pink Flamingos 2*," Waters told the *Guardian* in 2007. "He probably would've done it in the end, but he didn't want to. And he was right, in a way. He was already weary of the shit-eating thing. So to make a film where he would ride off on a turd at the end . . . If you read the script you can almost hear Divine's voice saying the lines, even though he never actually said them."

Besides Divine's uncertainty in the project, there was, more importantly, the simple matter that Waters could not find a backer for the film. At one point in 1985, there was serious consideration by Matt Polk, who founded Polk Audio, but the company finally backed out when deciding filmmaking wasn't a venture they wanted to pursue. Then the final tip into the abyss came with the death of Edith Massey in October 1984. Waters reports in *Trash Trio* that Troma Films and another producer made offers, but once Massey was gone, "there was not another actress in the world who could replace her."

At the time of announcing his plans to move on to a new project in 1985, Waters told the press that he planned to turn the script into his first novel. Instead, he wrote *Crackpot*. "Every time I've written a book, it's because one of my movies has fallen through. *Shock Value* was written when the budget fell through on *Polyester*. *Crackpot* happened the same way, because I was trying to do the sequel to *Pink Flamingos*. It was a two-year waste of my life. It scared me. I don't want to do that again." Besides, he had another script idea in mind that would take place in the 1950s. A movie, as he told the *Baltimore Sun* in February 1985, he planned to call *Hatchet Face* (see Chapter 15 for more details on how that panned out).

A Confederacy of Dunces

A favorite book of Waters and a classic novel that has never quite made it to the screen, no matter how often people have tried. Waters has stated it was the only book he read that he wanted to make into a film, and in the early 1980s, he pitched the idea to a Hollywood producer with Divine as Ignatius J. Reilly. The meeting had gone well, and Waters left a copy of his then-current book *Shock Value* with the producer as part of his resume. As it turns out, the producer had a good friend who was one of the victims of Charles "Tex" Watson. According to *Crackpot*, when Waters found out many months later, "I felt really awful. And, natch, I didn't get the job."

When asked by John Ives about the project in 1992, Waters replied: "I don't want to do that anymore, because when a book is revered by a specific audience, the movie could never be as good as the audience wants it to be. The old maxim may be true: 'Good books make bad movies and bad books make good movies.'" In the same interview, Waters also expressed interest in making a movie out of Mary McGarry Morris's 1991 novel *A Dangerous Woman*, which was made in 1993 and directed by Stephen Gyllenhaal.

Glamourpuss

The *New York Times* in April 1991 mentioned that Waters had landed a developmental deal with Paramount Pictures to write a script called *Glamourpuss*, a name Waters picked up from an article in *GQ*. (*Raving Beauty* was an alternate title Waters came up for the script as well.) Waters would write two scripts, neither of which were picked up by Paramount, which then put the project into "turnaround" (essentially allowing a project developed at one studio to be put up for sale to buy). Another unnamed studio picked it up, but eventually the idea was dropped sometime in 1992 and Waters moved on to the script for *Serial Mom*, which ironically also went through turnaround but was eventually made by Savoy Pictures.

The only time Waters opened up about the picture was with John Ives. The initial idea came to Waters while working on *Cry-Baby*: "It's basically about a Hollywood movie star who comes to Baltimore and falls in love with a truck driver. It's too easy a target to make an anti-Hollywood movie. This is about somebody who I would like in Hollywood. How she responds to being in Baltimore."

Waters began working on the script but then got sidetracked with an idea that came to him while writing an article for *Newsweek*, as he went on to explain to John Ives, "About how kids should rebel, about being black if you're white—I wanted to make a movie about that." The plot dealt with a white boy who wants to be black and who teams up with a "black fag hag, and together they [fight] a skinhead invasion of their community." Waters said that producers laughed in his face about the idea, although he appreciated Dawn Steel's response at Disney when she opened the pitch meeting by telling him, "Oh, well, sure, when I heard skinheads, I thought Disney!" She then admitted that she went with the pitch meeting namely because she had heard how good Waters's pitches were and wanted to hear one for herself.

Although the project never went forward, one character named Pecker, who was written in the *Glamourpuss* script as a movie-star stalker and then as a different character in early drafts of *Cecil B. DeMented*, finally became the main character in Waters's 1998 film *Pecker*.

Fruitcake

As mentioned in Joe Blevin's article on Splitsider.com from 2015, "Obscene and Unheard: The Unmade Films of John Waters," news broke on Jeff Jackson's website, *Dreamland News*, about Waters telling a librarian convention about his next planned film, to be called *Fruitcake*. On May 7, 2008, the *Hollywood Reporter* ran an article saying that the film was to be produced by This Is That Productions and Killer Films (who produced *A Dirty Shame*), while New Line Films passed on the project. ThinkFilm was in talks to take over at the time.

The *Hollywood Reporter* article went on to say that Johnny Knoxville and Parker Posey were "attached to star" in the film, which had a plot "officially under wraps, but is said to center on the title character, a boy named after his favorite dessert." His family "steals meat. A door-to-door meat salesman, which we have in Baltimore, will knock on your door and say 'Meatman.' You say, 'I want two porterhouses and a pound of ground beef.' And they shoplift it for you, bring it back, and you pay half of what's on the label. He runs away from home during the holidays after he and his parents are caught shoplifting meat, then meets up with a runaway girl raised by two gay men and searching for her birth mother."

In 2009, with at least Knoxville still attached, the project was looking for a new home, yet it seemed that the budget of the film was driving backers away. Waters told the *Baltimore Sun* in 2011, "I had two meetings this past week, but $4 to $5 million-budget independent movies are extinct." Waters would go into the money issue in 2014 with the newspaper. "They want me to go make it like I used to, but I have no desire to do that. I did that. I have seventeen movies; they're all playing everywhere in the world, more than ever. I can't afford to make a movie the way they want me to do it. I make way more writing these books." By 2017, when asked about the project—which by that point was ten years old, and it had been nearly fourteen years since the last film he directed—he dismissed it as being dead. Of course, there is always a chance that the project can be resurrected, but as Waters jokingly said in 2014, "Thank God I have five other careers."

And the career as a book writer continues to be strong, as seen in the next chapter.

21

If They Don't Have Books

Books Written by John Waters

I enjoy writing a book as much as making a movie. First of all, it's myself and a Bic pen and a pad. I don't have to raise millions of dollars. With a book, and with everything I've ever written, editors have encouraged me to be as bizarre as possible.

—John Waters on what he enjoys about writing books to the *Baltimore Sun*

Although he would eventually become known for his films, Waters would first venture into entertaining others through prose. "I wrote a story called 'Reunion' when I worked at a camp when I was thirteen years old. It was a horror story with gore and everything, and I read it to all the campers and they all freaked out and had nightmares and the parents called the camp and I got in trouble. That was the first thing I ever did with writing."

While Waters would write some occasional articles, it wasn't until 1981 that he released his first book: *Shock Value*, an autobiographical study that collected essays about the makings of a handful of his films, along with interviews and stories about people he knew and/or admired. As mentioned in the previous chapter, Waters admits he began writing the book when it looked like negotiations had stalled on what would become *Polyester*. After that, it would another six years before he would publish another book, *Crackpot*, which was another collection of essays—several of which had seen print in various publications. As with *Shock Value*, the book came out of necessity; Waters was struggling to finish and sell his script for what would become *Hairspray* after years of unsuccessfully pushing his *Flamingos Forever* script.

Over time, there have been several other books, two of which that each contain scripts from three of his films. Several of these books have appeared within the past ten years and have done well for him on the best-sellers list. There have also been a few books released pertaining to aspects of Waters's artwork (see Chapter 22 for more details on that career); some of these have been written solely by Waters, and others were written with his cooperation or collaboration.

There have been a handful of biographical books about Waters as well as a number of articles that Waters has written but that have not been collected in one of his books. However, this chapter looks solely at the writings directly linked to Waters over the past fifty-plus years.

"Inside a Home for Unwed Mothers" (*FACT* Magazine, Volume Three, Issue Five, September-October, 1966)

Written by Waters when he was twenty, this three-page article was his first published work for Ralph Ginzburg's magazine called *FACT*. In *Shock Value*, Waters discusses a friend of his girlfriend Mona who had become pregnant at the age of fourteen and sent to a home for unwed mothers. When the girl returned, she brought back with her "horror stories about her stay." Taking

fact: $1.25 VOLUME THREE ISSUE FIVE **A professor of ophthalmology says, "Everybody who puts on contact lenses will experience eye damage, and in many cases the damage will be permanent."**

The issue of *FACT* magazine featuring Waters's first published story, written under the pen name Jane Wierno.

that information, Waters constructed an article for the fact-based magazine "I made it up," Waters told Lithub.com. "I had a reputable beginning in publishing." To help with the first-person account, Waters used a pseudonym of Jane Wiemo. "I guess it's my drag name, my pen name," Waters said in the same interview.

The article is different in comparison to what we have become familiar with when reading Waters's work, and we should expect this difference from any young writer trying to impress others with their first published work. Most of the observations of "Jane" deal with girls crying while waiting for their pregnancies to conclude, and it's all done in a very serious tone. However, the girls being taken on a wagon ride by the strict staff will ring familiar to fans of *Polyester*, although there is no indication in the article, or in the movie, that the ride was an attempt to have the girls miscarry (and also there is no indication of there being a violent storm occurring at the time of the ride).

The article features artwork from Sergio Aragones, who is best known for his comic art for *Mad* magazine. "I was quite thrilled to find that I could live off my 'talent' as a writer," Waters wrote in *Shock Value*, "rather than having to search for some dismal summer job." His career as a filmmaker soon began to blossom, however, holding back his literary career for a few more years.

Shock Value: A Tasteful Book About Bad Taste (Delta Books, 1981; Thunder's Mouth Press, Updated Edition, 2003)

This was John Waters's first published book, which skips around through histories of his films (and over *The Diane Linkletter Story* entirely) up through *Desperate Living*, while *Polyester* is hinted at near the end of the book and is listed in the filmography at the back of the book. The book starts with a "making of" for *Pink Flamingos*, which was an obvious selling point. Other essays are autobiographical, dealing with Waters's upbringing, his friends, the city of Baltimore, his obsession with trials, and casting. There are also interviews with Divine and two of Waters's favorite directors: H. Gordon Lewis and Russ Meyers. Three chapters originally appeared in part or in full in *Oui* magazine in 1979, which is where his first published writing after *FACT* magazine appeared (the first article being "All My Trials").

Promotional photo of John Waters on the set of *Polyester* (1981), and just as his first book, *Shock Value*, was to be released.

The 1995 edition of the book from Thunder's Mouth Press features a five-page introduction that updates some information from where Waters left off back in 1981. The filmography at the end is also updated (yet still missing *The Diane Linkletter Story*), but no other changes were made to the interior text from the 1981 edition.

Crackpot: The Obsessions of John Waters (Vintage Books, 1986; Scribner, Updated Edition, 2003)

Similar to *Shock Value*, *Crackpot* is a collection of essays, some that deal with Waters's film career and others that deal with his life's "obsessions," such as a mini-biography of William Castle, teaching in prison, and his favorite art films. Fans of *Hairspray* in particular may find the book of interest due to the inclusion of an interview with Pia Zadora and interviews with participants on *The Buddy Deane Show*, the real teenage dance television program on which Waters based *Hairspray*. Twelve of the fifteen chapters in the 1986 edition appeared in full or in part in various magazines.

The 1987 paperback edition of the book shows Waters sitting by an old typewriter with a picture of Patty McCormack as "the Bad Seed" on the desk. (In documentary footage, the same picture of McCormack can be seen in Waters's home.) The 2003 edition replaces this photo with one of Waters covering his face with his hands. The 2003 edition includes a "director's commentary"—in other words, an introduction for the reprint, with some additional information, such as his seventy reasons to stop smoking and a list of 118 magazines he subscribed to at the time (some that no longer exist). The updated edition of the book also includes nine additional essays, making it twenty-one out of twenty-four chapters that had appeared in full or in part in various magazines over the years.

Director's Cut (Scalo Verlag Ac, 1997)

This book collects several of Waters's art pieces and uses stills from various movies, including his own, to tell a story. For fans of his movies who have rarely gotten a chance to see his art, the book is an excellent place to start. For those who want stories and not art, it is best to avoid. It includes 165 photos, most of which are in color.

The publication of the book led to one of the few fights Waters had with his parents in many years. "I told them I wanted to dedicate my book, *Director's Cut*, to them and they said, 'Oh, that's nice. We'd love that,'" Waters remembered to Todd Solondz in 2004. Waters warned them that the book had one piece in particular that was "really obscene," but his parents waved him off without even asking for the name of the piece. The piece, *Twelve Assholes and a Dirty Foot*, is self-explanatory, and Waters presented his parents with a copy of *Director's Cut* with the specific pages taped together in hopes that his parents would just ignore it. Naturally, his mother and father opened the pages, and they were shocked and upset.

"Later, I said to myself, 'What did you expect? You hand your parents a book and expect them to sit on their sofa in Baltimore and look at pictures of men's assholes?' Are they supposed to say, 'That's nice'?"

Art: A Sex Book (Thames 7 Hudson, 2003)

One of Waters's few book collaborations, *Art: A Sex Book*, was done with Bruce Hainley, and the book has text where the two discuss art by looking at 175 photos of contemporary artwork by artists such as Lichtenstein, Warhol, and others. One fascinating factor in the book is the idea of the two authors discussing their choices for each "room" of an exhibit, with the rooms being chapters in the book. This leads to the authors discussing their perceptions of art in general and, more specifically, sex in art. As with *Director's Cut*, it is a book for fans who want a better understanding of Waters's interpretation of art, but those looking for insight into his films may want to give it a pass.

Trash Trio (Vintage, 1988; Thunder's Mouth Press, Reissue, 1996; Thunder's Mouth Press, Updated Edition Re-Titled as *Pink Flamingos and Other Filth*, 2005)

Trash Trio collects the finished screenplays from two of Waters's films—*Pink Flamingos* and *Desperate Living*—along with the planned script for the never filmed *Flamingos Forever*. As Waters has noted in interviews and as was mentioned previously in an earlier chapter, the scripts provided within the book are based on the finished films and do not included scenes cut either before or after filming, so fans looking for bonus storylines or dialogue may be disappointed. The book contains several photos from the two movies as well as behind-the-scenes stills (such as the marquee of the Elgin Cinema when *Pink Flamingos* first premiered and Mole happily posing post-castration while filming *Desperate Living*).

As with other reprints, the 1996 Thunder's Mouth Press edition of the book changed the cover—from Waters sitting next to an old movie camera to the popular photo of Divine pointing a gun from *Pink Flamingos*. Another reprint occurred in 2005 and had a new cover and a new title—*Pink Flamingos and Other Filth*—to tie in with the other script book, *Hairspray, Female Trouble, and Multiple Maniacs: Three MORE Screenplays by John Waters*, released in 2005.

The 1996 and 2005 editions of the book include a two-page "Introduction to an Introduction," where Waters recasts *Pink Flamingos* with celebrities such as Paul Reubens and Lili Taylor as the Marbles, Sean Penn as Channing, and Juliette Lewis as Cookie.

John Waters: *Change of Life* (Harry N. Abrams, 2004)

Released in connection with Waters's art exhibit of the same name, *Change of Life* includes more of Waters's various photo layouts and altered photos as art pieces. Essays by Harvin Heiferman, Gary Indiana, Lisa Phillips, Brenda Richardson, and Todd Solondz appear, along with an interview with Waters.

Hairspray, Female Trouble, and Multiple Maniacs: Three More Screenplays (Thunder's Mouth Press, 2005)

As with *Trash Trio*, this book prints the scripts for three of Waters's films. The ten-page introduction features Waters discussing the movies and the cast for each. Numerous stills from the films along with behind-the-scenes photos appear.

John Waters: *Unwatchable* (Marianne Boesky Gallery, 2006)

Another collection of Waters's artwork, this ninety-six-page brochure is for his art exhibit *John Waters: Unwatchable*, which was at the Marianne Boesky Gallery from April through May 2006. Brenda Richardson provides an essay discussing Waters's artwork.

John Waters (Place Space) (AMMO Books, 2008)

Conceived and written by Todd Oldham and Cindy Sherman, this book doesn't have content written by Waters, but it was obviously done with his cooperation. The sixty-four-page book contains photos of the interiors of Waters's house in Baltimore. Considering how often Waters has given tours of his house to writers, it is little wonder that a book would finally appear being an end-all to the various documentation of his place. But when do we get an updated edition? (Yes, the quest never ends for the fans.)

Role Models (Farrar, Straus and Giroux, 2011)

Going back to the concept of *Shock Value* and *Crackpot*, *Role Models* is a collection of essays and interviews with people who Waters has been fascinated by in his life. The most serious of these—and one that Waters discussed in many interviews while promoting the book—is the chapter "Leslie," which is about "Manson girl" Leslie Van Houten. Some chapters, such as "Baltimore Heroes," are a bit depressing (the tale of Zorro, for example). More humorous is the attempted interview with Little Richard, which devolves into legalities before falling apart. Three of the ten essays appeared in altered form in other places before being collected in *Role Models*. Waters also recorded an audio version of the text.

Carsick: John Waters Hitchhikes Across America (Farrar, Straus, and Giroux, 2015)

The book is Waters's firsthand account of hitchhiking from Baltimore to San Francisco in May 2012. It is broken up into three sections, two of which are fiction. The first section deals with imagined "good" rides, with Waters being invited into exciting adventures with various people; the second section deals with unsettling, nightmarish "bad" rides that hilariously and sequentially end with Waters's death at the hands of an enraged moviegoer.

The third section deals with the real hitchhiking trip Waters takes, one which mixes boredom and an assortment of friendly faces who pick him up over the course of several days. It makes for a very pleasant read, but fans should be aware that more than half of the text is fictional rather than true, although the "bad rides" section is excellent.

Make Trouble (Alonquin Books of Chapel Hill, 2017)

This eighty-page book features illustrations by Eric Hanson. It is an adaptation of the commencement speech Waters gave to the graduating class of

2015 at Rhode Island School of Design. "I was the commencement speaker and they made me a doctor," Waters told *Huffington Post* soon after the event. "I got thrown out of every school I ever went to, so it was great. It was like the scarecrow at the end of *The Wizard of Oz*—I got the Doctor of Fine Arts, which immediately I said, 'My fee went up. I'm writing oxytocin prescriptions. And I want tenure.'"

With several pages featuring only a sentence with or without an illustration, the book has some good advice for people going out into the workforce but is a very quick read.

October 2017 saw the release of a 7-inch red vinyl single of the speech from Third Man Records.

Mister Know-It-All (Farrar, Straus and Giroux Forthcoming)

In April 2017, Waters told Alexander Chee that he was working on two books for Farrar, Straus and Giroux. "The first one is called *Mister Know-It-All*, which is detailed essays on how to avoid respectability at seventy." According to Brooklynvegan.com back in 2015, when Waters first began working on the book, it is a collection of essays that include topics such as "Why do gay people have to be nice now?" "Is it ever appropriate to take LSD when you are seventy years old?" and "How does it feel to claw your way to the top of Hollywood and then slide right back down again?"

Liar Mouth (Farrar, Straus and Giroux, Forthcoming)

The other book that Waters is contracted to write for Farrar, Straus and Giroux and is a novel that is sometimes listed as *Liarmouth*. The phrase can be heard in *Polyester*, when Francine confronts her daughter about her bad grades. The novel is supposedly about "a woman who steals suitcases at airports." When pressed on when the novel—Waters's first—would be released, he told Lithub.com: "Oh, god knows. I've got homework for the rest of my life. That's what a book advance feels like. Homework. Paid Homework."

Doesn't sound like too bad of a job.

22

Hardy Har

John Waters and His Artwork

All contemporary art should make you mad. Otherwise, what's the point? I like things that are original, and original is usually never easy to like. It's not about decoration; it's not about pretty. Most people should hate contemporary art. It hates you.

—John Waters on his art collection to *Baltimore Magazine* in 2007

E ver since 1964, when Waters first got a silver Warhol print of Jackie Kennedy from his girlfriend Mona, Waters has been collecting artwork. He even once wrote to *Life* Magazine in the early 1960s in defense of Warhol's work. In *Multiple Maniacs* you can see the Warhol piece, while nearby is clearly a Roy Lichtenstein one. It goes back even further however: "When I was about eight, I went to the Baltimore Museum. My aunt took me there, and I saw this little [Joan] Miro print, and I bought it and took it home. And when I had it home, all the other kids went, 'Ooh, that's the ugliest thing, you're an idiot,'" Waters told Dennis Cooper in 2004. To Waters, that reaction fit in with his growing need to rebel against the norms of his life. "I still like work like that, that is kind of artless and inspires contempt in people who generally hate contemporary art. It's the first thing I embraced."

His house and apartments are showcases for pieces by such artists, such as a Jess von der Ahe painting in the hallway of his house in Baltimore and an O. Tobias Wong piece that is a box holding capsules that, if swallowed, allows people to have bowel movements that contain gold flakes that will sparkle in the toilet. Certainly the most impressive is a piece by Gregory Green, which takes up the entirety of a third-floor guest room in his house. It is a room made to look like that of a lair for a bomber planning to blow up a baseball stadium in Baltimore. "It's the only piece the artist has ever done in a private home in the United States," Waters told *Baltimore Magazine* in 2007. The room has been decorated with most of the material to make a bomb and is roped off to keep people out of it. Once, the governor of Maryland was to come to a Christmas party at Waters's house. When security came in to check out his house ahead of time, Waters had to explain the bizarre guest room. "You should see their faces," Waters told *The New York Times*. "I always have a Gregory Green catalog right next to it, just in case: 'Hey, this is art! This is art!'"

Waters's house and apartments are pieces of art in themselves, with the layout of fake food, art, oddball items, and the claustrophobic collection of books everywhere. With such interest in coordinating art pieces in his home, it was only natural that he would turn to creating his own pieces as well—typically in the area of photography.

"I always was very interested in art when I was young," Waters told *Index Magazine* in 1997. "And then I was away from it for at least fifteen years, and then I got back heavily into going to it." Looking at photographic pieces he created with the magazine, he went on to say, "I did these for four-and-a-half years without telling one soul—even all my friends in the art world. I just didn't want to tell anybody, and I wanted to get a whole body of work." With this in mind, Waters set up an art studio in Hampden specifically just for his artwork only. "I have a studio," Waters mentioned to Dennis Cooper for *Bomb Magazine*, "and that's the only place I really ever think of ideas for my photographic pieces. So when I'm going to have a new show, I go over there, where I have envelopes full of photographs I've taken for possible future pieces."

Many of his pieces are that of photographs taken of frames of various movies, including his own earlier ones, which he believes have enough bad

NEUROTIC

JOHN WATERS

March 15 - April 14, 2012

Artist Reception:
Thursday, March 15, 6 - 8 PM

McClain Gallery
2242 Richmond Avenue Houston, Texas 77098
713.520.9988   www.mcclaingallery.com

Front: John Waters, Neurotic, 2009 4 C-prints, Edition 3/5 Each Image: 8 x 10 Inches, Framed: 22 1/2 x 26 1/2 inches. Left: John Waters Bad Directors Chair, 2006, Canvas, wood, steel, paint with leather bound script 46 x 24 1/2 x 23 inches, Edition 1/5, all images courtesy of the artist and Marianne Boesky Gallery, NY

A gallery invitation to one of the various art shows Waters has participated in over the years. Featured were pictures of some of his work, including this one showing his piece *Bad Directors Chair* (2006).

technical aspects to them. "See, if you primitively photograph badly photographed movies, it becomes a new kind of rawness that I believe can work in the contemporary art world." (*Bomb*) Many of the pieces have humorous touches to them, like a series of eight photos of Waters called "Self-Portrait #3" where all of the pictures have had the Waters's face obscured by some object. Portraits that show Waters, Lassie the Dog, and Justin Bieber, but manipulated to make it appear they have all had hideous facial surgery. Or like "Hair in the Gate," which shows stills from famous movies that are spoiled in their composition because a hair is in the frame of each photo like an OCD nightmare. There are also bigger pieces he has done that are interactive, such as "Hardy Har"—a photograph of flowers that squirts water on the viewer if they get too close to it, or sculpture, like a giant rubber snake called "Slimy jw," and a baby-stroller, "Bill's Stroller," that has a bondage leather harness and is covered with logos for gay clubs.

There are plenty of others, but such pieces work best when seen unexpectantly rather than described in various ways in text form here. Fortunately, for fans, Waters has done a number of art exhibits over the years that display his work, with his first show on his own being *Director's Cut* at the American Fine Arts. Co. in New York during November 1996, and later at Pacewildenstein Macgill (now known as Pace Gallery) in Los Angeles in 1997 and Galerie Emmanuel Perrotin in Paris during 1999. *Low Definition* was a series of shows between 1998 and 1999 where Waters showed off some of his movie-related photo-reconstructions, while *Hair in the Gate* was a similar exhibit that ran in New York, Provincetown, and Santa Fe in 2003.

Change of Life came between 2004 and 2006; arriving in New York, Switzerland, Pittsburgh and Newport Beach. *Unwatchable* came about in 2006, showing in New York, Louisville, and Zurich. This was followed by *Rear Projection*, which ran in New York and Los Angeles in 2009. Between 2010 and 2014, there were several one-off shows that featured only Waters's work, or as pieces in a group exhibit. *Beverly Hills John* in 2015 occurred in New York and London. As seen in the previous chapter, several of his pieces have been put together in book form for people to purchase, namely based around some of his exhibition titles, such as *Director's Cut*, *Unwatchable*, and *Change of Life*.

Such voyages into artwork extends to his Christmas cards that he sends out to friends every year that parody the season or sending out personal cards in some form. This has included a "Season's Greeting" card showing a photo of an auto accident destroying someone's Christmas, or one where

Steve Buscemi is dressed as Waters—including the mustache—with the card saying it is from Waters. 1994 saw one where Waters took a photo of Elizabeth Taylor from the film *Ash Wednesday* that shows her character after facial surgery looking remarkably like Waters and sent that. It would be a photo that Waters would later use in his art show as well. Atomic Books, the bookstore in Baltimore where Waters has all his fan mail directed, features a collage of the cards on one of their walls, showing Waters's creative streak that only a few ever get to see.

"It's a relief to not have to pretend that I'm appealing to everybody," Waters told *Baltimore Magazine* about the freedom artwork gives him over making movies. "In the movie business, you have to do that no matter what. When you go to sell a movie, you basically say it's going to cross over and everyone's going to love it. In the art world, you can be subtle, impenetrable, and harder to get—that's actually considered a good thing."

This sentiment is similar to one that Waters has mentioned for writing books. As his film career has slowed down, the books and artwork have taken its place in many ways. Fortunately for Waters, they have proven themselves to not only be avenues for his talents and humor, but ones that audiences have enjoyed as well.

23

Hawaiian Shirts

Actor in Films and Television

More people have seen that than all my movies put together. And there are people who only know me from seeing me on *The Simpsons*.
—John Waters to *Baltimore Magazine* on appearing as a character on the animated series

W aters has made it clear that he does not see himself as much of an actor, and he cringes at his work in his own movies when he has done roles because there wasn't anyone else to do them. His attitude about his ability as a performer began to change into the 1980s, when Waters established himself as a talkative and funny guest on numerous guest appearances on *Late Night with David Letterman* between 1982 and 1988. He also began appearing in various documentaries about his work and cult films. Once *Hairspray* came out, Waters was popping up everywhere, and by the 1990s, he had become a face with a distinctive voice instantly recognizable to not just fans but to the American public.

Besides narrating documentaries such as *Jessica the Hippo* for the Animal Planet cable channel and appearing on talk shows, Waters has slowly moved into doing some acting roles in which he plays either variations of himself (the "No Smoking in This Theater" ad, for example) or characters. Below is a list of most of his appearances on television and in movies over the past several years.

No Smoking in This Theater/Nuart Theatre Thank You/Shock Value Trailer (1982)

In 1982, Landmark Theatre Corporation agreed to do a Waters-related film series called the "Shock Value Film Festival" throughout its chain. The series would feature all of Waters's films along with ones from H. Gordon Lewis and Russ Meyer. The San Francisco-based theater chain at the time was partially owned by Gary Meyer, who owned the Nuart Theatre in Los Angeles, which had picked up *Pink Flamingos* in January 1974 and was still running the film on weekends as a "midnight movie" at the time.

To thank the Nuart for running *Pink Flamingos* for so long and to help promote the "Shock Value Film Festival," Waters went to New York to film short trailers, which were produced and directed by Douglas Brian Martin. Although not stated outright, it appears that the script for at least the "Shock Value Film Festival" trailer was written by Martin, as he noted in a 2006 response on the *Cinema Treasures* blog that "John wanted to change the script to use more common terms for anatomy and excretions, but I insisted on sticking to the script." Even with this discretion, the trailer was still banned by Texas due to Waters advising people to come see "movies featuring masturbation and coprophagy." The trailer for the "Shock Value Film Festival" runs a little over a minute.

The second trailer filmed that day was of Waters thanking the patrons of the Nuart Theatre for coming to see *Pink Flamingos* at the theater for "eight consecutive years," throughout which Waters was able to "make new movies, pay my rent, and [buy] endless cartons of Kool cigarettes."

The third and final trailer is the most famous, and it leaked its way to other theaters around the country to be seen before features in art theaters everywhere. The trailer has Waters telling patrons of the theater that there is no smoking allowed during the films. He does this while lusciously dragging on a Kool cigarette and asking the audience how anyone could sit through "a film, especially a European film, and not have a cigarette, but don't you wish you had one right now? Mmm, mmm, mmm." The film ends with Waters seductively sucking in the smoke and smiling. It is clear that Waters is having fun with this one and nearly begins to laugh at one point, causing him to slightly stumble with his words, but he gets through it, and it became a classic announcement to show before films in independent theaters.

Something Wild (1986)

This comedy from Jonathan Demme features Waters in a cameo as a shady used-car salesman who is willing to look the other way if the price is right. Waters at first balked at the stunt casting, as he didn't like seeing himself in his own movies, but he eventually agreed to do it more for a lark than anything else. It is the first time that he and Melanie Griffith worked together; Griffith would later star in Waters's *Cecil B. DeMented*. "I did it because I like

Jonathan [Demme] and I know him and he had a lot of cameos," Waters told *Exploitation Retrospect* in 1986.

Homer and Eddie (1989)

Waters appears briefly in this comedy film starring Whoopi Goldberg and Jim Belushi. His role as a robber appears prominently in the trailer, however.

21 Jump Street, "Awomp-Bomp-Aloobomp-Aloop-Bamboom" (1990)

Waters was working with Johnny Depp on *Cry-Baby* when he took on this small role as Mr. Bean, who kicks Depp's character and others off a bus for being disruptrive (this, after offering Depp's character a stiff Slim Jim).

Family Album (1994)

This two-part miniseries for NBC is an adaptation of a Danielle Steel novel, which sounds right up Waters's alley. Waters cameos as a film director named "Vincent."

Homicide: Life on the Street (1993 and 1995)

Waters appears in two episodes of this Baltimore-based series that fellow Dreamlanders—such as Pat Moran, Vincent Peranio, and Van Smith— worked on at one time or another. He is not credited in his first episode, "Law & Disorder," in 1993, but is credited as the bartender in the 1995 episode, "Smoke Gets in Your Eyes."

The Simpsons, "Homer's Phobia" (1997)

As mentioned at the beginning of this chapter, this appearance as "John"— the gay owner of a kitschy antique shop who befriends Homer and Bart—is probably Waters's best-known appearance anywhere, including his own movies. "When I was younger, I always wanted to be a Disney villain," Waters told Theringer.com in 2017. "And this was about as close to that as I got. Finally I was a cartoon character—and I kind of look like one anyway. So I was happy."

The episode would go on to win an Emmy and GLAAD Media Award. Director Mike B. Anderson worked with Waters on an animated series for MTV to be called *Uncle John* (featuring Waters as the star in animated form), but MTV bailed. "We never actually got paid," Waters told Theringer.com.

Anarchy TV (1998)

Waters appears briefly in this comedy film, which also features Mink Stole and deals with teenagers who fight to save their television station.

Frasier, "The Maris Counselor" (1998)

Waters does a voice-over in this episode of the comedy series starring Kelsey Grammer.

Sweet and Lowdown (1999)

Waters appears in this Woody Allen comedy-drama as Mr. Haynes. "[Allen] told Sean Penn and me what to do—different versions, all one big master shot. Took all of one morning. I left," Waters told Jamie Painter Young in 2000. Allen sought out Waters for the role. Waters auditioned for the role by saying to Allen, "I read a book where you said that when you write 'The End' on the first draft of your script, it's the first day of preproduction. Could that really be true?" When Allen said "Yes," Waters said, "I hate you."

Welcome to Hollywood (2000)

Waters appears as himself in this mockumentary about a young actor trying to make it in Hollywood.

Blood Feast 2: All U Can Eat (2002)

From Woody Allen to H. Gordon Lewis. Waters appears in one scene as a kinky reverend for Lewis, whom Waters interviewed for his book *Shock Value*.

Dead Like Me, "Haunted" (2004)

Waters has a role as an old man in a Waffle House in this supernatural series about grim reapers.

Seed of Chucky (2004)

In this fifth film in the killer Chucky Doll horror series, Waters plays Pete Peters, a tabloid journalist who, by accident, gets pictures of Chucky in action. Wanting the pictures, Chucky is about to attack Peters in his darkroom, where he is developing the pictures. Peters knocks over a shelf containing a bottle of sulfuric acid, which crashes on his head and kills him in a pretty hideous manner. It is one of Waters's most memorable roles in a movie, and one can suggest that Chucky's method of using a turkey-baster to impregnate a woman rings familiar to anyone who has seen *Pink Flamingos*.

'Till Death Do Us Part (2007)

A thirteen-episode series that ran on the cable network Court TV, with Waters narrating as the "Groom Reaper"—a "Rod Serling-like" character that would pop up in the action, breaking the fourth wall but going unnoticed by the other characters. Waters called the role "Vincent Price-ish" when asked to describe the character in the interview features on the DVD box set, although elements of Waters's past peek through at times, such as when he is petting the chicken at the beginning of the final episode.

Each thirty-minute episode featured a story about a bride and groom getting happily married and then things descending into chaos with one of the newlyweds killing the other by the end of the episode. The episodes would be set up as mysteries, so which person would be the murderer would remain unclear until the ending segment of the show. To play off of that, Court TV would interrupt the show at the halfway point and ask viewers to text their guesses as to who will kill the other.

By this time, Court TV was rapidly finding ratings falling off now that there were no longer any O. J. Simpson trials to run and began experimenting with more of a variety of shows, including comedies, which is how 'Till Death Do Us Part plays, with broad acting, bad puns by the

The DVD box set cover for the first and only season of *Till Death Do Us Part* (2007). Waters hosted each of the thirteen episodes as the "Vincent Price-ish" narrator.

narrator, and humorous results. In Canada, where the program was filmed, the show was called *Love You to Death*. A promotional comic book was released for the series and featured Waters's character as well.

My Name Is Earl, "Kept a Guy Locked in a Truck" (2007)

Waters appears in this episode as a happy funeral director who talks to Earl about staging a funeral for a man he finds in a stolen truck.

Each Time I Kill (2007)

Waters has a role as "movie watcher" in this movie written and directed by Doris Wishman, who made such films as *Blaze Starr Goes Nudist*, *Let Me Die a Woman*, and *Double Agent 73*. Wishman died in 2002, but the teenage horror film about a teenager who discovers that a magic locket gives her a physical trait of anyone she kills was not completed until 2006.

Hairspray (2007)

Waters appears as a flasher in the opening musical number in the musical remake of his 1988 movie.

The Lonely Island—"The Creep" (2011)

Created by the comedy team the Lonely Island, "The Creep" is a song that appears on their second album, *Turtleneck & Chain*. The team—Akiva Schaffer, Andy Samberg, and Jorma Taccone—had all worked at *Saturday Night Live*, and their video for the song appeared on the January 29, 2011, episode of the series. The video features Nicki Minaj and includes an intro and outro by Waters, performing as a type of evil Buddy Deane. The song is essentially about a wildly inappropriate and sexually creepy dance, with the trio appearing in the video dressed much like Waters, down to the pencil-thin mustache. Waters mentions in his book *Carsick* that people recognized him from the music video more than his films.

Mangus! (2011)

In this 2001 road-trip comedy, a legless teenager is determined to land the role of Jesus in his hometown's production of *Jesus Christ Superstar*. At one point, the boy hallucinates that he meets Jesus, who is played by John Waters.

Excision (2012)

Waters appears in this psychological horror film in the role of William. Waters's name and face appear prominently in the trailer. Traci Lords has a costarring role in the film.

The Culinary Adventures of Baron Ambrosia, "The Stomach Rumble of Baltimore" (2012)

This show on the Cooking Channel is based around a fictional character named Baron Ambrosia (Justin Fomal), who narrates a show about the cuisines of various real locations, only to get involved in (scripted) comedic adventures along the way. Waters appears as JW, an ex-boyfriend of Baron's new love who joins Baron in ribs and crab while determining Baron's demise.

Suburban Gothic (2014)

Waters has a small but memorable role in this horror-comedy by the same writer-director of *Excision*. Waters can be seen in his role at the end of the trailer for the film.

John Waters in his role from the film *Suburban Gothic* (2014).

Alvin and the Chipmunks: The Road Chip (2015)

Waters cameos as a first-class passenger onboard a flight with the chipmunks. "I've always wanted to be in an Alvin movie," Waters told the *Baltimore Sun*. "I talk about Alvin in my Christmas show. He's always been my mentor."

Groundbreakers (2015–2017)

Waters hosted this Playboy TV series featuring "classic" porn movies, with Waters providing background information on each film shown.

Feud, "Hagsploitation" (2017)

Previously discussed in the book, this miniseries deals with the feud between Bette Davis and Joan Crawford. In this late episode in the series, Waters briefly appears as moviemaker William Castle.

Voice Character

Besides *The Simpsons*, Waters has done a handful of voice characters for various animated series ranging from kid-friendly to . . . not so kid-friendly: *Superjail!*, "Ghosts" (2011); *Fish Hooks*, "Rock Yeti Lobster" (2012); *Mickey Mouse*, "Dog Show" (2013); "The Fancy Gentleman" (2018); *Mugworth* (2013); *Mr. Pickles*, "Coma" (2014); *Clarence*, "Plane Excited" (2016); *Liverspots and Astronots*, "The Exorcism of O-Dor" (2018).

24

Santa Claus Is a Black Man

The Musical Collections of John Waters

The fire has been enhanced to make it more dramatic. I guess I was too subtle.

—John Waters on the cover of his compilation
album *A John Waters Christmas*

Anyone who has seen one Waters movie knows how important music is to his films, particularly songs from his childhood and offbeat recordings. It's not unreasonable to get the vibe that Waters is asking us, the audience, "Isn't this song great? Can you imagine someone doing this and that you missed out on it until now?" (Yes, with *Mondo Trasho* there's also the feeling of "Can you stand hearing this song just one more time?" but that was not really Waters's intention in that case.) "When I turn in a script," Waters told the *New York Times* in 2007, "I almost always turn in a complete soundtrack with it. The studio executives are always surprised when that happens, but the music is another character in the movies. I use the songs like a punch line or a costume."

So when New Line began their own record line, it was natural for them to go to Waters and ask him about doing a compilation for Christmas in 2004. Waters agreed. The album sold well enough that it was followed by another compilation in 2007, also from New Line Records, called *A Date with John Waters*, featuring romantic songs.

When asked by *The Muse* in 2016 about the possibility of a third album, Waters stated: "I've actually wanted to do one called *Breaking Up with John Waters* because all the best music about love is about breaking up. How many good songs are about functional love? The best music is about horrible breakups and misery and being heartbroken." Waters went on to say that he had the perfect picture for such an album, which showed all the stars of *Cry-Baby* with a tear on their check, including Waters. However, Waters doesn't think it'll happen, saying, "I would probably sell one. And I still buy CDs as an old person."

A John Waters Christmas (New Line Records, 2004)

Tracks:
- "Fat Daddy"—Fat Daddy
- "Rudolph the Red-Nosed Reindeer"—Tiny Tim
- "Christmas Time Is Coming (A Street Carol)"—Stormy Weather
- "Happy Birthday Jesus (A Child's Prayer)"—Little Cindy
- "Here Comes Fatty Claus"—Rudolph and Gang
- "Little Mary Christmas"—Roger Christian
- "I Wish You a Merry Christmas"—Big Dee Irwin and Little Eva
- "Santa! Don't Pass Me By"—Jimmy Donley

The CD album cover for Waters's first CD compilation featuring various off beat or slightly disturbing Christmas songs.

- "Sleigh Ride"—Alvin and the Chipmunks
- "First Snowfall"—The Coctails
- "Santa Claus Is a Black Man"—AKIM & the Teddy Vann Production Company

The album cover is actually one of John Waters's earlier Christmas cards, showing Waters sitting next to a Christmas tree with plenty of gifts around it and noticing that many of the presents are on fire. The artwork was altered slightly to make the fire look bigger than it appeared on the original card.

"I've been trying to get Fat Daddy's song back in print for years," Waters told the *Washington Post* in 2004. "Every person in Baltimore who is of a certain age, white or black, remembers 'Fat Daddy from the North Pole, your Santa Claus with soul,' but the record's been out of print for ages."

Waters did run into issues with the last song on the album, both before and after the CD was released. The first was simply finding a copy of "Santa Claus is a Black Man" and having to eventually resort to eBay for a copy of the song that details a variation of "I Saw Mommy Kissing Santa Claus." Teddy Vann, who would later go on to co-write the Grammy-winning "Power of Love/Love Power" with Luther Vandross, had written it for his daughter Akim, who sings on the 1973 single. Which brings up the other problem— Vann didn't want Waters to use the song on the compilation, as Vann did not consider Waters "mainstream" enough for its use. According to the *New York Daily News* in 2008, Vann also felt Waters ridiculed the song in interviews. Whatever issues Vann had at the time, it appears things were worked out as the CD was rereleased in 2010 with the song still on the compilation.

A Date with John Waters (New Line Records, 2007)

Tracks:
- "Tonight You Belong To Me"—Patience & Prudence
- "Jet Boy Jet Girl"—Elton Motello
- "Ain't Got No Home"—Clarence "Frogman" Henry
- "I'd Love to Take Orders from You"—Mildred Bailey & Her Swing Band
- "In Spite of Ourselves"—John Prine
- "All I Can Do Is Cry"—Tina Turner
- "Big Girls Don't Cry"—Edith Massey
- "Imitation of Life"—Earl Grant

- "Sometimes I Wish I Had a Gun"—Mink Stole
- "Johnny, Are You Queer?"—Josie Cotton
- "The Right Time"—Ray Charles
- "Hit the Road to Dreamland"—Dean Martin
- "If I Knew You Were Comin' I'd've Baked a Cake"—Eileen Barton
- "Bewildered"—Shirley & Lee

Although the release of *A John Waters Christmas* came with the news that New Line planned to have a follow-up by Waters out in February 2005, it would be another two years before the Valentine's Day compilation would hit

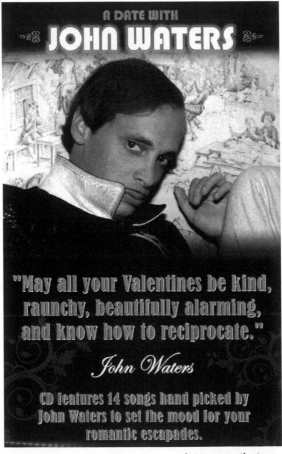

A poster promoting Waters's second CD compilation—this one full of questionable romantic musicial numbers, including songs sung by Mink Stole and Edith Massey.

the streets. The album cover shows Waters with a coy look on his face and includes commentary from him on the songs selected for the album. Included are two of the Dreamlanders: Edith Massey with "Big Girls Don't Cry," and Mink Stole with her song "Sometimes I Wish I Had a Gun," which is included on her 2013 album *Do Re Mink*.

Waters has stated that his soundtracks are like characters in his movies, and in a way, his two compilations are very much standalone characters as well. Both tell the stories he wanted and not always in the "trashy" way expected by some who know Waters only from his movies. It does make one wonder if it is time for someone to finally give Waters the opportunity to do at least one more for all of us.

25

A Lifetime of Penning Trashy Screenplays

The Awards of John Waters

There are two things that make you rich [in life]. You can buy every book you want without looking at the price; and secondly, you're never around assholes. And it took me fifty-something years to get to that position in my life, that you never are around assholes. That's power.

—John Waters to *Huffington Post* in 2015

On February 19, 2017, the Writers Guild of America presented John Waters with the Ian McLellan Hunter Career achievement award for his body of work. David Simon—who created the television series *The Wire*, which was filmed in Baltimore—gave him the award. "You'd be hard-pressed to find a greater and more influential enemy of normal than John Waters," Simon said at the ceremony. In his acceptance speech, Waters stated: "Every single weekday, I get up at 6:00 a.m. and go into my writing room and think up something fucked up. Writing is the only part of filmmaking I really love."

Surprisingly, for a man who reshaped a lot of our thinking when it comes to humor in the past fifty years, awards such as the one given to him at the WGA have not been as many as one would think. There have been a few, of course: In September 2015, the British Film Institute ran a retrospective of all of Waters's films (including his first three), while the Provincetown International Film Festival gave him the Filmmaker on the Edge Award in 1999. The audio version of *Carsick* was nominated for a Grammy in 2015 for Best Spoken Word Album, but being nominated isn't like wining in the category.

In 1997, the Chicago Underground Film Festival gave him the Jack Smith Lifetime Achievement Award, while the Phoenix Film Festival in 2003 gave him the Copper Wing Tribute Award. GLAAD presented him the Stephen F.

Kolzak Award in 2004. He also won the Timeless Award from the Gay and Lesbian Entertainment Critics Association in 2017. His latest personal award is that of becoming an officer of the Ordre des Arts ed des Lettres, which he received in France in 2018 in recognition to his contribution to the arts.

Nominations for his films first started with *Hairspray*, with six nominations from the Film Independent Spirit Awards and one from the Sundance Film Festival, but there were no winners. *Pecker* was nominated for the Grand Prix Asturias at the Gijon International Film Festival but did not win. The one win came with *A Dirty Shame* in 2005, with the film's trailer winning

John Waters from the press kit for *A Dirty Shame*. Perhaps one of his greatest awards is being one of the rare few writer-directors who can sell his movies on his name and face alone.

for "Trashiest Trailer" at the Golden Trailer Awards. Of course, the Broadway version of *Hairspray* won several Tony Awards. Some would say that it was a collaborative effort by others based on Waters's work, but if there hadn't been his 1988 movie that became a success in the first place, nothing that followed would have happened.

That's usually what happens to our innovators; the ones that work the hardest to create new, interesting ways of doing or even looking at things are usually the shoulders upon which the ones who get the awards stand. Waters went from being a kid knowing nothing about the camera, acting, or producing, but because of his zest for wanting to create for an audience, he picked up those skills and made movies. Because of his fearlessness when it came to promoting his work, at a point in a young filmmaker's career that would have had many cringing in terror, Waters threw himself into his work and into making sure someone saw it. It took time, a lot of hard work, and a lot of understanding from his friends and family, but he made it.

Throughout that process, we got a variety of films that refused to fit the formula of what any genre is supposed to represent. Waters may have started as an underground filmmaker, but his films weren't the serious studies of life's essential questions that were expected from the genre. His comedies were not like those of other popular writers and directors—we found our laughs not through sick jokes but through shock at how things can be told to us in a way that made us laugh. Nowadays, there are plenty of writers in Hollywood who put things in their comedies that go way past what Waters has done, but they're missing the main element that came with his work—there was heart behind it, and in the end good will always rise to the top. The films could be quite dark, but they always had some positive, uplifting element. His darkest early film, *Eat Your Makeup*, may have had women modeling themselves to death, but Waters couldn't just end the film with their dead bodies—the fantasy of death needed to have Prince Charming arrive to revive one of the girls for a happy ending. Waters has always claimed that *Female Trouble*, in a strange way, has a happy ending, as Dawn sees the electric chair as the "award" for all her good work in crime. She's happy to go out that way, and she actually really does love every fucking one of us. His absolutely darkest film, *Desperate Living*, ends with the population of Mortville free and dancing in the streets.

Waters's films deal with things we feel we have to shield our eyes from in order to live happy lives—death, bodily functions, the downward spiral of religion, the chance that at any moment we will crack under the strain and cause real damage to others and ourselves. Yet, every single one of his movies is ultimately a positive experience. The good guys in his movie—who would be the bad guys in anyone else's movie—win; the bad guys—or in most cases, the bad, bad guys against our good bad guys—lose. We may have to put up with a lot of muck and hard work, but ultimately a flower is going to grow from the muck if we give it a chance.

In some ways, Waters is the ultimate version of one of his characters in his movies. He makes these movies that are supposed to horrify us, but we love him for them. We look forward to his talks about taboo topics and see his contemporary artwork to get insights into ourselves. He is that good bad guy in his movies, who ultimately wins in the end.

Waters creates—it can be movies, stand-up lectures, artwork, or books—and he proves that by creating he can give something to all of us. What frustrates his critics is that they can never quite pigeonhole his work so they can put a stamp upon it. It's not underground, it's not drama, and while there's comedy, there's something more. It's life.

Waters has proved through determination in his films and in his career that life—in all its various oddball ways—is a journey upon which we need to make sure we see both the good and the ugly and appreciate what it is all about. His work reflects that and will tell those same stories to others for many years to come.

Life is its own award. And John Waters has won.

26

Not the Sleaze King

Nicknames That John Waters Does Not Want on His Tombstone, and One He Does

I guess it would be witty if—as my last movie—I just jumped in front of the camera and committed hara-kiri. That would shock people, and it would cement my reputation, wouldn't it? But I've always said the only thing I don't want to be ironic is my death.

—John Waters to Ben Nuckols of the Associated Press

Prince of Puke
The People's Pervert
Pope of Trash
Duke of Dirt
The Anal Ambassador
The Ayatollah of Assholes
Baron of Bad Taste
Sultan of Sleaze
The Filth King/The Sleaze King
Don Knotts
John Samuel Waters Jr.

John Samuel Waters Jr. in a posed photo from *Cry-Baby*. A man who is happy with that name, although he goes by many others, whether he wants to or not.

Bibliography

"Divine Director: Brando's My Guy." *New York Post*, December 13, 1996.

"John Waters: By the Book." *New York Times*, April 23, 2017.

"Judge Reluctantly Removes Indecent Exposure Case." *Baltimore Sun*, November 13, 1968.

"Obituary: Mark P. Isherwood." December 3, 2013, https://www.hathawayfunerals.com.

"Questions For: John Waters." *New York Times*, April 13, 1997.

"Reading with . . . John Waters." Accessed April 12, 2017, http://www.shelf-awareness.com/ issue.html?issue=2978#m36098

Abatemarco, Michael. "The Trashman: Filmmaker John Waters on Becoming a Household Name." *The New Mexican*, October 20, 2017.

Abraham, Amelia. "John Waters on the Terrible Trashy Films That Changed His Life." *Vice*, August 12, 2015, https://www.vice.com/en_us/article/dp5djk/the-films-that-made-me-john-waters.

Abrams, Simon. "John Waters Says All of His Films Are 'Completely' Politically Correct." *Esquire*, August 9, 2016.

Allman, Kevin. "John Waters: The Gambit Interview." *Best of New Orleans*, June 7, 2010.

Alvarez, Rafael. "Paul Swift, 'Eggman' in Waters's *Pink Flamingos*." *Baltimore Sun*, October 10, 1994.

Anderson, Lincoln. "John Waters, from Christmas Craziness to Caitlyn." *Villager*, December 3, 2015.

Appleford, Steve. "This Filthy World." *Los Angeles CityBeat*, October 11, 2007.

Baird, Kirk. "Filmmaker John Waters Brings His One-Man Show to BGSU." *Toledo Blade*, November 1, 2015.

Birmingham, Steve. "Interview with John Waters about his New Book *Role Models*." *Dog Canyon*, June 8, 2010.

Blair, Iain. "John Waters: A Polyester Sleaze Czar Turns Juvenile Delinquent with *Cry-Baby*." *BAM*, April 20, 1990.

Blevins, Joe. "John Waters: Change of Life," 2004, http://www.dreamlandnews.com/photo/change_of_life.shtml.

Bowman, Jon. "John Waters: A Bird Stranger than Pink Flamingos." *The Santa Fe New Mexican*, January 15, 1985.

Bramer, Mikki. "The Dreamers: John Waters." *Map Magazine*, 2011.

Bravo, Tony. "John Waters Presents Family-Unfriendly Stroller." *San Francisco Chronicle*, April 19, 2016.

Briley, Tom. "*Wizard of Oz* is Not Like the Classic." *Daily Times,* May 18, 1966.

Brooklyn Vegan Starr. "John Waters Working on Two New Books, Starts His Annual Christmas Show Tour This Weekend." November 23, 2015, http://www.brooklynvegan.com/john-waters-wor/.

Brooks, Claude Thomas. "Waters '. . . I've Always Tried to Sell Out.'" *In Motion Film and Video Production Magazine*, 1982.

Bruni, Frank. "Change of Coarse." *Detroit Free Press*, April 10, 1994.

Bruno, Paul. "Mink Stole." *Dirty Mag*, February 20, 2011.

Buster. "*Cry-Baby* Comparison: Theatrical Version and Director's Cut." January 21, 2012, https://www.movie-censorship.com/report.php?ID=453762.

Carr, Jay. "John Waters: Ex-Bad Boy?" *Boston Globe*, April 19, 1990.

Cerasaro, Pat. "In-depth Interview; John Waters Talks *Hairspray: In Concert, Hairspray 2,* Favorite Movie Musicals & More." January 19, 2013, https://www.broadwayworld.com/article/InDepth-InterView-John-Waters-Talks-HAIRSPRAY-IN-CONCERT-HAIRSPRAY-2-Favorite-Movie-Musicals-More-20130119.

Charles, Laura. "The *Cry-Baby* Crowd." *Baltimore Sun,* May 18, 1990.

Chee, Alexander. "John Waters: 'I Think I am Weirdly Politically Correct." April 27, 2017, http://lithub.com/john-waters-i-think-i-am-weirdly-politically-correct/.

Cohn, Michael. "John Waters: Change of Life." *NY Arts Magazine*, 2004.

Coldwell, Will. "John Waters on Baltimore." *Guardian*, November 28, 2014.

Cooper, Dennis. "John Waters." *Bomb Magazine*, April 1, 2004.

Corey, Mary. "Call Me a *Cry-Baby*." *Baltimore Sun*, March 13, 1989.

——. "Kitsch & Kin." *Baltimore Sun*, April 15, 1994.

Covert, Colin. "John Waters Talks (and Talks)." *Dispatch*, November 18, 2007.

Cowherd, Kevin. "'Sex Addicts' Take Will Make Her Life of Any Party." *Baltimore Sun*, November 20, 2003.

Curry, Bill. "Zipping to Baltimore for Egg Lady's Birthday." *Philadelphia Inquirer*, May 27, 1974.

Davies, Dave. "John Waters Argues for Murderer's Release." NPR, August 10, 2009.

Desroches, Steve. "National Legion of Decency Rates This Show 'O' for Morally Offensive." *Provincetown Magazine*, July 19, 2017.

Egan, James. *John Waters Interviews*. Jackson: University Press of Mississippi, 2011.

Elsasser, Glen. "Mild-Mannered King of the Gross-out: A Divine Sequel for *Pink Flamingos*." *Chicago Tribune*, July 1, 1984.

Engstrom, John. "John Waters: Schlepping through Suburbia with Cinema's Naughty Boy." *Advocate*, July 9, 1981.

Eyman, Scott. "The Dangerous Mind of John Waters." *Miami News*, February 17, 1988.

Fields, Danny and Fran Lebowitz. "*Pink Flamingos* and the Filthiest People Alive?" *Interview*, May 1973. Ford, Dave. "The King of Camp." *SF Weekly*, April 4, 1990.

Freund, Charles Paul. "John Waters, Filmdom's Bad Boy, Getting a 'Career Retrospective.'" *Baltimore Sun*, August 5, 1981.

Garner, Jack. "Waters's Work Anchors ImageOut Film Festival." *Democrat and Chronicle*, October 5, 2001.

George, Bill and Martin Falck. "The *Late Show* Presents the Divine World of John Waters." *Late Show*, 1974.

Giltz, Michael. "John Waters on *Faster, Pussycat! Kill! Kill!*" *New York*, January 16, 1995.

Goldstein, Gregg. "Johnny Knoxville, Parker Posey Join *Fruitcake*." *Hollywood Reporter*, Los Angeles, May 7, 2008.

Goldstein, Richard. "Drugs on Campus: Why Marijuana Use Surged in the 1960s." *Saturday Evening Post*, June 4, 1966.

Gomez, Patrick. "Ricki Lake Reveals Why Her Hair 'Never Recovered' After *Hairspray*." *People*, November 16, 2016.

Grant, James. "He Really Can't Help Himself." *Los Angeles Times*, April 10, 1994.

Grow, Kory. "John Waters on Restored *Multiple Maniacs*: A 'Movie to Scare Hippies.'" *Rolling Stone*, August 5, 2016.

Guillen, Michael. "Midnight Mass Interview with John Waters." June 25, 2007, http://screenanarchy.com/2007/07/midnight-mass-interview-with-john-waters.html.

Gunts, Edward. "Welcome to the 'Nuthouse.'" *Baltimore Sun*, March 5, 2009.

Halley, Peter and Bob Nickas. "John Waters." *Index Magazine*, 1997.

Harrington, Richard. "A Present from John Waters." *Washington Post,* December 3, 2004.

Harris, Joann. "Miles Beyond the Topless Bathing Suit." *Sun Magazine*, March, 31, 1968.

——. "You're a Star." *Baltimore Sun*, March 26, 1972.

Harmetz, Aljean. "Film: John Waters Cavorts in the Mainstream." *New York Times*, February 21, 1988.

Harrington, Richard. "Revenge of the Gross-Out King! John Waters's *Pink Flamingos* Enjoys a 25th-Year Revival." *Washington Post*, April 6, 1997.

Heilpern, John. "Uncharted Waters." *Vanity Fair*, June 2010.

Hiltner, George. "Stanzas Three: Thespians Free." *Baltimore Sun*, February 8, 1969.

Himes, Geoffrey. "John Waters's Love Songs, Suitably Bizarre." *New York Times*, 2007.

Holden, Stephen. "*Hairspray* Gives a Lift to Ruth Brown's Career." *Chicago Tribune*, April 7, 1988.

Hunter, Stephen. "John Waters: Never Quite Gone, He's Back Again." *Baltimore Sun,* October 5, 1986.

Hunter, Stephen. "Show Must Go On." *Baltimore Sun*, June 7, 1989.

Hutchins, Paul. "Big Mama of the Camp Cult." *Baltimore Sun*, December 9, 1973.

Hubert, Craig. "John Waters Tells the Story of His Mustache." *New York Times*, August 4, 2016.

Hunter, Stephen. "Kathleen Turner a *Serial Mom* in Waters's Latest Film." *Baltimore Sun*, February 2, 1993.

"It Came from Baltimore." *Cry-Baby*. Director's Cut DVD. Los Angeles: Universal, 2005.

Ives, John G. *American Originals: John Waters*. New York: Thunder's Mouth Press, 1992.

Jeffries, Stuart. "John Waters: 'I Want to Be Despised.'" *Guardian*, June 30, 2015.

Johnson, G. Allen. "John Waters on His Restored 2nd Feature *Multiple Maniacs*." *SFGate*, September 14, 2016.

Kaltenbach, Chris. "Waters's Latest: Sex by Pseudonym." *Baltimore Sun*, September 19, 2004.

——. "From *Hairspray* to the Highway." *Baltimore Sun*, June 4, 2014.

———. "In his New Book *Make Trouble*, John Waters Offers Inspiration. So Where Did He Get His?" *Baltimore Sun*, April 10, 2017.

Kasper, Rob. "Waters's 'Maniacal' Movie Eludes Censor Board's Ban." *Baltimore Sun*, January 9, 1981.

Kelly, Jacques and Frederick N. Rasmussen. "Film Censor Mary Avara, 90, Dies." *Baltimore Sun*, August 10, 2000.

Kelly, Jacques. "John S. Waters, 91." *Baltimore Sun*, June 12, 2008.

———. "John C. Whitaker, Who Served as Aide to President Nixon, Dies." *Baltimore Sun*, July 5, 2016.

Kinney, Tulsa. "John Waters: 3rd Degree." *Citybeat*, December 9–15, 2004.

Kronke, David. "*Boom!* Might Have Gone Bust, but John Waters Still Loved It." *Baltimore Sun*, September 20, 1998.

L'Ecuyer, Gerald. "On the Beltway and Back Streets." *Drive*, April 1990.

Lally, Kevin. "*Hairspray* Gets a 'Shocking' PG as Waters Looks Back at '62." *Film Journal*, March 1988.

Layton, Eric. "On the Waters Front." *Entertainment Today*, September 25, 1998.

Leland, John. "At Home with John Waters." *New York Times,* August 15, 2002.

Lemon, Brendan. "Inside John Waters." *Christopher Street*, New York, 1986.

Levy, Ariel. "Still Waters." *New York*, March 31, 2008.

Leroy, J. T. "What Price Hollywood?" *Filmmaker Magazine*, Summer 2000.

Lewis, John. "John Waters Inc." *Baltimore Magazine*, June 2007.

———. "Seeing Red," *Baltimore Magazine*, August 2013.

Lewis, Jon. *Hollywood v. Hard Core: How the Struggle over Censorship Saved the Modern Film Industry.* New York: New York University Press, 2000.

Limon, Erique. "Water Sheds." *Santa Fe Reporter*, October 15, 2013.

Loder, Kurt. "Random Notes." *St. Cloud Times*, December 13, 1980.

Lodi, Marie, "Talking about Sex, Trigger Warnings, and a Perfect Valentine's Day with John Waters." February 9, 2016, https://themuse.jezebel.com/talking-about-sex-trigger-warnings-and-a-perfect-valen-1757210162.

Long II, Robert. "Veteran Character Actor and a Class Act: The George Stover Interview." 2008, http://smashortrashindiefilmmaking.com/interviews/actor-george-stover/

Lowe, Susan. "Susan Lowe: Memoirs of a Dreamlander." *Film Threat*, December 28, 2004.

MacDonald, Scott. "John Waters's Divine Comedy." *Artforum*, January 1982.

Magnay, Jacquelin. "A Rude Word from John Waters." *Australian*, March 1, 2014.

Maier, Robert. *Low Budget Hell: Making Underground Movies with John Waters*. Davidson: Full Page Publishing, 2011.

Maier, Robert. "Divine Mauled by Press in Violent Scene Cut from *Polyester*." March 10, 2013, http://robertmaier.us/2012/03/10/divine-mauled-by-press-in-violent-scene-cut-from-polyester/.

Mandelbaum, Paul. "Kinkmeister." *New York Times*, April 7, 1991.

Marbella, Jean. "Drugs Behind Him, Matinee Idol Plays It Straight." *Baltimore Sun*, November 7, 1989.

McCabe, Bret. "John Waters on Hitchhiking Adventures and His Long-Ago Arrest at Johns Hopkins." HUB, September 22, 2014.

McGovern, Joe. "John Waters Explains that Infamous Divine-Lobster Scene in *Multiple Maniacs*." *Entertainment Weekly*, August 5, 2016.

McGrath, Nick. "John Waters: My Family Values." *Guardian*, September 18, 2005.

Meoli, Jon. "Unscripted Ending to Tale of Terror, Attack." *Baltimore Sun*, November 28, 2012.

Metz, Nina. "Filmmaker John Waters Gets Wicked in Chicago." *Chicago Tribune*, June 9, 2011.

Meyer, George. "John Waters's Films Are an Exercise in Bad, Bad Taste." *Tampa Tribune*, November 11, 1977.

Miller, Liz Shannon. "*Feud*: John Waters on Becoming William Castle and His Love of Great Gimmicks." April 9, 2017, http://www.indiewire.com/2017/04/feud-john-waters-william-castle-casting-ryan-murphy-1201803568/.

Miller, M. H. "What It's Like to Live with Art that Doesn't Love You Back," *The New York Times*, New York, September 22, 2017.

Morgan, Kim. "Talking with John Waters." *Sight & Sound*, August 11, 2015.

Morris, John A. "Sykesville's Main Street to Star in John Waters Film." *Baltimore Sun,* April 2, 1989.

——. "Sykesville Relishes its Day in the Movies." *Baltimore Sun*, May 28, 1989.

Mueller, Cookie. "Pink Flamingos." September 3, 2014, https://www.mookychick.co.uk/feminism/uk-feminism/pink_flamingos.php.

Murphy, Ryan. "Hollywood's Drama Queens Looking for Lighter Roles." *Los Angeles Times*, January 4, 1993.

Musto, Michael. "*Desperate Living*: Not a Pretty Picture." *Soho Weekly News*, October 20, 1977.

Myers, Marc. "The Divine Childhood Home of John Waters." *Wall Street Journal*, April 11, 2017.

Nuckols, Ben. "Gentler Filmmaker Emerges from Waters." *Tallahassee Democrat*, August 20, 2000.

Ollove, Michael. "Archivist Finds Fast Friendships on Movie Sets." *Baltimore Sun*, November 23, 1999.

Ollover, Michae. "Delightfully Deviant." *Baltimore Sun*, April 19, 1998.

Patches, Matt. "John Waters Discusses 50 Years of John Waters Movies, and Why He Refuses to Go Backward." 2014, https://thedissolve.com/features/interview/730-john-waters-discusses-50-years-of-john-waters-movi/.

Pearce, Mary Vivian. "The Cinematic Unabomber." *Paper*, September 2000.

Peary, Gerald. "John Waters in Provincetown." *Provincetown Arts Magazine*, 1997.

——. "John Waters—*Pecker*." 1997, http://www.geraldpeary.com.

Peters, Jenny. "Plimpton Finds Place in Pecking Order." *Daily Times*, October 7, 1998.

Pogrebin, Robin. "Riding High with a Big, Bouffant Hit; After 25 Years of Paying Dues, an Independent Producer Scores with *Hairspray*." *New York Times*, October 16, 2002.

Postel, Louis. "A Lot of People Were Upset That We Put the Baby in the Refrigerator . . ." *Provincetown Magazine*, 1977.

Powell, Fiona Russell. "Divinely Yours." *Face*, September 1984.

Rasmussen, Frederick. "Jean E. Hill." *Baltimore Sun*, August 27, 2013.

Rasmussen, Frederick. "Patricia Waters, Mother of Filmmaker John Waters, Dies at 89." *Baltimore Sun*, February 10, 2014.

Raymond, Gerard. "Interview: Mink Stole Talks *The Mutilated*, John Waters, & More." *Slant*, November 10, 2013.

Rizzo, Frank. "Patty Hearst Enjoys New Role as One of 'Odd People' in *Cry-Baby*." *Los Angeles Times*, April 6, 1990.

Roberts, Vida. "Killer Outfits." *Baltimore Sun,* April, 7, 1994.

Rooney, David. "An Evening with John Waters: Critic's Notebook." *Hollywood Reporter*, July 1, 2013.

Ross, Jonathan. "John Waters." *Guardian*, November 17, 1998.

Rothbart, Daniel. "Excerpts from an Interview with John Waters." December 2000, http://semioticstreet.com/waters.html.

Rousuck, J. Wynn. "*Hairspray* to Spritz on Broadway." *Baltimore Sun*, February 15, 2000.

Sefcovic, Enid. "*Pink Flamingos* to Land in Baltimore." *News American*, April 24, 1973.

Sherman, Pat. "The Pope of Trash Basks in the Joy of Holiday Madness." *San Diego City Beat*, December 14, 2005.

Shister, Gail. "Actress Rockets to Fame with Young-Adult Talk Show." *Titusville Herald,* October 5, 1992.

Shulman, Randy. "Waters World." *Metro Weekly*, December 3, 2009.

Siegel, Alan. "When *The Simpsons* Came out of the Closet." February 8, 2017, https://www.theringer.com/2017/2/8/16038570/simpsons-homers-phobia-john-waters-gay-lgbt-representation-tv-849196024467.

Signorile, Michelangelo. "John Waters Says He Never Actually Came Out as Gay Because Nobody Asked." *Huffington Post*, June 24, 2015.

Smith, Jane A. "Edith Massey, Actress in Waters Films, Dies at 66." *Baltimore Sun*, October 25, 1984.

Smith, Liz. "Kathleen Likes Film's Ending Fine." *Detroit Free Press*, October 14, 1993.

Stewart, Jenny. *"A Dirty Shame."* 2005, http://www. planetout.com.

Solondz, Todd. "Interview with John Waters." *John Waters: Change of Life.* New York: Harry N. Abrams, 2004.

Suebsaeng, Asawn. "John Waters on Police Brutality in Baltimore, Sex in Voting Booths, and the Insanity of Fox News." *Daily Beast*, May 30, 2015.

Tarpinian, Katherine. "We Talked to John Waters about Facelifts, *Kiddie Flamingos*, and His New Art Show." January 8, 2015, https://creators.vice.com/en_us/article/vvybzd/we-talked-to-john-waters-about-his-new-art-show.

Teeman, Tim. "John Waters: 'Doing the Show Is an Effective Anti-Alzheimer's Exercise." *Guardian*, November 2, 2013.

Trunick, Austin. "John Waters on His 1994 Cult Classic *Serial Mom*." *Under the Radar*, May 8, 2017.

Visco, Geraldine. "With Lincoln Center Retrospective, John Waters Runs Deep." September 5, 2014, https://hyperallergic.com/147599/with-lincoln-center-retrospective-john-waters-runs-deep/.

Waters, John. *Shock Value*. New York: Dell Publishing, 1981.

———. *Role Models*. New York: Farrar, Straus and Giroux, 2010.

———. "John Waters's Provincetown." *Civilian Magazine*, May 28, 2014.

———. "My Childhood Home." *Lapham's Quarterly*, Winter 2017.

White, Terri. "John Waters Interview: 'I Didn't Become a Drug Addict Because I Always Had to Make a Movie.'" *TimeOut*, September 4, 2014.

Willistein, Paul. "John Waters: Riding the Roller Coaster of Life." *Morning Call*, June 21, 1987.

Wise, Damon. "The Filth and the Fury." *Guardian*, September 28, 2007.

Wolgamott, L. Kent. "His Filthy World: John Waters on His Life, Movies and *The Howdy Doody Show*." *Lincoln Journal Star*, April 18, 2015.

Woodward, Daisy. "How LSD Adventures Inspired John Waters's *Multiple Maniacs*." *AnOther Magazine*, February 13, 2017.

Young, Jamie Painter. "DeMented at Heart." *Back Stage West*, August 3, 2000.

Zuich, Fred and Robbie Busch. "Reluctantly Ironic: John Waters Just Can't Resist." *Cups*, Winter 1998.

Index

Adams, Bob, 50–51, 156
Anger, Kenneth, 13, 95, 103–104, 106, 289
Avara, Mary, 148–149, 167–168, 184

Babb, Howard, 95–97, 100, 101, 117
Baby Doll, 84, 93–94, 110–111
Baltimore, 2–3, 13–14, 19, 21, 34, 35, 36, 37, 39, 40–43, 45, 46, 48, 52, 54, 57, 58, 64, 70, 72, 78–90, 94, 100, 101, 102, 108, 121, 123–124, 133, 135, 137, 148, 156, 157, 163, 164, 167, 177–179, 181–184, 191, 195, 198, 203, 214, 217, 226, 229–231, 233, 234, 241, 252, 254–256, 258, 266, 271, 272, 275, 279, 280, 283–284, 291, 294–296, 302, 305–307, 315, 317, 321, 323, 325–326, 328, 331, 334, 339, 343, 346
Bergman, Ingmar, 95, 96, 102, 106–107, 108, 150
Black, Lizzy Temple, 57, 124, 129
Blair, Selma, 298, 301–302, 304, 305
Bono, Sonny, 221, 223, 225, 226
Boom!, 12, 109–110
Bunuel, Luis, 95, 102–103, 233

Carsick, 13, 326, 338, 346
Castle, William, xii, 99–101, 114–115, 117, 166, 288, 322, 340
Cecil B. DeMented, 20, 29, 31, 33, 37, 40–43, 50–52, 54, 57, 82, 94, 143, 174, 231, 280, 281, 286–297, 305, 314, 317, 333
Coffey, Elizabeth, 154, 173
Crackpot, xii, 97, 100–101, 114, 115, 218, 229, 243, 315, 316, 319, 322–323, 326
Cry-Baby (1990 movie), 17, 29, 33, 37, 41–43, 45, 50–52, 54–56, 66, 83, 89, 105, 112, 174, 224, 227, 245–262, 268, 269, 314, 316, 334, 341–342, 350
Cry-Baby (Broadway musical), 260–262

Depp, Johnny, 245, 247–249, 251, 254–256, 258, 334
Desperate Living, xii, 29, 33, 34, 37, 39–43, 45, 48, 50–52, 57, 58, 73, 81, 87, 107, 108, 109, 137, 164, 174, 185–200, 205, 206, 215, 228, 294, 321, 324, 348
Diane Linkletter Story, The, 29, 33, 34, 118, 126–128, 144, 217, 321, 322
Dirty Shame, A, 7, 28, 29, 33, 37, 40–43, 50–52, 54, 56, 57, 84, 188, 229, 268, 281, 296, 298–311, 314, 317, 347
Divine Trash, xii
Divine, xii, 4, 7, 12, 20, 22, 29, 32–36, 38, 42–44, 48–50, 56, 58, 59–77, 82–85, 87–89, 101, 102, 106, 110–114, 118, 122, 124, 127, 129–137, 139, 141–146, 149, 150, 151–165, 167, 169, 171, 174–176, 178–182, 184, 189, 200, 201, 204, 205, 207, 210–212, 214, 215, 218, 220–222, 225–228, 234, 259, 268, 270, 313–316, 321, 324
Dorff, Stephen, 286, 291–292
Dorothy, the Kansas City Pothead, 120–122
Dreamland (people), xii,12, 27, 28–58, 72, 116, 119, 122, 123, 133, 142, 150, 205, 227, 228, 251, 334, 345
Dreamland (production company), xii, 28, 95, 122, 126, 142, 150, 193

Eat Your Makeup, 29, 31–34, 37, 38, 40, 47, 48, 57, 67, 81, 118, 124–126, 348

Feirstein, Harvey, 1, 237, 240, 241, 242, 243
Fellini, Federico, 101–102, 137, 313
Female Trouble, xii, 4, 7, 8, 12,21, 24, 29, 32–34, 37, 39–45, 47–51, 57, 58, 61, 68, 70, 71, 75, 77, 81, 83, 113, 114, 124, 137, 146, 150, 154, 164, 166, 169, 170, 171–184, 190–191, 195, 205, 215, 218, 232, 251, 313, 324, 325, 348

Feud, xii, 100–101, 108, 340

Figgs, George, 40–41, 121, 124, 139, 186, 303

Flamingos Forever, 229, 313–315, 319, 324

Furlong, Edward, 75, 278, 279, 282

Gruber, Howard, 47–48, 88, 124, 140, 150, 288

Hag in a Black Leather Jacket, 4, 29, 31, 32, 37, 66, 81, 116, 117–120, 124

Hairspray (1988 movie), 7, 29, 30, 33, 34, 37, 42, 43, 50–54, 58, 61, 75, 76, 83, 84, 89, 150, 167, 169, 174, 203, 205, 214, 217, 220–244, 253, 254, 256, 259, 259, 260, 269, 279, 285, 301, 313, 319, 322–323, 324, 325, 332, 347

Hairspray (Broadway musical), 1, 90, 235–238, 240–241, 260–261, 302, 348

Hairspray (movie musical), 238–242, 338

Hairspray Live!, 52, 236, 242–244

Harry, Debbie, 213–214, 220, 223, 225, 226

Hearst, Patricia, 20–21, 52–54, 83–84, 245, 249–252, 256, 265, 271, 284, 288, 293, 303

Heatherton, Joey, 224. 245, 250–251,

Hill, Jean, 51–52, 61, 185, 187, 188, 192, 194, 221, 226, 228–229, 303, 315

Hunter, Tab, 20, 73–74, 77, 201, 204, 210–211, 213, 214, 215, 251, 315

Isaak, Chris, 298, 302

Isherwood, Mark, 39, 122, 123, 129, 134

Kiddie Flamingos, 169

Knoxville, Johnny, 56–57, 298, 301–302, 307, 310, 317–318

Kuchar Brothers, xii, 95, 101, 104, 105–107

Lake, Ricki, 52–53, 220, 221, 225, 227, 228, 232, 240, 242, 246, 247, 249, 251, 260, 263, 267–268, 270, 279, 280, 286, 293, 303

Leisenring, John, 48, 129

Lewis, H. Gordon, xii, 97–99, 101, 106, 267, 288, 321, 332, 336

Lochary, David, 4, 15, 29, 34–37, 42, 44, 57, 60, 63–64, 82, 119, 122–124, 127, 130, 132, 134, 135, 136, 139, 141, 142, 144, 147, 150, 155, 157, 160, 164, 172, 174, 190

Lords, Traci, 54, 55, 66, 112, 245, 247, 249, 251, 258, 264, 268, 339

Lowe, Susan, 39, 41, 44, 45, 48, 50, 73, 87, 131, 140, 180, 185, 187, 189, 193, 194, 203, 205, 227, 251, 268, 280, 293

Maier, Robert, 166, 174, 179, 181, 190, 191, 193, 195, 211–213, 251, 254, 313

Make Trouble, 326–327

Maryland Board of Censors, 148–149, 195, 215, 283,

Massey, Edie, 29, 41, 43, 45–47, 50, 56, 74, 111, 140, 142, 150, 151, 161, 171, 174, 182, 186, 192, 195, 201, 205, 211, 212, 216, 219, 313–315, 343–345

Mason, Christine, 174,

McGuire, Kim, 56, 245, 247, 249

Melin, Marina, 40, 124–125, 131, 173, 186, 205

Meyer, Russ, 99, 106, 112–113, 321, 332

Milstead, Harris Glenn, (see Divine)

Mill, Danny, 29, 79, 151, 154, 158–159, 160, 165,

Mondo Trasho, 4, 7, 20, 29, 30, 32–34, 37, 39, 40, 41, 44, 48, 51, 57, 58, 68, 79, 84, 86, 89, 104, 107, 108, 113, 126, 129–138, 142, 148, 149, 154, 156, 170, 178, 180, 205, 341

Montgomery, Mona, 31–32, 40, 86, 119

Moran, Pat, 6, 13, 33–34, 36, 37, 38, 44, 52, 55, 60, 65, 66, 95, 121–122, 123, 130, 154, 157, 162, 174, 179, 181, 188, 192, 195, 199, 211, 217, 230, 234, 249, 251, 257, 303, 334

Morgan, Scott, 268, 303

Morrow, Rick, 58, 132, 139, 150

Mueller, Cookie, 15, 48–50, 67, 87, 140, 142, 150, 151, 154, 157–159, 160, 171, 176, 177, 178, 186, 205, 280

Multiple Maniacs, 3, 9, 14, 16, 17, 21, 29, 30, 32, 33, 34, 37, 39, 40–49, 51, 57, 58, 62, 68, 76, 79, 81, 84, 86–89, 98, 101, 103, 126–127, 133, 137, 139–150, 154, 157, 163, 170, 175, 176, 232, 324, 325, 328

New Line Cinema, 108, 160, 163–166, 169–170, 182–183, 190, 193, 200, 207–210, 213–216, 229–230, 233, 235, 238, 243, 259, 285, 307, 317, 341–343

Pearce, Mary Vivian, 20, 22, 29–31, 32, 37, 38, 42, 44, 64, 79, 81, 86, 87, 104, 107, 108, 119, 120, 122–124, 127, 129, 134–136, 139, 151, 154, 157, 158, 159, 164, 172, 174, 186, 205, 227, 251, 268, 280, 293, 314
Pecker, 9, 29, 32, 33, 37, 40–43, 50–54, 57, 84, 205, 217, 268, 270, 275–285, 294, 317, 347
Peranio, Vincent, 34, 41–45, 67, 87, 142, 144, 156, 173, 190, 192, 194, 251, 283, 304, 334
Peter Pan, 3, 92, 242
Pink Flamingos, xii, 3, 4, 6, 7, 18, 21, 23, 29, 30, 32–36, 39, 40, 42–51, 57, 61, 68–71, 74, 79, 80, 82–84, 90, 99, 100, 103, 110, 111, 114, 123, 124, 132, 137, 146, 147, 148, 151–170, 175, 177–180, 183, 190, 191, 211, 215–216, 217–219, 231, 285, 293, 294, 314–315, 321, 324–325, 336
Polyester, xii, 3, 7, 16, 20, 29, 30, 33, 34, 37, 40–43, 45, 47–52, 58, 69, 73–74, 76, 77, 100, 114, 116, 137, 166, 174, 177, 188, 200, 201–216, 229, 250, 264, 312, 313, 315, 319, 321, 322, 327
Pop, Iggy, 17, 112, 246, 249, 251, 253
Provincetown, 14, 15, 20, 22, 23, 31, 35, 37, 40, 42, 48, 50, 51, 57, 58, 67–68, 78, 79, 81, 85–88, 89, 90, 93, 125, 132, 137, 142, 170, 177, 191, 207, 330, 346

Renay, Liz, 185, 188–189, 194, 199
Ricci, Christina, 275, 278, 279, 280
Roggero, Charles, 174, 190, 195, 212
Role Models, xii, 12, 17, 19, 112, 154, 281, 326
Roman Candles, 4, 9, 29, 31–34, 37–39, 66, 81, 105, 118, 122–125, 189

Salvia Films (see New Line Cinema)
Serial Mom, 12, 20, 29, 33, 37, 40–43, 50, 52–56, 108, 219, 229, 232, 249, 262, 263–274, 281–283, 294, 316,

Skidmore, Bob, 32, 64, 119, 122–124, 131, 132, 280
Skidmore, Margie, 32, 57, 124, 129, 131, 139
Shock Value, xii, 3, 4, 5, 7–10, 13, 21, 22, 27, 31, 32, 35, 38, 40, 49, 57, 61, 63–66, 78, 81, 82, 94, 97–99, 121, 124, 125, 136, 137, 147, 154, 155, 158, 162, 164, 166, 175, 177–179, 184, 189–192, 194–196, 199, 315, 316, 319–322, 326, 336
Smith, Van, 41, 42–43, 44, 68, 69, 70, 106, 142, 154, 157–158, 180, 181, 190, 251, 279, 318, 334
Soul, Maelcum, 13, 33, 38–39, 57, 121–124, 217
Stole, Mink, 17, 19, 21, 22, 29, 35–38, 44, 50, 58, 67, 71, 76, 81–83, 87, 93, 122, 123, 129, 132, 134–136, 140–143, 146, 157–160, 162, 172, 185, 187, 191, 194–195, 201, 205, 220, 227, 245, 250, 251, 263, 267, 277, 280, 287, 293, 298, 303, 314, 335, 344–345
Stover, George, 58, 174, 199, 212, 227,
Swift, Paul, 39–40, 142, 150, 151, 188

Turner, Kathleen, 159, 266–267, 271–272

Ullman, Tracey, 298, 299, 301, 302, 305

Van Houten, Leslie, 19–21, 154, 326

Walsh, Susan, 51, 171, 176
Warhol, Andy, 13, 60, 72, 95, 104–105, 106, 122, 149, 251, 288, 291, 324, 328
Waters, John (on art), 323–325
Waters, John (on drugs), 5, 10–11, 13–16, 22, 126
Waters, John (on education), 8–11, 217–219
Waters, John (on family), 1–7,
Waters, John (on reading and books), 11–13, 23, 84, 85, 86–87, 89, 316, 329
Waters, John (on religion), 8–9, 92–94, 101, 103, 118
Waters, John (on trials), 19–21, 53, 79, 175, 217 273–274, 321
Waters, John (on work), 6, 23–27, 89
Waters, John (on writing), xii, 6, 15, 89, 90, 132, 177, 201, 207, 252, 269–270, 313, 318, 319–327, 346

Waters, John Samuel Sr., 2, 4, 5, 7, 22–23, 71, 125, 126, 133, 137, 142, 155, 177, 180–181, 185, 323
Waters, Kathleen, 3–4
Waters, Patricia (Trish), 3–4, 6,
Waters, Patricia, 2, 5, 6, 7, 119, 143–144, 180–181, 185, 323
Waters, Stephen, 3–4,
Waterston, Sam, 263, 267, 271

Wendl, Alan J., 54, 222, 227, 246, 249, 280, 293, 300, 303
Wilroy, Channing, 51, 68, 151, 189, 251, 280, 293
Williams, Tennessee, 12, 14, 109–110, 111
Wizard of Oz, 107–108, 121, 123, 133, 327

Yeaton, Brook, 34, 55, 188, 305
Yeaton, Chuck, 34, 181, 189, 195, 228

THE FAQ SERIES

AC/DC FAQ
by Susan Masino
Backbeat Books
9781480394506.................$24.99

Armageddon Films FAQ
by Dale Sherman
Applause Books
9781617131196........................$24.99

The Band FAQ
by Peter Aaron
Backbeat Books
9781617136139 ....$19.99

Baseball FAQ
by Tom DeMichael
Backbeat Books
9781617136061........................$24.99

The Beach Boys FAQ
by Jon Stebbins
Backbeat Books
9780879309879.................$22.99

The Beat Generation FAQ
by Rich Weidman
Backbeat Books
9781617136016 ....$19.99

Beer FAQ
by Jeff Cioletti
Backbeat Books
9781617136115 ....$24.99

Black Sabbath FAQ
by Martin Popoff
Backbeat Books
9780879309572.................$19.99

Bob Dylan FAQ
by Bruce Pollock
Backbeat Books
9781617136078 ....$19.99

Britcoms FAQ
by Dave Thompson
Applause Books
9781495018992 ....$19.99

Bruce Springsteen FAQ
by John D. Luerssen
Backbeat Books
9781617130939.................$22.99

A Chorus Line FAQ
by Tom Rowan
Applause Books
9781480367548 ....$19.99

The Clash FAQ
by Gary J. Jucha
Backbeat Books
9781480364509 ....$19.99

Doctor Who FAQ
by Dave Thompson
Applause Books
9781557838544....................$22.99

The Doors FAQ
by Rich Weidman
Backbeat Books
9781617130175 ....$24.99

Dracula FAQ
by Bruce Scivally
Backbeat Books
9781617136009 ....$19.99

The Eagles FAQ
by Andrew Vaughan
Backbeat Books
9781480385412........................$24.99

Elvis Films FAQ
by Paul Simpson
Applause Books
9781557838582.....................$24.99

Elvis Music FAQ
by Mike Eder
Backbeat Books
9781617130496......................$24.99

Eric Clapton FAQ
by David Bowling
Backbeat Books
9781617134548 ....$22.99

Fab Four FAQ
*by Stuart Shea and
Robert Rodriguez*
Hal Leonard Books
9781423421382........................$19.99

Fab Four FAQ 2.0
by Robert Rodriguez
Backbeat Books
9780879309688..................$19.99

Film Noir FAQ
by David J. Hogan
Applause Books
9781557838551.....................$22.99

Football FAQ
by Dave Thompson
Backbeat Books
9781495007484 ....$24.99

Frank Zappa FAQ
by John Corcelli
Backbeat Books
9781617136030........................$19.99

Godzilla FAQ
by Brian Solomon
Applause Books
9781495045684 ....$19.99

The Grateful Dead FAQ
by Tony Sclafani
Backbeat Books
9781617130861........................$24.99

Guns N' Roses FAQ
by Rich Weidman
Backbeat Books
9781495025884 ....$19.99

Haunted America FAQ
by Dave Thompson
Backbeat Books
9781480392625.................$19.99

Horror Films FAQ
by John Kenneth Muir
Applause Books
9781557839503.....................$22.99

James Bond FAQ
by Tom DeMichael
Applause Books
9781557838568....................$22.99

Jimi Hendrix FAQ
by Gary J. Jucha
Backbeat Books
9781617130953........................$22.99

Prices, contents, and availability
subject to change without notice.

Johnny Cash FAQ
by C. Eric Banister
Backbeat Books
9781480385405 .... $24.99

KISS FAQ
by Dale Sherman
Backbeat Books
9781617130915 .... $24.99

Led Zeppelin FAQ
by George Case
Backbeat Books
9781617130250 .... $22.99

Lucille Ball FAQ
*by James Sheridan
and Barry Monush*
Applause Books
9781617740824 .... $19.99

M.A.S.H. FAQ
by Dale Sherman
Applause Books
9781480355897 .... $19.99

Michael Jackson FAQ
by Kit O'Toole
Backbeat Books
9781480371064 .... $19.99

Modern Sci-Fi Films FAQ
by Tom DeMichael
Applause Books
9781480350618 .... $24.99

Monty Python FAQ
*by Chris Barsanti, Brian Cogan,
and Jeff Massey*
Applause Books
9781495049439 .... $19.99

Morrissey FAQ
by D. McKinney
Backbeat Books
9781480394483 .... $24.99

Neil Young FAQ
by Glen Boyd
Backbeat Books
9781617130373 .... $19.99

Nirvana FAQ
by John D. Luerssen
Backbeat Books
9781617134500 .... $24.99

Pearl Jam FAQ
*by Bernard M. Corbett and
Thomas Edward Harkins*
Backbeat Books
9781617136122 .... $19.99

Pink Floyd FAQ
by Stuart Shea
Backbeat Books
9780879309503 .... $19.99

Pro Wrestling FAQ
by Brian Solomon
Backbeat Books
9781617135996 .... $29.99

Prog Rock FAQ
by Will Romano
Backbeat Books
9781617135873 .... $24.99

Quentin Tarantino FAQ
by Dale Sherman
Applause Books
9781480355880 .... $24.99

Robin Hood FAQ
by Dave Thompson
Applause Books
9781495048227 .... $19.99

**The Rocky Horror
Picture Show FAQ**
by Dave Thompson
Applause Books
9781495007477 .... $19.99

Rush FAQ
by Max Mobley
Backbeat Books
9781617134517 .... $19.99

Saturday Night Live FAQ
by Stephen Tropiano
Applause Books
9781557839510 .... $24.99

Seinfeld FAQ
by Nicholas Nigro
Applause Books
9781557838575 .... $24.99

Sherlock Holmes FAQ
by Dave Thompson
Applause Books
9781480331495 .... $24.99

The Smiths FAQ
by John D. Luerssen
Backbeat Books
9781480394490 .... $24.99

Soccer FAQ
by Dave Thompson
Backbeat Books
9781617135989 .... $24.99

The Sound of Music FAQ
by Barry Monush
Applause Books
9781480360433 .... $27.99

South Park FAQ
by Dave Thompson
Applause Books
9781480350649 .... $24.99

Star Trek FAQ
(Unofficial and Unauthorized)
by Mark Clark
Applause Books
9781557837929 .... $19.99

Star Trek FAQ 2.0
(Unofficial and Unauthorized)
by Mark Clark
Applause Books
9781557837936 .... $22.99

Star Wars FAQ
by Mark Clark
Applause Books
9781480360181 .... $24.99

Steely Dan FAQ
by Anthony Robustelli
Backbeat Books
9781495025129 .... $19.99

Stephen King Films FAQ
by Scott Von Doviak
Applause Books
9781480355514 .... $24.99

Three Stooges FAQ
by David J. Hogan
Applause Books
9781557837882 .... $22.99

TV Finales FAQ
*by Stephen Tropiano and
Holly Van Buren*
Applause Books
9781480391444 .... $19.99

The Twilight Zone FAQ
by Dave Thompson
Applause Books
9781480396180 .... $19.99

Twin Peaks FAQ
*by David Bushman and
Arthur Smith*
Applause Books
9781495015861 .... $19.99

UFO FAQ
by David J. Hogan
Backbeat Books
9781480393851 .... $19.99

Video Games FAQ
by Mark J.P. Wolf
Backbeat Books
9781617136306 .... $19.99

The Who FAQ
by Mike Segretto
Backbeat Books
9781480361034 .... $24.99

The Wizard of Oz FAQ
by David J. Hogan
Applause Books
9781480350625 .... $24.99

The X-Files FAQ
by John Kenneth Muir
Applause Books
9781480369740 .... $24.99

Prices, contents, and availability subject to change without notice.